# Treatise on Human Nature

## Other Titles of Interest from St. Augustine's Press

Thomas Aquinas, *Treatise on Law*. Translated by Alfred J. Freddoso

Thomas Aquinas, *Commentary on Aristotle's Nicomachean Ethics*

Thomas Aquinas, *Commentary on Aristotle's De Anima*

Thomas Aquinas, *Commentary on Aristotle's Metaphysics*

Thomas Aquinas, *Commentary on Aristotle's Posterior Analytics*. Translated by Richard Berquist

Thomas Aquinas, *Commentary on Aristotle's Physics*

Thomas Aquinas, *Disputed Questions on Virtue*. Translated by Ralph McInerny

Thomas Aquinas, *Commentary on the Epistle to the Hebrews*. Translated by Chrysostom Baer, O. Praem.

Thomas Aquinas, *Commentaries on St. Paul's Epistles to Timothy, Titus, and Philemon*. Translated by Chrysostom Baer, O. Praem.

John of St. Thomas, *Introduction to the Summa Theologiae of Thomas Aquinas*. Translated by Ralph McInerny.

John Poinsot [John of St. Thomas], *Tractatus de Signis Poinsot: The Semiotic of John Poinsot*.

St. Augustine, *On Order [De Ordine]*. Translated by Silvano Borruso.

St. Augustine, *The St. Augustine LifeGuide: Words to Live by from the Great Christian Saint*. Translated by Silvano Borruso,

Plato, *The Symposium of Plato: The Shelley Translation*. Translated by Percy Bysshe Shelley.

Aristotle, *Aristotle – On Poetics*. Trans. by Seth Benardete and Michael Davis

Aristotle, *Physics, Or Natural Hearing*. Translated by Glen Coughlin.

Peter Kreeft, *Socratic Logic: A Logic Text Using Socratic Method, Platonic Questions, and Aristotelian Principles*

Josef Pieper, *Happiness and Contemplation*

Josef Pieper, *Scholasticism: Personalities and Problems*

Josef Pieper, *The Silence of St. Thomas*

Josef Pieper, *Enthusiasm and Divine Madness: On the Platonic Dialogue Phaedrus*

Francisco Suarez, *On Creation, Conservation, & Concurrence:•Metaphysical Disputations 20–22*. Translated by Alfred J. Freddoso

Francisco Suarez, *Metaphysical Demonstration of the Existence of God*. Translated by John P. Doyle

Jacques Maritain, *Natural Law: Reflections on Theory and Practice*

Fulvio di Blasi, *God and the Natural Law: A Rereading of Thomas Aquinas*

Joseph Bobik, *Veritas Divina: Aquinas on Divine Truth*

Joseph Owens, C.Ss.R., *Aristotle's Gradations of Being in Metaphysics E–Z*

# Treatise on Human Nature
## The Complete Text
### (*Summa Theologiae* I, Questions 75–102)

Thomas Aquinas

Translated by Alfred J. Freddoso

ST. AUGUSTINE'S PRESS
South Bend, Indiana
2010

Manufactured in the United States of America

1 2 3 4 5 6   16 15 14 13 12 11 10

**Library of Congress Cataloging in Publication Data**
Thomas, Aquinas, Saint, 1225?–1274.
[Summa theologica. Pars 1. Quaestio 75–102. English]
Treatise on human nature: the complete text
(Summa theologiae I, Questions 75–102) / Thomas Aquinas;
translated by Alfred J. Freddoso.
p. cm.
Includes index.
ISBN 978-1-58731-881-8 (paperbound: alk. paper)
1. Theological anthropology – Catholic Church.
2. Catholic Church – Doctrines.  I. Freddoso, Alfred J.  II. Title.
BT741.3.T4913 2010
233'.5 – dc22          2010027396

∞ *The paper used in this publication meets the minimum requirements of the*
*American National Standard for Information Sciences – Permanence of*
*Paper for Printed Materials, ANSI Z39.48-1984.*

ST. AUGUSTINE'S PRESS
www.staugustine.net

# Table of Contents

# QUESTION 75

## The Essence of the Human Soul

Now that we have considered the spiritual creature and the corporeal creature, we must consider man, who is composed of a spiritual and a corporeal substance (*ex spirituali et corporali substantia componitur*). We will consider first the nature of man (questions 75–89) and then the production of man (questions 90–102).

Now the theologian's role is to consider man's nature with respect to the soul and not the body, except insofar as the body is related to the soul. And so the first part of our consideration will have to do with the soul. Since, according to Dionysius, *De Caelesti Hierarchia*, chap. 11, there are three aspects of spiritual substances, viz., their essence, their power, and their operation, we will consider, first, that which has to do with the essence of the soul (questions 75–76); second, that which has to do with the soul's powers or capacities (*virtutem vel potentias*) (questions 77–83); and, third, that which has to do with the soul's operations (questions 84–89).

On the first point there are two things to consider. The first is the soul itself in its own right (question 75), and the second is the union of the soul with the body (question 76).

On the first topic there are seven questions: (1) Is a soul a body? (2) Is the human soul something subsistent? (3) Are the souls of brute animals subsistent? (4) Is the soul a man or is a man instead something composed of a soul and a body? (5) Is the soul composed of form and matter? (6) Is the human soul incorruptible? (7) Is the soul the same in species as an angel?


## Article 1

### Is a soul a body?

It seems that a soul is a body:

**Objection 1:** A soul is a mover of a body. But it does not give motion without being moved, both because (a) it seems that nothing can be a mover unless it is moved, since nothing gives to another what it itself does not have—e.g., something that is not itself hot does not give heat—and because (b) if something is an unmoved mover, then, as *Physics* 8 shows, it is a cause of a motion that is everlasting (*sempiternum*) and uniform (*eodem modo se habentem*)—which does not appear to be the case with the motion of an animal, which is from the soul Therefore, a soul is a mover that is moved. But every mover that is moved is a body. Therefore, a soul is a body.

**Objection 2:** Every cognition is effected by means of some sort of likeness. But a body cannot bear a likeness to an incorporeal thing. Therefore, if a soul were not a body, it would not be able to have any cognition of corporeal things.

**Objection 3:** A mover must have some contact with the thing moved. But only bodies have contact. Therefore, since a soul moves a body, it seems that a soul is a body.

**But contrary to this:** In *De Trinitate* 6 Augustine says that a soul "is simple in comparison to a body, since it is not spread out with its mass (*mole*) through a region in space (*per spatium loci*)."

**I respond:** In order to inquire into the nature of a soul, one must take for granted that what is called a 'soul' (*anima*) is a first principle of life in those things around us that are alive; for we say that living things are 'ensouled' (*animata*) and that things which lack life are 'not ensouled' (*inanimata*).

There are two operations by which life is especially made manifest, viz., cognition and movement. The ancient philosophers, unable to transcend the imagination, posited bodies as the principle of these operations, and they claimed that bodies alone are entities and that what is not a body is nothing. Accordingly, they claimed that a soul is a certain sort of body.

Even though the falsity of this view can be shown in many ways, we will make use of just the one way in virtue of which it is most surely and most generally clear that a soul is not a body:

It is evident that not every principle of a vital operation is a soul, since otherwise an eye would be a soul, given that it is a principle of seeing; and the same thing would have to be said of others among the soul's instruments. Instead, we are claiming that a soul is the *first* principle of life. For even though a body can in some sense be a principle of life, in the way that the heart is a principle of life in an animal, nonetheless, a body cannot be the *first* principle of life. For it is clear that *being a principle of life*, or *being alive* (*vivens*), cannot belong to a body by reason of its being a body; otherwise, each body would be alive or would be a principle of life. Therefore, the fact that a body is alive—or is even a principle of life—is something that belongs to it by virtue of the fact that it is a body of a given sort (*tale corpus*). But the fact that a body is actually of a given sort (*actu tale*) is due to a principle that is called its act (*eius actus*). Therefore, a soul, i.e., a first principle of life, is the *act of a body* and not itself a body—just as heat, i.e., a principle of heating, is a certain act of a body and not itself a body.

**Reply to objection 1:** Since everything that is moved is moved by another, and since this cannot go on *ad infinitum*, one must admit that not every mover is moved. For since to be moved is to go from potentiality to actuality, a mover gives what it has to the moveable thing insofar as it makes that thing to be actually such-and-such (*esse in actu*).

Now as is shown in *Physics* 8, there is a sort of mover that is completely unmoveable and that is moved neither *per se* nor *per accidens*; and this sort of mover can effect a motion that is always uniform (*semper uniformem*). On the other hand, there is another sort of mover that is moved *per accidens* and not *per se*, and because of this it does not effect a motion that is always uniform; a soul is a mover of this sort. Finally, there is a sort of mover that is moved *per se*, viz., a body.

Since the ancient natural philosophers believed that only bodies exist, they claimed that (a) every mover is itself moved and that (b) a soul is moved *per se* and is a body.

**Reply to objection 2:** It is not necessary that a likeness of the thing of which there is a cognition should exist *in actuality* in the *nature* of that which has the cognition. Instead, if something is such that it has cognition first in potentiality and afterwards in actuality, then a likeness of the thing of which there is cognition exists only *in potentiality*, and not in actuality, in the *nature* of the thing having the cognition—just as a color exists in the pupil only in potentiality and not in actuality. Hence, it is not necessary for there to be an actual likeness of corporeal entities in the nature of a soul; rather, it is necessary only that likenesses of this sort should exist in a soul in potentiality.

However, since the ancient natural philosophers were ignorant of the distinction between actuality and potentiality, they claimed that a soul is a body in order that it might have cognition of bodies; and they claimed that it is composed of the principles of all bodies in order that it might have cognition of all bodies.

**Reply to objection 3:** There are two sorts of contact, contact of *quantity* and contact of *power* (*contactus quantitatis et virtutis*). In the case of the first sort of contact, a body is touched only by a body. In the case of the second sort of contact, a body can be touched by an incorporeal entity that moves the body.

## Article 2

### Is a human soul something subsistent?

It seems that a human soul is not something subsistent:

**Objection 1:** That which is subsistent is said to be a *this-something* (*hoc aliquid*). Yet it is not the soul that is a *this-something*, but rather that which is composed of a soul and a body. Therefore, a soul is not something subsistent.

**Objection 2:** Anything that is subsistent can be said to operate. But a soul is not said to operate, since, as *De Anima* 1 puts it, "To say that a soul senses or understands is like saying that a soul weaves or builds." Therefore, a soul is not something subsistent.

**Objection 3:** If a soul were something subsistent, then it would have an operation without a body (*operatio sine corpore*). But none of its operations occurs without a body (*nulla est sine corpore*)—not even the act of intellective understanding, since the soul cannot have an act of understanding without phantasms, and phantasms cannot exist without a body. Therefore, a human soul is not something subsistent.

**But contrary to this:** In *De Trinitate* 10 Augustine says, "If anyone discerns the nature of the mind and sees that it is a substance, but not a corporeal substance, he will see that those who think it is a corporeal substance make this mistake because they attach to the soul those things, viz., the images of bodies, without which they cannot think of any nature." Therefore, the nature of a human mind is not only incorporeal but also a substance, i.e., something subsistent.

**I respond:** One must claim that the principle of intellectual operations, which we call a man's soul, is an incorporeal and subsistent principle. For it is clear that by means of his intellect a man is able to have cognition of the natures of all bodies. But that which is able to have cognition of given things must be such that it has nothing of those things in its own nature, since what exists in it naturally would in that case impede the cognition of those other things. For instance, we see that a sick tongue infected with bilious and bitter humors (*infecta cholerico et amaro humore*) is unable to perceive anything sweet; instead, everything seems bitter to it. Therefore, if an intellectual principle had within itself the nature of any sort of body, it would be unable to have cognition of all bodies. But each body has some determinate nature. Therefore, it is impossible that this intellectual principle should be a body. And, similarly, it is impossible that it should have intellective understanding through a bodily organ, since the determinate nature of that bodily organ would likewise prevent its having cognition of all bodies—in just the same way that if some determinate color exists not only in the pupil but also in the glass vase, then a liquid poured into that vase seems to be of that same color.

Therefore, the intellectual principle itself, which is called the *mind* or the *intellect*, has an operation on its own (*habet operationem per se*) in which the body does not share. But nothing can operate on its own unless it subsists on its own (*nihil potest per se operari nisi quod per se subsistit*). For to operate belongs to a being that is actualized, and so a thing operates in the way in which it exists. It is for this reason that we say that it is the hot thing (*calidum*), rather than the heat (*calor*), that gives warmth. It follows, then, that the human soul, which is called the intellect or mind, is something incorporeal and subsistent.

**Reply to objection 1:** The term '*this-something*' can be taken in two senses. In the first sense it is taken for any subsistent thing, whereas in the second sense it is taken for a subsistent thing that is complete in the nature of some species. The first sense excludes inherence of the sort that belongs to an accident or material form; the second sense excludes in addition the incompleteness that belongs to a part. Hence, a hand could be called a *this-something* in the first sense, but not in the second sense.

So, then, since the human soul is a part of the human species, it can be called a *this-something*, i.e., subsistent, in the first sense, but not in the second sense. For in the second sense what is called a *this-something* is that which is composed of a soul and a body.

**Reply to objection 2:** Aristotle is making this assertion (*verba illa dicit*) not to express his own opinion, but rather to express the opinion of those who were claiming that to have intellective understanding is to be moved. This is clear from what he says just before the cited passage.

An alternative reply is that to act on its own (*per se agere*) befits something that exists on its own (*per se existenti*). But the phrase 'exists on its own' (*per se existens*) can sometimes be predicated of a thing as long as it is not inherent like an accident or a material form, even if it is a part. On the other hand, what is said to subsist properly and *per se* is such that it is neither inherent in the aforementioned ways nor a part. In this sense, neither an eye nor a hand could be said to subsist on its own, and so neither could it be said to operate on its own. Hence, the operations of the parts are attributed to the whole *by means of* the parts (*per partes*). For we say that a man sees by means of his eye, and that he touches by means of his hand.

This is different from saying that a hot thing gives warmth by means of its heat (*per calorem*), since there is no sense in which the heat gives warmth, properly speaking. Therefore, one can claim that a soul understands in the same sense in which an eye sees, but that it is more proper to say that the man understands by means of his soul.

**Reply to objection 3:** The body is not required for the intellect's action as an organ by means of which that action is exercised; rather, the body is required for the sake of the action's object (*ratione obiecti*). For a phantasm is related to intellective understanding in the way that a color is related to seeing. But needing the body in this sense does not rule out the intellect's being subsistent; otherwise, it would be the case that because it needs external sensible things in order to have sensation, an animal is not something subsistent.

## Article 3

### Are the souls of brute animals subsistent?

It seems that the souls of brute animals are subsistent:

**Objection 1:** Man agrees with the other animals in genus. But as has been shown (a. 2), man's soul is subsistent. Therefore, the souls of the other animals are likewise subsistent.

**Objection 2:** Something sentient is related to what is sensible in the same way that something intellective is related to what is intelligible. But the intellect understands intelligible things without the body. Therefore, the senses apprehend sensible things without the body. But the souls of brute animals are sentient. Therefore, they are subsistent, for the same reason that the human soul, which is intellective, is subsistent.

**Objection 3:** A brute animal's soul moves its body. But a body is moved and does not effect movement. Therefore, a brute animal's soul has an operation without its body.

**But contrary to this:** In *De Ecclesiasticis Dogmatibus* it says, "We believe that man alone has a soul that is a substance (*anima substantiva*), whereas the souls of animals are not substances."

**I respond:** The ancient philosophers did not draw a distinction between sensation and intellective understanding, and they attributed both of them to a corporeal principle, as has already been explained (a. 1).

Now Plato did distinguish intellective understanding from sensation, but he attributed both of them to an incorporeal principle, arguing that just as intellective understanding belongs to the soul in its own right, so too does sensing. And from this it followed that even the souls of brute animals are subsistent.

Aristotle, on the other hand, claimed that, among the works of the soul, only intellective understanding is exercised without a corporeal organ. By contrast, sensing and the resulting operations of the sentient soul clearly occur with bodily changes; for instance, in the act of seeing the pupil is changed by the species of color, and the same thing is clear with the other senses.

And so it is clear that the sentient soul does not have any proper operation of its own (*non habet aliquam operationem propriam per seipsam*); instead, every operation of the sentient soul belongs to the conjoined entity (*est coniuncti*). From this it follows that since the souls of brute animals do not operate on their own (*per se*), they are not subsistent; for each thing has its *esse* in the same way that it has its operation (*similiter unumquodque habet esse et operationem*).

**Reply to objection 1:** Even though man agrees with the other animals in genus, he nonetheless differs from them in species, and a difference in species is accompanied by a difference in form. Nor does it have to be the case that every difference of form makes for a diversity of genera.

**Reply to objection 2:** There is a sense in which the sentient part of the soul (*sensitivum*) is related to sensible things in the way that the intellective part (*intellectivum*) is related to intelligible things, viz., each is in potentiality with respect to its objects.

However, there is another sense in which they are related in different ways to their objects; for the sentient part is acted upon by the sensible object via a corporeal change, and hence an excessiveness in the sensible objects harms the sensory power (*excellentia sensibilium corrumpit sensum*). This does not occur in the case of the intellect, for an intellect that is having an intellective understanding of the most intelligible objects is more able afterwards to understand lesser objects. What's more, even though the body gets tired out in intellective understanding, this is incidental (*per accidens*), given that the intellect needs the operation of the sentient powers to prepare phantasms for it.

**Reply to objection 3:** There are two sorts of moving powers.

There is one which *commands* movement (*imperat motum*), viz., the appetitive power. And its operation in the sentient soul does not occur without the body. Rather, anger and joy and all passions of this sort exist along with some change in the body.

The second sort of moving power is one which *executes* movement (*exequens motum*) and through which the members of the body are rendered capable of obeying the appetite. This power's act is to be moved and not to effect motion.

Hence, it is clear that to effect movement is not an act that the sentient soul has without the body.

## Article 4

### Is the [human] soul the man?

It seems that the [human] soul is the man:

**Objection 1:** 2 Corinthians 4:16 says, "Though our outward man is corrupted, yet the inward man is renewed day by day." But what is 'inward' in a man is the soul. Therefore, the soul is the interior man.

**Objection 2:** The human soul is a certain substance. But it is not a universal substance. Therefore, it is a particular substance. Therefore, it is a hypostasis or person. But it is not a person unless it is a human person. Therefore, the soul is the man, since a human person is a man.

**But contrary to this:** In *De Civitate Dei* 19 Augustine commends Varro for thinking that "a man is neither the soul alone nor the body alone, but the soul and the body together."

**I respond:** There are two ways to understand the claim that the soul is the man.

In the first way, it is understood to mean that (a) *man* is a soul and yet that (b) *this* man, e.g., Socrates, is not a soul but is instead composed of a soul and a body. I bring this position up because some have claimed that the form alone belongs to the nature of the species, whereas the matter is part of the individual and not of the species.

However, this cannot be true. For what pertains to the nature of the species is what is signified by the definition. But in the case of natural things the definition signifies both the form and the matter—and not just the form. Hence, the matter is part of the species in the case of natural things—not, to be sure, *designated* matter (*materia signata*), which is a principle of individuation, but rather *common* matter (*materia communis*). For just as it is of the nature of *this* man to be composed of *this* soul and *this* flesh and *these* bones, so it is of the nature of *man* to be composed of a soul and flesh and bones, since whatever belongs to the substance of the species must belong in a general way (*communiter*) to the substance of all the individuals contained under that species.

In the second way, the claim that the soul is the man is understood to mean that *this* soul is *this* man. To be sure, this claim could be sustained if one asserted that the sentient soul's operations are its own without the body, since in that case all the operations attributed to the man would belong to the soul alone. But it is the entity that performs the entity's operations. Hence, it is the man that performs the man's operations. But it has been shown (a. 3) that an act of sensing is not an operation belonging only to the soul. Therefore, since sensing is one of the man's operations, even if not his proper operation, it is clear that a man is something composed of a soul and a body and is not the soul alone.

However, Plato, who claimed that sensing is proper to the soul, was able to hold that a man is a soul making use of a body.

**Reply to objection 1:** According to the Philosopher in *Ethics* 9, each thing seems to be mainly what is principal in it, in the way that a city is said to do what the mayor of the city (*rector civitatis*) does. It is in this sense that what is principal in a man is something called the man. In some cases this is the intellective part of man, which is indeed principal and is called the 'interior' man, and in other cases it is the sentient part along with the body, which is principal in the opinion of those who are engaged only with sensible things. And the latter is called the 'exterior' man.

**Reply to objection 2:** Not every particular substance is a hypostasis or person; rather, a hypostasis or person is a particular substance that has the *complete* nature of a species. Hence, a hand or foot cannot be called a hypostasis or a person. And, likewise, neither can a soul, since it is a part of a human nature (*pars speciei humanae*).

## Article 5

### Is a [human] soul composed of matter and form?

It seems that a [human] soul is composed of matter and form:

**Objection 1:** Potentiality (*potentia*) is contrasted with actuality (*actus*). But everything that exists in actuality participates in the *First Actuality* (*primus actus*), who is God and through participation in whom all things exist and are good and are alive—as is clear from Dionysius's teaching in *De Divinis Nominibus*. Therefore, everything that exists in potentiality participates in the *first potentiality* (*prima potentia*). But the first potentiality is primary matter (*materia prima*). Therefore, since a human soul in some sense exists in potentiality, which is clear from the fact that a man is sometimes engaged in intellective understanding [only] in potentiality, it seems that a human soul participates in primary matter as one of its parts.

**Objection 2:** Anything in which the properties of matter are found is such that matter is found in it. But the properties of matter are found in a soul. These properties are *to be a subject* (*subiici*) and *to undergo change* (*transmutari*). For a soul is the subject of knowledge and of virtue, and it undergoes a change from ignorance to knowledge and from vice to virtue. Therefore, there is matter in the soul.

**Objection 3:** As *Metaphysics* 8 says, anything that does not have matter does not have a cause of its *esse*. But a soul has a cause of its *esse*, since it is created by God. Therefore, a soul has matter.

**Objection 4:** Anything that is just a form and does not have matter is pure and infinite actuality (*actus purus et infinitus*). But this belongs to God alone. Therefore, a soul has matter.

**But contrary to this:** In *Super Genesim ad Litteram* 7 Augustine shows that a soul is made neither from corporeal matter nor from spiritual matter.

**I respond:** A soul does not have matter. This can be seen in two ways.

The first way stems from *the nature of a soul in general*. For it belongs to the nature of a soul to be the form of a body. Therefore, either it is (a) a form as regards the whole of itself or (b) a form as regards some part of itself. If it is a form as regards the whole of itself, then it is impossible that a part of it should be matter—given that 'matter' means a being that exists only in potentiality. For a form *qua* form is an actuality, whereas what exists just in potentiality cannot be part of an actuality. For potentiality is incompatible with actuality, since it is divided off against actuality. On the other hand, if a soul is a form as regards some part of itself, then we will call that part 'the soul', and we will call the matter of which it is primarily the actuality 'the first animated thing'.

The second way stems from *the specific nature of a human soul insofar as it is intellective*. For it is clear that whatever is received in a thing is received in it according to the mode of the receiver. So each thing is such that there is cognition of it insofar as its form exists in the one who has cognition of it. But an intellective soul has cognition of an entity in that entity's nature taken absolutely (*in sua natura absolute*); for instance, it has cognition of a rock insofar as the rock is a rock taken absolutely. Therefore, the form of a rock taken absolutely, i.e., according to its proper formal notion (*secundum propriam rationem formalem*), exists in the intellective soul. Thus, an intellective soul is an absolute form and not something composed of matter and form. For if an intellective soul were composed of matter and form, then the forms of the things would be received in it as individuals, and so the soul would know them only as singulars, just as happens in the case of the sentient powers, which receive the forms of things in a corporeal organ. For matter is a principle of individuation for forms.

Therefore, it follows that an intellective soul, along with every intellectual substance that has cognition of forms taken absolutely, lacks a composition of form and matter.

**Reply to objection 1:** The First Actuality is the universal source of all actualities (*universale principium omnium actuum*), since it is infinite and has "everything virtually within itself to begin with," as Dionysius puts it. Hence, things participate in it not as parts, but rather according to the diffusion of its procession (*secundum diffusionem processionis ipsius*). Now since potentiality is receptive of actuality, it must be proportioned to the actuality. But the received actualities that proceed from the infinite First Actuality and are participations in it are diverse. Hence, there cannot be a single potentiality that receives all the actualities, in the way that there is a single actuality that flows into (*influens*) all the participated actualities; otherwise, the receptive potentiality would equal the active power of the First Actuality.

However, the receptive potentiality that exists in an intellective soul is different from the receptive potentiality of primary matter, as is clear from the differences in what is received. For primary matter receives individual forms, whereas the intellect receives absolute forms. Hence, a potentiality of the sort that exists in the intellective soul does not indicate that the soul is composed of matter and form.

**Reply to objection 2:** To be a subject (*subiici*) and to undergo change (*transmutari*) belong to matter insofar as it is in potentiality. Therefore, just as an intellect's potentiality is different from primary matter's potentiality, so the notions of *being a subject of* and *undergoing change* are different in the two cases. For it is insofar as it is in potentiality with respect to intelligible species that the intellect is the subject of knowledge and undergoes a change from ignorance to knowledge.

**Reply to objection 3:** The form is a cause of the matter's *esse*, along with the agent. Hence, insofar as the agent brings the matter to the actuality of the form by transforming it, it is a cause of *esse* for it. But if something is a subsistent form, it does not have *esse* through any formal principle; nor does it have a cause that changes it from potentiality to actuality. Hence, after the cited passage, the Philosopher concludes that in the case of things composed of matter and form "the cause is none other than that which moves the thing from potentiality to actuality, whereas things that do not have matter are all simply beings that are truly something."

**Reply to objection 4:** Everything that is participated in is related to what participates in it as its actuality. But if a created form is posited as subsisting *per se*, then it must participate in *esse*, since "its very life," or whatever else is said of it, "participates in *esse* itself," as Dionysius puts it in *De Divinis Nominibus*, chap. 5. Now participated *esse* is limited to the capacity of that which participates. Hence, God alone, who is His own *esse* itself, is pure and infinite actuality (*actus purus et infinitus*). On the other hand, in intellectual substances there is a composition of actuality and potentiality—not, to be sure, a composition of form and matter, but rather a composition of form and participated *esse*. Hence, an intellectual substance is said by some to be composed of *that by which* it exists and *that which* exists (*componi ex quo est et quod est*). For *esse* itself is *that by which* something exists.


## Article 6

### Is the human soul corruptible?

It seems that the human soul is corruptible:

**Objection 1:** Things whose principles and processes are similar seem to have similar ends as well. But the principle of generation for men is similar to the principle of generation for beasts, since they are made from the earth. Again, the processes of life are similar in both cases, since "all things breathe alike, and man has no more than the beast," as Ecclesiastes 3:19 puts it. Therefore, as Ecclesiastes 3 concludes, "Death (*interitus*) for a man and a beast is one, and the condition of both is equal." But the souls of brute animals are corruptible. Therefore, the human soul is likewise corruptible.

**Objection 2:** Everything that is made *ex nihilo* is reducible to nothingness, since the end must correspond to the beginning. But as Wisdom 2:2 says, "We are born from nothing"—which is true not only with respect to the body but also with respect to the soul. Therefore, as that same passage concludes, "After this we shall be as if we had never existed"—even with respect to the soul.

**Objection 3:** No entity exists without its proper operation. But the soul's proper operation, which is to understand intellectively in conjunction with a phantasm (*intelligere cum phantasmate*), cannot exist without a body, since the soul understands nothing without a phantasm and, as *De Anima* says, "there is no phantasm without the body." Therefore, the soul does not remain after the body has been destroyed.

**But contrary to this:** In *De Divinis Nominibus*, chap. 4, Dionysius says that out of God's goodness human souls are such that they are "intellectual" and have "an incorruptible substantival life."

**I respond:** One must claim that the human soul, which we call the intellective principle, is incorruptible.

For a thing is corrupted in one of two ways, either (a) *per se* or (b) *per accidens.*

But it is impossible for anything subsistent to be generated or corrupted *per accidens*, i.e., generated or corrupted because something else is generated or corrupted. For *being generated* and *being corrupted* belong to a thing in the same way as does its *esse*, which is acquired through generation and lost through corruption. Hence, that which has *esse per se* can be generated or corrupted only *per se*, whereas things that do not subsist, such as accidents and material forms, are said to be made and corrupted through the generation and corruption of composite things. Now it was shown above (a. 3) that only human souls, and not the souls of brute animals, are subsistent *per se*. Hence, the souls of brute animals are corrupted when their bodies are corrupted, whereas the human soul could not be corrupted unless it were corrupted *per se*.

However, this is wholly impossible—not only in the case of the human soul, but in the case of any subsistent thing that is just a form. For it is clear that what belongs to a thing because of its very self (*secundum se*) is inseparable from that thing. But *esse* belongs *per se* to form, i.e., to actuality. This is why matter acquires *esse* in actuality to the extent that it acquires form, whereas corruption occurs in it to the extent that form is separated from it. But it is impossible for a form to be separated from itself. Hence, it is impossible that a subsistent form should cease to exist.

Even if one conceded that the soul is, as some claim, composed of form and matter, he would still have to claim that it is incorruptible. For there is corruption only where there is contrariety, since instances of generation and corruption are from contraries into contraries; hence, the celestial bodies are incorruptible because they do not have a matter that is subject to contrariety. But there cannot be any contrariety within the intellective soul. For it receives *esse* in its own mode, and the things that are received in it exist without contrariety. For within the intellect the concepts of contraries (*rationes contrariorum*) are not themselves contraries; rather, there is a single science of the contraries. Therefore, it is impossible for the intellective soul to be corruptible.

Again, an indication of this can be also be found in the fact that each thing naturally desires *esse* in its own mode. But in things with cognition, desire follows upon cognition. Now the senses have cognition of *esse* only in the here and now, whereas the intellect apprehends *esse* absolutely speaking and with respect to all of time. Hence, everything that has an intellect naturally desires to exist always. But a natural desire cannot be in vain. Therefore, every intellectual substance is incorruptible.

**Reply to objection 1:** As is made clear in Wisdom 2, Solomon introduces this argument on behalf of the foolish. Thus, the claim that man and the other beasts have a similar principle of generation is true with respect to the body; for all animals are alike in being made from the earth. However, it is not true with respect to the soul; for the soul of brute animals is produced by a corporeal power, whereas the human soul is produced by God. In order to indicate this, Genesis says of the other animals, "Let the earth bring forth the living soul" (1:24), whereas of man it says, "He breathed into his face the breath of life" (2:7). And so Ecclesiastes 12:7 concludes, "The dust returns to the earth, from where it came, and the spirit returns to God, who made it."

Likewise, the process of life is similar with respect to the body; on this score Ecclesiastes 3:19 says, "All things breathe alike," and Wisdom 2:2 says, "The breath in our nostrils is smoke . . ." But the process is not similar with respect to the soul. For a man has intellective understanding, whereas brute animals do not.

Hence, the claim that man has nothing more than the beast is false. And so death is similar with respect to the body, but not with respect to the soul.

**Reply to objection 2:** Just as a thing is said to be able to be created not through any passive potentiality (*per potentiam passivam*) but only through the active power (*per potentiam activam*) of the creator, who is able to produce something *ex nihilo*, so too when a thing is said to be able to be reduced to nothingness, this does not imply a potentiality for *non-esse* within the *creature*, but instead implies within the *creator* a power not to communicate *esse* (*in creatore potentia ad hoc quod esse non influat*). By contrast, a thing is said to be able to be corrupted because there exists *within it* a potentiality for *non-esse*.

**Reply to objection 3:** To understand intellectively in conjunction with a phantasm is the proper operation of the soul insofar as it is united to the body. However, when it is separated from the body, it will have another mode of understanding like that of other substances that are separated from a body. This will be explained more fully below (q. 89, a. 1).

## Article 7

### Does a [human] soul belong to the same species as an angel?

It seems that a [human] soul belongs to the same species as an angel (*anima et angelus sint unius speciei*):

**Objection 1:** Each thing is ordered to its proper end by the nature of its species, through which it has an inclination toward that end. But the soul's end is the same as an angel's, viz., eternal beatitude. Therefore, they belong to the same species.

**Objection 2:** The ultimate specific difference is the most noble, since it brings the nature of the species to completion. But in an angel and in a soul there is nothing more noble than intellectual *esse*. Therefore, an angel and a soul agree in their ultimate specific difference. Therefore, they belong to the same species.

**Objection 3:** A soul seems to differ from an angel only in being united to a body. But since the body lies outside the soul's essence, it does not seem relevant to its species. Therefore, an angel and a soul belong to the same species.

**But contrary to this:** Things that have diverse natural operations differ in species. But an angel and a soul have diverse natural operations. For as Dionysius says in *De Divinis Nominibus*, chap. 7, "Angelic minds have simple and beatific acts of intellective understanding (*simplices et beatos intellectus*), not inferring (*non congregantes*) their knowledge of God from visible things"—whereas a little later he says the opposite about the soul. Therefore, a soul and an angel do not belong to the same species.

**I respond:** Origen claimed that all angels and human souls belong to the same species. As was explained above (q. 47, a. 2), he said this because he held that the different grades found among such substances were incidental, stemming from free choice.

But this cannot be the case, since among incorporeal substances there is no numerical diversity without a diversity of species and without natural inequality.

For if incorporeal substances are not composed of matter and form but are instead subsistent forms, then it will clearly be necessary for there to be a diversity of species among them. For it is unintelligible that there should be a separated form that is not the only one of its species (*una unius speciei*)—just as, if whiteness were separated, then there could be only one whiteness, since *this* whiteness differs from *that* whiteness only because it is the whiteness of *this* thing or the whiteness of *that* thing. Now diversity in species is always accompanied by a natural diversity; for instance, among the species of color one is more perfect than another, and likewise for the other species. This is because the differences that divide the genus are contraries. But contraries are related to one other as the perfect and the imperfect, since the sources of contrariety are, as *Metaphysics* 10 says, the disposition and [corresponding] privation.

The same thing would follow even if substances of the sort in question were composed of matter and form. For if the matter of *this* thing is distinct from the matter of *that* thing, then it must be the case either that (a) the form is the source (*principium*) of the distinction between the matters, in the sense that the matters are diverse because of their relation to diverse forms, in which case it still follows that there is a difference in species and a natural inequality, or that (b) the matter is the source of the distinctness of the forms, in which case *this* matter can be said to be distinct from *that* matter only because of a distinction in quantity (*secundum divisionem quantitativam*)—something that has no place in the case of incorporeal substances such as an angel or a soul.

Hence, it is impossible for an angel and a soul to belong to the same species.

Now we will show below (q. 76, a. 2) how it is that many souls belong to the same species.

**Reply to objection 1:** This argument goes through in the case of an end that is proximate and natural. However, eternal beatitude is an end that is ultimate and supernatural.

**Reply to objection 2:** The ultimate specific difference is the most noble because it is maximally determinate, in the way in which an actuality is more noble than the corresponding potentiality. However, in this sense *intellectual* (*intellectuale*) is not the most noble, because it is indeterminate and common with respect to the many grades of intellectuality, just as *sentient* (*sensibile*) is indeterminate and common with respect to the many grades within sentient *esse*. Hence, just as it is not the case that all sentient beings belong to the same species, so neither is it the case that all intellectual beings belong to the same species.

**Reply to objection 3:** Even though the body does not belong to the essence of the soul, the soul is by the nature of its essence such that it can be united to the body (*sit corpori unibilis*). Hence, it is not the soul, but rather the composite, that properly speaking belongs to a species. And the very fact that the soul needs the body in a certain way for its operation shows that the soul has a lower grade of intellectuality than does an angel, who is not united to a body.

# QUESTION 76

## The Union of the Soul with the Body

Next we must consider the union of the soul with the body. On this topic there are eight questions:

(1) Is the intellective principle united to the body as a form? (2) Is the intellective principle multiplied in accord with the multiplication of the bodies, or is there a single intellect for all men? (3) Are there any other souls in a body whose form is an intellective principle? (4) Are there any other substantial forms in such a body? (5) What sort of body does it have to be that has an intellective principle as its form? (6) Is the intellective principle united to the sort of body in question by the mediation of some accident? (7) Is the intellective principle united to the sort of body in question by the mediation of some other body? (8) Does the soul exist as a whole in each part of the body?

## Article 1

### Is the intellective principle united to the body as its form?

It seems that the intellective principle is not united to the body as its form:

**Objection 1:** In *De Anima* 3 the Philosopher says that the intellect is "separated" and that it is not the actuality of a body. Therefore, it is not united to the body as its form.

**Objection 2:** Every form is specified (*determinatur*) in accord with the nature of the matter whose form it is; otherwise, a proportionality between the form and the matter would not be required. Therefore, if the intellect were united to the body as its form, then since each body has a determinate nature, it would follow that the intellect has a determinate nature. And in that case, as is clear from what was said above (q. 75, a. 2), the intellect would not have cognition of all things—which is contrary to the nature of the intellect. Therefore, the intellect is not united to the body as its form.

**Objection 3:** If a given receptive potentiality is the actuality of a body, then it receives its form materially and individually, since what is received exists in the receiver in accord with the mode of the receiver (*receptum est* *in recipiente secundum modum recipientis*). But the form of a thing that is understood intellectively is not received materially and individually in the intellect; instead, it is received immaterially and universally. Otherwise, the intellect would not have cognition of immaterial things and universals, but would instead have cognition only of singulars, in the way that the senses do. Therefore, the intellect is not united to the body as its form.

**Objection 4:** A power (*potentia*) and [corresponding] action belong to the same thing, since it is the same thing that is able to act and that acts. But as is clear from what was said above (q. 75, a. 2), an intellectual action does not belong to a body. Therefore, neither is an intellectual power a power that belongs to a body. But a power or potentiality (*virtus sive potentia*) cannot be more abstract or more simple than the essence from which that power or potentiality is derived. Therefore, the intellect's substance is not the form of the body.

**Objection 5:** That which has *esse per se* is not united to a body as its form. For a form is that *by which* something exists, and so the *esse* of a form does not belong to the form itself in its own right (*secundum se*). But as was explained above (q. 75, a. 2), the intellective principle does have *esse* in its own right and is subsistent. Therefore, it is not united to the body as its form.

**Objection 6:** That which exists in a thing in its own right (*secundum se*) exists in it always. But a form is such that it is united to matter in its own right. For it is through its essence, and not through any accident, that it is the actuality of the matter; otherwise, what comes to be from the matter and the form would be unified accidentally and not substantively. Therefore, a form cannot exist without its proper matter. But as was shown above (q. 75, a. 6), since the intellective principle is incorruptible, it persists without being united to a body, after its body has been corrupted. Therefore, the intellective principle is not united to the body as its form.

**But contrary to this:** According to the Philosopher in *Metaphysics* 8, the difference is taken from a thing's form. But the constitutive difference of *man* is *rational*, which is said of man because of his intellective principle. Therefore, the intellective principle is the form of a man.

**I respond:** One must claim that the intellect, which is the principle of an intellectual operation, is the form of the human body.

For that by which something operates first and foremost (*primo operatur*) is the form of that to which the operation is attributed. For instance, that by which the body is first and foremost made healthy is health, and that by which the soul first and foremost knows is knowledge; hence, health is a form belonging to the body, and knowledge is a form belonging to the soul. The reason for this is that nothing acts except insofar as it is actually such-and-such, and so that by which it is actually such-and-such is that by which it acts. But it is obvious that the soul is that by which the body is first and foremost alive. And since life is made manifest by different operations within the different grades of living things, the soul is that by which we perform each of these vital works. For instance, the soul is that by which we first and foremost assimilate nourishment (*nutrimur*), have sensory cognition (*sentimus*), and move from place to place (*movemur secundum locum*); and, similarly, the soul is that by which we first and foremost have intellective understanding (*intelligimus*). Therefore, this principle by which we first and foremost have intellective understanding—regardless of whether it is called the intellect or the intellective soul—is the form of the body. This is Aristotle's demonstration in *De Anima* 2.

Now if someone wants to claim that the intellective soul is not the form of the body, then he has to find a sense in which the action in question, viz., intellective understanding, is an action that belongs to *this* man. For each of us experiences that it is he himself who understands. But as is clear from the Philosopher in *Physics* 5, there are three ways in which an action is attributed to someone. For he is said to effect something, or to act, either (a) *by himself as a whole* (*secundum se totum*), as in 'The physician heals'; or (b) *by a part of himself*, as in 'The man sees with his eyes"; or (c) *incidentally* (*per accidens*), as in 'The one who is white is building', since it is incidental to a builder that he is white. Thus, when we say that Socrates (or Plato) understands, it is obvious that this is not being attributed to him incidentally, since it is attributed to him insofar as he is a man, and 'man' is predicated essentially of him. Therefore, either (a) one must claim that Socrates has intellective understanding by himself as a whole, as Plato posited when he claimed that a man is an intellective soul, or (b) one must claim that the intellect is a part of Socrates. However, as was shown above (q. 75, a. 4), the first answer cannot hold up. For it is the very same man who perceives that he both understands and senses, and yet sensation does not exist without the body. Hence, the body must be a part of the man. Therefore, it follows that the intellect by which Socrates has intellective understanding is a part of Socrates in such a way that the intellect is somehow united to Socrates' body.

In *De Anima* 3 the Commentator claims that this union is effected by the intelligible species, which has two subjects, viz., (a) the potential intellect (*intellectus possibilis*) and (b) the phantasms that exist in the bodily organs. And so it is through the intelligible species that the potential intellect is connected with the body of *this* man or *that* man.

However, this sort of connection or union is not sufficient for the intellect's action to be *Socrates'* action. This is clear from a comparison with sensation, on the basis of which Aristotle proceeds to a consideration of what is involved in intellective understanding. For as *De Anima* 3 explains, phantasms are related to the intellect as colors are related to the visual power (*ad visum*). Therefore, species of the phantasms exist in the potential intellect in the same way that species of the colors exist in the visual power. But it is clear that the action of the visual power is not attributed to a wall in virtue of the fact that the colors whose likenesses are in the visual power exist in that wall. For we do not say that the wall *sees*; rather, we say that the wall *is seen*. Therefore, from the fact that species of the phantasms exist in the potential intellect it does not follow that Socrates, in whom the phantasms exist, *understands*; rather, what follows is that he or, better, his phantasms *are understood*.

Again, some have wanted to claim that the intellect is united to the body as its mover, and that a single entity is made up of the intellect and the body in such a way that the intellect's action can be attributed to the whole.

However, there are a number of things wrong (*multipliciter vanum*) with this claim:

First, the intellect moves the body only through the appetite, whose movement presupposes the intellect's operation. Therefore, it is not because Socrates is moved by the intellect that he understands; to the contrary, it is because he understands that Socrates is moved by the intellect.

Second, Socrates is an individual in a nature whose essence is unified (*una*) and composed of matter and form. If the intellect were not his form, it would follow that it lies outside his essence, and in that case the intellect would be related to the whole Socrates as a mover is related to the thing moved. But intellective understanding is an action that comes to rest within the agent and that, unlike the action of heating, does not pass into another. Therefore, it cannot be the case that understanding is attributed to Socrates by virtue of his being moved by the intellect.

Third, a mover's action is never attributed to the thing moved except as an instrument, in the way that the carpenter's action is attributed to the saw. Therefore, if it is because of his mover's action that understanding is attributed to Socrates, then it follows that understanding is attributed to him as an instrument. But this contradicts the Philosopher, who claims that intellective understanding does not occur by means of a corporeal instrument.

Fourth, even though the action of a part may be attributed to the whole—in the way that the eye's action is attributed to the man—still, the action of one part is never attributed to another part, except perhaps incidentally. For we do not say that the hand sees in virtue of the fact that the eye sees. Therefore, if Socrates and his intellect are made one in the way in question, then the intellect's action cannot be attributed to Socrates. On the other hand, if (a) Socrates is a whole composed by the union of the intellect to the other things belonging to Socrates and if (b) the intellect is nonetheless united to the other things belonging to Socrates only as a mover, then it follows that Socrates is not a single thing absolutely speaking (*non sit unum simpliciter*) and hence is not an entity absolutely speaking. For an entity is a being in the same sense in which it has oneness (*sic enim aliquid est ens quomodo et unum*).

Therefore, the only way left is the one proposed by Aristotle, viz., that *this* man understands because the intellective principle is *his form*. Thus, it is clear from the intellect's very operation that the intellective principle is united to the body as its form.

The same point can also be made clear from the nature of the human species, since the nature of an entity is shown by its operation. But the proper operation of a man *qua* man is to have intellective understanding, since it is through this operation that he transcends all the animals. Hence, in the *Ethics* Aristotle locates ultimate happiness in this operation, as in something proper to man. Therefore, man must be assigned his species in accord with the principle of this operation, since each thing is assigned a species by reference to its proper form. Therefore, it follows that the intellective principle is the proper form of man.

But note that the more noble a form is, the more it dominates corporeal matter, and the less immersed it is in it, and the more it exceeds it in its operation or power. Hence, we see that the form of a mixed body has certain operations that are not caused by the qualities of the elements. And the further one proceeds in nobility among forms, the more the power of the form exceeds elemental matter; for instance, the vegetative soul exceeds it more than does the form of a metal, and the sentient soul exceeds it more than does the vegetative soul. But the human soul ranks first in nobility among forms. Hence, by its power it exceeds corporeal matter to such a degree that it has a certain operation and power that corporeal matter does not share in at all. And this power is called the intellect.

Now notice that if someone were to claim that the soul is composed of matter and form, he could in no way agree that the soul is the form of the body. For given that form is actuality, whereas matter is being only in potentiality, there is no way in which what is composed of matter and form can in its own right as a whole be the form of something else. Still, as was explained above (q. 75, a. 5), if some part of it is a form, then we will call that which is form 'the soul' and that whose form it is 'the first animated thing'.

**Reply to objection 1:** As the Philosopher says in *Physics* 2, the highest (*ultima*) among natural forms, and the one that completes the natural philosopher's investigation, viz., the human soul, is (a) separated, to be sure, and yet (b) in matter. The latter he proves from the fact that "man, along with the sun, generates a man out of matter." On the other hand, it is separated with respect to its intellective power, since the intellective power is not a power that belongs to any corporeal organ in the way that the visual power is an act that belongs to the eye. For intellective understanding is an act that cannot be exercised by means of a corporeal organ, in the way that the act of seeing is exercised. Still, the soul exists in matter to the extent that the soul itself, to which the power of understanding belongs, is the form of the body and the terminus of human generation.

So, then, the reason why the Philosopher says in *De Anima* 3 that the intellect is "separated" is that it is not a power that belongs to any corporeal organ.

**Reply to objection 2 and objection 3:** This makes clear the replies to the second and third objections. For the fact that the intellective power is not an act belonging to the body is sufficient both (a) for a man's being able to understand all things through his intellect and (b) for the intellect's understanding immaterial things and universals.

**Reply to objection 4:** Because of its perfection, the human soul is not a form that is immersed in corporeal matter or entirely encompassed (*totaliter comprehensa*) by it. And so nothing prevents it from being the case that a certain power of the soul is not an act belonging to the body, even though the soul is by its essence the form of the body.

**Reply to objection 5:** The soul communicates the *esse* in which it itself subsists to the corporeal matter that, along with the intellective soul, makes up a single entity, with the result that the *esse* that belongs to the whole composite is also the *esse* of the soul itself. This is not the case with other forms that are not subsistent. And it is for this reason that the human soul, but not other forms, remains in its own *esse* after its body has been destroyed.

**Reply to objection 6:** It is fitting for the soul in its own right to be united to the body, in the same way that it is fitting for a lightweight body to be high up. And just as a lightweight body remains lightweight when separated from its proper place and retains its aptitude for, and inclination toward, its proper place, so too the human soul remains in its *esse* when it has been separated from its body—even while retaining its natural aptitude for, and inclination toward, union with the body.

## Article 2

### Is the intellective principle multiplied as the bodies are multiplied?

It seems that the intellective principle is not multiplied as the bodies are multiplied, but that instead there is just a single intellect for all men (*sit unus intellectus in omnibus hominibus*):

**Objection 1:** No immaterial substance is numerically multiplied within a single species. But the human soul is an immaterial substance; for as was shown above (q. 75, a. 5), it is not composed of matter and form. Therefore, it is not the case that there are many human souls belonging to a single species. But all men belong to a single species. Therefore, there is a single intellect for all men (*unus intellectus omnium hominum*).

**Objection 2:** When a cause is removed, its effect is removed. Therefore, if human souls were multiplied as the bodies are multiplied, it would seem to follow that when the bodies are removed, what remains is not a multitude of souls, but just a single one of all the souls. But this is heretical, since the difference between rewards and punishments would disappear.

**Objection 3:** If my intellect is distinct from your intellect, then my intellect is a certain individual, and likewise your intellect; for they are particulars that differ numerically and agree in a single species. But whatever is received in a thing exists in that thing according to the mode of the receiver. Therefore, the species of things are received individually in my intellect and in your intellect. But this is contrary to the nature of the intellect, because the intellect has cognition of universals.

**Objection 4:** What is understood (*intellectum*) exists in an intellect when that intellect has an act of understanding (*in intellectu intelligente*). Therefore, if my intellect is distinct from your intellect, then what is understood by me must be distinct from what is understood by you (*aliud sit intellectum a me et aliud intellectum a te*). And so what is understood will be counted as an individual (*individualiter numeratum*), and it is only in potentiality that it will be understood intellectively; and so it will be necessary to abstract a common intention from the two things understood, since from any two different things it is possible to abstract a common intelligible thing But this is contrary to the nature of the intellect, since if it were so, then the intellect would not seem to be distinct from the power of imagining (*a virtute imaginativa*). Therefore, it seems to follow that there is a single intellect for all men.

**Objection 5:** When a student receives knowledge from a teacher, one cannot say that the teacher's knowledge generates knowledge in the student, since otherwise knowledge would be an active form in the way that heat is—which is clearly false. Therefore, it seems that numerically the same knowledge that is in the teacher is communicated to the student. But this is impossible unless there is a single intellect for the two of them. Therefore, it seems that there is a single intellect for the student and the teacher—and, consequently, for all men.

**Objection 6:** In his book *De Quantitate Animae* Augustine says, "If I were to claim that there are as many human souls as that, I would laugh at myself." But it is especially with respect to the intellect that the soul seems to be one. Therefore, there is a single intellect for all men.

**But contrary to this:** In *Physics* 2 the Philosopher says that particular causes are related to particulars in the same way that universal causes are related to universals. But it is impossible for a soul that is one in species to belong to animals that are diverse in species. Therefore, it is impossible for an intellective soul that is one in number to belong to things that are numerically diverse.

**I respond:** It is altogether impossible for there to be a single intellect for all men.

This is utterly obvious if, in keeping with Plato's opinion, the man is the intellect itself. For it would follow that if there is just one intellect for Socrates and Plato, then Socrates and Plato are a single man and are distinct from one another only in what lies outside the essence of both. And in that case the distinction between Socrates and Plato will be no different from the distinction between a man wearing a tunic and the same man wearing a cape (*distinctio non alia quam hominis tunicati et cappati*)—which is completely absurd.

It is likewise clear that this is impossible if, in keeping with Aristotle's opinion, the intellect is thought of as a part, i.e., a power, of that soul which serves as the form of a man. For it is impossible that many numerically diverse things should have a single form, just as it is impossible that numerically diverse things should have a single *esse*. For the form is the source of *esse* (*principium essendi*).

Similarly, it is clear that the claim in question is impossible regardless of how one thinks of the intellect's union with *this* man and *that* man:

(a) For instance, it is obvious that if they are a single principal agent and two instruments, then one can say that there is a single agent absolutely speaking but more than one action—just as, if a single man touches different things with his two hands, there will be one toucher and two touches.

(b) Conversely, if they are a single instrument and two different principal agents, then there would be more than one agent but a single action—in the same way that if many men are dragging a boat with a single rope, there will be many draggers but only a single dragging.

(c) On the other hand, if they are a single principal agent and a single instrument, then there will be one agent and one action—just as, when a blacksmith strikes with one hammer, there is one striker and one striking.

But it is clear that however the intellect might be united to or connected with *this* man or *that* man, the intellect has preeminence over the other things that belong to a man. For instance, the sentient powers obey the intellect and serve it. Therefore, if one supposed that two men had more than one intellect but a single sensory power—for instance, if the two men had a single eye—then there would be more than one man seeing but just a single act of seeing (*visio*). But if there is a single intellect, then no matter how different the other powers used by the intellect as instruments are, Socrates and Plato could not in any way be called anything but a single knower (*intelligens*). And if we add that the very act of intellective understanding (*ipsum intelligere*), which is the intellect's action, is not effected by any organ other than the intellect itself, it will follow further that there is both a single agent and a single action; that is, it will follow that all men are a single knower and that there is a single act of understanding (I mean with respect to the same intelligible object).

To be sure, my intellectual action and yours could be diversified by a diversity of phantasms—that is, by the fact that the phantasm of a rock in me is different from the one in you—if the phantasm itself, differing in the two of us, were the form of the potential intellect. For a single agent produces different actions corresponding to different forms; for instance, there are different acts of seeing (*visiones*) corresponding to the different forms of things in the same eye.

However, the phantasm is not itself the form of the potential intellect; rather, the form of the potential intellect is the intelligible species that is abstracted from the phantasms. But in a single intellect there is just one intelligible species that is abstracted from different phantasms of the same species. For instance, it is clear that in one man there can be different phantasms of a rock, and yet what is abstracted from all of them is a single intelligible species of a rock, through which that one man's intellect understands the nature *rock* by means of a single operation, despite the diversity of the phantasms. Therefore, if there were a single intellect for all men, then the diversity of the phantasms existing in *this* man and *that* man could not, as the Commentator imagines in *De Anima* 3, cause a diversity of intellectual operations in *this* man and *that* man.

Therefore, what follows is that it is altogether impossible and absurd to posit a single intellect for all men.

**Reply to objection 1:** Even though the intellective soul, just like an angel, has no matter *out of which* it is made (*non habeat materiam ex qua sit*), it is nonetheless the form of a certain matter—something that is not true of an angel. And so corresponding to the division of matter (*secundum divisionem materiae*) there are many souls of a single species, whereas it is altogether impossible for there to be many angels of a single species.

**Reply to objection 2:** Each thing has oneness in the same way that it has *esse* and, as a result, the same judgment should be made about the multiplication of a thing as about its *esse*. But it is obvious that by its own *esse*, the intellectual soul is united to the body as its form and, yet, when the body is destroyed, the intellectual soul remains with its *esse*. For the same reason, a multitude of souls corresponds to the multitude of bodies, and, yet, when the bodies are destroyed, the souls remain multiplied in their *esse*.

**Reply to objection 3:** The *individuality* (*individuatio*) of that which has intellective understanding, or of the species through which it understands, does not rule out its understanding universals; otherwise, given that intellects are certain subsistent substances and thus particulars, they would not be able to understand universals. Rather, it is the *materiality* of a cognitive [power] and of the species through which it has cognition that impedes the cognition of a universal. For just as every action follows the mode of the form by which its agent acts—in the way that the action of giving warmth follows the mode of heat—so too a cognition follows the mode of the species by which the knower has the cognition. But it is obvious that a common nature is made distinct and is multiplied in accord with the individuating principles, which come from the side of the matter. Therefore, if the form by which a cognition comes to be is a material form that is not abstracted from the conditions of matter, then it will be a likeness of the nature of a species or genus insofar as that nature is made distinct and multiplied by individuating principles, and so the nature will not be able to be known in its commonality. By contrast, if the species is abstracted from the conditions of the material individual, then it will be a likeness of the nature in the absence of the principles that divide and multiply it; and it is in this way that there is cognition of a universal.

Also, as far as this present point is concerned, it makes no difference whether there is a single intellect or more than one. For even if there were just one intellect, it would have to be a certain individual (*aliquem quendam*), and the species through which it has intellective understanding would have to be a certain individual (*aliquam quandam*).

**Reply to objection 4:** What is understood intellectively is a single thing, regardless of whether there is a single intellect or many. For what is understood exists in the intellect not in its own right (*non secundum se*) but as a likeness. For as *De Anima* 3 says, "It is not the rock, but a likeness of the rock, that exists in the soul." And yet, except when the intellect is reflecting upon itself, what is understood is the rock, and not a likeness of a rock; otherwise, scientific knowledge would be about intelligible species and not about the things.

Now it is possible for diverse things to be assimilated to one and the same thing by means of diverse forms. And since cognition comes to be by an assimilation of the knower to the thing known (*secundum assimilationem cognoscentis ad rem cognitam*), it follows that it is possible for the same thing to be known by different knowers. This is clear in the case of the senses; for many knowers see the same color by means of different likenesses. Similarly, many intellects have intellective understanding of a single thing that is understood (*plures intellectus intelligunt unam rem intellectam*).

According to Aristotle's position, the only difference between the senses and the intellect is that a thing is sensed in accord with the disposition it has outside the soul, in its particularity, whereas the nature of a thing, which is what there is intellective understanding of, exists, to be sure, outside the soul, but outside the soul it does not have the very mode of existence according to which it is understood. For a common nature is understood intellectively with its individuating principles set aside, but it does not have this mode of existing outside the soul. However, according to Plato's position, the thing that is understood intellectively exists outside the soul in the same mode as that in which it is understood; for he claimed that the natures of things are separated from matter.

**Reply to objection 5:** The student's knowledge is different from the teacher's. In what follows (q. 117, a. 1) we will show how it is caused.

**Reply to objection 6:** Augustine's meaning is that there are not so many souls that they cannot be united in a single concept of the species.


### Article 3

### Are there, in addition to the intellective soul, other souls in a man that differ from it in their essence, viz., a sentient soul and a nutritive soul?

It seems that there are, in addition to the intellective soul, other souls in a man that differ from it in their essence, viz., a sentient soul and a nutritive soul:

**Objection 1:** The corruptible and the incorruptible cannot belong to the same substance. But as is clear from what was said above (q. 75, a. 6), the intellective soul is incorruptible, whereas the other souls, viz., the sentient soul and the nutritive soul, are corruptible. Therefore, it cannot be the case that in a man the intellective soul, the sentient soul, and the nutritive soul have a single essence.

**Objection 2:** If someone replies that in a man the sentient soul is incorruptible, then against this:

As *Metaphysics* 10 says, "The corruptible and the incorruptible differ in genus." But the sentient soul is corruptible in a horse and in a lion and in other brute animals. Therefore, if the sentient soul were incorruptible in a man, it would not be of the same genus in a man and in a brute animal. But something is called 'an animal' from the fact that it has a sentient soul. Therefore, *animal* will not be a single genus common to both man and the other animals—which is absurd.

**Objection 3:** In *De Generatione Animalium* the Philosopher claims that the embryo is an animal before being a man. But this cannot be the case if the same essence belongs to both the sentient soul and the intellective soul, since something is an animal through the sentient soul and a man through the intellective soul. Therefore, it is not the case that in a man the sentient and intellective souls have a single essence.

**Objection 4:** In *Metaphysics* 8 the Philosopher says that the genus is taken from the matter and the difference from the form. But *rational*, which is the constitutive difference of man, is taken from the intellective soul, whereas something is called an *animal* because it has a body animated by a sentient soul. Therefore, the intellective soul is related to a body animated by a sentient soul as form to matter. Therefore, it is not the case that in a man the intellective soul is the same in essence as the sentient soul. Rather, the intellective soul presupposes the sentient soul as a material suppositum.

**But contrary to this:** *De Ecclesiasticis Dogmatibus* says, "Unlike Jacob and the other Syrians, we do not say that there are two souls in one man—the one an animal soul, by which the body is animated and which is mixed with the blood, and the other a spiritual soul, which gives rise to reason. To the contrary, we say that in a man there is one and same soul which both vivifies the body by its association with it and conducts itself by its reason."

**I respond:** Plato held that there are diverse souls in the one body and even, corresponding to the organs, distinct souls to which he attributed the various vital operations—claiming that the nutritive power resides in the liver, the concupiscible power in the heart, and the cognitive power in the brain.

In *De Anima* Aristotle argues against this opinion as regards the parts of the soul that use corporeal organs in their operations; he does so by appealing to the fact that in animals that live after having been divided, the different operations of the soul, such as sensation and appetition, are found in each part. But this would not be so if different principles of the soul's operations—i.e., souls diverse in their essence—were distributed among the different parts of the body. However, as regards the intellective soul, he seems to leave it in question whether it is separate from the other parts of the soul "only conceptually or also spatially" (*solum ratione, an etiam loco*).

Now Plato's position could be sustained if one claimed that the soul is united to the body not as a form but as a mover, as Plato did in fact claim. For nothing absurd follows if the same moveable thing is moved by different movers, especially with respect to different parts.

However, if we claim that the soul is united to the body as a form, it seems altogether impossible for many souls, differing in their essence, to exist in a single body. This can be made clear in three ways:

First, an animal would not have oneness absolutely speaking (*non esset simpliciter unum*) if it had more than one soul. For nothing has oneness absolutely speaking except because of a single form through which the thing has *esse*, since the fact that an entity is a being and the fact that it is unified derive from the same source. And so things that are denominated from different forms, e.g., *white man*, do not have oneness absolutely speaking. Therefore, if the fact that a man is living were derived from one form, viz., the vegetative soul, and the fact that he is an animal were derived from a second form, viz., the sentient soul, and the fact that he is a man were derived from a third form, viz., the rational soul, then it would follow that a man does not have oneness absolutely speaking—in just the way Aristotle argued against Plato in *Metaphysics* 8 that if the idea *animal* were different from the idea *bipedal*, then a bipedal animal would not have oneness absolutely speaking. It is for this reason that in *De Anima* 1 he asks, in opposition to those who posit diverse souls in the body, what it is that contains those souls, i.e., what it is that is constituted as one thing from them. One cannot reply that they are made one by the body's oneness, since it is the soul that contains the body and makes it to have oneness, rather than vice versa.

Second, the position in question is seen to be impossible by appeal to the modes of predication. For things derived from different forms are such that either (a) they are predicated of one another *per accidens*, if the forms are not ordered to one another, as when we say that what is white is sweet, or (b), if the forms are ordered to one another, then there will be *per se* predication in the second mode of *per se* predication, since the subject occurs in the definition of the predicate. For instance, a surface is a prerequisite for color, and so if we say that a body with a surface is colored, this will be the second mode of *per se* predication. Therefore, if the form from which something is called 'an animal' were different from the form from which it is called 'a man', then either (a) one of them would be able to be predicated of the other only *per accidens*, if they have no ordering with respect to one another, or (b) there would be a predication in the second mode of *per se* predication, if one of the souls were a prerequisite for the other. But both of these alternatives are manifestly false. For *animal* is predicated *per se* of *man* and not *per accidens*; nor does *man* occur in the definition of *animal*—just the opposite. Therefore, the form through which something is an animal must be the same form through which something is a man; otherwise, a man would not truly be something that is an animal, so that *animal* might be predicated *per se* of *man*.

Third, the position in question is seen to be impossible from the fact that when one operation of the soul is intense, it impedes the other operations.

But this would not be possible if the principle of the actions were not one in essence.

Therefore, one should claim that in a man the sentient, intellective, and nutritive souls are numerically the same (*eadem numero*).

Now just how this is possible can easily be seen if one attends to the differences among species and forms. For the species and forms of things are found to differ with respect to the more perfect and the less perfect. For instance, within the order of things, the living are more perfect than the non-living, and animals are more perfect than plants, and men are more perfect than brute animals; and within each of these genera there are diverse levels. This is why in *Metaphysics* 8 Aristotle compares the species of things to numbers, which themselves differ in species insofar as the number *one* (*unitas*) is added or subtracted. And in *De Anima* 2 he compares the different types of soul to shapes that are such that one of them contains the other, in the way that a pentagon contains a tetragon and goes beyond it. So, then, the intellective soul has within its power whatever the sentient soul of brutes animals has and whatever the nutritive soul of plants has. Therefore, just as a surface with a pentagonal shape is not tetragonal through one shape and pentagonal through another shape—since the tetragonal shape would be superfluous, given that it is contained within the pentagon—so neither is Socrates a man through one soul and an animal through another soul; instead, it is through one and the same soul that he is a man and an animal.

**Reply to objection 1:** The sentient soul does not have incorruptibility by virtue of its being sentient; rather, incorruptibility is owed to it by virtue of its being intellective. Therefore, when a soul is merely sentient, it is corruptible, whereas when it is intellective in addition to being sentient, then it is incorruptible. For even though sentience does not bestow incorruptibility (*incorruptio*), it nonetheless cannot rob what is intellective of its incorruptibility.

**Reply to objection 2:** It is the composites, and not the forms, that are collected together into a genus or species. Now man is corruptible, just as the other animals are. Hence, the difference with respect to corruptibility and incorruptibility, which has to do with the forms, does not make man differ in genus from the other animals.

**Reply to objection 3:** The embryo first has a soul that is merely sentient, but when this is cast off, there comes a more perfect soul that is both sentient and intellective (*qua abiecta advenit perfectior anima quae est simul sensitiva et intellectiva*). This will be shown in more detail below (q. 118, a. 2).

**Reply to objection 4:** It is not necessary for there to be among natural things a diversity that corresponds to the diverse concepts (*rationes*) or logical intentions (*intentiones logicae*) that follow upon our mode of understanding. For reason can apprehend one and the same entity in diverse ways. Therefore, since, as has been explained, the intellective soul contains within its power what the sentient soul has and more besides, reason is able to consider what pertains to the power of the sentient soul separately as something imperfect and material (*quasi imperfectum et materiale*), so to speak. And since it finds this to be common to men and other animals, it forms the concept of the genus from it. On the other hand, it takes that in which the intellective soul exceeds the sentient soul as formal and perfective (*quasi formale et completivum*), and from this it formulates the specific difference of man.

### Article 4

#### Is there in man any other form besides the intellective soul?

It seems that there is in man some other form besides the intellective soul:

**Objection 1:** In *De Anima* 2 the Philosopher says, "The soul is the actuality of a physical body that has life in potentiality." Therefore, the soul is related to the body as form to matter. But a body has a substantial form through which it is a body. Therefore, in the body there is a substantial form prior to the soul.

**Objection 2:** Man, along with every animal, is a self-mover. But as *Physics* 8 shows, everything that moves itself is divided into two parts, one of which effects the motion and the other of which is moved. Now the part that effects the motion is the soul. Therefore, the other part must be such that it is capable of being moved. But as *Physics* 5 says, primary matter cannot be moved, since it is an entity only in potentiality, whereas everything that is moved is a body. Therefore, in man—and in every animal—there must be a second substantial form through which the body is constituted.

**Objection 3:** There is an ordering among forms according to their relation to primary matter, since 'prior' and 'posterior' are predicated relative to some principle. Therefore, if in man there were no substantial form besides the rational soul, and if instead the rational soul directly inhered in primary matter, then it would follow that the rational soul belongs to the order of the most imperfect forms, viz., those that directly inhere in matter.

**Objection 4:** The human body is a mixed body. But a mixture cannot be made just of matter (*non fit secundum materiam tantum*), since in that case it would be a mere corruption. Therefore, the forms of the elements, which are substantial forms, must remain in a mixed body. Therefore, in the human body there are other substantial forms besides the intellective soul.

**But contrary to this:** A single entity has just a single substantival *esse*. But it is the substantial form that gives substantival *esse*. Therefore, a single entity has just one substantial form. But the soul is the substantial form of man. Therefore, it is impossible for there to be in a man any substantial form other than the intellective soul.

**I respond:** If one claimed, as did the Platonists, that the intellective soul is united to the body only as its mover and not as its form, then he would have to assert that in a man there is another substantial form through which the body moved by the soul is constituted in its own *esse*. However, if, as we have already claimed above (a. 1), the intellective soul is united to the body as its substantial form, then it is impossible for any other substantial form besides it to be found in a man.

To see this clearly, note that a substantial form differs from an accidental form in that an accidental form gives such-*esse* (*esse tale*) and not *esse* absolutely speaking (*esse simpliciter*); for instance, heat makes its subject *to be hot* and not *to be* absolutely speaking. And so when an accidental form appears, one does not say that something is made or generated absolutely speaking (*fieri vel generari simpliciter*); rather, one says that it comes to be such-and-such (*fieri tale*) or that it comes to be disposed in a certain way (*fieri aliquo modo habens se*). Similarly, when an accidental form disappears, one does not say that something is corrupted absolutely speaking (*corrumpi simpliciter*); rather, one says that it is corrupted in a certain respect (*corrumpi secundum quid*). By contrast, a substantial form gives *esse* absolutely speaking, and so at its appearance something is said to be generated absolutely speaking, and at its disappearance something is said to be corrupted absolutely speaking. This is why the ancient natural philosophers, who thought that primary matter is some actual being (e.g., fire or air or something of this sort), claimed that nothing is either generated or corrupted absolutely speaking; instead, as *Physics* 1 reports, they maintained that every instance of coming-to-be is an instance of being-altered. Therefore, if it were true that besides the intellective soul there are other preexistent substantial forms in the matter through which the soul's subject is an actual being, then it would follow that the soul does not give *esse* absolutely speaking, and that consequently it is not a substantial form, and that at the soul's appearance there is no generation absolutely speaking, and that at its disappearance there is no corruption absolutely speaking; instead, there would be generation or corruption only in a certain respect. But all of these claims are manifestly false.

Hence, one should reply that (a) there is no substantial form in a man other than the intellective soul alone, and that (b) just as the intellective soul virtually contains the sentient soul and the nutritive soul, so too it virtually contains all the lower forms, and that (c) it brings about by itself alone whatever the more imperfect forms bring about in other things. And the same should be said of the sentient soul in brute animals and of the nutritive soul in plants and, in general, of all the more perfect forms in relation to the less perfect forms.

**Reply to objection 1:** Aristotle did not say merely that the soul is "the actuality of a body." Rather, he said that the soul is "the actuality of an organic physical body that has life in potentiality," and that this potentiality "does not exclude the soul." Hence, the soul is also clearly included in what the soul is called the actuality of, in the same manner of speaking in which one says that heat is the actuality of what is hot, and that light is the actuality of what is bright—not that it is bright taken separately without the light, but that it is bright because of the light. Likewise, the soul is said to be the actuality of a body, etc., because it is through the soul that it is a body, and that it is organic, and that it has life in potentiality. And first actuality is said to be in potentiality with respect to second actuality, i.e., operation; for this potentiality does not rule out, i.e., exclude, the soul.

**Reply to objection 2:** It is not through its own *esse*, or insofar as it is united to the body as its form, that the soul moves the body; instead, it moves the body through its moving power, the actualization of which presupposes that the body has already been brought into actuality through the soul. So through its moving power the soul is the part that effects movement, and the animated body is the part that is moved.

**Reply to objection 3:** In matter there are different grades of perfection, e.g., *to exist* (*esse*), *to live* (*vivere*), *to sense* (*sentire*), and *to understand intellectively* (*intelligere*). Now the next in line (*secundum*), which supervenes on what is prior to it, is always more perfect than what is prior to it. Therefore, a form that gives only the first grade of perfection to matter is the least perfect, while a form that gives the first and second and third grades, and so on, is the most perfect, even though it inheres directly in the matter (*tamen materiae immediata*).

**Reply to objection 4:** Avicenna claimed that (a) the substantial forms of the elements maintain their integrity in a mixed thing, but that (b) a mixture comes into existence insofar as the contrary qualities of the elements are moderated to a mean (*reducuntur ad medium*).

But this is impossible. For the diverse forms of the elements can exist only in diverse parts of matter, and the diversity of those parts must presuppose dimensions, without which matter cannot be divisible. But matter subject to dimensions is found only in bodies, and diverse bodies cannot exist in the same place. Hence, it follows that the elements in a mixed thing are distinct from one another in place. Hence, there will not be a *genuine mixture* (*vera mixtio*), i.e., a mixture with respect to the whole, but instead there will be a *mixture with respect to the senses* (*mixtio ad sensum*), which consists of very small entities positioned close to one another.

Averroes, on the other hand, claimed in *De Caelo* 3 that, because of their imperfection, the forms of the elements lie midway between accidental forms and substantial forms, and so they admit of more and less. And so in a mixture they are remitted and moderated to a mean, and a single form is fused together from them.

But this is even more impossible. For the substantival *esse* of any given thing consists in something indivisible, and, as *Metaphysics* 8 puts it, every addition or subtraction changes the species, just as with numbers. Hence, it is impossible that any substantial form should admit of more and less. Nor is it any less impossible for something to lie midway between a substance and an accident.

And so, in keeping with what the Philosopher says in *De Generatione et Corruptione* 1, one should reply that the forms of the elements remain in a mixed thing *virtually* but *not in actuality*. For what remains are the qualities which, though less intense (*remissae*), are proper to the elements, and it is in these qualities that the power of the elemental forms resides. And the quality of this sort of mixture is a proper disposition for the substantial form of the mixed body, e.g., the form of a rock or of any type of soul.

## Article 5

### Is it fitting for an intellective soul to be united to the sort of body in question?

It seems that it is not fitting for an intellective soul to be united to the sort of body in question:

**Objection 1:** The matter has to be proportionate to the form. But the intellective soul is an incorruptible form. Therefore, it is not fitting for it to be united to a corruptible body.

**Objection 2:** The intellective soul is a maximally immaterial form; an indication of this is that it has an operation in which corporeal matter does not share. But the more subtle a body is, the less it has of matter. Therefore, the soul should have been united to the most subtle sort of body, viz., fire, and not to a body that is mixed and rather earthy (*non corpori mixto et terrestri magis*).

**Objection 3:** Since the form is the principle of the species, it is not the case that diverse species spring from a single form. But the intellective soul is a single form. Therefore, it should not be united to a body that is composed of parts of dissimilar species.

**Objection 4:** There ought to be a more perfect subject (*perfectius susceptibile*) for a more perfect form. But the intellective soul is the most perfect of forms. Therefore, since the bodies of the other animals are naturally provided with covering, e.g., fur instead of clothes and hooves instead of shoes, and since they are also naturally endowed with weapons such as claws, teeth, and horns, it seems that the intellective soul should not have been united to an imperfect body, i.e., one deprived of these sorts of assistance.

**But contrary to this:** In *De Anima* 2 the Philosopher says that the soul is "the actuality of an organic physical body that has life potentially."

**I respond:** Since the form does not exist for the sake of the matter, but instead the matter exists for the sake of the form, the reason why the matter is the way that it is has to be taken from the form (*ex forma oportet rationem accipere quare materia sit talis*), and not vice versa.

Now as was established above (q. 55, a. 2), within the order of nature the intellective soul occupies the lowest grade among intellectual substances. For unlike the angels, the intellective soul is not endowed by nature with knowledge of the truth, but instead, as Dionysius puts it in *De Divinis Nominibus*, chap. 7, it must gather its knowledge from divisible things by way of the senses.

Now nature is not lacking in necessities, and so the intellective soul had to possess not only the power of intellective understanding, but also the power of sensing. But the action of the senses does not exist in the absence of a corporeal instrument. Therefore, the intellective soul had to be united to a body of a sort that could serve as an appropriate instrument of the sensory power (*conveniens organum sensus*). But all the other senses are grounded in the sense of touch, and the organ of touch must be a medium between those contraries that the sense of touch apprehends, viz., hot and cold, moist and dry, etc. And in this way it is in potentiality with respect to the contraries and able to sense them. Hence, the more the organ of touch is drawn toward a balanced composition (*reductum ad aequalitatem complexionis*), the more sensitive the sense of touch will be. But the intellective soul has the sentient power most fully, because, as Dionysius says in *De Divinis Nominibus*, what belongs to the lower exists more perfectly in the higher. Hence, the body to which the intellective soul is united had to be a mixed body that, among all others, was more drawn toward a balanced composition. And because of this, among all the animals man has the best sense of touch. And among men themselves, those who have a better sense of touch have better intellective understanding. An indication of this is that as, *De Anima* 2 points out, "We see that those who are refined in body are very capable mentally."

**Reply to objection 1:** Someone might want to evade this objection by claiming that man's body was incorruptible before sin.

But this reply does not seem adequate. For prior to sin, man's body was immortal not by nature, but by a gift of God's grace. Otherwise, his immortality would not have been taken away because of sin, just as a demon's immortality was not taken away because of sin.

And so one must reply in an alternative way, viz., that there are two conditions in which matter is found: (a) one is chosen in order that it might be appropriate for the form, and (b) the other follows from a necessity of a prior disposition. For instance, a craftsman chooses iron as the matter for the form of a saw because of iron's aptness for cutting through hard material, whereas the fact that the teeth of the saw can become blunt and rusted follows from a necessity of the matter. So, then, the intellective soul needs a body that has a balanced composition, but it thereby follows, from a necessity of the matter, that the body is corruptible.

Now if someone objects that God could have circumvented this necessity, the appropriate reply is that, as Augustine says in *Super Genesim ad Litteram* 2, when it comes to the constitution of natural things, one takes into account not what God can do, but instead what is fitting for the nature of things. Still, God provided in this case by applying the remedy against death through the gift of grace.

**Reply to objection 2:** It is not because of the intellectual operation itself, taken in its own right, that the intellective soul needs the body; rather, it needs the body because of the sentient power, which requires an instrument with balanced composition (*organum aequaliter complexionatum*). And this is the reason why the intellective soul had to be united to this sort of body and not to a simple element or to a mixed body in which fire dominated quantitatively. For because of fire's excessively active power, such a body could not have had a balanced composition. On the other hand, this body, with its balanced composition, has a certain dignity because of its remoteness from the contraries, and in this feature it is in some sense similar to a celestial body.

**Reply to objection 3:** It is not the parts of an animal, such as the eye, the hand, the flesh and bone, etc., that belong to a species, but rather the whole animal. And so it cannot be said, properly speaking, that these parts are diverse in *species*; rather, they are diverse in *disposition*. And this fact is traced to the intellective soul, which, even though it is one in essence, is nonetheless, because of its perfection, complex in its power (*multiplex in virtute*). And so for the diverse operations it needs diverse dispositions in the parts of the body to which it is united. Because of this, we see that there is more diversity in the parts of perfect animals than in the parts of imperfect animals, and more diversity in animals than in plants.

**Reply to objection 4:** Since the intellective soul comprehends universals, it has power with respect to infinitely many things. And so it was impossible for nature to have given it determinate natural judgments (*determinatae existimationes naturales*) or even determinate aids or defenses or coverings like those of the other animals, whose souls have apprehension and power with respect to a limited range of particulars (*ad aliqua particularia determinata*). In place of all of these, man by nature has reason and hands, which are "the instruments of instruments" (*organa organorum*), since by use of them man is able to make instruments of infinitely many kinds and for the sake of infinitely many effects.

## Article 6

### Is the intellective soul united to the body through the mediation of certain accidental dispositions?

It seems that the intellective soul is united to the body through the mediation of certain accidental dispositions:

**Objection 1:** Every form is in a matter that is proper to it and disposed for it. But the dispositions for a form are certain accidents. Therefore, certain accidents must be presupposed in the matter prior to the substantial form—and so prior to the soul, since the soul is a substantial form.

**Objection 2:** Diverse forms of a single species require diverse parts of matter. But diverse parts of matter can be thought of only as corresponding to the division of dimensional quantities. Therefore, dimensions have to be presupposed in the matter prior to those substantial forms that are multiplied within a single species.

**Objection 3:** The spiritual is applied to the corporeal through a virtual contact. But the soul's virtue (*virtus*) is its power (*potentia*). Therefore, it seems that the soul is united to the body by the mediation of power, which is a certain accident.

**But contrary to this:** As *Metaphysics* 7 says, an accident is posterior to its substance "both temporally and conceptually." Therefore, no accidental form can be thought of as existing in the matter prior to the soul, which is the substantial form.

**I respond:** If the soul were united to the body as its mover, then nothing would prevent its being the case—indeed, it would have to be the case—that certain dispositions mediate between the soul and the body, viz., (a) on the part of the soul, a power by which it moves the body, and (b) on the part of the body, a certain aptitude by which the body is able to be moved by the soul.

However, if, as has already been explained (a. 1), the intellective soul is united to the body as its substantial form, then it is impossible for any accidental disposition to mediate (*cadat media*) between the body and the soul—or, for that matter, between *any* substantial form and its matter. The reason is that there is a certain order in which the matter is in potentiality to all its corresponding actualities, and so the actuality that is the first of all the actualities, absolutely speaking, must be thought of as the first one that is in the matter. But the first among all the actualities is *esse*. Therefore, it is impossible to think of the matter as being hot or quantified before thinking of it as existing in actuality. But *esse* in actuality is had through the substantial form, which makes a thing to exist absolutely speaking, as has already been explained (a. 4). Hence, it is impossible that any accidental disposition should exist in the matter prior to the substantial form or, consequently, prior to the soul.

**Reply to objection 1:** As is clear from what was said above (a. 4), a more perfect form virtually contains whatever belongs to the lower forms. And so one and the same existent form perfects the matter with respect to diverse grades of perfection. For it is one and the same form in essence through which a man is (a) a being in actuality, (b) a body, (c) a living being, (d) an animal, and (e) a man. But it is clear that every genus is such that its proper accidents follow from it. Therefore, just as the matter is thought of as being complete in its *esse* (*perfecta secundum esse*) prior to its being thought of as a body (*ante intellectum corporeitatis*), and so on, so too the accidents that are proper to it as a being are thought of as preceding its being a body (*ante corporeitatem*). And so dispositions are thought of as being present in the matter prior to the form with respect to the form's later effects, but not with respect to all its effects.

**Reply to objection 2:** Quantitative dimensions are accidents that follow upon the thing's being a body, which belongs to the matter as a whole (*accidentia consequentia corporeitatem, quae toti materiae convenit*). Hence, once the matter is thought of as existing under the corporeity and dimensions, it can then be thought of as being divided into distinct parts, so that it might receive diverse forms corresponding to further grades of perfection. For even though, as has been explained (a. 4), it is in essence the same form that gives the diverse grades of perfection to the matter, there are nonetheless differences according to reason's consideration of it.

**Reply to objection 3:** A spiritual substance that is united to a body only as its mover is united to it through its power, i.e., virtually (*per potentiam vel virtutem*). But the intellective soul is united to the body as a form through its own *esse*.

Still, it is through the soul's power or virtue that it oversees (*administrat*) the body and moves it.

## Article 7

### Is the soul united to the animal body by the mediation of a body?

It seems that the soul is united to the animal body by the mediation of another body:

**Objection 1:** In *Super Genesim ad Litteram* 7 Augustine says, "The soul oversees (*administrat*) the body through light, i.e., fire, and air, which are more similar to a spirit." But fire and air are bodies. Therefore, the soul is united to the human body by the mediation of a body.

**Objection 2:** If something is such that when it is taken away, the union of things that had been united is dissolved, then it seems to be a mediator between those things. But when breathing (*spiritus*) ceases, the soul is separated from the body. Therefore, breath, which is a subtle body, is a mediator in the union of the body and the soul.

**Objection 3:** Things that are distant from one another are united only through a medium. But the intellective soul is distant from the body, both because it is incorporeal and because it is incorruptible. Therefore, it seems that it is united to the body by the mediation of something that is an incorruptible body. And this seems to be some sort of celestial light, which harmonizes the elements and makes them one.

**But contrary to this:** In *De Anima* 2 the Philosopher says, "one need not ask if the soul and body are one, just as one need not ask whether the wax and the shape are one." But the shape is united to the wax without the mediation of any other body. Therefore, the soul is likewise united to the body without the mediation of a body.

**I respond:** If, as the Platonists hold, the soul were united to the body only as a mover, then it would be appropriate to claim that certain other bodies intervene between man's soul—or that of any animal—and his body. For it is appropriate that a mover should effect motion in a distant thing through the mediation of things that are closer.

However, if, as has already been explained (a. 1), the soul is united to the body as its form, then it is impossible that it should be united to it by the mediation of a body. The reason for this is that a thing is called *one* in the same way that it is called *a being*. But it is the form that through itself makes a thing to exist in actuality, since it is an actuality through its own essence and so does not give *esse* through any mediator. Hence, the oneness of an entity composed of matter and form is due to the form itself, which is united to the matter in its own right as the actuality of the matter. Nor, with the exception of the agent, is there anything else that makes the matter to exist in actuality—as *Metaphysics* 8 explains.

Hence, the views of those who claimed that certain bodies mediate between man's soul and body are clearly false. Certain Platonists among them asserted that (a) the intellective soul has an incorruptible body that is naturally united to it and from which it is never separated, and that (b) it is by the mediation of this body that the intellective soul is united to a corruptible human body.

Others claimed that it is united to the body by the mediation of a corporeal spirit.

Still others said that it is united to the body by the mediation of light, which they claimed to be a body and a fifth essence by nature, so that (a) the vegetative soul is united to the body by the mediation of the light of the starry heaven, (b) the sentient soul is united by the mediation of the light of the crystalline heaven, and (c) the intellectual soul is united by the mediation of the light of the empyrean heaven. All of this is clearly fictitious and ridiculous, since (a) light is not a body, (b) the fifth essence enters only virtually and not materially into the composition of mixed bodies, given that it is not subject to alteration (*inalterabilis*), and (c) the soul is directly united to the body as the form of its matter.

**Reply to objection 1:** Augustine is talking about the soul insofar as it moves the body; this is why he uses the word 'oversight' (*administratio*). And it is true that the grosser parts of the body are moved by the more subtle ones. As the Philosopher puts it in *De Causa Motus Animalium*, the first instrument of the moving power is an animal spirit.

**Reply to objection 2:** The reason why the union of the soul to the body ceases when breath ceases is not that breath is a mediator, but that the disposition by which the body is disposed toward such a union is destroyed. Still, breath is a mediator in effecting movement as the first instrument of motion.

**Reply to objection 3:** If the conditions of the body and the soul are thought of separately, then there are several senses in which the soul is distant from the body. Hence, if the two of them had *esse* separately from one another, then many mediators would have to intervene. But since the soul is the form of the body, it does not have *esse* separately from the body's *esse*, instead, it is united to the body directly through its own *esse*. In the same way, if any form at all is thought of as an actuality, it has a great distance from matter, which is a being only in potentiality.

## Article 8

### Does the soul exist as a whole in each part of the body?

It seems that the soul does not exist as a whole in each part of the body:

**Objection 1:** In *De Causa Motus Animalium* the Philosopher says, "It is not necessary for the soul to be in each part of the body; rather, if it is in some principle of the body, then it will vivify the other parts, since all of them are apt by nature to effect their proper movement."

**Objection 2:** The soul is in the body whose actuality it is. But it is the actuality of an organic body. Therefore, it exists only in an organic body. But not every part of the human body is an organic body. Therefore, the soul does not exist as a whole in each part of the body.

**Objection 3:** *De Anima* 2 says that the soul as a whole is related to the whole body of the animal in the same way that a part of the soul is related to a part of the body, e.g., the power of vision to the pupil. Therefore, if the whole soul exists in each part of the body, then it will follow that each part of the body is an animal.

**Objection 4:** Every power of the soul is grounded in the very essence of the soul. Therefore, if the whole soul is in each part of the body, then it will follow that every power of the soul exists in every part of the body—and so vision will exist in the ear and hearing in the eye. But this is absurd.

**Objection 5:** If each part of the body were such that the soul as a whole exists in it, then each part of the body would be directly dependent on the soul. Therefore, it would not be the case that one part of the body depends upon another, or that one part is more important than another—which is manifestly false. Therefore, the soul does not exist as a whole in each part of the body.

**But contrary to this:** In *De Trinitate* 6 Augustine says, "In each body the soul exists as a whole in the whole and as a whole in each part of it."

**I respond:** As we have already explained in the other articles, if the soul were united to the body only as a mover, then one could claim that it is not in every part of the body, but is just in the one part of the body by which it moves the other parts.

However, since the soul is in fact united to the body as its form, it must exist in the whole body and in each part of the body. For it is a substantial form and not an accidental form. But a substantial form is the perfection not only of the whole, but of each part. For since a whole consists of its parts, a form of a whole that does not give *esse* to each part of a body is a form which is, like the form of a house, itself a composition and an ordering [of parts]; and a form of this sort is an accidental form. The soul, by contrast, is a substantial form, and so it has to be the form and actuality not only of the whole but also of each part. And so just as, when the soul departs, [the body] is only equivocally called an animal and a man, like an animal in a picture or one made out of stone, so it is with the hands and eyes, or bones and flesh—as the Philosopher explains. An indication of this is that when the soul departs, no part of the body retains its proper function (*proprium opus*), whereas anything that retains its species retains the operation of that species. Now an actuality exists in that of which it is the actuality. Hence, the soul has to be in the whole body and in each part of the body.

From here we can consider the claim that the soul exists *as a whole* in each part of the body. For there are three kinds of wholes, corresponding to the three types of division in which a whole is divided into parts. One type is a whole divided into *quantitative parts*, e.g., a whole line or a whole body. Next, there is the type of whole divided into *rational* or *essential parts* (*partes rationis et essentiae*), as when what is defined is divided into the parts of the definition, or when what is composed is resolved into its matter and form. The third type is a whole power (*totum potentiale*), which is divided into *virtual parts* (*partes virtutis*).

Now the first type of wholeness belongs to forms only *per accidens* and then only to those forms that have a uniform relation (*habent indifferentem habitudinem*) to a quantitative whole and to its parts. For instance, as far as its own nature is concerned, a [patch of] whiteness (*albedo*) is equally in a whole surface and in each part of the surface, and so the whiteness is incidentally (*per accidens*) divided when the surface is divided. By contrast, a form that requires diversity in the parts—such as a soul, and especially the soul of a perfect animal—is not related in the same way to the whole and to the parts, and so it is not divided *per accidens* when the quantity is divided. So, then, quantitative wholeness cannot be attributed to the soul either *per se* or *per accidens*.

On the other hand, the second kind of wholeness, which involves a completeness of concept or of essence, belongs to forms properly and *per se*. And the same holds for a wholeness of power (*totalitas virtutis*), since a form is a principle of operation.

Therefore, if one were asking whether or not whiteness exists as a whole in the whole surface and in each of the parts, it would be necessary to draw a distinction. For if the question were about a quantitative whole that has whiteness *per accidens*, then the whiteness would not exist as a whole in each of the parts. And the same would have to be said of a complete power, since the whiteness that exists in the whole surface is able to affect vision more than is the whiteness that exists in some small part (*particula*) of the surface. On the other hand, if the question were about the specific and essential whole (*de totalitate speciei et essentiae*), then whiteness as a whole is in each part of the surface.

However, since, as has been explained, the soul does not have a quantitative wholeness either *per se* or *per accidens*, it is enough to say that the soul exists as a whole in each part of the body with respect to a wholeness of perfection and essence, but not with respect to a completeness of power. For it is not the case that the soul is in each part of the body with respect to each of its powers; rather, it is in the eye with respect to the power of seeing (*secundum visum*) and in the ear with respect to the power of hearing (*secundum auditum*), and so on for the others.

Note, however, that since the soul requires diversity in the parts, it is not related in the same way to the whole and to the parts. Rather, it is related to the whole in the first place and *per se* (*primo et per se*), since the whole is what it properly and proportionately perfects; by contrast, it is related to the parts secondarily (*per posterius*), insofar as they are ordered toward the whole.

**Reply to objection 1:** The Philosopher is talking about the soul's moving power.

**Reply to objection 2:** The soul is the actuality of an organic body in the sense that the organic body is what it perfects in the first place and proportionately.

**Reply to objection 3:** An animal is composed of the soul and the whole body, which the soul perfects in the first place and proportionately. But the soul is not in a part in this same way. Hence, it is not necessary for a part of an animal to be an animal.

**Reply to objection 4:** Some powers of the soul, viz., the intellect and will, are in it insofar as it exceeds the whole capacity of the body, and powers of this sort are not said to be in any part of the body. However, other powers are common to the soul and the body, and so it is not necessary for each of these powers to be in whatever part the soul is; instead, a power is just in that part of the body that is proportionate to its operation.

**Reply to objection 5:** One part of the body is said to be more important (*principalior*) than another because of the diverse powers whose organs are parts of the body. A more important part of the body is one that is an organ of a more important power or one that serves that power in a more important way.

# QUESTION 77

## The Powers of the Soul in General

Next we must consider what pertains to the powers of the soul—first in general (question 77), and then specifically (questions 78–83). On the first topic there are eight questions: (1) Is the essence of the soul the soul's own power? (2) Is there just a single power of the soul, or are there many powers? (3) How are the powers of the soul distinguished from one another? (4) What is the ordering of the powers with respect to one another? (5) Is the soul the subject of all the powers? (6) Do the powers flow from the essence of the soul (*fluant ab essentia animae*)? (7) Does one power arise from another? (8) Do all the powers of the soul remain in it after death?

### Article 1

### Is the very essence of the soul the soul's power?

It seems that the very essence of the soul is the soul's power (*potentia*):

**Objection 1:** In *De Trinitate* 9 Augustine says, "Mind, knowledge, and love exist in the soul substantially or, what amounts to the same thing, essentially." And in *De Trinitate* 10 he says, "Memory, understanding, and will constitute one life, one mind, one essence."

**Objection 2:** The soul is more noble than primary matter. But primary matter is its own power or potentiality (*potentia*). Therefore, *a fortiori*, so is the soul.

**Objection 3:** A substantial form is more simple than an accidental form; an indication of this is that a substantial form is not intensified or remitted, but consists in what is indivisible. But an accidental form is its own power itself (*ipsa sua virtus*). Therefore, *a fortiori*, so is the substantial form, i.e., the soul.

**Objection 4:** The sentient power is that by which we have sensation, and the intellective power is that by which we have intellective understanding. But according to the Philosopher in *De Anima* 2, it is first and foremost (*primo*) the soul by which we sense and understand. Therefore, the soul is its own powers.

**Objection 5:** Everything that does not belong to a thing's essence is an accident. Therefore, if the soul's power lies outside its essence, it follows that the soul's power is an accident. But this is contrary to Augustine in *De Trinitate* 9, where he says that the aforementioned powers "are not in the soul as in a subject, in the way that color or shape or any other quality or quantity is in a body; for nothing like that goes beyond the subject it is in, whereas the mind is able to love and to know other things as well."

**Objection 6:** "A simple form cannot be a subject." But the soul is a simple form, since, as was explained above (q. 75, a. 5), it is not composed of form and matter. Therefore, it cannot be the case that the soul's power is in it as in a subject.

**Objection 7:** An accident is not the principle of a substantival difference. But *sentient* and *rational* are substantival differences, and they are taken from sensation and reason, which are powers of the soul. Therefore, the soul's powers are not accidents. And so it seems that the soul's power is its essence.

**But contrary to this:** In *De Caelesti Hierarchia*, chap. 11, Dionysius says, "The celestial spirits are divided into essence, power, and operation." So, *a fortiori*, in the case of the soul, the essence is one thing and the virtue or power (*virtus sive potentia*) is something else.

**I respond:** It is impossible to maintain that the soul's essence is its power, even though some have made this claim. For present purposes, this will be shown in two ways:

First, since *potentiality* (*potentia*) and *actuality* (*actus*) divide *being* and every genus of being, potentiality and actuality have to be referred back to the same genus. And so, if an actuality is not in the genus of substance, then the potentiality corresponding to it cannot be in the genus of substance. Now the soul's operation is not in the genus of substance; rather, it is only in the case of God that His operation is His substance. Hence, God's power, which is a principle of operation, is the very essence of God. But as was explained above for the case of angels (q. 54, a. 3) as well, this cannot be true either of the soul or of any other creature.

Second, this is likewise obviously impossible in the case of the soul. For in its essence the soul is an actuality. Therefore, if the soul's essence were itself an immediate principle of operation, then whatever has a soul would always actually be engaging in [all of the] vital works, in the same way that whatever has a soul is always actually alive. For the soul, just insofar as it is a form, is not an actuality ordered toward any further actuality, but is instead the ultimate terminus of generation. Hence, the fact that the soul is in potentiality with respect to some further actuality is not something that belongs to it because of its *essence*, just insofar as it is a form; rather, it is something that belongs to it because of its *power*.

And so insofar as the soul itself is the subject of its own power, it is called a *first actuality* that is ordered toward a *second actuality*. But a thing that has a soul is not always in actuality with respect to [all the] vital works (*non semper esse in actu operum vitae*). Hence, in the definition of the soul one likewise says that the soul is "the actuality of a body having life in potentiality," where this potentiality "does not exclude the soul." Therefore, it follows that the soul's essence is not its power. For nothing is in potentiality with respect to an actuality insofar as it itself is an actuality.

**Reply to objection 1:** Augustine is talking about the mind insofar as it knows itself and loves itself. So, then, insofar as the knowledge and love are referred back to the mind itself as what is known and loved, they are substantially or essentially in the soul, since it is the soul's very substance or essence that is being known and loved. And this is likewise the way to understand what he says in the other place, viz., "[Memory, understanding, and will constitute] one life, one mind, one essence."

An alternative reply is that, as some claim, this last passage is rendered true by the way in which a *whole of power* (*totum potestativum*) is predicated of its parts, where this sort of whole lies between a *universal whole* (*totum universale*) and an *integral whole* (*totum integrale*). For a universal whole is present to each part with its whole essence and power, in the way that *animal* is predicated of *man* and *horse*, and in this sense is properly predicated of each part. By contrast, an integral whole is not in each part either with its whole essence or with its whole power; and so it is not in any way predicated of each part—though in a certain way, albeit improperly, it is predicated of all the parts taken together, as when we say that the walls, the roof, and the foundation are a house. Lastly, a whole of power (*totum potentiale*) is present to each part with its whole essence but not with its whole power; and there is a sense in which it can be predicated of each part, but not as properly as a universal whole is. And it is in this sense that Augustine is claiming that memory, understanding, and will are a single essence of the soul.

**Reply to objection 2:** The actuality with respect to which primary matter is in potentiality is the substantial form. And this is why the power or potentiality (*potentia*) of the matter is not distinct from its essence (*non est aliud quam eius essentia*).

**Reply to objection 3:** Acting belongs to the composite, in the same way that the *esse* belongs to the composite; for acting belongs to that which exists. But the composite has *esse* substantivally through its substantial form, whereas it acts through a power that follows upon its substantial form. Hence, a power of the soul is related to the soul in the way that an active accidental form is related to the agent's substantial form, e.g., in the way that heat is related to the form of fire.

**Reply to objection 4:** The very fact that an accidental form is a principle of action is something it derives from the substantial form. And so the substantial form is the *first* principle of action, but not the *proximate* principle of action. This is the sense in which the Philosopher is claiming that "the soul is that by which we understand and sense."

**Reply to objection 5:** If *accident* is taken in the sense in which it is divided off against *substance*, then there cannot be anything between a substance and an accident, since they are divided off as an affirmation and a negation, viz., *existing in a subject* and *not existing in a subject*. And in this sense, since the soul's power is not its essence, it must be an accident contained within the second species of *quality*.

On the other hand, if *accident* is taken in the sense in which it is posited as one of the five universals, then there is something between a substance and an accident. For whatever is essential to a thing pertains to *substance*, but not everything that lies outside of the essence can be called an accident; rather, an accident is only that which is not caused by the essential principles of the species. For a *property* (*proprium*) does not belong to the thing's essence, but is caused by the essential principles of the thing, and so it lies between an essence and an accident taken in the present sense. In this way, the powers of the soul can be said to lie between a substance and an accident in the sense that they are natural properties of the soul.

As for Augustine's claim that knowledge and love are not in the soul as accidents are in a subject, this is to be understood in the way explained above; that is, knowledge and love are being related to the soul insofar as the soul is that which is being loved and known—and not insofar as the soul is that which is knowing and loving. In this way his argument goes through. For if the love were in the-soul-as-loved as in a subject, then it would follow that an accident transcends its own subject, since there are also other things loved through the soul.

**Reply to objection 6:** Even though the soul is not composed of matter and form, it nonetheless has potentiality mixed in with it, as was explained above (q. 75, a. 5). And so it can be the subject of an accident.

The cited proposition, [viz., "A simple form cannot be a subject,"] has a place in the case of God, who is Pure Actuality, and it is in the material on God that Boethius introduces this proposition.

**Reply to objection 7:** Insofar as *rational* and *sentient* are differences, they are taken not from the powers of sentience and reason, but from the sentient and rational soul itself. Yet because substantial forms, which are unknown to us in their own right, are known through their accidents, nothing prevents accidents from sometimes being used [in definitions] in place of substantival differences.

### Article 2

### Does the soul have more than one power?

It seems that the soul does not have more than one power (*non sint plures potentiae animae*):

**Objection 1:** The intellective soul comes closest to a likeness of God. But in God there is a single and simple power. Therefore, the same holds for the intellective soul.

**Objection 2:** The higher a power is, the more unified it is. But the intellective soul exceeds all other forms in its power. Therefore, it is especially the case that it ought to have a single power or potentiality (*unam virtutem seu potentiam*).

**Objection 3:** Operating belongs to that which exists in actuality. But as was established above (q. 76, a. 3–4), it is through one and the same essence of the soul that a man has *esse* with respect to the diverse grades of perfection. Therefore, it is through one and the same power of the soul that he carries out the diverse operations of those diverse grades.

**But contrary to this:** In *De Anima* 2 the Philosopher posits a multiplicity of powers of the soul.

**I respond:** One must claim that the soul has a multiplicity of powers (*plures potentias*). To see this clearly, note that as the Philosopher says in *De Caelo* 2, the lowest things cannot attain perfect goodness, but they do attain a certain imperfect goodness by means of a few movements; and things higher than these acquire perfect goodness by means of many movements; and still higher things acquire perfect goodness by means of a few movements; and the highest perfection is found in those things that possess perfect goodness without any movements at all—in the same way that someone who is least disposed to health cannot attain perfect health, but does attain some measure of health by means of a few medicines; and someone who is better disposed to health can attain perfect health, but by means of many medicines; and someone who is still better disposed can attain perfect health by means of a few medicines; and someone who is the best disposed to health has perfect health without any medicines at all.

Therefore, one should reply that the things below man attain certain particular goods and so have a few limited operations and powers, whereas man can attain universal and perfect goodness, since he is able to possess beatitude. However, he is, according to nature, in the lowest order of beings to whom beatitude belongs, and so the human soul needs many and diverse operations and powers. By contrast, the angels have a lesser diversity of powers, whereas in God there is no power or action at all beyond His essence.

There is also another reason why the human soul abounds in a diversity of powers, viz., that it is at the boundary between spiritual and corporeal creatures (*est in confinio spiritualium et corporalium creaturarum*), and so the powers of both sorts of creatures come together in it.

**Reply to objection 1:** The intellective soul comes closer to a likeness of God than do lower creatures in the very fact that it is able to attain perfect goodness—even if through many diverse operations, a point on which it falls short of higher beings.

**Reply to objection 2:** A unified power is higher as long as it extends to just as many effects. But a multiplicity of powers is higher if more effects are subject to it.

**Reply to objection 3:** There is a single substantival *esse* for a single entity, but it is possible for there to be many operations. And so there is a single essence of the soul, but many powers.

### Article 3

### Are the powers distinguished from one another by their acts and objects?

It seems that the powers are not distinguished from one another by their acts and objects:

**Objection 1:** Nothing is contracted to a species by anything posterior to it or extrinsic to it. But the act is posterior to the corresponding power, whereas the object is extrinsic to the power. Therefore, it is not through their acts or objects that the powers are distinguished from one another in species.

**Objection 2:** Contraries differ from one another to the maximal degree. Therefore, if powers were distinguished from one another by their objects, it would follow that there is no one power with respect to contraries. But this is obviously false in almost all the relevant cases; for instance, the same visual power has black and white [as objects], and the same sense of taste has the sweet and the bitter [as objects].

**Objection 3:** When a cause is removed, its effect is removed. Therefore, if the differences among the powers stemmed from differences among their objects, the same object would not belong to diverse powers. But this is obviously false; for instance, the same thing is such that the cognitive power has cognition of it and the appetitive power desires it.

**Objection 4:** That which is a *per se* cause of something is a cause of that thing in all cases. But certain diverse objects belonging to diverse powers also belong to some one power. For instance, color and sound belong to the sense of sight and the sense of hearing, which are diverse powers; and yet they also belong to the unified common sensory power (*ad unam potentiam sensus communis*). Therefore, powers are not distinguished from one another by differences in their objects.

**But contrary to this:** Things that are posterior are distinguished by appeal to what is prior. But in *De Anima* 2 the Philosopher says that "acts and operations are conceptually prior to the corresponding powers and prior still to them are their opposites," i.e., their objects. Therefore, powers are distinguished from one another by their acts and objects.

**I respond:** A power, insofar as it is a power, is ordered toward an act. Hence, the nature of the power (*ratio potentiae*) has to be taken from the act toward which it is ordered and, as a result, the nature of the power must vary as the nature of the act varies. But the nature of the acts varies with the diverse nature of the objects.

Now every action belongs to either an *active power* or a *passive power*. The object is related to the act of a *passive* power as its source (*principium*) and moving cause; for instance, color is a source of the act of seeing (*principium visionis*) insofar as it moves the visual power (*inquantum movet visum*). On the other hand, the object is related to the act of an *active* power as its terminus and end; for instance, the object of the power to grow is a full size (*quantum perfectum*), which is the end of growth. Now an action receives its species from these two things, viz., either from its source or from its end, i.e., its terminus; for instance, heating differs from cooling insofar as the former proceeds from what is hot, viz., the active principle, to the hot, whereas the latter proceeds from what is cold to the cold. Hence, it must be the case that powers vary according to their acts and objects.

Note, however, that what is incidental (*per accidens*) does not make for a diversity of species. For instance, since being of a certain color is incidental to an animal, the species that belong to *animal* do not vary according to differences in color; instead, they vary according to the difference in what accrues *per se* to an animal, viz., by differences belonging to the sentient soul, which is sometimes found accompanied by reason and sometimes found without reason. Hence, *rational* and *non-rational* are differences that divide *animal* and constitute its diverse species.

So, then, not just any variation in the objects makes for a variation in the powers of the soul; rather, what makes for a variation is a difference in something that the power is related to *per se*. For instance, the sensory power is related *per se* to *sensible quality* (*passibilem qualitatem*), which is divided *per se* into *color*, *sound*, etc.; and so the sentient power that has to do with color (the sense of sight) is distinct from the sentient power that has to do with sound (the sense of hearing). But it is incidental to sensible qualities such as color whether a thing is a musician or a grammarian, large or small, a man or a rock. And so it is not by differences of this latter sort that the powers of the soul are distinguished.

**Reply to objection 1:** Even though the act is posterior to the power in *esse*, it is nonetheless prior in intention and conceptually, in the way that the end is prior to the agent. And even though the object is extrinsic, it is nonetheless a principle and end of the action; and those things that are intrinsic to the thing are proportioned to the principle and to the end.

**Reply to objection 2:** If a power is related *per se* to one of two contraries as its object, then the other contrary must be related to some other power. However, a power of the soul relates *per se* not to the proper natures of the contraries, but rather to a nature that is common to both of the contraries; for instance, the sense of sight is related *per se* not to the nature *white*, but to the nature *color*. And the reason for this is that the one contrary is in some sense the nature of the other, since they are related as the perfect and the imperfect.

**Reply to objection 3:** Nothing prevents what is the same in subject from being conceptually diverse. And in this sense it can be related to diverse powers of the soul.

**Reply to objection 4:** A higher power is related *per se* to a more universal conception of its object (*respicit universaliorem rationem obiecti*) than a lower power is. For the higher a power is, the more things it extends to. And so more things agree in the single conception of the object that the higher power is related to *per se*, and yet those things differ from one another in the conceptions that the lower powers are related to *per se*. And this is how diverse objects belong to diverse lower powers, even though they fall under a single higher power.

## Article 4

### Is there any ordering among the powers of the soul?

It seems that there is no ordering among the powers of the soul (*in potentiis animae non sit ordo*):

**Objection 1:** There is no 'before' (*prius*) or 'after' (*posterius*) among things that fall under the same division; rather, they are naturally 'simultaneous' (*naturaliter simul*). But the powers of the soul are divided off against one another. Therefore, there is no ordering among them.

**Objection 2:** The powers of the soul are related to their objects and to the soul itself. But from the side of the soul, there is no ordering among the powers, since the soul is one. Likewise, from the side of the objects, there is no ordering among the powers, since the objects are diverse and wholly disparate, as is clear in the case of color and sound. Therefore, there is no ordering among the powers of the soul.

**Objection 3:** In powers that are ordered with respect to one another one finds that the operation of the one depends on the operation of the other. But it is not the case that the act of one power of the soul depends on the act of another; for instance, the sense of sight can act without the sense of hearing, and vice versa. Therefore, it is not the case that there is an ordering among the powers of the soul.

**But contrary to this:** In *De Anima* 2 the Philosopher compares the parts or powers of the soul to shapes. But shapes have an ordering with respect to one another. Therefore, so do the powers of the soul.

**I respond:** Since the soul is one, whereas the powers are many, and since a multitude proceeds from one thing in a certain order, there must be an ordering among the powers of the soul.

In fact, three types of ordering are found among them. Two of these types have to do with the dependence of one power on another, while the third is taken from an ordering among their objects.

Now there are two ways to think of the dependence of one power on another: the first concerns an *ordering of nature*, insofar as what is perfect is naturally prior to what is imperfect; and the second concerns an *ordering of time and generation*, insofar as the perfect arises from the imperfect.

According to the first type of ordering among the powers, the intellective powers are prior to the sentient powers, and so they direct them and command them. Similarly, the sentient powers are prior in this type of ordering to the powers of the nutritive soul.

According the second type of ordering, the converse holds. For the powers of the nutritive soul are prior, in the line of generation, to the powers of the sentient soul and so prepare the body for the actions of the sentient powers. And the same holds for the powers of sentient soul with respect to the powers of the intellective soul.

On the other hand, according to the third type of ordering, certain of the sentient powers (*vires sensitivae*) have an ordering with respect to one another, viz., the sense of sight, the sense of hearing, and the sense of smell. For the visible is naturally prior to the other [objects], since it is common to both higher and lower bodies. And the audible sound exists in the air, which is naturally prior to the mixing of the elements that the odoriferous follows upon.

**Reply to objection 1:** The species of certain genera are related as 'before' and 'after', e.g., the genera *number* and *shape*, as far as their *esse* is concerned—even though the species in question are said to be 'simultaneous' insofar as they bear the predication of a common genus.

**Reply to objection 2:** The relevant ordering of the powers of the soul is (a) on the part of the soul, which has an aptitude for diverse acts in a certain order, even though it is one in essence, and (b) on the part of the objects, and also (c) on the part of the acts, as has been explained.

**Reply to objection 3:** This argument goes through in the case of those powers among which there is an ordering only of the third type. By contrast, those powers that are ordered according to the other two modes are related in such a way that the act of the one is dependent on the act of the other.

## Article 5

### Are all the soul's powers in the soul as in a subject?

It seems that all the soul's powers are in the soul as in a subject:

**Objection 1:** The powers of the soul are related to the soul in the same way that the powers of the body are related to the body. But the body is the subject of the corporeal powers. Therefore, the soul is the subject of the powers of the soul.

**Objection 2:** The operations of the soul's powers are attributed to the body because of the soul; for, as is explained in *De Anima* 2, "the soul is first and foremost (*primum*) that by which we have sensation and intellective understanding." But the powers are the proper principles of the operations of the soul. Therefore, the powers are first and foremost (*per prius*) in the soul.

**Objection 3:** In *Super Genesim ad Litteram* 12 Augustine says that the soul senses (*sentit*) certain things but not through the body—indeed, without the body—e.g., fear and things of that sort, whereas it senses other things through the body. But if the sentient power were not in the soul alone as in a subject, it would not be able to sense anything without a body. Therefore, the soul is the subject of the sentient power and, by parity of reasoning, of all the other powers as well.

**But contrary to this:** In *De Somno et Vigilia* the Philosopher says, "Sensing is proper neither to the soul nor the body, but to the conjoined being." Therefore, the sentient power is in the conjoined being as in a subject. Therefore, it is not the case that the soul is by itself (*sola*) the subject of all its own powers.

**I respond:** The subject of an operative power is that which is able to operate, since every accident denominates its proper subject. But the thing that is able to operate is the same as the thing that does operate. Hence, "what has the power" as a subject "is that to which the operation belongs," as the Philosopher likewise says at the beginning of *De Somno et Vigilia*.

Now it is clear from what was said above (q. 75, a. 2–3 and q. 76, a. 1) that certain operations that are exercised without a corporeal organ, e.g., intellective understanding and willing, belong to the soul. Hence, the powers that are the principles of these operations are in the soul as in a subject.

However, there are certain operations of the soul that are exercised through corporeal organs, e.g., the act of seeing with the eyes and the act of hearing with the ears. And the same holds for all the other operations of the nutritive and sentient parts of the soul. And so the powers that are the principles of such operations are in the conjoined being as in a subject, and not in the soul alone.

**Reply to objection 1:** All the powers are said to belong to the soul not as a *subject* but as a *principle*, since it is through the soul that the conjoined being is able to carry out such operations.

**Reply to objection 2:** All the powers in question are in the soul prior to being in the conjoined being, but as in a *principle* and not as in a *subject*.

**Reply to objection 3:** Plato's opinion was that sensing is an operation proper to the soul, just as intellective understanding is, and in many matters related to philosophy Augustine makes use of Plato's opinions by reciting them without asserting them.

Now as far as the matter at hand is concerned, there are two possible ways to understand the claim that the soul senses some things with the body and some without the body:

In the first way, the phrases 'with the body' (*cum corpore*) and 'without the body' (*sine corpore*) modify *the act of sensing* insofar as it proceeds from the one who is sensing. And given that the phrases are taken in this way, nothing has sensation without a body, since the action of sensing cannot proceed from the soul except through a corporeal organ.

In the second way, the phrases modify the act of sensing on the part of *the object that is sensed*. And given that the phrases are taken in this way, the soul senses some things 'with the body', i.e., as existing in the body, as when it senses a wound or something of that sort, whereas it senses other things 'without the body', i.e., as existing not in the body but only in the soul's apprehension, as when it senses that it is sad or joyful about something that has been heard.

## Article 6

### Do the powers of the soul flow from its essence?

It seems that the powers of the soul do not flow from its essence (*non fluant ab eius essentia*):

**Objection 1:** Diverse things do not proceed from one simple thing. But the essence of the soul is one and simple. Therefore, since the powers of the soul are many and diverse, they cannot proceed from the soul's essence.

**Objection 2:** That from which something else proceeds is a cause of that thing. But the soul's essence cannot be called a cause of the powers, as is clear to one who runs through each of the genera of causes. Therefore, the powers of the soul do not flow from its essence.

**Objection 3:** 'Emanation' names a certain movement. But as *Physics* 7 proves, nothing is moved by itself—except perhaps by reason of a part, as when an animal is said to be moved by itself because one part of it is the mover and another part the thing moved. Again, as *De Anima* 1 proves, the soul is not moved. Therefore, it is not the case that the soul in itself is a cause of its own powers.

**But contrary to this:** The powers of the soul are certain properties that are natural to it. But a subject is a cause of its proper accidents and thus, as is clear from *Metaphysics* 7, is mentioned in the definition of its accident. Therefore, the powers of the soul proceed from the soul's essence as from a cause.

**I respond:** A substantial form and an accidental form agree in some things and differ in others. They agree in that both are actualities and each is such that because of it something in some way exists in actuality. However, there are two ways in which they differ:

First, a substantial form makes something to exist absolutely speaking, and its subject is a being only in potentiality. By contrast, an accidental form does not make a thing to exist absolutely speaking, but makes it to be such-and-such qualitatively (*esse tale*), or to be such-and-such a size (*esse tantum*), or to be related in some way (*esse aliquo modo se habens*); for its subject is a being in actuality. Hence, it is clear that actuality is found in a substantial form prior to being found in its subject; and because the first thing in any genus is the cause, the substantial form causes *esse* in actuality in its subject. By contrast, actuality is found in the subject of an accidental form prior to being found in the accidental form, and so the actuality of the accidental form is caused by the actuality of the subject. Hence, insofar as the subject exists in potentiality, it is receptive of the accidental form, whereas insofar as it exists in actuality, it is productive of the accidental form. (I am making this claim about a proper and *per se* accident, since with respect to extraneous accidents the subject is receptive only, while an extrinsic agent produces such an accident.)

The second difference between a substantial form and an accidental form is that because what is less important (*minus principale*) exists for the sake of what is more important (*principalius*), the matter exists for the sake of the substantial form, whereas, conversely, the accidental form exists for the sake of the completion of its subject.

Now it is clear from what has been said (a. 5) that the subject of the soul's powers is either (a) just the soul itself, which, as was explained above (q. 75, a. 3), can, insofar as it has some sort of potentiality (*secundum quod habet aliquid potentialitatis*), be the subject of an accident, or (b) the composite. But the composite exists in actuality because of the soul. Hence, it is clear that all the soul's powers—whether their subject is the soul by itself or the composite—flow from the soul's essence as their principle. For it has already been explained that an accident (a) is caused by its subject insofar as its subject exists in actuality and (b) is received in its subject insofar as its subject exists in potentiality.

**Reply to objection 1:** Many things can naturally proceed from a single simple thing according to a certain order, and this, once again, because of the diversity of the things receiving them. So, then, from a single essence of the soul there proceed many and diverse powers, both because of the ordering among the powers, and also because of the diversity of the corporeal organs.

**Reply to objection 2:** The subject is a *final cause* and, in some sense, an *acting cause* of its proper accidents—and also a *material cause*, insofar as it receives the accidents. And from this one can infer that the soul's essence is a cause of all the soul's powers as an *end* and an *active principle*, whereas it is a cause of some of its powers as their *subject*.

**Reply to objection 3:** The emanation of the proper accidents from a subject is not through any sort of transmutation but through a sort of natural resultancy (*per aliquam naturalem resultationem*), in the manner in which one thing naturally results from another, e.g., color from light.


## Article 7

### Does one power arise from another?

It seems that it is not the case that one power arises from another:

**Objection 1:** Things that begin to exist at the same time are such that the one does not arise from the other. But all the powers of the soul are co-created together with the soul. Therefore, it is not the case that one of those powers arises from another.

**Objection 2:** A power of the soul arises from the soul as an accident arises from its subject. But one power of the soul cannot be the subject of another, since an accident does not have accidents. Therefore, it is not the case that one power arises from another.

**Objection 3:** An opposite does not arise from its opposite, but instead each of them arises from something similar to it in species. But the powers of the soul are divided off from one another as opposites, in the way that diverse species are divided off from one another as opposites. Therefore, it is not the case that one of them arises from another.

**But contrary to this:** Powers are known through their acts. But the act of one power is caused by another power; for instance, an act of imagining (*actus phantasiae*) is caused by an act of sensing. Therefore, one power of the soul is caused by another.

**I respond:** Among things that proceed in a certain natural ordering from one first thing, just as the first thing is a cause of all of them, so what is closer to the first thing is in some sense a cause of what is more remote from the first thing. But it was shown above (a. 4) that there is a multiple ordering among the powers of the soul. And so one power of the soul proceeds from the soul's essence by the mediation of another power. But since (a) the soul's essence is related to the powers both as an active and final principle and also as a receptive principle (either separately by itself or together with the body), and since (b) that which is an agent and an end is more perfect, whereas that which is a receptive principle is as such less perfect, it follows that those powers of the soul which are prior in the order of perfection and nature are principles of the other powers in the manner of an end and an active principle. For we see that the sensory power exists for the sake of the intellect, and not vice versa. Again, the sensory power is a certain deficient participation in the intellect, and so according to its natural origin it in some sense arises from the intellect in the way that what is imperfect arises from what is perfect.

Conversely, along the path of receptive principles, the more imperfect powers are principles with respect to the others, in the same way that the soul, insofar as it has the sentient power, is thought of as a subject and as a sort of material [cause] with respect to the intellect. And because of this, the less perfect powers are prior on the path of generation, since the animal is generated before the man.

**Reply to objection 1:** Just as a power of the soul flows from the soul's essence—not through a transmutation but through a sort of natural resultancy—and yet is simultaneous with it, so the same holds for one power with respect to another.

**Reply to objection 2:** An accident cannot *per se* be the subject of an accident, but one accident is received in the substance prior to another, in the way that quantity is received before quality. And in this sense the one accident is said to be the subject of the other—in the way that a surface is said to be the subject of a color—because it is by the mediation of the one accident that the substance receives the other accident. And something similar can be said about the powers of the soul.

**Reply to objection 3:** The powers of the soul are opposed to one another by an opposition of what is perfect to what is imperfect, in the way that the species of number and shape are opposed to one another. However, this sort of opposition does not prevent one power from arising from another, since what is imperfect naturally proceeds from what is perfect.

## Article 8

### Do all the powers of the soul remain in a soul that is separated from its body?

It seems that all the powers of the soul remain in a soul that is separated from its body:

**Objection 1:** In *De Spiritu et Anima* it says, "The soul recedes from the body, taking the sensory power and power of imagination with it, along with reason, and intellect, and understanding, and concupiscibility, and irascibility."

**Objection 2:** The powers of the soul are the soul's natural properties. But a property always exists in, and is never separated from, that of which it is a property. Therefore, the powers of the soul remain in it even after death.

**Objection 3:** The soul's powers, even its sentient powers, are not weakened when the body is weakened, since, as *De Anima* 1 says, "If an old man received the eyes of a young man, he would see in the same way that a young man does." But weakening is a path to corruption. Therefore, the powers of the soul are not corrupted when the body is corrupted; instead, they remain in the separated soul.

**Objection 4:** As the Philosopher shows, memory is a power of the sentient soul. But memory remains in a separated soul; for in Luke 16:25 the rich glutton, whose soul is in hell, is told, "Remember that you received good things in your life." Therefore, memory remains in a separated soul and, consequently, so do the other powers of the sentient part of the soul.

**Objection 5:** Joy and sadness exist in the concupiscible power, which is a power of the sentient part of the soul. But it is obvious that separated souls are sad or joyful about the rewards or punishments they have. Therefore, the concupiscible power remains in a separated soul.

**Objection 6:** In *Super Genesim ad Litteram* 12 Augustine says that just as when the body lies senseless though not yet wholly dead, the soul sees certain things by means of an imaginative vision, so the same holds when the soul is completely separated from its body through death. But the imagination is a power of the sentient part of the soul. Therefore, the power of the sentient part remains in a separated soul and, consequently, so do all the other powers.

**But contrary to this:** In *De Ecclesiasticis Dogmatibus* it says, "A man is composed of just two substances, the soul with its reason and the flesh with its senses." Therefore, when the flesh is dead, the sentient powers do not remain.

**I respond:** As has already been explained (a. 5–7), all the powers of the soul have the soul alone as their *principle*.

However, certain of the powers, viz., the intellect and the will, have the *soul alone* as their subject, and powers of this sort must remain in the soul after its body has been destroyed.

By contrast, certain of the powers, viz., all the powers of the sentient and nutritive parts of the soul, have the *conjoined being* as their subject. Now when a subject is destroyed, its accidents cannot remain. Hence, when the conjoined being is corrupted, powers of the sort in question do not remain in actuality but remain only *virtually* in the soul as in their principle or root. And so the claim made by some, viz., that powers of this sort remain in the soul even after the body is corrupted, is false. And the further claim that the acts of these powers remain in a separated soul is all the more false, since no action belongs to these powers except through a corporeal organ.

**Reply to objection 1:** The book in question has no authority. Hence, what is written in it is rejected just as easily as it is asserted.

Still, one can reply that the soul takes powers of the sort in question along with it virtually and not actually.

**Reply to objection 2:** The powers which we claim do not remain actual in the separated soul are properties not of the soul alone, but of the conjoined being.

**Reply to objection 3:** Powers of the sort in question are said not to be weakened when the body is weakened because the soul, which is a virtual principle of these powers, remains immutable.

**Reply to objection 4:** Memory as referred to here (*illa recordatio*) is taken in the sense in which Augustine posits memory in the mind, and not in the sense in which it is posited as a part in the sentient soul.

**Reply to objection 5:** Sadness and joy are in the separated soul not with respect to the sentient appetite, but with respect to the intellective appetite—as is also the case with the angels.

**Reply to objection 6:** Augustine is speaking here by way of inquiry and not by way of assertion. That is why he retracts some of the things that were said in this place.

# QUESTION 78

## The Specific Powers of the Soul

Next we have to consider the specific powers of the soul. It is relevant to the theologian's inquiry to ask specifically only about the intellective and appetitive powers, in which the virtues are found. But because knowledge of these powers in some way depends on the others, our inquiry concerning the specific powers of the soul will have three parts. For we have to consider, first, those powers that are preparatory for intellective understanding (question 78); second, the intellective powers (question 79); and, third, the appetitive powers (questions 80–83).

On the first topic there are four questions: first, concerning the genera of the powers of the soul; second, concerning the species of the vegetative part of the soul; third, concerning the exterior sensory powers; and fourth, concerning the interior sensory powers.

## Article 1

### Are there five kinds of power that belong to the soul?

It seems that there are not five kinds of power that belong to the soul, viz., (a) the vegetative, (b) the sentient, (c) the appetitive, (d) the power to effect movement with respect to place, and (e) the intellective:

**Objection 1:** The powers of the soul are called the soul's 'parts'. But there are only three parts of the soul commonly enumerated by everyone, viz., the vegetative soul, the sentient soul, and the rational soul. Therefore, there are only three kinds of power that belong to the soul, and not five.

**Objection 2:** The powers of the soul are the principles of the vital works (*principia operum vitae*). But there are four senses in which something is said to be alive (*vivere*). For in *De Anima* 2 the Philosopher says, "There are many senses of 'to be alive' (*multipliciter ipso vivere dicto*), so that something is said to be alive even if just one of the following is present: intellective understanding; sensing; movement and standing still with respect to place; and movement with respect to nourishment, decrease, and increase." Therefore, given that the appetitive is left out, there are just four genera of the powers of the soul.

**Objection 3:** What is common to all the powers ought not to be designated as a special kind of soul. But appetition (*appetere*) belongs to each of the powers of the soul. For the sense of sight desires a fitting visible object, and thus Ecclesiasticus 40:22 says, "The eye will desire favor and beauty (*gratiam et speciem*) but, more than these, green sown fields (*virides sationes*)." And by the same line of reasoning, each of the other powers desires an object fitting for itself. Therefore, the appetitive should not be posited as a special type of power belonging to the soul.

**Objection 4:** As is explained in *De Anima* 3, in animals the principle that effects movement is either the sensory power, the intellect, or the appetite. Therefore, the principle that effects movement should not be posited as a special kind of soul beyond the ones mentioned above.

**But contrary to this:** In *De Anima* 2 the Philosopher says, "We claim that the powers are the vegetative, the sentient, the appetitive, the power to effect movement with respect to place, and the intellective."

**I respond:** There are five *kinds of power* that belong to the soul, and they are enumerated above. Three are called *souls* (*animae*), whereas four are called *ways of being alive* (*modi vivendi*).

The reason for this difference is that the different *souls* are distinguished by the fact that there are diverse ways in which the soul's operation exceeds the operation of the corporeal nature; for the whole of the corporeal nature is subject to the soul (*tota natura corporalis subiacet animae*) and is related to it as its matter and instrument.

Thus, there is a certain operation of the soul that exceeds corporeal nature to the extent that it is not even exercised through a corporeal organ; and this is the operation of the *rational soul*.

Again, there is another operation of the soul, lower than this one, which is, to be sure, effected through a corporeal organ, but not through any corporeal quality (*fit per organum corporale non tamen per aliquam corpoream qualitatem*); and this is the operation of the *sentient soul*. For even though *hot* and *cold* and *moist* and *dry* and other corporeal qualities of this sort are required for the operation of the sensory power, they are nonetheless not required in such a way that the sentient soul's operation proceeds by the mediation of the power of such qualities; instead, they are required only for appropriately disposing the organ.

Again, the lowest operation of the soul is that which is effected through a corporeal organ and by the power of a corporeal quality. Yet this operation exceeds the operation of corporeal nature because the motions of bodies are from an exterior principle, whereas operations of the sort in question are from an intrinsic principle—something that is common to all the operations of the soul, since anything with a soul (*omne animatum*) moves itself in some way. And this is the operation of the *vegetative soul*; for, as *De Anima* 2 explains, digestion and what follows upon digestion are effected instrumentally by the action of heat.

By contrast, the *kinds of powers* belonging to the soul are distinguished by their objects. As was explained above (q. 77, a. 3), the higher a power is, the more universal the object it is related to. But the object of the soul's operation can be thought of in a three-step ordering:

For the object of some of the soul's operations is just the body that is united to the soul. And this kind of power belonging to the soul is the *vegetative*, since the vegetative power acts only on the body to which the soul is united.

Again, there is another kind of power belonging to the soul that has a more universal object, viz., all bodies that can be sensed (*omne corpus sensibile*), and not just the body united to the soul.

And there is yet another kind of power belonging to the soul that has a still more universal object, viz., not just all the bodies that can be sensed but every being in general (*universaliter omne ens*).

From this it is clear that these last two kinds of power belonging to the soul have an operation not only with respect to the conjoined being, but also with respect to extrinsic beings. But since something that operates must in some way be conjoined to the object with respect to which it operates, it is necessary for an extrinsic being that is the object of an operation of the soul to be related to the soul in two ways:

First, it must be related to the soul in such a way that it is apt to be conjoined to the soul and to exist in the soul through a likeness of itself (*per suam similitudinem*); and in this regard there are two kinds of power, viz., the *sentient power* with respect to the less general object (*respectu obiecti minus communis*), i.e., the sensible body, and the *intellective power* with respect to the most general object of all, i.e., being in general (*ens universale*).

Second, the soul is itself inclined toward and tends toward the exterior being. And in accord with this relation there are two kinds of power belonging to the soul, viz., the *appetitive power*, according to which the soul is related to an extrinsic being as to an end, which is the first thing in intention, and the *power of effecting movement with respect to place*, insofar as the soul is related to the exterior being as to a terminus of operation and motion; for every animal effects movement in order to obtain something that is desired and intended.

Lastly, the *ways of being alive* are distinguished in a manner that corresponds to the grades of living things. For some living things, viz., *plants*, are such that only the vegetative is present in them. Some are such that, in addition to the vegetative, the sentient is also present, but not movement with respect to place; these are the *immobile animals* such as small shellfish (*conchilia*). Still other living things are such that they have, in addition, movement with respect to place; these are the *perfect animals*, which require many things for their life and so need movement in order to be able to find the necessities that are situated at some distance from them. Finally, there are some living beings, viz., *men*, in whom the intellective is combined with the others. However, as *De Anima* 2 explains, the appetitive does not constitute a separate grade of living thing, since appetite exists in everything in which sentience exists.

**Reply to objection 1 and objection 2:** The first two objections are answered by what has been said.

**Reply to objection 3:** A *natural appetite* is an inclination which an entity has by its nature toward something; hence, it is by a natural appetite that every power desires what is fitting for it. However, an *animal's appetite* follows upon an apprehended form. And for an appetite of this sort a special power of the soul is required; the power of apprehension (*apprehensio*) is not by itself sufficient. For a thing is desired insofar as it exists in its own nature. But it does not exist with its own nature in the apprehensive power; instead, it exists there by means of a likeness.

Hence, it is clear that it is only for its own act that the sense of sight naturally desires the visible thing; that is, it desires to see it. By contrast, an animal, through its appetitive power, desires the thing seen not only in order to see it, but also for its other uses. And if the soul needed the things perceived by the sensory powers only for the sake of the actions of those powers—i.e., only in order that it might sense those things—then it would not be necessary to posit the appetitive as a special genus among the powers of the soul. For in that case the natural appetite of the powers would be sufficient.

**Reply to objection 4:** Even though the appetitive and sensory powers are principles for effecting movement in perfect animals, it is nonetheless not the case that the appetitive and sensory powers as such are sufficient to effect movement without some other power being added to them. For immobile animals have appetitive and sensory powers, and yet they do not have the power to effect movement. Moreover, this power to effect movement exists not only in the appetitive and sensory powers insofar as they command movement, but also in the parts of the body themselves, in order that they might readily obey the appetitive power of the soul that moves them. An indication of this is that when the members of the body lose their natural disposition, they do not obey the appetitive power with respect to movement.

## Article 2

### Are the parts of the vegetative soul appropriately enumerated as the nutritive, the augmentative and the generative?

It seems that the parts of the vegetative soul are not appropriately enumerated as the nutritive, the augmentative and the generative:

**Objection 1:** Powers (*vires*) of this sort are called 'natural'. But the powers (*potentiae*) of the soul go beyond natural powers (*supra vires naturales*). Therefore, powers (*vires*) of this sort should not be posited as powers of the soul (*potentiae animae*).

**Objection 2:** What is common to both living and non-living things should not be counted as a power of the soul. But generation is common to all generable and corruptible things, both living and non-living. Therefore, the generative power should not be posited as a power of the soul.

**Objection 3:** The soul is more powerful than a corporeal nature is. But it is by the very same active power that a corporeal nature communicates both the species and appropriate size (*speciem et debitam quantitatem*). Therefore, *a fortiori*, the same holds for the soul. Therefore, the augmentative power of the soul is not distinct from the generative power.

**Objection 4:** Each thing is conserved in *esse* by that through which it has *esse*. But it is the generative power through which an entity acquires the *esse* of a living thing. Therefore, a living thing is conserved through that same power. But as *De Anima* 2 explains, it is the nutritive power that is ordered toward the conservation of a living thing, since it is a power that is able preserve its subject. Therefore, the nutritive power should not be distinguished from the generative power.

**But contrary to this:** In *De Anima* 2 the Philosopher says that the works of this soul are "to generate and to make use of nourishment," and again, "to effect growth" (*augmentum facere*).

**I respond:** There are three powers of the vegetative part [of the soul]. For as has been explained (a. 1), the vegetative part has as its object the very body that is alive through the soul, and there are three operations of the soul that are necessary for such a body.

One operation is that through which it acquires *esse*, and this is what the *generative* power is ordered toward. The second is that through which the living body acquires its appropriate size, and this is what the *augmentative* power is ordered toward. The third operation is that through which the body of a living thing is preserved both in *esse* and in its appropriate size, and this is what the *nutritive* power is ordered toward.

However, there is a certain difference among these powers that has to be noted. For the nutritive and augmentative powers have their effect in the thing in which they exist, since it is the very body that is united to the soul that grows and is conserved through the augmentative and nutritive powers that exist in that same soul. By contrast, the generative power has its effect not in the same body but in another body, since nothing generates its very own self. And so the generative power in a certain sense approaches the dignity of the sentient soul, which has an operation with respect to exterior things—even though the sentient soul has this sort of operation in a more excellent and universal way—since, as is clear from Dionysius in *De Divinis Nominibus*, chap. 7, the highest manifestation of a lower nature attains to the lowest manifestation of a higher nature.

And so, as *De Anima* 2 says, among these three powers it is the generative that is closer to the boundary [with the sentient] and more important and more perfect; for it is an already perfected entity that "has the role of making another entity like itself." Moreover, the augmentative and nutritive powers serve the generative power, while the nutritive power serves the augmentative.

**Reply to objection 1:** Powers of the sort in question are called 'natural' both (a) because they have an effect that is similar to that of nature, which likewise communicates *esse*, size, and conservation (though these powers do it in a higher way), and also (b) because these powers exercise their actions by the instrumentality of the active and passive powers that are the principles of natural actions.

**Reply to objection 2:** Among inanimate things, generation is totally from the outside (*ab extrinseco*). By contrast, the generation of living things has a higher mode, through something that belongs to the living being itself, viz., its seed (*semen*), in which there resides a principle that gives form to the body. And so in a living thing there has to be a power through which this sort of seed is prepared; and this is the generative power.

**Reply to objection 3:** Since the generation of living things is by means of seed, the animal that is generated must be small in size at the beginning. Because of this, it has to have a power of the soul through which it is brought to its appropriate size. By contrast, an inanimate body is generated from determinate matter by an extrinsic agent, and so it receives both its species and quantity simultaneously in accord with the condition of the matter.

**Reply to objection 4:** As has already been explained (a. 1), the operation of the vegetative principle is brought to completion by the mediation of heat, the role of which is to consume moisture. And so in order to restore the moisture that is lost, the vegetative principle needs to have a nutritive power through which food is converted into the substance of the body. This is likewise necessary for the action of the augmentative and generative powers.

## Article 3

### Are the five exterior sensory powers appropriately distinguished?

It seems that the five exterior sensory powers (*sensus*) are not appropriately distinguished:

**Objection 1:** The senses have cognition of accidents. But there are many kinds of accidents. Therefore, since powers are distinguished by their objects, it seems that the sensory powers are multiplied according to the number of the kinds of accidents.

**Objection 2:** Shape and size and the other accidents that are called 'common sensibles' are not '*per accidens* sensibles', but are instead divided off against the latter in *De Anima* 2. But it is a diversity of *per se* objects that diversifies powers. Therefore, since shape and size differ more from color than sound does, it seems that, *a fortiori*, there should be another sentient power that has cognition of shape and size rather than of color and sound.

**Objection 3:** A single sense has cognition of a single pair of contraries (*unus sensus est unius contrarietatis*); for instance, the sense of sight has cognition of white and black. But the sense of touch has cognition of several pairs of contraries, viz., hot and cold, moist and dry, etc. Therefore, the sense of touch is not a single sensory power, but a number of them. Therefore, there are more than five sensory powers.

**Objection 4:** Species are not divided off against their genus. But the sense of taste is a sort of sense of touch. Therefore, it should not be posited as another sense over and beyond the sense of touch.

**But contrary to this:** In *De Anima* 3 the Philosopher says that "there is no other sensory power beyond these five."

**I respond:** Some want to take the explanation for the distinctions among, and number of, the exterior sensory powers from the organs in which one or another of the elements dominates—either water or air or something of that sort. Others take the explanation from the medium, either the conjoined medium or the extrinsic medium, be it air or water or something else of that sort. Still others take it from the diverse natures of the sensible qualities, depending on whether the quality in question belongs to a simple body or whether instead it follows upon complexity.

However, none of these views is satisfactory. For the powers do not exist for the sake of the organs; rather, the organs exist for the sake of the powers. Hence it is not because there are diverse organs that there are diverse powers. Rather, nature instituted diversity in the organs in order that they might correspond to a diversity of powers. Similarly, nature provided the diverse media for the diverse sensory powers, insofar as this was appropriate for the acts of the powers. And it is the intellect—and not the sensory powers—that has cognition of the natures of the sensible qualities.

Therefore, the explanation for the number of, and distinctions among, the exterior sensory powers has to be taken from what is proper and *per se* to the sensory powers themselves. Now a sensory power is a passive power that is susceptible to being affected by an exterior sensible thing. Therefore, the exterior things that effect the changes are what a sensory power perceives *per se*, and the sensory powers are distinguished from one another in a way that corresponds to the diversity of such things.

Now there are two kinds of change, *natural change* (*immutatio naturalis*) and *spiritual change* (*immutatio spiritualis*). A change is *natural* insofar as the form of the thing that effects the change is received with its natural *esse* in the thing changed, e.g., heat in a thing that is heated. The change is *spiritual* insofar as the form of the thing that effects the change is received with spiritual *esse* in the thing changed, e.g., the form of a color in the pupil, which does not thereby become colored. And for the operation of a sensory power what is required is a spiritual change, through which an *intention* of the sensible form (*intentio formae sensibilis*) comes to exist in the organ of the sensory power. Otherwise, if a natural change were by itself sufficient for sensing, then every natural body would have sensation whenever it was altered.

Now in certain sensory powers, e.g., the *sense of sight*, there is only a spiritual change, whereas in the other sensory powers the spiritual change is accompanied by a natural change either on the part of the object alone or on the part of the organ as well.

On the part of the object, the natural change is with respect to place in the case of sound, which is the object of the *sense of hearing*. For sound is caused by vibration and movement in the air. And as for alteration, in the case of odor, which is the object of the *sense of smell*, a body has to be altered in some way through heat in order to give off an odor.

On the part of the organ, a natural change is involved in the *sense of touch* and the *sense of taste*; for instance, when a hand touches something hot, it itself becomes hot; and the tongue is moistened by the moistness of various tastes. By contrast, the organ of the sense of smell and the organ of the sense of hearing do not undergo any natural change in sensing, except incidentally.

Now since the sense of sight does not involve a natural change in either the organ or the object, it is maximally spiritual, and it is the most perfect and the most general of all the sensory powers. And after the sense of sight comes the sense of hearing, and then the sense of smell, both of which involve a natural change on the part of the object; for as *Physics* 8 proves, local motion is more perfect than, and naturally prior to, the motion of alteration. On the other hand, the sense of touch and the sense of taste are the most material; the distinction between them will be explained in a moment (*ad* 3 and *ad* 4 below). The reason why the first three senses are not effected through a conjoined medium is so that no natural change will touch the organ, as occurs with these last two sensory powers.

**Reply to objection 1:** Not all accidents have the power to effect change (*vim immutativam*) in their own right; rather, only qualities of the third species are such that alteration occurs because of them. And so only qualities of this sort are the objects of the sensory powers; for as *Physics* 7 explains, "A sensory power is altered in the same way that inanimate bodies are."

**Reply to objection 2:** Size and shape and other such accidents, which are called *common sensibles*, lie between *per accidens sensibles* and *proper sensibles*, where the latter are the objects of the sensory powers.

For the proper sensibles effect change in the sensory powers directly and primarily (*primo et per se*), since they are the qualities that effect alterations.

By contrast, the common sensibles are all traced back to quantity. In the case of size and number, it is clear that they are species of quantity, whereas shape is a quality that involves quantity, since the nature of a shape consists in its being the boundary of a magnitude (*terminatio magnitudinis*) On the other hand, motion and rest are sensed insofar as the subject is related in one or more ways to (a) the magnitude of an object or of its spatial distance (in the case of augmentation or local motion), or to (b) sensible qualities (in the case of alteration). And so to sense motion and rest is in a certain way to sense one thing and many things.

Now a quantity is the proximate subject of a quality that effects alteration; for instance, a surface is the proximate subject of a color. And so the common sensibles do not effect change primarily and directly in a sensory power. Rather, they effect such change by means of a sensible quality; for instance, a surface effects change in a sensory power by means of its color.

And yet the common sensibles are not *per accidens* sensibles, since common sensibles make for variations in the way that a sensory power is affected. For instance, a sensory power is affected in different ways by a large surface and by a small surface, since the whiteness itself is also called large or small and so is divided in accord with its proper subject.

**Reply to objection 3:** As the Philosopher seems to say in *De Anima* 2, the sense of touch is one in genus but divided into many species of sensory power; and this is why it has diverse pairs of contraries as objects. However, these species are not separated from one another by organ, but are instead spread throughout the whole body, and so the distinction among them is not obvious. On the other hand, the sense of taste, which perceives the sweet and the bitter, is joined together with the sense of touch in the tongue, but not throughout the whole body, and so it is easily distinguished from the sense of touch.

However, one could reply that all these pairs of contraries are such that (a) each belongs to a single proximate genus and (b) all of them together belong to a common genus that is the object of the sense of touch according to its common nature. But this common genus is unnamed, in the same way that the proximate genus of *hot* and *cold* is unnamed.

**Reply to objection 4:** According to what the Philosopher says, the sense of taste is that species of the sense of touch which exists just in the tongue, and it is distinct not from the sense of touch in general but from those species of the sense of touch that are spread throughout the body.

On the other hand, if the sense of touch is just a single sensory power because of the single common nature of its object, one will have to say that the sense of taste is distinguished from the sense of touch by reason of different sorts of changes. For as far as its organ is concerned, and given the quality which is its proper object, the sense of touch is affected by a natural change and not just a spiritual change. The organ of the sense of taste, however, is not necessarily affected with a natural change by the quality that is its proper object, in such a way, namely, that the tongue itself becomes sweet or bitter; instead, it is affected by the preparatory quality on which taste is based, viz., moistness, which is an object of the sense of touch.

## Article 4

### Are the interior sensory powers appropriately distinguished?

It seems that the interior sensory powers are not appropriately distinguished:

**Objection 1:** What is common is not divided off [on the same level] over against what is proper (*commune non dividitur contra proprium*). Therefore, the common sensory power (*sensus communis*) should not be enumerated among the interior sentient powers, over against the proper exterior sensory powers.

**Objection 2:** One should not posit an interior apprehensive power for any object that a proper and exterior sensory power is sufficient for. But the proper exterior sensory powers are sufficient for judging sensible things, since each sensory power judges with respect to its own proper object. These sensory powers seem likewise sufficient for perceiving their own acts; for instance, since the action of a sensory power in some sense lies between the power and the object, it seems that the sense of sight is much more capable of perceiving its own act of seeing, as something closer to itself, than of seeing color—and so on for the other sensory powers. Therefore, it was unnecessary to posit an interior power, called the 'common sensory power', for this purpose.

**Objection 3:** According to the Philosopher, the power of imagining (*vis phantastica*) and the power of remembering (*vis memorativa*) are passions of the primary sentient power. But a passion is not divided off over against its subject. Therefore, memory (*memoria*) and imagination (*phantasia*) should not be posited as powers distinct from the sensory power.

**Objection 4:** The intellect is less dependent on the sensory power than is any power of the sentient part of the soul. But the intellect does not have cognition of anything unless it receives it from the sensory power; for as

*Posterior Analytics* 1 says, "Whoever lacks one of the sensory powers lacks one sort of knowledge." Therefore, *a fortiori*, one should not posit a power of the sentient part, called the estimative power (*vis aestimativa*), to perceive intentions that are not perceived by the sensory power.

**Objection 5:** Acts of the cogitative power (*vis cogitativa*), i.e., comparing and composing and dividing, and acts of the power of reminiscing (*vis reminiscitiva*), i.e., using a sort of syllogism to conduct an inquiry, are no less distant from the acts of the estimative power and of the power of remembering than acts of the estimative power are from an act of imagining (*ab actu phantasiae*). Therefore, either the cogitative power and power of reminiscing should be posited as powers distinct from the estimative power and the power of remembering, or else the estimative power and the power of remembering should not be posited as powers over and beyond the power of imagining.

**Objection 6:** In *Super Genesim ad Litteram* 12 Augustine posits three types of vision: (a) *corporeal vision*, which is effected through the sensory power; (b) *spiritual vision*, which is effected through the power of imagining or fantasizing (*per imaginationem sive phantasiam*); and (c) *intellectual vision*, which is effected through the intellect. Therefore, there is no interior power other than the power of imagining that lies between the sensory powers and the intellect.

**But contrary to this:** In his *De Anima* Avicenna posits five interior sentient powers, viz., "the common sensory power (*sensus communis*), the imaging power (*phantasia*), the imaginative power (*potentia imaginativa*), the estimative power (*potentia aestimativa*), and the power of remembering (*potentia memorativa*)."

**I respond:** Since nature is not lacking in what is necessary, there must be as many actions of the sentient part of the soul as are sufficient for the life of a perfect animal. And if these actions cannot all be traced back to a single principle, then they require diverse powers, since a power of the soul is nothing other than a proximate principle for the soul's operation.

Note, then, that the life of a perfect animal requires that the animal apprehend a thing not only in the presence of the sensible object, but also in its absence. Otherwise, since an animal's movement and action follow upon apprehension, the animal would not move in order to find out about a thing that is absent—just the opposite of what appears to be true, especially in the case of perfect animals, which move purposefully (*moventur motu processivo*), since they are moving toward something absent that has been apprehended. Therefore, through its sentient soul the animal must not only receive the species of sensible things when it is presently being affected by those things, but must also retain and conserve the species. But among corporeal things, to receive and to retain are traced back to diverse principles; for instance, moist things are good at receiving but bad at retaining, and the opposite holds for dry things. Hence, since the sentient power is the act of a corporeal organ, a power that receives sensible species must be different from a power that conserves them.

Again, note that if an animal moved solely because of sensibly pleasurable or painful things, one would have to posit in the animal only an apprehension of forms that the sensory power perceives and with respect to which it takes delight or feels revulsion. But an animal has to seek out or flee from certain things not only because they are pleasant or unpleasant to sense, but also because of other kinds of suitability and utility, or harm—as, for instance, when a sheep, seeing a wolf coming, flees not because of the ugliness of the wolf's color or shape, but because of the danger to sheep's nature; or as when a bird collects straw not because the straw delights its senses, but because this is useful for building a nest. Therefore, an animal has to perceive intentions of this sort which the exterior sensory powers do not perceive. And for this sort of perception there has to be some distinct principle, since perception of sensible forms comes from changes effected by the sensible thing, whereas the perception of the intentions just alluded to does not.

So, then, the *proper sensory powers* and the *common sensory power* are ordered toward the reception of sensible forms. (The distinction between them will be explained below.)

On the other hand, the *imaging power* or *power of imagining* (*phantasia vel imaginatio*)—they are the same—is ordered toward the retention or conservation of forms. For the imaging (or imagining) power is, as it were, a sort of treasury of forms that have been received through the sensory power.

Now the *estimative power* (*vis aestimativa*) is ordered toward apprehending intentions that are not [presently] being received through the sensory power, whereas the *power of remembering* (*vis memorativa*), which is a treasury of intentions of this sort, is ordered toward conserving them. An indication of this is that, in animals, the source of remembering comes from some intention of this sort, e.g., that something is harmful or agreeable. And the very nature of the past, which the power of remembering attends to, is intertwined with intentions of this sort.

Now note that as far as sensible forms are concerned, there is no difference between man and the other animals, since they are affected in similar ways by sensible exterior things. However, there is a difference with respect to the intentions we have just been talking about. For the other animals perceive intentions of this sort only by a sort of natural instinct, whereas man also perceives them through a certain comparison (*per quandam collationem*). And so what in animals is called the *natural estimative power*, in man is called the *cogitative power*, which arrives at intentions of this sort through a certain comparison. Hence, it is also called *particular reason*, and physicians assign it a determinate organ, viz., the middle part of the head; for it compares intentions of individuals in the way in which *intellective reason* compares intentions of universals.

As for the power of remembering, man has not only *memory* (*memoria*), like the other animals, in the immediate recording of past things, but also *reminiscence* (*reminiscentia*) in inquiring quasi-syllogistically into the memory of the past by means of individual intentions.

Now Avicenna posits a fifth power, between the estimative power and the power of imagining, which composes and divides the imagined forms—as is clear, for instance, when from the imagined form of gold and imagined form of a mountain we compose a single form of a golden mountain, which we never actually see. But this operation is not apparent in animals other than man, in whom the power of imagining power is sufficient for this. In his book *De Sensu et Sensibilibus* Averroes likewise attributes this action to the power of imagining.

And so it is necessary to posit just four interior powers of the sentient part of the soul, viz., the common sensory power (*sensus communis*), the power of imagining (*vis imaginativa*), the estimative power (*vis aestimativa*), and the power of remembering (*vis memorativa*).

**Reply to objection 1:** The interior sensory power is called 'common' not through predication, like a genus, but as the common root and principle of the exterior senses.

**Reply to objection 2:** A proper sensory power judges a proper sensible by distinguishing it from other things that fall under the same sensory power, e.g., distinguishing white from black or green. But neither the sense of sight nor the sense of taste can distinguish white from sweet, since whatever makes a distinction between two things must have cognition of both of them. Hence, the judgment regarding this distinction must belong to the common sensory power, which is such that (a) all the apprehensions of the senses are referred to it as to a common terminus, and such that (b) it also perceives the intentions of the sensory powers, as when someone sees that he is seeing. For the latter cannot be done through a proper sensory power, which has cognition only of the sensible form by which it is changed. The act of seeing is perfected in such a change, and from this change there follows another change in the common sensory power, which perceives the act of seeing.

**Reply to objection 3:** Just as one power arises from the soul by the mediation of another power in the way explained above (q. 77, a. 7), so too the soul is the subject of one power by the mediation of another. It is in this sense that the power of imagining and the power of remembering are called passions of the primary sentient power (*passiones primi sensitivi*).

**Reply to objection 4:** Even though the intellect's operation arises from the sensory power, nonetheless, in the entity apprehended through the sensory power the intellect knows many things that the sensory power is unable to perceive. The same holds for the estimative power, though on a lower level.

**Reply to objection 5:** The cogitative power and power of remembering have an eminence in man not because they are proper to the sentient part of the soul, but—by a sort of overflow—because of their affinity for and nearness to universal reason. And so they are not different powers from the ones in other animals, but the same powers, and yet more perfect.

**Reply to objection 6:** Augustine is calling 'spiritual vision' the vision which is effected by the likenesses of bodies in the absence of the bodies. From this it is clear that spiritual vision is common to all interior apprehensions.

# QUESTION 79

## The Intellective Powers

Next we ask about the intellective powers. On this topic there are thirteen questions: (1) Is the intellect a power of the soul, or is it the soul's essence? (2) If it is a power, is it a passive power? (3) If it is a passive power, should one posit an active intellect (*intellectus agens*)? (4) Is the active intellect a part of the soul? (5) Is there a single active intellect for everyone? (6) Does memory exist in the intellect? (7) Is it a power distinct from the intellect? (8) Is reason a power different from the intellect? (9) Are higher reason and lower reason distinct powers? (10) Is intellective understanding (*intelligentia*) a distinct power over and beyond the intellect? (11) Are the speculative intellect and the practical intellect distinct powers? (12) Is *synderesis* a power of the intellective part of the soul? (13) Is conscience a power of the intellective part of the soul?

## Article 1

### Is the intellect a power of the soul, or is it instead the soul's essence?

It seems that the intellect (*intellectus*) is not a power of the soul, but is instead the soul's essence:

**Objection 1:** The intellect (*intellectus*) seems to be the same thing as the mind (*mens*). But the mind is the essence of the soul and not a power of the soul; for in *De Trinitate* 9 Augustine says, "'Mind' (*mens*) and 'spirit' (*spiritus*) are not predicated as relations (*relative*), but instead point to the essence." Therefore, the intellect is the very essence of the soul.

**Objection 2:** The diverse kinds of power that belong to the soul are united in the soul's essence alone and not in any one power. But as *De Anima* 2 says, the appetitive and the intellective are diverse kinds of power belonging to the soul. And yet they come together in the mind (*mens*); for in *De Trinitate* 10 Augustine locates intellective understanding (*intelligentia*) and willing (*voluntas*) in the mind. Therefore, the mind or intellect (*mens et intellectus*) is the very essence of the soul and not one of its powers.

**Objection 3:** According to Gregory in his homily on the feast of the Ascension, "Man has intellective understanding along with the angels."

But the angels are called 'minds' and 'intellects'. Therefore, the mind or intellect of a man is the soul itself and not one of the powers of the soul.

**Objection 4:** It is because a substance is immaterial that it is intellective. But the soul is immaterial through its essence. Therefore, it seems that the soul is intellective through its essence.

**But contrary to this:** As is clear from *De Anima* 2, the Philosopher posits the intellective as a power of the soul.

**I respond:** Given what was said above (q. 54, a. 3 and q. 77, a. 1), one should reply that the intellect is a power of the soul and not the very essence of the soul. The only time the immediate principle of an operation is the very essence of a thing is when the operation itself is the thing's *esse*. For an essence is related to its *esse* in the same way that a power is related to its operation, i.e., its act. But it is only in the case of God that His intellective understanding (*intelligere*) is the same as His *esse*. Hence, it is only in the case of God that His intellect is His essence, whereas in other intellectual creatures the intellect is a certain power of the one who has intellective understanding (*quaedam potentia intelligentis*).

**Reply to objection 1:** 'Sense' (*sensus*) is sometimes taken for a power and sometimes for the sentient soul itself, since the sentient soul is denominated by the name of its principal power, viz., the sensory power. Likewise, the intellective soul is sometimes denominated by the name 'intellect' as by its principal power. For instance, *De Anima* 1 says, "The intellect is a certain substance." And this is also the sense in which Augustine says that the mind is 'spirit' or 'essence'.

**Reply to objection 2:** The appetitive and the intellective are diverse kinds of power belonging to the soul, corresponding to diverse types of objects. But the appetitive agrees in part with the intellective and in part with the sentient as regards the mode of operating with a corporeal organ and the mode of operating without a corporeal organ. For appetite follows upon apprehension. This is why Augustine locates willing (*voluntas*) in the mind (*mens*) and the Philosopher puts it in reason (*ratio*).

**Reply to objection 3:** In the angels there are no powers other than the intellective power and the will, which follows upon intellective understanding. And the reason why an angel is called a 'mind' or an 'intellect' is that all his power consists in this. By contrast, the soul has many other powers, such as the sentient and nutritive powers. And so the two cases are not parallel.

**Reply to objection 4:** The immateriality of an intelligent created substance is not itself its intellect; rather, it is because of its immateriality that it has the power to have intellective understanding (*virtutem ad intelligendum*). Hence, the intellect does not have to be the substance of the soul; all it has to be is the soul's virtue and power (*virtus et potentia*).

## Article 2

### Is the intellect a passive power?

It seems that the intellect is not a passive power:

**Objection 1:** Each thing is acted upon or suffers (*patitur*) in accord with its matter, whereas it acts by reason of its form. But the intellective power follows upon the immateriality of an intelligent substance. Therefore, it seems that the intellect is not a passive power.

**Objection 2:** As was explained above (q. 75, a. 6), the intellective power is incorruptible. But as *De Anima* 3 says, if the intellect is passive, then it is corruptible. Therefore, the intellective power is not passive.

**Objection 3:** As Augustine says in *Super Genesim ad Litteram* 12 and as Aristotle says in *De Anima* 3, to act is more noble than to be acted upon. But all the powers of the vegetative part of the soul are active, and yet they are the lowest among the powers of the soul. Therefore, *a fortiori*, the intellective powers, which are the highest, are all active powers.

**But contrary to this:** In *De Anima* 3 the Philosopher says, "To have intellective understanding (*intelligere*) is in some way to be acted upon."

**I respond:** 'To suffer' or 'to be acted upon' (*pati*) has three senses:

First, its most proper sense, viz., when something that belongs to a thing by its nature or by a proper inclination is taken away from it—as, for instance, when water loses its coldness by being heated, or when a man gets sick or becomes sad.

Second, a less proper sense, viz., when someone is said to suffer or be acted upon by reason of the fact that something is taken away from him, whether or not the thing in question is agreeable to him. In this sense, someone is said to suffer or be acted upon not only when he gets sick but also when he gets well, not only when he becomes sad but also when he becomes joyful, or when he is altered or moved in any way at all.

Third, a thing is said to be acted upon in a general sense (*pati communiter*) solely by reason of the fact that what is in potentiality in some respect receives what it was in potentiality with respect to, without losing anything at all. In this sense, anything that goes from potentiality to

actuality can be said to suffer or be acted upon, even when it is being perfected. And this is the sense in which for us to have intellective understanding is to be acted upon.

This is clear from the following line of reasoning:

As was explained above (q. 78, a. 1), an intellect has its operation with
respect to being in general (*ens in universali*). Therefore, we can think
about whether a given intellect is in potentiality or in actuality by considering how that intellect is related to being in general (*ens universale*).

For there is an intellect that is related to being in general (*ens universale*) as the actuality of all being (*actus totius entis*), and this is the divine
intellect, i.e., God's essence, in which all being preexists virtually and in
its origin, as in its first cause. And so God's intellect is not in potentiality
but is instead pure actuality (*actus purus*).

By contrast, no created intellect can be related as actuality to the whole
of being in general (*ut actus respectu totius entis universalis*), since in that
case it would have to be an unlimited being (*ens infinitum*). Hence, by the
very fact that it is created, a created intellect is not the actuality of all intelligible things, but is instead related to intelligible things themselves as
potentiality is related to actuality.

Now there are two ways in which potentiality is related to actuality.
There are some potentialities that are always being perfected by an actuality, as we claimed above (q. 58, a. 1) concerning the matter of the celestial
bodies. On the other hand, there are some potentialities that are not always
actualized (*non semper in actu*) but instead proceed from potentiality into
actuality, as is the case with generable and corruptible things. Thus, the
angelic intellect is always in actuality with respect to its intelligible
things—and this because of its closeness to the first intellect, which, as was
just explained, is pure actuality. By contrast, the human intellect, which is
the lowest in the order of intellects and furthest from the perfection of
God's intellect, is in potentiality with respect to intelligible things, and at
the start it is "like a blank slate on which nothing has been written," as the
Philosopher puts it in *De Anima* 3. This is manifestly obvious from the fact
that at the start we have intellective understanding only in potentiality, and
afterwards we are brought to have intellective understanding in actuality.

So, then, it is clear that for us to have intellective understanding is for
us to be acted upon, in the third sense of being acted upon. And, as a result,
our intellect is a passive power.

**Reply to objection 1:** This argument goes through for the first and
second senses of being acted upon, which are proper to primary matter.

However, the third sense of being acted upon belongs to anything that is in potentiality and is then brought to actuality.

**Reply to objection 2:** According to some, the passive intellect is the sentient appetite, in which the passions of the soul reside and which, in *Ethics* 1, is called "rational by participation" because it obeys reason. On the other hand, according to others, the passive intellect is the cogitative power, which is named 'particular reason'. In both cases, 'passive' is being taken in accord with the first two senses of being acted upon, insofar as such an 'intellect', so-called, is the act of a corporeal organ.

However, the intellect which is in potentiality with respect to intelligible things and which Aristotle for this reason names the 'passive intellect' (*intellectus possibilis*) is passive only in the third sense. For it is not the act of a corporeal organ. And so it is incorruptible.

**Reply to objection 3:** The agent is more noble than the patient as long as the action and passion are being referred back to the same thing; however, it is not always the case if they are being referred back to diverse things. Now the intellect is a passive power with respect to the whole of being in general, whereas the vegetative power is active with respect to a particular being, viz., the conjoined body. Hence, nothing prevents what is passive in the one way from being more noble than what is active in the other way.

## Article 3

### Is it appropriate to posit an active or agent intellect?

It seems that it is inappropriate to posit an active or agent intellect (*intellectus agens*):

**Objection 1:** Our intellect is related to intelligible things in the same way that the sensory power is related to sensible things. But it is not the case that because the sensory power is in potentiality with respect to sensible things, an active sensory power is posited; instead, only a passive sensory power is posited. Therefore, since our intellect is in potentiality with respect to intelligible things, it seems that only a passive intellect (*intellectus possibilis*) and not an active intellect (*intellectus agens*) should be posited.

**Objection 2:** If someone replies that there is also an agent, such as light, involved in sensing, then against this: Light is required for vision insofar as it makes the medium actually lucid; for color itself is in its own right the mover of what is lucid. By contrast, in the case of the intellect's operation there is no medium posited that has to be actualized (*quod necesse sit fieri in actu*). Therefore, it is unnecessary to posit an active intellect.

**Objection 3:** A likeness of the agent is received in the patient according to the mode of the patient. But the passive intellect is an immaterial power (*virtus immaterialis*). Therefore, the intellect's immateriality is sufficient for its being the case that forms are received in it in an immaterial mode (*immaterialiter*). but a form is actually intelligible by the very fact that it is immaterial. Therefore, there is no need to posit an active intellect in order that it might make the species actually intelligible (*ad hoc quod faciat species intelligibiles in actu*).

**But contrary to this:** In *De Anima* 3 the Philosopher says, "Just as in every nature, so also in the soul, there is something by which it becomes all things and something by which it makes all things." Therefore, it is appropriate to posit an active intellect.

**I respond:** According to Plato's opinion, there was no need to posit an active intellect in order to make things actually intelligible (*ad faciendum intelligibilia in actu*)—though, as will be explained below (a. 4 and q. 84, a. 6), positing an active intellect was perhaps necessary in order to provide the 'intelligible light' for the one having intellective understanding (*ad praebendum lumen intelligibile intelligenti*). For Plato held that the forms of natural things subsist without matter and are consequently intelligible, since a thing is actually intelligible by virtue of being immaterial. He called them 'species' or 'ideas' (*species sive ideas*), and he said that it was by participating in these ideas that (a) corporeal matter is formed in the sense that the individuals are naturally constituted in their own genera and species, and that (b) our intellects are formed in the sense of having knowledge (*scientia*) of the genera and species of things.

By contrast, since Aristotle did not hold that the forms of natural things subsist without matter and since forms that exist in matter are not actually intelligible, it followed that the natures or forms of sensible things—natures that we have intellective understanding of—are not actually intelligible. But nothing is brought from potentiality into actuality except by some actual being, in the way that the sensory power is brought into act by what is actually sensible. Therefore, it was necessary to posit some power on the part of the intellect that would render them actually intelligible by abstracting the species from material conditions. And this is why it is necessary to posit an active intellect.

**Reply to objection 1:** Sensible things are actualized outside the soul, and so there is no need to posit an active sensory power. And in this way it is clear that (a) in the nutritive part of the soul all the powers are active, whereas (b) in the sentient part all of them are passive, and (c) in the intellective part there is something active and something passive.

**Reply to objection 2:** There are two opinions about what the effect of light is:

Some claim that light is required for vision because it makes the colors actually visible. And given this view, the active intellect is required for intellective understanding in a way similar to, and for the same reason that, light is required for seeing.

By contrast, according to others, light is required for seeing not in order that the colors might become actually visible, but in order that the medium might become actually lucid, as the Commentator claims in *De Anima* 2. And given this view, the analogy by which Aristotle assimilates the active intellect to light consists in the fact that just as light is necessary for seeing something, so the active intellect is necessary for understanding something intellectively—but not for the same reason.

**Reply to objection 3:** Assuming that an agent already exists, it is quite possible for its likeness to be received in different ways in diverse patients because of their diverse dispositions. But if there is no preexistent agent, then the patient's disposition makes no difference in this regard.

Now as regards the nature of sensible things, which do not subsist outside of matter, there is nothing in the nature of the things that is actually intelligible. And so the immateriality of the passive intellect would not be sufficient for the intellective understanding of those things if there were no active intellect present to make them actually intelligible by way of abstraction.

## Article 4

### Is the active intellect something that belongs to our soul?

It seems that the active intellect is not something that belongs to our soul:

**Objection 1:** The active intellect's effect is to illuminate for the sake of intellective understanding. But this illumination is effected by something higher than the soul—this according to John 1:9 ("This was the true light, which enlightens every man who comes into this world"). Therefore, it seems that the active intellect is not something that belongs to the soul.

**Objection 2:** In *De Anima* 3 the Philosopher says of the active intellect (*intellectui agenti*) that it "is not such that it is sometimes engaged in intellective understanding and sometimes not (*non aliquando intelligit et aliquando non intelligit*)." But our soul is not always engaged in intellective understanding; rather, sometimes it is engaged in intellective understanding and sometimes not. Therefore, the active intellect is not something that belongs to our soul.

**Objection 3:** An agent and a patient are sufficient for something's being done. Therefore, if the passive intellect, which is a passive power, belongs to our soul, and if the active intellect, which is an active power, does, too, then it will follow that a man is always able to engage in intellective understanding when he wants to. But this is obviously false. Therefore, the active intellect is not something that belongs to our soul.

**Objection 4:** In *De Anima* 3 the Philosopher says that the active intellect is "a substantival being in actuality (*substantia actu ens*)." But there is nothing that is both in actuality and in potentiality in the same respect. Therefore, if the passive intellect, which is in potentiality with respect to all intelligible things, is something that belongs to our soul, then it seems impossible for the active intellect to be something that belongs to our soul.

**Objection 5:** If the active intellect is something that belongs to our soul, then it must be a power. For it is neither a passion nor a habit, since habits and passions do not have the character of an agent with respect to the 'passions of the soul'; rather, a passion is the action itself as belonging to the passive power, whereas a habit is something that follows upon actions. But every power of the soul flows from the essence of the soul. Therefore, it would follow that the active intellect proceeds from the essence of the soul. And so it would not be in the soul through participation in any higher intellect—which is just wrong. Therefore, the active intellect is not something that belongs to our soul.

**But contrary to this:** In *De Anima* 3 the Philosopher says, "It is necessary for these differences to exist in the soul," viz., the passive intellect and the active intellect.

**I respond:** The active intellect of which the Philosopher speaks is something that belongs to the soul.

To see this clearly, note that beyond the human intellective soul it is necessary to posit a higher intellect from which the soul obtains its power to engage in intellective understanding. For it is always the case that what participates in something and is changeable and imperfect requires prior to itself something that is such-and-such through its essence, unchangeable, and perfect. But the human soul is called 'intellective' through participation in an intellectual power. An indication of this is that the human soul is intellective not as a whole, but rather with respect to a part of itself. Moreover, it arrives at an intellective understanding of truth discursively and through a movement, by way of argument. Again, it has imperfect intellective understanding, both because it does not understand all things and also because in the case of those things that it does understand, it proceeds from potentiality to actuality. Therefore, there must be some higher intellect by which the soul is assisted in engaging in intellective cognition. Thus, some have claimed that it is this intellect, separated with respect to its substance, which is the active intellect and which, by illuminating the phantasms, renders things actually intelligible.

However, granted that there is some such separated active intellect, it is nonetheless still necessary to posit within the human soul itself a power which is a participation in that higher intellect and through which the human soul renders things actually intelligible. As in the case of other perfect natural entities, there are, in addition to the universal agent causes, proper powers that are derived from the universal agents and given to individual perfect things. For instance, it is not the sun alone that generates a man; rather, there is in man a power to generate man—and the same holds for the other perfect animals. But among lower things there is none more perfect than the human soul. Hence, one must claim that within the human soul there is a power, derived from a higher intellect, through which it can illuminate phantasms. We know this from experience when we perceive ourselves abstracting universal forms from particular conditions—which is what it is to render things actually intelligible. But as was explained above (q. 76, a. 1) when we were discussing the passive intellect, an action belongs to a being only through some principle that formally inheres in it. Therefore, the power that is the principle of this action must be something within the soul. This is why Aristotle compared the active intellect to light, which is something received in the air.

Plato, on the other hand, compared the separated intellect impressed on our souls to the sun, as Themistius reports in his commentary on *De Anima* 3. Now according to the teaching of our Faith, this separated intellect is God Himself, who is the creator of the soul and in whom alone the soul is beatified, as will become clear below (q. 90, a. 3 and *ST* 1–2, q. 3, a. 7). Hence, it is because of Him that the human soul participates in the intellectual light—this according to Psalm 4:7 ("The light of your countenance, O Lord, is signed upon us").

**Reply to objection 1:** The true light in question illuminates as a universal cause, because of which, as has been explained, the human soul participates in a certain particular power.

**Reply to objection 2:** The Philosopher is talking about actually engaging in intellective understanding and not about the active intellect. Hence, a little before this he had said of the former that it is the same as actual knowledge of the thing.

An alternative reply is that if he is indeed talking about the active intellect, what he means is that it is not because of the active intellect (*non est ex parte intellectus agentis*) that we are sometimes engaged in intellective understanding and sometimes not; instead, it is because of the intellect that is in potentiality.

**Reply to objection 3:** If the active intellect were related to the passive intellect as an active object is related to a power, in the way that something visible in actuality is related to the power of sight, then it would follow that we have intellective understanding of all things immediately, since the active intellect's function is to fashion all things.

As things stand, however, the active intellect behaves not as an object but as that which renders the objects actual, and what is required for this, besides the presence of the active intellect, are (a) the presence of phantasms, (b) well-disposed sentient powers, and (c) the exercise of the right sort of act. For through one thing that is understood intellectively other things come to be understood as well; for instance, propositions come to be understood through terms, and conclusions come to be understood through first principles. And as far as this is concerned, it makes no difference whether the active intellect is something that belongs to the soul or something separated.

**Reply to objection 4:** The intellective soul is, to be sure, actually immaterial, but it is in potentiality with respect to the determinate species of things. Conversely, the phantasms are in actuality likenesses of certain species, but they are immaterial in potentiality. Hence, nothing prevents one and the same soul, insofar as it is actually immaterial, from having (a) one power—a power called the active intellect—through which it renders things actually immaterial by abstracting them from the conditions of individual matter, and (b) another power that is receptive of this sort of species—and this power is called the passive intellect insofar as it is in potentiality with respect to species of this sort.

**Reply to objection 5:** Since the essence of the soul is immaterial and is created by the highest intellect, there is no problem with a power proceeding from it—just as other powers of the soul do—which is a participation in the highest intellect and by which it abstracts from matter.

## Article 5

### Is there a single active intellect for everyone?

It seems that there is a single active intellect for everyone:

**Objection 1:** Nothing that is separated from a body is multiplied as bodies are multiplied. But as *De Anima* 3 says, the active intellect is "separated." Therefore, it is not multiplied in the many bodies of men, but is the same in everyone

**Objection 2:** The active intellect fashions the universal, which is one in many. But that which is the cause of oneness is *a fortiori* one. Therefore, there is a single active intellect for everyone.

**Objection 3:** All men agree in the first conceptions of the intellect. But they assent to these conceptions through the active intellect. Therefore, all men agree in having a single active intellect.

**But contrary to this:** In *De Anima* 3 the Philosopher says that the active intellect is like light. But it is not the case that the same light exists in diverse illuminated things. Therefore, it is not the case that the same active intellect exists in diverse men.

**I respond:** The truth with regard to this question depends on what has already been said (a. 4).

For if the active intellect were not something that belongs to the soul but were instead a separated substance, then there would be a single active intellect for all men. And this is how those who posit the oneness of the intellect understand the situation.

On the other hand, if the active intellect is something that belongs to the soul as one of its powers, then one must claim that there are many active intellects corresponding to the plurality of souls, and that they are multiplied as men are multiplied, as was explained above (q. 76, a. 2). For it is impossible for numerically one and the same power to belong to diverse substances.

**Reply to objection 1:** The Philosopher proves that the active intellect is separated from the premise that the passive intellect is separated. For, as he points out, the active intellect is more noble than the passive intellect. But the reason why the passive intellect is called 'separated' is that it is not the act of any corporeal organ. And it is in this sense, too, that the active intellect is said to be 'separated'—and not in the sense that it is a separated substance.

**Reply to objection 2:** The active intellect is a cause of the universal by abstracting it from matter. What is required for this is not that it be [numerically] one in everyone who has an intellect, but rather that it be one in everyone as regards its relation to those things from which it abstracts the universal and with respect to which the universal is one. And this feature belongs to the active intellect insofar as it is immaterial.

**Reply to objection 3:** All things of the same species share in an action that follows upon the nature of the species, and, consequently, they share in the power that is the principle of that action—but not in the sense that the power is numerically the same in all of them. Now to have cognition of the first intelligible things (*cognoscere prima intelligibilia*) is an action that follows upon the human species. Hence, all men must share in the power that is the principle of that action, and this is the power of the active intellect. But it is not necessary for this power to be numerically the same in everyone; what is necessary is that it should be derived from a single principle in each of them. And so the fact that men share in the first intelligible things points to the oneness of the separated intellect that Plato compares to the sun, but not to the oneness of the active intellect that Aristotle compares to light.

### Article 6

#### Does memory exist in the intellective part of the soul?

It seems that memory does not exist in the intellective part of the soul:

**Objection 1:** In *De Trinitate* 12 Augustine says that what belongs to the higher part of the soul "are not things that are common to men and beasts." But memory is common to men and beasts; for in the same place he says, "Beasts can sense corporeal things through their bodily senses and commit those things to memory." Therefore, memory does not belong to the intellective part of the soul.

**Objection 2:** Memory is of past things. But 'past' expresses a determinate time. Therefore, memory provides cognition of a thing under the rubric of a determinate time (*sub determinato tempore*), i.e., it provides cognition of something under the rubric of a *here* and *now*. But this feature belongs to the sensory power and not to the intellective power. Therefore, memory exists only in the sentient part of the soul and not in the intellective part.

**Objection 3:** What is conserved in the memory are the species of things that are not actually being thought about. But this cannot occur in the intellect, since the intellect becomes actualized (*fit in actu*) by being formed by an intelligible species (*per hoc quod informatur specie intelligibili*), and for the intellect to be actualized is just for it to be actually engaged in intellective understanding (*intellectum esse in actu est ipsum intelligere in actu*). And so the intellect understands in actuality all the things whose species it has within it. Therefore, it is not the case that memory exists in the intellective part.

**But contrary to this:** In *De Trinitate* 10 Augustine says, "Memory, intellective understanding (*intelligentia*), and will are one mind."

**I respond:** Since it is the nature of memory to conserve species of things that are not actually being apprehended, the first thing that has to be considered is whether intelligible species are able to be conserved in this way in the intellect.

Avicenna, for one, claimed that this is impossible. For, he said, this sort of thing happens in the sentient part of the soul with respect to certain powers, insofar as they are acts of corporeal organs in which species can be conserved without actual apprehension. But in the intellect, which lacks a corporeal organ, nothing exists except as actually intelligible (*nisi intelligibiliter*). Hence, if the likeness of a thing exists in the intellect, then that thing is such that it is actually being understood intellectively. So, then, according to him, as soon as someone ceases to be having an actual intellective cognition of a given thing, the species of that thing ceases to exist in the intellect. Moreover, if he once again wants to have an intellective cognition of that thing, then he must turn to the active intellect, which Avicenna posits as a separated substance, in order for the intelligible species to flow from it into the passive intellect. And from the exercise and practice of turning to the active intellect, there follows in the passive intellect, according to him, a certain facility of turning to the active intellect, a facility that he claimed is the habit of knowledge (*habitum scientiae*). Therefore, according to this position, there is nothing conserved in the intellective part of the soul that is not actually being considered. Hence, on this view memory cannot be posited in the intellective part of the soul.

However, this opinion is manifestly incompatible with what Aristotle says. For in *De Anima* 3 he says that (a) "when the passive intellect becomes each of the things in knowing them, it is said to be actually knowing them (*dicitur qui secundum actum*)," and that (b) "this happens when it is able to act *through itself*; thus, even at that point it is in some sense in potentiality, though not in the same way as it was before it learned or discovered the relevant thing." Now the passive intellect is said to 'become each thing' insofar as it receives the species of each thing. Therefore, by the fact that it receives the species of intelligible things, it is such that it is able to operate when it wants to, but not such that it is always operating; for even then it is in some sense in potentiality, though in a different way from the way it was in potentiality before it had intellective cognition. More specifically, it is in potentiality in the way in which someone who knows something habitually is in potentiality with respect to actually considering that thing.

Moreover, the position described above is contrary to reason. For what is received in a thing is received in it in accord with the mode of what receives it. But the intellect has a more stable and unchanging nature than does corporeal matter. Therefore, if corporeal matter holds on to the forms it receives not only while actually acting through them but also after it has ceased to act through them, then *a fortiori* the intellect will receive intelligible species in an unchangeable and permanent way, regardless of whether they are taken from sensible things or flow forth from some higher intellect.

So, then, if 'memory' is taken to mean merely a power that conserves species, then one must claim that memory exists in the intellective part of the soul. On the other hand, if it is also part of the concept of memory that its object is something past insofar as it is past, then memory will exist only in the sentient part of the soul, which apprehends particulars, and not in the intellective part. For since 'the past insofar as it is the past' signifies being under the rubric of a determinate time, it involves the condition of a particular.

**Reply to objection 1:** Insofar as it conserves species, memory is not common to us and the beasts. For species are conserved not in the sentient part of the soul alone, but rather in the conjoined being, since the power of remembering is the act of an organ. By contrast, the intellect conserves species in its own right, without a connection to any corporeal organ. Hence, in *De Anima* 3 the Philosopher says, "The soul is the locus of species—not the whole soul, but the intellect."

**Reply to objection 2:** Pastness (*praeteritio*) can apply to two things, viz., the *object* that one has cognition of, and the *act of cognition*.

These two are joined together in the sentient part of the soul, which apprehends a thing when it is changed by a present sensible object. Hence, an animal remembers at the same time both (a) that it was *sensing at a prior time* in the past and (b) that it was sensing some *past sensible object*.

By contrast, as far as the intellective part is concerned, pastness is incidental to, and does not belong *per se* to, the intellect's *object*. For the intellect has an intellective understanding of a man insofar as he is a man, and it is incidental to a man insofar as he is a man that he exists in the present or in the past or in the future.

On the other hand, as far as the *act* is concerned, pastness can be taken account of *per se* in the intellect as well as in the sensory power. Our soul's having an intellective cognition is a particular act that exists at this or that time, since a man is said to be having an intellective cognition now or yesterday or tomorrow. This is not incompatible with the status of intellection (*non repugnat intellectualitati*), since even though this sort of act of intellective cognition is a particular, it is nonetheless an immaterial act, as was explained above concerning the intellect (q. 76, a. 1). And so just as the intellect has an intellective understanding of itself even though it itself is a singular intellect, so it has an intellective understanding of its own act of intellective understanding, which is a singular act existing in either the present or the past or the future.

So, then, insofar as it concerns past things, the nature of memory is preserved in the intellect by the fact that it understands intellectively that it has previously had an intellective understanding—but not by its having an intellective understanding of a past thing insofar as that thing has a *here* and *now*.

**Reply to objection 3:** An intelligible species sometimes exists in the intellect only in potentiality, and in such a case the intellect is said to be in potentiality. On the other hand, an intelligible species sometimes exists in the intellect because of the full completion of the act (*secundum ultimam completionem actus*), and in such a case the intellect is said to be actually engaged in intellective understanding (*tunc intelligit actu*). And sometimes the intellect is in a middle state between potentiality and actuality, and in that case the intellect is said to be habituated (*in habitu*); and it is in this mode that the intellect conserves species, even when it is not actually engaged in intellective understanding.

## Article 7

### Is intellective memory a power distinct from the intellect?

It seems that intellective memory is a power distinct from the intellect:

**Objection 1:** In *De Trinitate* 10 Augustine posits in the mind "memory, intellective understanding (*intelligentia*), and will." But it is clear that memory is a power distinct from the will. Therefore, it is likewise a power distinct from the intellect.

**Objection 2:** The nature of the distinctions among the powers is the same in the case of the sentient part of the soul as it is in the case of the intellective part. But as was explained above (q. 78, a. 4), in the sentient part memory is a power distinct from the sensory power. Therefore, memory in the intellective part of the soul is a power distinct from the intellect.

**Objection 3:** According to Augustine, memory, intellective understanding, and will are equal to one another, and one of them arises from another. But this could not be the case if memory were the same power as the intellect. Therefore, it is not the same power.

**But contrary to this:** It is part of the nature of memory that it is a treasury or locus where species are conserved. But as has been pointed out (a. 6), in *De Anima* 3 the Philosopher attributes this role to the intellect. Therefore, in the intellective part of the soul it is not the case that memory is a power distinct from the intellect.

**I respond:** As has been explained (q. 77, a 3), the powers of the soul are distinguished by the diverse natures of their objects, since the nature of each power consists in its being ordered toward what it is related to, i.e., its object. It was also explained above (q. 59, a. 4) that if a power is by its proper nature ordered toward an object taken under some general concept of the object, that power will not be diversified by the diversity of particular differences; for instance, the visual power, which relates to its object under the concept *being colored*, is not diversified by the difference between *white* and *black*.

Now the intellect is related to its object under the common conception *being* (*respicit suum obiectum secundum communem rationem entis*), since the passive intellect is that by which the intellect becomes all things. Hence, there is no difference among beings by which the passive intellect is diversified. Yet the passive intellect is diversified as a power from the active intellect because, with respect to the very same object, there must be one principle that is an active power and makes a thing to be an object in actuality, and another principle that is a passive power and is moved by the object now existing in actuality. And so the active power is related to its object as a being in actuality is related to a being in potentiality, whereas the passive power's relation to its object is just the opposite, as a being in potentiality is related to a being in actuality. So, then, there can be no difference among the powers in the intellect except the difference between the passive and the active.

Hence, it is clear that memory is not a power distinct from the intellect; for it pertains to the nature of a passive power to conserve as well as to receive.

**Reply to objection 1:** Even though in *Sentences* 1, dist. 3 the claim is made that memory, intellective understanding, and will are three "powers," this is nonetheless not what Augustine means. For in *De Trinitate* 14 he explicitly says, "If memory (*memoria*), intellective understanding (*intelligentia*), and will (*voluntas*) are taken to be always present in the soul regardless of whether they are being thought of, then they seem to belong to memory alone. At present, by 'intellective understanding' I mean that by which we understand when we are thinking, and by 'will' I mean love or affection (*dilectio*), which joins together the child with the parent." From this it is clear that Augustine is not using these words for three powers, but that he is instead taking 'memory' for the soul's habitual retention, whereas he is taking 'intellective understanding' for an act of the intellect and 'will' for an act of the will.

**Reply to objection 2:** The past and the present can be proper differences that diversify sentient powers, but they cannot, for the reason stated above (a.6), be proper differences that diversify intellective powers.

**Reply to objection 3:** Intellective understanding arises from memory in the way that an act arises from a habit. And it is in this sense, too—and not as one power with respect to another—that memory is equal to intellective understanding.

### Article 8

### Is reason a power distinct from the intellect?

It seems that reason (*ratio*) is a power distinct from the intellect (*intellectus*):

**Objection 1:** In *De Spiritu et Anima* it says, "When we wish to ascend from the lower to the higher, the first thing to occur to us is the sensory power, then the imagination, next reason (*ratio*), after that the intellect (*intellectus*)." Therefore, reason is a power distinct from the intellect, just as imagination is distinct from reason.

**Objection 2:** In *De Consolatione Philosophiae* Boethius says that the intellect is related to reason in the way that eternity is related to time. But being in eternity does not belong to the same power as does being in time. Therefore, reason and intellect are not the same power.

**Objection 3:** Man shares intellect with the angels and sensory power with the brute animals. But reason, which is proper to man and by which man is called a 'rational' animal, is a power distinct from the sensory power. Therefore, by parity of reasoning, reason is a power distinct from the intellect, which belongs properly to the angels and is the source of their being called 'intellectual' beings.

**But contrary to this:** In *Super Genesim ad Litteram* 3 Augustine says, "That by which man exceeds the non-rational animals is reason (*ratio*), or mind (*mens*), or intellective understanding (*intelligentia*), or whatever other word it is most appropriately called by." Therefore, reason and intellect and mind are a single power.

**I respond:** Reason and intellect cannot be diverse powers in man. This is seen clearly if the acts of the two of them are examined. For to have intellective understanding (*intelligere*) is simply to apprehend intelligible truth, whereas to engage in discursive reasoning (*ratiocinari*) is to proceed from one thing that is understood to another in order to come to a cognition of intelligibile truth (*veritatem intelligibilem cognoscere*). And so as Dionysius says in *De Divinis Nominibus*, chap. 7, angels, who by their nature have perfect possession of the cognition of intelligible truth, do not have to proceed from one thing to another, but instead apprehend the truth about things simply and without discursive reasoning (*simpliciter et absque discursu*). By contrast, as he says in the same place, men arrive at the understanding of intelligible truth by proceeding from one thing to another, and this is why they are called 'rational'.

Therefore, it is clear that to engage in discursive reasoning (*ratiocinari*) is related to having intellective understanding (*intelligere*) in the way that moving (*moveri*) is related to coming to rest (*quiescere*), or in the way that coming to acquire (*acquirere*) is related to possessing (*habere*)—where the one is complete (*perfecti*) and the other incomplete (*imperfecti*). And since motion always proceeds from what is unmoved and terminates in what is at rest, so it is that (a) on the path of *inquiry* (or *discovery*) (*secundum viam inquisitionis vel inventionis*) human reasoning proceeds from some things that are simply understood, viz., first principles, and, again, (b) on the path of *judgment* (*in via iudicii*) it returns through analysis (*resolvendo*) to the first principles and in light of them examines what has been discovered. Now it is clear that even among natural things, moving and coming to rest are traced back to one and the same power and not to diverse powers, since it is through the same nature that a thing moves to a place and rests in that place. Therefore, *a fortiori*, it is through the same power that we have intellective understanding and reason discursively. And so it is clear that in man reason and intellect are the same power.

**Reply to objection 1:** This enumeration is made in accord with an ordering of acts and not in accord with a distinction among powers—though the book in question does not have much authority in any case.

**Reply to objection 2:** The reply is clear from what has been said. For eternity is related to time in the way that what is unchanging is related to what is changing. And so Boethius is likening intellective understanding to eternity and discursive reasoning to time.

**Reply to objection 3:** The other animals are inferior to man to such an extent that they cannot attain to the cognition of the truth that reason seeks. Man, however, attains in an imperfect way the understanding of intelligible truth had by the angels. And so the angels' cognitive power is not of a different genus from the cognitive power of reason, but is instead related to it as the perfect is related to the imperfect.


### Article 9

### Are higher reason and lower reason diverse powers?

It seems that higher reason and lower reason are diverse powers:

**Objection 1:** In *De Trinitate* 12 Augustine says that the image of the Trinity exists in the higher part of reason but not in the lower part. But the parts of the soul are its powers. Therefore, higher reason and lower reason are two distinct powers.

**Objection 2:** Nothing takes its origin from itself. But lower reason takes its origin from higher reason and is regulated and directed by it. Therefore, higher reason is a power distinct from lower reason.

**Objection 3:** In *Ethics* 6 the Philosopher says that the *scientific* (*scientificum*) part of the soul, by which the soul knows necessary things, is a different principle and different part of the soul from the *opinative* and *ratiocinative* part (*alia pars animae ab opinativo et ratiocinativo*), by which it has cognition of contingent things. And he proves this by appealing to the fact that "parts of the soul that differ in genus are ordered toward things that differ in genus." Now the contingent and the necessary differ in genus as the corruptible and the incorruptible. But since the necessary is the same as the eternal and the temporal is the same as the contingent, it seems that (a) what the Philosopher is calling the 'scientific' part is the same as higher reason, which, according to Augustine, "tends toward considering and consulting eternal things," and that (b) what the Philosopher is calling the 'ratiocinative' or 'opinative' part is the same as lower reason, which, according to Augustine, "tends toward dealing with temporal things." Therefore, higher reason is a power of the soul that is distinct from lower reason.

**Objection 4:** Damascene says, "From the imagination comes opinion. Then the mind, judging that the opinion is true or false, judges with respect to truth, and then it is called 'mind' (*mens*), from 'measuring' (*mentio*). Therefore, what is called 'intellect' has to do with those things that have already been judged and truly determined." So, then, the opinative part, which is lower reason, is different from 'mind' and 'intellect', which can be interpreted as higher reason.

**But contrary to this:** In *De Trinitate* 12 Augustine says that higher and lower reason are distinguished only as functions (*non nisi per officia distinguuntur*). Therefore, they are not two distinct powers.

**I respond:** As higher and lower reason are understood by Augustine, they cannot in any way be two distinct powers of the soul. For he says, "Higher reason tends toward considering and consulting eternal things"—'considering' in the sense that it looks at them in themselves, and 'consulting' in the sense that takes from them rules for acting. On the other hand, he says that lower reason "tends toward temporal things." Now these two sorts of things, viz., the temporal and the eternal, are related to our cognition in such a way that the one is the medium for the cognition of the other. For on the path of *discovery*, we go by way of temporal things to a cognition of eternal things—this according to the Apostle in Romans 1:20 ("The invisible things of God are clearly seen, being understood through the things that have been made")—whereas on the path of *judgment*, we pass judgment on temporal things by reference to eternal things, once we have cognition of them, and we go on to deal with temporal things in light of the nature of eternal things.

Now it is possible for a medium and that which is arrived at through the medium to belong to diverse *habits*, in the way that the first indemonstrable principles belong to the habit of understanding (*intellectus*), whereas the conclusions deduced from them belong to the habit of scientific knowledge (*scientia*). And so from the principles of geometry it is possible to draw a conclusion in another science, viz., the science of perspective.

However, both the medium and ultimate end belong to the same *power* of reason. For an act of reason is, as it were, a movement that arrives at one thing from another; but the same moving thing that passes through the medium is the one that arrives at the terminus. Hence, higher and lower reason are one and the same power of reason. They are distinguished, according to Augustine, by the functions of their acts and by diverse habits, for wisdom (*sapientia*) is attributed to higher reason and scientific knowledge (*scientia*) to lower reason.

**Reply to objection 1:** The term 'part' can be used in a way corresponding to any sort of partition. Therefore, it is because reason is divided by diverse functions that higher and lower reason are called parts (*parti tiones*)—and not because they are diverse powers.

**Reply to objection 2:** Lower reason is said to be derived (*deduci*) from higher reason, or regulated by it, insofar as the principles that lower reason makes use of are derived from and directed by the principles of higher reason.

**Reply to objection 3:** The 'scientific' part of the soul that the Philosopher is talking about is not the same thing as higher reason. For necessary knowable things are also found among temporal things, and there is natural science and mathematics with respect to them. On the other hand, since the opinative and ratiocinative part has to do only with contingent things, it is concerned with less than lower reason is.

But neither should one claim simply that there is one power by which the intellect has cognition of necessary things and another power by which it has cognition of contingent things. For it has cognition of both in accord with the same type of object, viz., in accord with the natures *being* and *true*. Hence, necessary things, which have perfect *esse* in truth, are such that the intellect has perfect cognition of them as far as their 'what-ness' (*quidditas*) is concerned, and it is by appeal to the 'what-ness' that the intellect infers (*demonstrat*) their proper accidents. On the other hand, contingent things are such that the intellect has imperfect cognition of them, even as they themselves have imperfect *esse* and truth. However, the actual perfect and imperfect do not diversify powers; instead, they diversify acts with regard to their mode of acting and, as a result, they diversify the principles of the acts and the habits themselves.

And the reason why the Philosopher posited the scientific and the ratiocinative as two parts of the soul is not that they are two distinct powers, but that they are distinguished according to their diverse aptitudes for receiving diverse habits. And it was the diversity of the habits that he wanted to inquire about in that place. For even if contingent things and the necessary things differ in their proper genera, they nonetheless agree in the common nature *being*, which is what the intellect looks to and which contingent and necessary things are related to in diverse ways as the imperfect and the perfect.

**Reply to objection 4:** This distinction of Damascene's has to do with a diversity of acts and not with a diversity of powers. For 'opinion' signifies an act of the intellect that is drawn to one part of a contradiction with fear of the other part. And to 'pass judgment on', or to 'measure', is an act of the intellect that applies firm principles to the examination of proposed objects; and this is what the name 'mind' is taken from. On the other hand, to 'have intellective understanding' is to adhere with a sort of approbation to what has been judged.


## Article 10

### Is intellective understanding a power distinct from the intellect?

It seems that intellective understanding (*intelligentia*) is a power distinct from the intellect (*intellectus*):

**Objection 1:** In *De Spiritu et Anima* it says, "When we wish to ascend from the lower to the higher, the first thing to occur to us is the sensory power, then the imagination, next reason (*ratio*), after that the intellect (*intellectus*), and after that intellective understanding (*intelligentia*)." But imagination and the sensory power are distinct powers. Therefore, so are intellect and intellective understanding.

**Objection 2:** In *De Consolatione Philosophiae* 5 Boethius says, "The sensory power, the imagination, reason (*ratio*), and intellective understanding (*intelligentia*) all see the man himself in different ways." But the intellect (*intellectus*) is the same power as reason (*ratio*). Therefore, it seems that intellective understanding is a power distinct from the intellect, in the same way that reason is a power distinct from the imagination and the sensory power.

**Objection 3:** As *De Anima* 2 says, "Acts are prior to powers." But intellective understanding (*intelligentia*) is a certain act divided off from the other acts that are attributed to the intellect. For Damascene says, "The first movement is called intellective understanding (*intelligentia*), and when there is intellective understanding with respect to something, this is called an intention (*intentio*); and when the soul is stable and configured to that of which there is intellective understanding (*permanens et figurans* *animam ad id quod intelligitur*), this is called thinking things out (*excogi-tatio*); and when thinking things out remains the same and the soul exam-ines itself and passes judgement, this is called *phronesis*, i.e., wisdom (*sapientia*); and *phronesis* extended in time (*dilatata*) makes for cogitation (*cogitatio*), i.e., orderly interior speech (*interius dispositum sermonem*), from which, they say, comes forth speech expressed by the tongue." Therefore, it seems that intellective understanding is a certain special power.

**But contrary to this:** In *De Anima* 3 the Philosopher says, "Intellective understanding (*intelligentia*) is of indivisibles, in which there is nothing false." But this sort of cognition belongs to the intellect. Therefore, intellective understanding is not a distinct power over and beyond the intellect.

**I respond:** The name 'intellective understanding' (*intelligentia*) signi-fies the very act of the intellect, viz., to have intellective understanding (*intelligere*). However, in certain books translated from Arabic, the sepa-rated substances that we call angels are called 'intelligences' (*intelligenti-ae*), perhaps because they are always actually engaged in intellective understanding. By contrast, in the books translated from Greek they are called 'intellects' (*intellectus*) or 'minds' (*mentes*).

So, then, intellective understanding (*intelligentia*) is distinguished from the intellect (*intellectus*) not as one power from another, but as an act from a power. Such a division is found also among the philosophers. For instance, they sometimes posit four 'intellects', viz., the *active intellect* (*intellectus agens*), the *passive intellect* (*intellectus possibilis*), the *habitu-al intellect* (*intellectus in habitu*), and the *acquired intellect* (*intellectus adeptus*). Of these four, the active intellect and passive intellect are diverse powers, just as in all other cases the active power is one thing and the cor-responding passive power is another. However, the other three are distin-guished as three states of the passive intellect, which (a) sometimes is only in potentiality, and in that case it is called the *passive intellect*; (b) some-times is in first actuality, i.e., knowledge (*scientia*), and in that case it is called the *habitual intellect*; and (c) sometimes is in second actuality, i.e., actual consideration, and in that case it is called the *intellect in act or actu-ality* (*intellectus in actu*) or acquired intellect (*intellectus adeptus*).

**Reply to objection 1:** Assuming that this authority should be taken seriously, 'intellective understanding' is being posited as an act of the intel-lect. And so it is divided off against the intellect as an act is divided off against its corresponding power.

**Reply to objection 2:** Boethius is taking 'intellective understanding' (*intelligentia*) for an act of the intellect that transcends the act of reason. Hence, in the same place he says that reason belongs only to the human race, just as intellective understanding belongs only to God, since it is proper to God to understand all things without any inquiry at all.

**Reply to objection 3:** All these acts enumerated by Damascene belong to a single power, viz., the intellective power. First, the intellective power simply apprehends something, and this act is called *intellective understanding* (*intelligentia*). Second, it orders what it apprehends either toward having cognition of something else or toward acting, and this is called *intention* (*intentio*). When it persists in inquiring into that which it intends, then this is called *thinking things out* (*excogitatio*). And when it examines what has been thought out with respect to some things that have certitude, it is said to know (*scire*) or to be wise (*sapere*)—which is *phronesis* or wisdom (*sapientia*), since, as *Metaphysics* 1 says, it belongs to wisdom to pass judgment. And from the fact that it holds something as certain and as having been examined, it thinks about how it might be possible to make it manifest to others; this is the *ordering of interior speech* (*dispositio interioris sermonis*), and from this flows *exterior speech* (*exterior locutio*). For it is not every difference among acts that makes for diverse powers; instead, as was explained above (q. 78, a. 4), it is only the sort of difference that cannot be traced back to the same principle.

## Article 11

### Are the speculative intellect and the practical intellect diverse powers?

It seems that the speculative intellect and the practical intellect are diverse powers:

**Objection 1:** As *De Anima* 2 makes clear, the apprehensive power and the power that effects movement are diverse powers. But the speculative intellect is purely apprehensive, whereas the practical intellect is a power that effects movement. Therefore, they are diverse powers.

**Objection 2:** Powers are diversified by the diverse natures of their objects. But the object of the speculative intellect is the true, whereas the object of the practical intellect is the good; and these objects differ in nature. Therefore, the speculative intellect and practical intellect are diverse powers.

**Objection 3:** In the intellective part of the soul, the practical intellect is related to the speculative intellect in the way that, in the sentient part of the soul, the estimative power is related to the power of imagining. But as was explained above (q. 78, a. 4), the estimative power differs from the power of imagining as one power from another. Therefore, the practical intellect and speculative intellect differ in the same way.

**But contrary to this:** *De Anima* 3 says that the speculative intellect becomes practical by extension. But it is not the case that one power is changed into another. Therefore, the speculative intellect and practical intellect are not diverse powers.

**I respond:** The practical intellect and speculative intellect are not diverse powers. The reason for this, as was explained above (q. 77, a. 3), is that something related incidentally to the nature of a power's object does not diversify the power. For instance, it is incidental to what is colored that it is a man, or that it is large or small; hence, all things of this sort are apprehended by one and the same visual power.

Now it is incidental to what is apprehended by the intellect that it is ordered or not ordered toward an action—but it is in this that the speculative intellect and the practical intellect differ. For the speculative intellect orders what it apprehends only toward the consideration of truth and not toward an action, whereas the practical intellect is such that it does order what it apprehends toward an action. And this is just what the Philosopher says in *De Anima* 3, viz., that "the speculative intellect differs from the practical intellect in its end." Hence, each is denominated from its end, the one being speculative, and the other practical, i.e., operative (*operativus*).

**Reply to objection 1:** The practical intellect is a power that effects movement not in the sense that it executes movement, but in the sense that it directs one toward movement. This feature belongs to it because of the mode of its apprehension.

**Reply to objection 2:** The true and the good include one another, since the true is a certain good (otherwise it would not be desirable) and the good is in a certain sense true (otherwise it would not be intelligible). Therefore, just as the true can be an object of desire insofar as it has the nature of a good, as when someone desires to have cognition of the truth, so the object of the practical intellect is a good that can be ordered toward action, under the concept of the true. For the practical intellect has cognition of truth in the same way that the speculative intellect does, but it orders the truth it has cognition of toward action.

**Reply to objection 3:** As was explained above (a. 7), there are many differences that diversify the sentient powers but do not diversify the intellective powers.

## Article 12

### Is synderesis a special power distinct from the others?

It seems that synderesis (*synderesis*) is a special power distinct from the others:

**Objection 1:** Things that fall under the same division seem to belong to the same genus. But in Jerome's Gloss on Ezechiel 1:6, synderesis is divided off against the irascible, the concupiscible, and the rational, all of which are powers. Therefore, synderesis is a certain power.

**Objection 2:** Opposites belong to the same genus. But synderesis and sensuality (*sensualitas*) appear to be opposites, since synderesis always inclines one toward what is good, whereas sensuality always inclines one toward what is bad; this is why sensuality is signified by a serpent, as is clear from Augustine in *De Trinitate* 12. Therefore, it seems that synderesis is a power in the same way that sensuality is.

**Objection 3:** In *De Libero Arbitrio* Augustine says that present in nature's court of judgment (*in naturali judicatorio*) are certain "rules and seeds of the virtues, both true and unchangeable," and these we call synderesis. Therefore, since, as Augustine claims in *De Trinitate* 12, the unchangeable rules by which we make judgments have to do with the higher part of reason, it seems that synderesis is the same as reason. And so it is a power.

**But contrary to this:** According to the Philosopher, the rational powers bear a relation to opposites. However, synderesis does not bear a relation to opposites, but inclines one only toward what is good. Therefore, synderesis is not a power. For if it were a power, it would have to be a rational power, since it is not found in brute animals.

**I respond:** Synderesis is a habit and not a power, even though some have claimed that synderesis is a certain power higher than reason (*ratio*) and others have claimed that it is reason itself—not reason insofar as it is reason, but reason insofar as it is a nature.

To see this clearly, note that, as was explained above (a. 8), since man's discursive reasoning (*ratiocinatio*) is a movement, it proceeds from the intellective understanding of certain things (*ab intellectu aliquorum*) that serve as unchangeable principles—viz., things known naturally without reason's inquiry—and likewise terminates in an intellective understanding, insofar as we make judgments on the basis of principles naturally known in themselves (*per principia per se naturaliter nota*) about the things that we discover by reasoning discursively. But it is clear that practical reason reasons about actions (*de operabilibus*) in the same way that speculative reason reasons about speculative objects (*de speculativis*). Therefore, just as we have been naturally endowed with principles regarding speculative objects (*principia speculabilium*), so too we have been naturally endowed with principles regarding actions (*principia operabilium*).

Now the first principles regarding speculative objects that we have been naturally endowed with do not involve any special power, but instead involve a special habit, which is called the *intellective understanding of principles* (*intellectus principiorum*), as is clear from *Ethics* 6. Hence, the principles that we have been naturally endowed with regarding actions do not involve a special power, either, but instead involve a special natural habit, which we call *synderesis*. Hence, synderesis is said to goad us toward what is good and to murmur about what is bad (*instigare ad bonum et murmurare de malo*), insofar as (a) we proceed to discover things on the basis of the first principles and (b) we pass judgment about what has been discovered.

It is clear, then, that synderesis is a natural habit and not a power.

**Reply to objection 1:** Jerome's division is made according to a diversity of acts and not a diversity of powers. But diverse acts can belong to the same power.

**Reply to objection 2:** Similarly, the opposition between sensuality and synderesis is made by reference to an opposition of acts and not an opposition of diverse species within a single genus.

**Reply to objection 3:** Unchangeable natures of the sort in question are the first principles of actions, concerning which one cannot be in error. And they are attributed to reason as a power and to synderesis as a habit. Hence, we make natural judgments by means of both, viz., reason and synderesis.


### Article 13

### Is conscience a power?

It seems that conscience (*conscientia*) is a power:

**Objection 1:** Origen says that conscience is "the spirit corrector" and "companion teacher of the soul, by which the soul is separated from what is bad and adheres to what is good." But 'spirit' names a power in the soul, either the mind—this according to Ephesians 4:23 ("Be renewed in the spirit of your mind")—or the imagination; hence, it is also called an imaginative spiritual vision, as is clear from Augustine in *Super Genesim ad Litteram* 12. Therefore, conscience is a power.

**Objection 2:** Nothing is subject to sin except a power of the soul. But conscience is subject to sin; for Titus 1:15 says, "Their mind and conscience are defiled." Therefore, it seems that conscience is a power.

**Objection 3:** Conscience must be either an act or a habit or a power. But it is not an act, since in that case it would not always remain in a man. Nor is it a habit, since in that case there would be many such habits and not just one; for in our acting we are directed by many cognitive habits. Therefore, conscience is a power.

**But contrary to this:** Conscience can be laid aside (*deponi potest*), but a power cannot be laid aside. Therefore, conscience is not a power.

**I respond:** Properly speaking, conscience is an act and not a power. This is clear both from the name 'conscience' and also from what is attributed to conscience by common linguistic usage.

For according to the strict meaning of the word, conscience implies an ordering of knowledge toward something, since 'conscience' means 'knowledge with another' (*cum alio scientia*). But the application of knowledge to something is accomplished through an act. Hence, from the meaning of the name it is clear that conscience is an act.

The same thing is evident from what is attributed to conscience. For conscience is said to testify, to bind (*ligare*), or to goad (*instigare*), and also to accuse (*accusare*) or rebuke (*remordere*), or to restrain (*reprehendere*). And all of these follow upon the application of our cognition or knowledge to the things we do. This application is accomplished in three ways. First, insofar as we recognize that we have done or not done something—this according to Ecclesiastes 7:23 ("Your conscience knows that you have often spoken ill of others"), and it is in this sense that conscience is said to *testify*. Second, our knowledge is applied when through our conscience we judge that something should be done or should not be done, and it is in this sense that conscience is said to *goad* or *bind*. Third, our knowledge is applied when through our conscience we judge that something that has been done was good to do or was not good to do (*quod est factum sit bene factum vel non bene factum*), and it is in this sense that conscience is said to *excuse* (*excusare*) or to *accuse* (or *rebuke*).

Now it is clear that all these things follow upon the actual application of knowledge to what we do. Hence, properly speaking, 'conscience' names an act. However, since habits are the principles of acts, sometimes the name 'conscience' is attributed to the first natural habit, viz., synderesis, in the way that in the Gloss on Ezechiel 1:6 Jerome calls synderesis 'conscience', and in the way that Basil calls natural judgment 'conscience', and in the way that Damascene says that conscience is the law of our intellect. For it is common for causes and effects to be named by one another.

**Reply to objection 1:** Conscience is 'spirit' in the sense that 'spirit' is standing in for 'mind', since conscience is a sort of dictate of the mind.

**Reply to objection 2:** Defilement (*inquinatio*) is said to exist in a conscience not in the sense that conscience is the subject of the defilement, but in the sense that what is known exists in the cognition of it, i.e., insofar as someone knows himself to be defiled.

**Reply to objection 3:** Even if the act does not always remain in its own right, it nonetheless remains at all times in its cause, which is the power and the habit. And even if there are many habits by which a conscience is informed, all of them nonetheless have their efficacy from a single first habit, viz., from the habit with respect to the first principles, which is called 'synderesis'. This is why, as was noted above, this habit especially is sometimes called conscience.

# QUESTION 80

## The Appetitive Powers in General

Next we have to consider the appetitive powers. And on this topic there are four things to be considered: first, the appetitive powers in general (question 80); second, the sentient appetite (*sensualitas*) (question 81); third, the will (question 82); and, fourth, free choice (question 83).

On the first topic there are two questions: (1) Should appetite be posited as a special power of the soul? (2) Is the division of appetite into the sentient appetite and the intellective appetite a division into diverse powers?

### Article 1

#### Is appetite a special power of the soul?

It seems that appetite (*appetitus*) is not a special power of the soul:

**Objection 1:** No power should be assigned to the soul with respect to what is common to living and non-living things. But to desire (*appetere*) is common to living and non-living things, since, as *Ethics* 1 says, the good is "what all things desire." Therefore, appetite is not a special power of the soul.

**Objection 2:** Powers are distinguished by their objects. But it is the very same thing that we have cognition of and that we desire. Therefore, it is unnecessary for there to be a distinct appetitive power in addition to the apprehensive power.

**Objection 3:** What is common is not divided off from what is proper. But every power of the soul desires some particular desirable thing, viz., the object that is fitting for it. Therefore, there is no need to countenance a power which is distinct from the others and which is called the appetitive power with respect to the object *desirable in general* (*appetibile in communi*).

**But contrary to this:** In *De Anima* 2 the Philosopher distinguishes the appetitive from the other powers. Likewise, in *De Fide Orthodoxa* 2 Damascene distinguishes the appetitive powers from the cognitive powers.

**I respond:** It is necessary to posit an appetitive power in the soul. To see this clearly, note that every form has some inclination following upon it, in the way that fire is by its form inclined toward the highest place and toward generating what is similar to itself.

However, in those things that participate in cognition the form exists in a higher mode than in things that lack cognition.

For among those things that lack cognition, the form determines each thing only to its own singular *esse*, which is likewise its *natural esse*. Therefore, a natural inclination, which is called *natural appetite*, follows upon this sort of natural form.

By contrast, among things that have cognition, each is determined to its own proper natural *esse* through a natural form, yet in such a way that it is receptive to the species of other things, in the way that the sensory power receives the species of all sensible things and the intellect receives the species of all intelligible things. The result is that man's soul is in a certain sense all things through its sensory power and intellect, and in this respect things that have cognition come close in a certain sense to a likeness of God, "in whom all things preexist," as Dionysius says. Therefore, just as forms exist in a higher mode in things that have cognition, beyond the mode of natural forms, so there must exist in them an inclination beyond the natural inclination called 'natural appetite'. And this higher inclination involves the appetitive power of the soul, through which an animal is able to desire what it apprehends and not merely to desire what it is inclined toward by its natural form.

So, then, it is necessary to posit an appetitive power of the soul.

**Reply to objection 1:** As has been explained, in things that have cognition, desire (*appetere*) is found in a mode higher than the common mode in which it is found in all things in general. And so there must be a power of the soul that is prescribed for this (*oportet ad hoc determinari aliquam potentiam animae*).

**Reply to objection 2:** What is apprehended and desired is the same in subject but conceptually diverse. For a thing is apprehended as a sensible or intelligible being, but it is desired as something fitting or good. Now what is required for a diversification of powers is a *conceptual* diversity in the objects of those powers, and not a *material* diversity.

**Reply to objection 3:** Each power of the soul is a sort of form or nature, and it has a natural inclination toward something. Hence, it is by a *natural appetite* that each power of the soul desires an object fitting for itself. Beyond this, there is *animal appetite*, which follows upon apprehension and by which something is desired not because it is fitting for the act of this or that power, in the way that the visual power (*visio*) is for seeing and the power of hearing (*auditio*) is for hearing, but because it is fitting for the animal absolutely speaking.

## Article 2

### Are the sentient appetite and the intellective appetite diverse powers?

It seems that the sentient appetite and the intellective appetite are not diverse powers:

**Objection 1:** As was explained above (q. 77, a. 3), powers are not diversified by incidental differences. But the difference between being apprehended by the sensory power and being apprehended by the intellect is incidental to a desirable object. Therefore, the sentient appetite and the intellective appetite are not diverse powers.

**Objection 2:** Intellective cognition is of universals, and this is what distinguishes it from sentient cognition, which is of singulars. But there is no room for this distinction in the case of appetite; for since appetite is a movement from the soul toward the things—i.e., toward singulars—every desire seems to be a desire for a singular thing. Therefore, it is not the case that the intellective appetite should be distinguished from sentient appetite.

**Objection 3:** Just as the appetitive power falls as a lower power under the apprehensive power, so it is with the power to effect movement. But the power to effect movement that follows upon man's intellective understanding is not distinct from the power to effect movement that follows upon sensory cognition in the other animals. Therefore, by parity of reasoning, neither is the appetitive power in man distinct from the appetitive power in the other animals.

**But contrary to this:** In *De Anima* 3 the Philosopher distinguishes two appetites, and he says that the higher appetite moves the lower appetite.

**I respond:** It is necessary to claim that the intellective appetite is a power distinct from the sentient appetite. For an appetitive power is a passive power that is naturally moved by what is apprehended; hence, as is explained in *De Anima* 3 and *Metaphysics* 12, the desirable apprehended thing is an unmoved mover, whereas the appetite is a moved mover. But things that are passive and movable are distinguished in a way that corresponds to the distinction among active movers, since what effects movement must be proportioned to what is moved, and what is active must be proportioned to what is passive. And the passive power itself has its proper nature from being ordered toward its active counterpart (*ipsa potentia passiva propriam rationem habet ex ordine ad suum activum*). Therefore, since what is apprehended by the intellect is different in genus from what is apprehended by the sensory power, it follows that the intellective appetite is a power distinct from the sentient appetite.

**Reply to objection 1:** The difference between being apprehended by the sensory power and apprehended by the intellect is not incidental to what is desirable. Rather, this feature belongs to it *per se*, since what is desirable moves the appetite only insofar as it is apprehended. Hence, differences in what is apprehended are *per se* differences in what is desired. And so the appetitive powers are distinguished by the differences in the apprehended things as by their proper objects.

**Reply to objection 2:** Even if the intellective appetite is led toward things which are singulars outside the soul, it is nonetheless led toward them under some universal notion (*secundum aliquam rationem universalem*)—as when it desires something because it is good. Hence, in the *Rhetoric* the Philosopher says that there can be hatred with respect to a universal, as when "we hate every type of thief." Similarly, through the intellective appetite we can desire immaterial goods that the sensory power does not apprehend—e.g., knowledge, virtue, and other things of this sort.

**Reply to objection 3:** As is explained in *De Anima* 3, a general opinion (*opinio universalis*) does not effect movement except by the mediation of a particular case (*mediante particulari*). Similarly, a higher appetite effects movement by the mediation of a lower appetite. This is why the power to effect movement that follows upon the intellect is not distinct from the power to effect movement that follows upon the sensory power.

# QUESTION 81

## The Sentient Appetite

Next we have to consider sensuality or the sentient appetite (*sensualitas*). And on this topic there are three questions: (1) Is sensuality a purely appetitive power? (2) Is it divided into the irascible and the concupiscible as into diverse powers? (3) Do the irascible and concupiscible powers obey reason?

## Article 1

## Is sensuality a purely appetitive power?

It seems that sensuality (*sensualitas*) is not a purely appetitive power, but a cognitive power as well:

**Objection 1:** In *De Trinitate* 12 Augustine says, "The soul's sensual movement, which is concentrated in the bodily senses, is common to us and the beasts." But the bodily senses fall under the cognitive powers. Therefore, sensuality is a cognitive power.

**Objection 2:** Whatever falls under the same division seems to belong to the same genus. But in *De Trinitate* 12 Augustine divides sensuality off against higher reason and lower reason, both of which involve cognition. Therefore, sensuality is likewise a cognitive power.

**Objection 3:** In a man's temptations sensuality takes the place of the serpent. But in the temptation of the first parents the serpent's role was to introduce and propose the sin, and this role belongs to a cognitive power. Therefore, sensuality is a cognitive power.

**But contrary to this:** Sensuality is defined as "a desire for things that have to do with the body."

**I respond:** The name 'sensuality' (*sensualitas*) seems to be taken from 'sensual movement' (*sensualis motus*)—which is what Augustine is talking about in *De Trinitate* 12—in the way that the name of a power is taken from its act, e.g., the visual power (*visus*) from the act of seeing (*visio*).

Now sensual movement is a desire (*appetitus*) that follows upon sentient apprehension. For an act of the apprehensive power is not called a movement in as proper a sense as the action of the appetitive power is, since the apprehensive power's operation finds its perfection in the fact that the things apprehended exist in the one apprehending them, whereas the appetitive power's operation finds its perfection in the fact that the one who has the desire is inclined toward the desirable thing. And so the apprehensive power's operation is more like rest, whereas the operation of an appetitive power is more like a movement. Hence, 'sensual movement' means the operation of an appetitive power. And so 'sensuality' is a name of the sentient appetite.

**Reply to objection 1:** Augustine's claim that the soul's sensual movement is concentrated in the bodily senses means not that the senses are included under sensuality, but rather that the movement of sensuality is a certain inclination toward the bodily senses, viz., when we desire the things that are apprehended by the bodily senses. And in this way the bodily senses are, as it were, entries (*praeambulae*) into sensuality.

**Reply to objection 2:** Sensuality is divided off from higher reason and lower reason insofar as they all share in the act of motion. For the cognitive power, which is what higher and lower reason belong to, is a power that effects movement, just like the appetitive power, which sensuality belongs to.

**Reply to objection 3:** The serpent not only displayed and proposed the sin, but also incited them to commit the sin (*inclinavit in effectum peccati*). And it is in this last respect that sensuality is signified by the serpent.

## Article 2

### Is the sentient appetite divided into the irascible and the concupiscible as into diverse powers?

It seems that the sentient appetite is not divided into the irascible (*irascibilis*) and the concupiscible (*concupiscibilis*) as into diverse powers:

**Objection 1:** As *De Anima* 2 explains, the same power of the soul is related to a pair of contraries, in the way that the power of seeing is related to both white and black. But the agreeable (*conveniens*) and the harmful (*nocivum*) are contraries. Therefore, since the concupiscible has to do with the agreeable and the irascible with the harmful, it seems to be the same power of the soul that is both irascible and concupiscible.

**Objection 2:** The sentient appetite is directed only at things that are agreeable to the senses. But what is agreeable to the senses is the object of the concupiscible power. Therefore, there is no sentient appetitive power that differs from the concupiscible power.

**Objection 3:** Hatred (*odium*) resides in the irascible power; for in *Super Matthaeum* Jerome says, "Let us have in the irascible power a hatred for vices." But since hatred is the contrary of love (*amor*), it is in the concupiscible power. Therefore, the same power is both concupiscible and irascible.

**But contrary to this:** Gregory of Nyssa and Damascene posit two powers, the irascible and the concupiscible, as parts of the sentient appetite.

**I respond:** The sentient appetite is generically one faculty (*una vis*), which is called sensuality, but it is divided into two powers, which are the species of the sentient appetite, viz., the irascible and the concupiscible. To see this clearly, consider that in a natural corruptible thing there has to be not only (a) an inclination toward pursuing what is agreeable and avoiding what is harmful, but also (b) an inclination toward resisting the corrupting or contrary things that pose an obstacle to what is agreeable and that inflict what is harmful—in just the way that fire has a natural inclination not only (a) to recede from a lower place that is not agreeable to it and to tend toward a higher place that is agreeable to it, but also (b) to resist what corrupts it or impedes it.

Therefore, since the sentient appetite is an inclination that follows upon sentient apprehension in the way that a natural appetite is an inclination that follows upon a natural form, it must be the case that in the sentient part of the soul there are two appetitive powers: (a) one through which the soul is simply inclined to pursue those things that are agreeable according to the senses and to avoid those things that are harmful, and this is called the *concupiscible* power; and (b) a second through which the animal resists aggressors that pose obstacles to what is agreeable and that inflict harm, and this is called the *irascible* power. Hence, the object of the irascible power is said to be what is difficult (*arduum*), because the irascible power tends toward overcoming contraries and winning out over them.

Moreover, these two inclinations are not reducible to a single principle. For sometimes the soul, in opposition to the inclination of the concupiscible power, inflicts hardships upon itself in order to fight off contraries in accord with the inclination of the irascible power. The passions of the irascible power even seem to fight against the passions of the concupiscible power, since, in most cases, aroused concupiscence diminishes anger, and aroused anger diminishes concupiscence.

This point is also clear from the fact that the irascible power is, as it were, a promoter and defender of the concupiscible power when it rises up against obstacles to those agreeable things sought by the concupiscible power, and when it fights against the harmful things that the concupiscible power shrinks from. And for this reason all the passions of the irascible power take their origin from passions of the concupiscible power and terminate in the latter. For instance, anger arises from an inflicted pain and, having gained vengeance, terminates in joy. It is also for this reason that, as is explained in *De Animalibus* 8, struggles among animals are over concupiscible objects like food and sexual pleasure.

**Reply to objection 1:** The concupiscible power is directed toward both the agreeable and the disagreeable. By contrast, the irascible power is directed toward resisting the disagreeable that stands in opposition to it.

**Reply to objection 2:** Just as, in keeping with what was pointed out above (q. 78, a. 2), among the apprehensive powers of the sentient part of the soul there is an estimative power that perceives things that are not presently affecting the sensory powers, so also in the sentient appetite there is a power that does not seek what is appropriate for delighting the senses, but instead seeks something that is appropriate insofar as it is useful to the animal for its own defense. And this is the irascible power.

**Reply to objection 3:** Hatred absolutely speaking belongs to the concupiscible power. However, because of the pugnacity caused by hatred, it can also be relevant to the irascible power.

## Article 3

### Do the irascible and concupiscible powers obey reason?

It seems that the irascible and concupiscible powers do not obey reason:

**Objection 1:** The irascible and concupiscible powers are parts of sensuality. But sensuality does not obey reason; this is why it is signified by the serpent, as Augustine points out in *De Trinitate* 12. Therefore, the irascible and concupiscible powers do not obey reason.

**Objection 2:** Whatever obeys a given thing does not fight against it. But the irascible and concupiscible powers fight against reason—this according to the Apostle in Romans 7:23 ("But I see another law in my members, fighting against the law of my mind"). Therefore, the irascible and concupiscible powers do not obey reason.

**Objection 3:** Just as the appetitive power is lower than the rational part of the soul, so too is the sentient [apprehensive] power. But the sentient [apprehensive] part of the soul does not obey reason, since we do not hear or see when we want to. Therefore, it is likewise not the case that the powers of the sentient appetite, viz., the irascible and the concupiscible, obey reason.

**But contrary to this:** Damascene says that what is "obedient to" reason and susceptible to persuasion "by reason is divided into concupiscence (*concupiscentia*) and anger (*ira*)."

**I respond:** There are two ways in which the irascible and concupiscible powers obey the higher part of the soul, where one finds the intellect (or reason) and will. The first of these ways has to do with reason, and the second has to do with the will.

The irascible and concupiscible powers obey *reason* with respect to their *acts*. The explanation for this is that in the other animals the sentient appetite is apt to be moved by the estimative power, in the way that a sheep, taking the wolf to be an enemy, fears it. But as was explained above (q. 78, a. 4), in man the estimative power is replaced by the cogitative power, which some call 'particular reason' because it brings together intentions of individuals (*collativa intentionum individualium*). This is why the sentient appetite is apt to be moved by the cogitative power in a man. Now particular reason is itself apt to be moved and directed by 'universal reason', and so there are syllogisms in which singular conclusions are derived from universal propositions. Thus, it is clear that universal reason gives commands to (*imperat*) the sentient appetite, which is divided into the concupiscible and irascible, and that this appetite obeys it. And since deriving singular conclusions from universal principles is the work of discursive reason and not of simple intellective understanding (*non est opus simplicis intellectus sed rationis*), the irascible and concupiscible powers are said to obey reason rather than the intellect. Moreover, anyone can experience within himself that when he applies universal considerations, anger and fear and other such [passions] are mitigated or, as the case may be, instigated.

Likewise, the sentient appetite is subject to the *will* as regards *execution*, which is brought about by the power that effects movement. For in the other animals movement follows immediately upon an appetitive act (*appetitum*) of the concupiscible and irascible powers; for instance, when the sheep becomes fearful of the wolf, it immediately flees, since in sheep there is no higher appetitive act that might resist this movement. By contrast, a man is not immediately moved by an appetitive act of the concupiscible or irascible powers; rather, he awaits the command of the will (*expectatur imperium voluntatis*), which is a higher appetite. For in the case of all

ordered powers that effect movement, a mover effects movement only by
the power of the first mover; thus, the lower appetite is not sufficient to
effect movement unless the higher appetite consents—which is what the
Philosopher is saying in *De Anima* 3: "The higher appetite moves the lower
appetite in the way that a higher sphere moves a lower sphere."

Therefore, these are the ways in which the irascible and concupiscible
powers are subject to reason.

**Reply to objection 1:** Sensuality is signified by the serpent as regards
what is proper to the sentient part of the soul, whereas 'irascible' and 'concupiscible' name the sentient appetite as regards its act, to which the irascible and concupiscible powers are induced by reason, as has been
explained.

**Reply to objection 2:** As the Philosopher says in *Politics* 1, "One
finds in the animal both despotic rule (*despoticus principatus*) and constitutional rule (*politicus principatus*). For the soul rules the body with a
despotic rule, whereas the intellect rules the appetite with a constitutional
and royal rule." Despotic rule is that by which someone rules slaves, who
do not have the ability to resist the ruler in any of his commands, since they
have nothing of their own (*quia nihil sui habent*). By contrast, political and
royal rule is that by which someone rules free men, who, even if they are
subject to the rule of the leader, nonetheless have something of their own
(*habent aliquid proprium*) by which they are able to resist the leader's command.

So, then, the soul is said to rule the body with despotic rule because
the bodily members cannot in any way resist the soul's rule, but instead at
the soul's desire the hand and foot move immediately, along with any mem-
ber of the body that is apt to be moved by a voluntary movement. By contrast, the intellect, i.e., reason, is said to rule the irascible and concupiscible powers with constitutional rule, since the sentient appetite has something of its own by which it is able to resist reason's command. For the sentient appetite is apt to be moved not only by the estimative power in other
animals and the cognitive power (which is ruled by universal reason) in
man, but also by the power of imagining and the sensory power. Hence, we
experience the irascible and concupiscible powers resisting reason when
we sense or imagine something pleasant that reason forbids, or something
unpleasant that reason prescribes. And so the fact that the irascible and
concupiscible powers fight against reason in some cases does not rule out
their being obedient to reason.

**Reply to objection 3:** The exterior sensory powers need for their acts exterior sensible things by which they are affected and whose presence is not within reason's power. By contrast, the interior powers, both appetitive and apprehensive, do not need exterior things. And so they are subject to the command of reason, which is able not only to instigate or mitigate the affections of the appetitive power, but also to form the phantasms that belong to the power of imagining.

# QUESTION 82

## The Will

Next we have to consider the will. And on this topic there are five questions: (1) Does the will desire anything by necessity? (2) Does the will desire everything by necessity? (3) Is the will a more eminent power than the intellect? (4) Does the will move the intellect? (5) Is the will divided into the irascible and the concupiscible?

## Article 1

### Is there anything the will desires by necessity?

It seems that the will desires nothing by necessity (*nihil ex necessitate appetat*):

**Objection 1:** In *De Civitate Dei* 5 Augustine says that if something is necessary, then it is not voluntary. But everything that the will desires is voluntary. Therefore, nothing that the will desires (*appetit*) is desired necessarily (*est necessario desideratum*).

**Objection 2:** According to the Philosopher, rational powers are directed toward opposites. But the will is a rational power, since, as *De Anima* 3 says, the will exists in reason. Therefore, the will is directed toward opposites. Therefore, it is not determined to anything by necessity (*ad nihil de necessitate determinatur*).

**Objection 3:** Because of the will we are masters of our own acts (*domini nostrorum actuum*). But we are not masters of what exists by necessity (*ex necessitate*). Therefore, no act of the will can exist by necessity (*de necessitate*).

**But contrary to this:** In *De Trinitate* 13 Augustine says, "Everyone desires beatitude with one accord (*una voluntate*)." But if this fact were contingent and not necessary, then in at least a few cases it would not be true. Therefore, there is something the will wills by necessity (*voluntas ex necessitate aliquid vult*).

**I respond:** There are many senses of 'necessity' (*necessitas*). Now the necessary is what is *not able not to be.*

One way in which this feature belongs to something is in virtue of an *intrinsic principle*—either a *material* intrinsic principle, as when we say that it is necessary for everything composed of contraries to be corrupted, or a *formal* intrinsic principle, as when we say that it is necessary for a triangle to have three angles equal to two right angles. This is *natural and absolute necessity* (*necessitas naturalis et absoluta*).

In a second way, some things are *not able not to be* in virtue of some *extrinsic principle*—either an *end* or an *agent*. In virtue of an *end*, as when without this thing one cannot attain a given end at all, or one cannot attain it in a satisfying way (*bene*); it is in this sense that food is said to be necessary for life, or that a horse is said to be necessary for a journey. This is called the *necessity of the end* (*necessitas finis*), and it is also sometimes called utility (*utilitas*). On the other hand, some things are not able not to be because of an *agent*, as when someone is coerced by some agent in such a way that he cannot do the contrary. And this is called the *necessity of coercion* (*necessitas coactionis*).

The necessity of coercion is altogether at odds with the will (*omnino repugnat voluntati*). For what is contrary to a thing's inclination we call 'violent'. But the movement of the will is itself an inclination toward something. And so just as something is called 'natural' because it accords with a natural inclination (*inclinatio naturae*), so something is called 'voluntary' because it accords with the will's inclination. Therefore, just as it is impossible for something to be simultaneously both violent and natural, so it is impossible for something to be, absolutely speaking, both coerced (or violent) and voluntary.

However, the necessity of the end is not at odds with the will when the end can be arrived at in just one way; for instance, given that one wills to cross the sea, a necessity arises in the will for willing a ship.

Similarly, a *natural necessity* is not at odds with the will, either. At the very least, it is necessary that just as the intellect adheres by necessity to its first principles, so too the will adheres by necessity to its final end, which is beatitude. For as *Physics* 2 says, the end plays the role in matters of action (*in operativis*) that a [first] principle plays in speculative matters (*in speculativis*). For what belongs to something naturally and immutably must be the foundation and source (*fundamentum et principium*) of everything else, since in each thing what is primary is its nature, and all movement proceeds from something immovable.

**Reply to objection 1:** Augustine should be understood to be talking about the necessity of coercion. By contrast, natural necessity "does not destroy the will's freedom," as Augustine himself says in the same book.

**Reply to objection 2:** Insofar as the will wills something naturally, it is more like the intellective understanding of natural principles than it is like reason, which is directed toward opposites. Hence, in this sort of case the will is more an *intellectual* power than a *rational* power.

**Reply to objection 3:** We are masters of our own actions insofar as we are able to choose *this* or *that*. But as *Ethics* 3 says, choice (*electio*) is about the means to an end and not about the end. Hence, the desire for the ultimate end is not among those acts of which we are the masters.

## Article 2

### Does the will will by necessity everything it wills?

It seems that the will wills by necessity everything it wills:

**Objection 1:** In *De Divinis Nominibus* 4 Dionysius says, "Evil lies beyond the will." Therefore, it is by necessity that the will tends toward the good proposed to it

**Objection 2:** The will's object is related to the will as a mover to what is moved. But the movement of what is moved follows necessarily from the mover. Therefore, it seems that the will's object moves it by necessity.

**Objection 3:** Just as what is apprehended by the sensory power is an object of the sentient appetite, so what is apprehended by the intellect is an object of the intellective appetite, which is called the will. But what is apprehended by the sensory power moves the sentient appetite by necessity; for in *Super Genesim ad Litteram* Augustine says that animals are moved by what they see. Therefore, it seems that what is apprehended by the intellect moves the will by necessity.

**But contrary to this:** Augustine says, "The will is that by which one sins and that by which one lives in an upright way"—and so it is directed toward opposites. Therefore, it is not the case that the will wills by necessity everything it wills.

**I respond:** The will does not will by necessity everything it wills. To see this clearly, note that, as has already been explained (a.1), the will adheres to its ultimate end in the same way that the intellect adheres naturally and by necessity to its first principles.

Now some intelligible things do not have a necessary connection to the first principles, e.g., contingent propositions, the denial of which does not imply the denial of the first principles. Propositions like these are such that the intellect does not assent to them by necessity.

On the other hand, there are some propositions which are necessary and which have a necessary connection with the first principles, e.g., demonstrable conclusions, the denial of which implies the denial of the first principles. These propositions are such that the intellect assents to them by necessity once it recognizes the necessary connection of the conclusions to the principles by way of a demonstrative deduction; however, it does not assent to them by necessity before it recognizes the necessity of the connection by way of the demonstration.

Something similar holds for the will as well.

For there are some particular goods which do not have a necessary connection to beatitude and in the absence of which someone can have beatitude (*potest esse beatus*). The will does not adhere to goods of this sort by necessity.

On the other hand, there are some particular goods which have a necessary connection to beatitude and by which a man adheres to God, in whom alone true beatitude consists. However, before the necessity of this sort of connection is demonstrated by the certitude of the vision of God, the will does not adhere to God by necessity, or to the things that are of God. On the other hand, the will of one who sees God through His essence adheres to God necessarily, in the same way that we now will by necessity to have beatitude.

Thus, it is clear that the will does not will by necessity everything it wills.

**Reply to objection 1:** The will tends toward nothing except under the notion of the good (*sub ratione boni*). But because the good is complex (*quia bonum est multiplex*), the will is not determined by necessity to one alternative (*non ex necessitate determinatur ad unum*).

**Reply to objection 2:** A mover causes movement by necessity in the movable thing when the power of the mover exceeds the movable thing in such a way that the totality of the movable thing's possibilities is subject to the mover (*ita quod tota eius possibilitas moventi subdatur*). But since the will's possibilities encompass a universal and perfect good (*possibilitas voluntatis sit respectu boni universalis et perfecti*), it is not the case that the totality of its possibilities is subject to any particular good. And so no particular good moves it by necessity.

**Reply to objection 3:** The sentient power is not a power that brings together diverse things in the way that reason does; instead, it simply apprehends some one thing. And this is why one thing determinately moves the sentient appetite. By contrast, reason brings together many things, and for this reason the intellective appetite, i.e., the will, is able to be moved by many things and is not moved by any one of them with necessity.

## Article 3

### Is the will a higher power than the intellect?

It seems that the will is a higher power than the intellect:

**Objection 1:** The good or the end is the object of the will. But the end is the first and highest of all causes. Therefore, the will is the first and highest of all powers.

**Objection 2:** Natural entities proceed from the imperfect to the perfect. And this is also apparent among the powers of the soul; for they proceed from the sensory power to the intellect, which is the more noble. But there is a natural progression from an act of the intellect to an act of the will. Therefore, the will is a more perfect and more noble power than the intellect.

**Objection 3:** Habits are proportioned to their powers in the way that perfections are proportioned to the things they perfect. But the habit by which the will is perfected, viz., charity, is more noble than the habits by which the intellect is perfected; for 1 Corinthians 13:2 says, "If I should know all mysteries . . . and if I should have all faith . . . and have not charity, I am nothing." Therefore, the will is a higher power than the intellect.

**But contrary to this:** In *Ethics* 10 the Philosopher claims that the highest power of the soul is the intellect.

**I respond:** There are two ways to think about the eminence of two things with respect to one another: (a) absolutely speaking (*simpliciter*) and (b) relatively speaking (*secundum quid*). Something is thought of as such-and-such absolutely speaking insofar as it is such-and-such in its own right (*secundum seipsum tale*), whereas it is thought of as such-and-such relatively speaking insofar as it such-and-such in relation to something else (*secundum respectum ad alterum*).

Thus, if the intellect and the will are considered *in their own right*, then the intellect is the more eminent. This is apparent from a comparison of their objects to one another. For the intellect's object is more simple and more absolute than the will's object, since the notion *desirable good* is itself an object of the intellect (*objectum intellectus est ipsa ratio boni appetibilis*), whereas it is the desirable good, whose notion exists in the intellect, that is the will's object. But the more simple and abstract something is, the higher and more noble it is in its own right. And so the intellect's object is higher than the will's object. Therefore, since the proper nature of a power has to do with the object it is ordered toward, it follows that the intellect is in its own right and absolutely speaking higher and more noble than the will.

On the other hand, *relatively speaking* and in relation to something else, the will is in some cases higher than the intellect, viz., because the will's object exists in a higher entity than the intellect's object does. For instance, I might claim that hearing is, relatively speaking, more noble than seeing, because some entity that makes a sound is more noble than some entity that is colored, even though color is more simple and more noble than sound. For as was explained above (q. 16, a. 1 and q. 27, a. 4), the intellect's action consists in the nature of what is understood existing in the one who understands, whereas the act of the will is perfected in the will's being inclined toward that thing as it exists in itself. And this is why in *Metaphysics* 6 the Philosopher says that the good and the bad, which are objects of the will, exist in the things, whereas the true and the false, which are objects of the intellect, exist in the mind. Therefore, when an entity in which a given good exists is more noble than the soul itself, in which the nature as understood exists, then the will is higher than the intellect in relation to such an entity. But when the entity in which a given good exists is inferior to the soul, then the intellect is higher than the will in relation to such an entity. Hence, the love of God is better than the cognition of God, whereas, conversely, the cognition of corporeal things is better than the love of corporeal things.

Still, absolutely speaking, the intellect is more noble than the will.

**Reply to objection 1:** The notion of a cause is taken from a comparison of the one thing to the other, and in such a comparison the notion of the good is the most important; but 'true' is said, rather, in an absolute sense, and it signifies the notion of the good itself. Hence, even the good is something true.

On the other hand, the true is itself a certain good, because the intellect is an entity, and the true is its end. And among other ends this end is the most excellent, just as the intellect is the most excellent among the powers.

**Reply to objection 2:** What is prior in generation and in time is less perfect, since in one and the same thing potentiality temporally precedes actuality and imperfection temporally precedes perfection.

However, what is prior absolutely speaking and according to the order of nature is more perfect, since this is the sense in which actuality is prior to potentiality. And it is in this sense that the intellect is prior to the will—as a mover is prior to what is moved, and as what is active is prior to what is passive. For it is the good as intellectively understood that moves the will.

**Reply to objection 3:** This argument goes through for the will taken in comparison to what is above the soul. For the virtue of charity is the virtue by which we love God.

## Article 4

### Does the will move the intellect?

It seems that the will does not move the intellect:

**Objection 1:** The mover is more noble than and prior to what is moved, since the mover is an agent and, as Augustine says in *Super Genesim ad Litteram* 12 and the Philosopher in *De Anima* 3, an agent is more noble than its patient. But as was explained above (a. 3), the intellect is prior to and more noble than the will. Therefore, the will does not move the intellect.

**Objection 2:** A mover is not moved by the thing it moves, except perhaps incidentally. But the intellect moves the will, since the desirable thing as apprehended by the intellect is an unmoved mover, whereas the appetite is a moved mover. Therefore, the intellect is not moved by the will.

**Objection 3:** We can will only what is understood intellectively. Therefore, if the will moves the intellect to intellective understanding by willing to have intellective understanding, then another act of intellective understanding will have to precede this act of willing, and another act of willing will have to precede that act of intellective understanding, and so on *ad infinitum*—which is impossible. Therefore, it is not the case that the will moves the intellect.

**But contrary to this:** Damascene says, "It is within our power to learn an art or not to learn it, as we will." But something is within our power through the will, and we learn an art through the intellect. Therefore, the will moves the intellect.

**I respond:** There are two ways in which something is said to effect movement.

The first way is in the manner of an *end*, in the sense in which an end is said to move an agent. It is in this way that the intellect moves the will, since the will's object is a good as intellectively understood, and it moves the will as an end.

The second way in which something is said to effect movement is in the manner of an *agent*—in the way in which the thing that effects an alteration moves the thing that is altered, and in the way in which the thing that gives an impulse moves the thing that is impelled. This is the way in which the will moves the intellect and all the powers of the soul, as Anselm explains in *De Similitudinibus*.

The reason for this is that in the case of all ordered active powers, the power that is directed toward a universal end moves the powers that are directed toward particular ends. This is apparent both in natural matters and political matters. For the heavens, which act for the sake of conserving generable and corruptible things in general, move all the lower bodies, each of which acts for the sake of conserving its own species or even the individual. Again, a king, who intends the common good of the whole kingdom, moves by his commands all the heads of the cities (*praepositi civitatum*), who devote themselves to ruling the individual cities.

Now the will's object is the good and the end in general (*bonum et finis in communi*). But each power is directed toward some proper good that is appropriate for it, in the way that the power of sight is directed toward the perception of color, and in the way that the intellect is directed toward the cognition of what is true. And so the will moves all the powers of the soul to their acts in the manner of an agent—except for the natural powers of the vegetative part of the soul, which are not subject to our choice.

**Reply to objection 1:** The intellect can be thought of in two ways: first, insofar as it apprehends being and truth in general (*est apprehensivus entis et veri universalis*), and, second, insofar as it is a certain entity and particular power that has a determinate act.

Similarly, the will can be thought of in two ways: first, according to the universality of its object, i.e., insofar as it desires the good in general (*appetitiva boni communis*), and, second, insofar as it is a certain determinate power of the soul having a determinate act.

Thus, if the intellect and will are compared with respect to the nature of the universality of both their objects, it has already been explained above (a. 3) that in this sense the intellect is absolutely speaking higher and more noble than the will.

Moreover, if the intellect is thought of with respect to the universality of its object and the will insofar as it is a certain determinate power, then, once again, the intellect is higher than and prior to the will, since the will itself, along with its act and its object, is contained under the notions *being* and *true*, which the intellect apprehends. Hence, the intellect has intellective understanding of the will and of its act and its object, just as it has intellective understanding of the other specific things it understands, such as a rock or a piece of wood, which are contained under the common notions *being* and *true*.

However, if the will is thought of with respect to the general notion of its object, which is the good, and the intellect is thought of insofar as it is a certain specific entity and power, then the intellect is contained under the common notion *good* as a certain specific good, along with the act of intellective understanding itself and its object, which is the true; each of them is a certain specific good. And in this respect the will is higher than the intellect and able to move it.

From these considerations it is apparent that the reason why these powers include one another by their acts is that the intellect understands that the will wills, and the will wills that the intellect understand. And by a similar line of reasoning, the good is contained under the true insofar as the good is a certain true thing that is understood, and the true is contained under the good insofar as the true is a certain desired good.

**Reply to objection 2:** As has already been explained, the intellect moves the will in a way different from the way in which the will moves the intellect.

**Reply to objection 3:** There is no need to proceed to infinity; instead, one stops with the intellect as the first thing. For an apprehension must precede every movement of the will, but it is not the case that a movement of the will precedes every apprehension. Rather, the source of counsel and understanding is an intellective principle that is higher than our intellect, viz., God. Aristotle likewise makes this claim in *Eudemian Ethics* 7, and in this way he shows that there is no infinite regress.

## Article 5

### Should the irascible and the concupiscible be distinguished in the higher appetite, i.e., the will?

It seems that the irascible and the concupiscible should be distinguished in the higher appetite, i.e., the will:

**Objection 1:** The name of the concupiscible power is taken from desire (*a concupiscendo*) and the name of the irascible power is taken from anger (*ab irascendo*). But there are some instances of desire (*concupiscentia*) that can involve only the intellective appetite, i.e., the will, and cannot involve the sentient appetite, e.g., the desire for wisdom (*concupiscentia sapientiae*) of which Wisdom 6:21 says, "The desire for wisdom leads to the everlasting kingdom." There are likewise instances of anger that can involve only the intellective appetite and cannot involve the sentient appetite, as when we are angry about vices; hence, in *Super Matthaeum* Jerome says, "Let us have in the irascible power a hatred for vices." Therefore, the irascible and the concupiscible should be distinguished in the intellective appetite, just as in the sentient appetite.

**Objection 2:** According to what is commonly said, charity exists in the concupiscible power, whereas hope exists in the irascible power. But charity and hope cannot exist in the sentient appetite, since they are intelligible objects and not sensible objects. Therefore, the concupiscible and the irascible should be posited in the intellective part of the soul.

**Objection 3:** *De Spiritu et Anima* says, "The soul has these powers [viz., the irascible, the concupiscible, and the rational] before it is mixed with the body." But no power of the sentient part belongs just to the soul; instead, as was explained above (q. 77, a. 5), it belongs to the conjoined being. Therefore, the irascible and the concupiscible exist in the will, i.e., in the intellective appetite.

**But contrary to this:** Gregory of Nyssa says that the non-rational part of the soul is divided into the desirous power and the irascible power (*dividitur in desiderativum et irascitivum*); and Damascene says the same thing in *De Fide Orthodoxa* 2. Moreover, in *De Anima* 3 the Philosopher says that "the will exists in reason, whereas concupiscence and anger, or desire and vehemence (*animus*), exist in the non-rational part of the soul."

**I respond:** The irascible and the concupiscible are not parts of the intellective appetite, which is called the will. For, as was explained above (q. 59, a. 4 and q. 79, a. 7), a power that is ordered toward an object under a common notion is not diversified by special differences contained under that common notion. For instance, since the power of sight is directed to the visible under the notion *colored*, visual powers are not multiplied according to the diverse species of color. However, if there were a power that was directed toward what is white insofar as it is white and not insofar as it is colored, then it would be diverse from a power directed toward what is black insofar as it is black.

Now the sentient appetite is not directed toward the common notion *good*, since the sensory powers do not apprehend the universal. And so the parts of the sentient appetite are diversified in a way that corresponds to the diverse notions of particular goods. For the concupiscible is directed at the proper notion of the good insofar as it is pleasant to the senses and agreeable to the nature, whereas the irascible is directed toward the notion of the good insofar as it repels and attacks that which inflicts harm.

The will, however, is directed toward the good under the common notion *good*. And so it is not the case that appetitive powers are diversified within it, i.e., within the intellective appetite, in such a way that within the intellective appetite there would be a distinct irascible power and a distinct concupiscible power—just as it is not the case that apprehensive powers are multiplied in the intellect, even though they are multiplied among the sensory powers.

**Reply to objection 1:** Love (*amor*), concupiscence (*concupiscentia*), and other things of this sort are taken in two ways.

For sometimes they are taken insofar as they are certain passions, bringing with them a certain arousal of feeling (*cum concitatione animi*). This is the way they are commonly taken, and when they are taken in this way, they exist only in the sentient appetite.

In the second way, they signify a simple affection, without passion or an arousal of feeling. Taken in this way, they are acts of the will, and in this sense they are likewise attributed to the angels and to God. But insofar as they are taken in this way, they involve only a single power, which is called the will, and not diverse powers.

**Reply to objection 2:** The will can be called irascible insofar as it wills to fight off evil not from the force of passion, but by the judgment of reason. And, in the same way, it can be called concupiscible because of its desire for the good. And this is the sense in which charity and hope exist in a concupiscible power and an irascible power, i.e., they are in the will insofar as it is ordered toward acts of this sort.

This is likewise the way one can interpret what *De Spiritu et Anima* says, viz., that the irascible and the concupiscible belong to the soul before it is united to the body (insofar as one understands this to be a natural ordering and not a temporal ordering)—even though it is unnecessary to pay heed to what this particular book says.

**Reply to objection 3:** From this the answer to the third objection is obvious.

# QUESTION 83

## Free Choice

Next we ask about free choice (*liberum arbitrium*). And on this topic there are four questions: (1) Does man have free choice? (2) What is free choice: a power, an act, or a habit? (3) If it is a power, is it an appetitive power or a cognitive power? (4) If it is an appetitive power, is it the same power as the will, or a distinct power?

## Article 1

### Does man have free choice?

It seems that man does not have free choice (*liberum arbitrium*):

**Objection 1:** Anyone who has free choice does what he wants to. But a man does not do what he wants to; for Romans 7:15 says, "For the good which I will, I do not; but the evil which I will not, that I do." Therefore, man does not have free choice.

**Objection 2:** Anyone who has free choice is such that it is up to him to will or not to will, to act or not to act. But this is not the way it is with man; for Romans 9:16 says, "It is not up to him that wills"—i.e., it is not up to him to will—"nor up to him that runs . . ."—i.e., it is not up to him to run. Therefore, man does not have free choice.

**Objection 3:** As *Metaphysics* 1 says, "The free is that which is a cause of itself." Therefore, that which is moved by another is not free. But God moves the will; for Proverbs 21:1 says, "The heart of the king is in the hand of the Lord; wherever He will He shall turn it," and Philippians 2:13 says, "it is God who works in us both to will and to accomplish. Therefore, man does not have free choice.

**Objection 4:** Anyone who has free choice is the master of his own acts. But man is not the master of his own acts, since, as Jeremiah 10:23 says, "The way of a man is not his; neither is it in a man . . . to direct his own steps." Therefore, man does not have free choice.

**Objection 5:** In *Ethics* 3 the Philosopher says, "Each man is such that the end appears to him in a way that corresponds to what he is like (*qualis est*)." But what we are like is not within our power; rather, it is ours by nature. Therefore, it is natural to us that we should follow a given end. Therefore, this does not come from free choice.

**But contrary to this:** Ecclesiasticus 15:14 says, "God made man from the beginning, and left him in the hand of his own counsel"—and the Gloss adds, ". . . that is, left him with freedom of choice."

**I respond:** Man has free choice. Otherwise, deliberations, exhortations, precepts, prohibitions, rewards, and punishments would make no sense (*frustra essent*).

To see this clearly, note that some things act without judgment, e.g., a rock moving downward and, similarly, all things that lack cognition.

Other things act with judgment, but not with *free* judgment, viz., brute animals. For instance, a sheep, seeing a wolf, judges by a natural judgment—and not by a free judgment—that it should run away from the wolf, since it makes this judgment by natural instinct (*ex naturali instinctu*) and not by comparing alternatives (*non ex collatione*). And the same holds for every judgment made by brute animals.

Now a man acts by judgment, since through his cognitive power he judges that something should be pursued or avoided. But the reason why he acts by *free* judgment and is able to go in alternative ways (*potens in diversa ferri*) is that in the case of a particular action this judgment arises from a comparison made by reason (*ex collatione quadam rationis*) and not from natural instinct. For with respect to contingent matters, reason has an openness with respect to opposites (*ratio habet viam ad opposita*), as is clear from dialectical syllogisms and rhetorical persuasions. But particular actions (*operabilia*) are contingent matters, and so with respect to them the judgment of reason is related to different alternatives and is not determined to just one (*ad diversa se habet et non est determinatum ad unum*). Accordingly, by the very fact that he is rational, man must have free choice.

**Reply to objection 1:** As was explained above (q. 81, art. 3), even though the sentient appetite obeys reason, it is still able to resist it in some cases by having desires that are contrary to what reason dictates. This, then, is the good that a man does not do when he wants to, viz., not to have a desire contrary to reason—as Augustine's gloss on the same passage explains.

**Reply to objection 2:** This passage from the Apostle should not be interpreted to mean that man does not will by free choice or that he does not run by free choice. Rather, it should be interpreted to mean that free choice is not sufficient for these things unless it is moved and assisted by God.

**Reply to objection 3:** Free choice is a cause of its own movement in the sense that through free choice a man moves himself to act. However, freedom does not require that what is free should be the first cause of itself—just as, in order for something to be a cause of another, it is not required that it be the first cause of that thing. Therefore, God is the first cause and moves both natural causes and voluntary causes. And just as, in the case of natural causes, He does not, by moving them, deprive their acts of being natural, so too He does not, by moving voluntary causes, deprive their actions of being voluntary, but instead He brings this very thing about in them (*sed potius hoc in eis facit*). For within each thing He operates in accord with what is proper to that thing (*secundum eius proprietatem*).

**Reply to objection 4:** Man's way is said not to be within his power with respect to the *execution* of his choices, in which a man can be impeded, whether he wants to be or not. However, the choices themselves (*electiones ipsae*) exist *within us*, assuming God's assistance.

**Reply to objection 5:** There are two senses of 'what a man is like' (*qualitas hominis*): (a) natural and (b) subsequent (*superveniens*).

The *natural* sense of what a man is like can be understood either with respect to *the intellective part of the soul* or with respect to *the body and the powers associated with the body*. Thus, given what man is naturally like because of the intellective part of the soul, a man naturally desires his ultimate end, viz., beatitude. As was explained above (q. 82, art. 1 and 2), this is a natural appetite and is not subject to free choice. On the other hand, as regards the body and the powers associated with the body, a man can be what he is like naturally insofar as he has a certain temperament (*complexio*) or disposition because of the influence of corporeal causes which cannot affect the intellective part of the soul, since that part of the soul is not the actuality of a body (*non est alicuius corporis actus*). So, then, given what each man is like according to his corporeal makeup (*secundum corpoream qualitatem*), the end will strike him in a certain way, since a man is inclined by this sort of disposition to choose something or to reject it. However, inclinations of this sort are subject to the judgment of reason, which, as was explained above (q. 81, a. 3), the lower appetite obeys. Hence, this is not prejudicial to freedom of choice.

Now the *subsequent* qualities (*qualitates supervenientes*) are those such as habits and passions, in accord with which someone is more inclined toward one alternative than toward another. Yet even these inclinations are subject to the judgment of reason, and the qualities themselves are also subject to reason, since it is within our power (a) to acquire such qualities, either by causing them or by disposing ourselves to them (*vel causiter vel dispositive*), or (b) to exclude them from ourselves. And there is nothing here that is incompatible with freedom of choice.

## Article 2

### Is free choice a power?

It seems that free choice is not a power:

**Objection 1:** Free choice (*liberum arbitrium*) is nothing other than free judgment (*liberum iudicium*). But 'judgment' names an act and not a power. Therefore, free choice is not a power.

**Objection 2:** Free choice is said to be "a faculty of will and reason (*facultas voluntatis et rationis*)." But 'faculty' names a facility with respect to a power, and this sort of facility occurs through a habit. Therefore, free choice is a habit. Also, Bernard says that free choice "is a habit of the soul, free for itself." Therefore, it is not a power.

**Objection 3:** No natural power is destroyed by sin (*tollitur per peccatum*). But free choice is destroyed by sin; for Augustine says, "A man who uses free choice badly loses both himself and free choice." Therefore, free choice is not a power.

**But contrary to this:** Nothing except a power, it seems, is the subject of a habit. But free choice is the subject of grace, with the assistance of which it chooses the good. Therefore, free choice is a power.

**I respond:** Even though, according to the proper signification of the term, 'free choice' names a certain act, nevertheless, in the common usage of speakers, what we call free choice is the principle of this act, viz., that by which a man judges freely (*quo homo libere iudicat*).

Now the principles of our acts include both powers and habits; for we are said to have cognition both through [the habit of] knowledge (*per scientiam*) and through the intellective power (*per intellectivam potentiam*). Therefore, free choice has to be either a power or a habit or a power along with a habit.

But there are two ways in which it is clear that free choice is neither a habit nor a power along with a habit.

First, if it were a habit, it would have to be a natural habit, since it is natural to man to have free choice. But there is no natural habit available to us for the things that fall under free choice, since the things with respect to which we have natural habits, e.g., assenting to first principles, are such that we are inclined toward them naturally, and things that we are inclined toward naturally do not fall under free choice—as has already been explained in the case of the desire for beatitude (q. 82, a. 1 and 2). Hence, it is contrary to the proper notion of free choice that it be a natural habit, but for it to be a non-natural habit is contrary to its status as something natural (*contra naturalitatem eius*). And so it follows that free choice is in no way a habit.

Second, as *Ethics* 2 says, a habit is something according to which we are related either in a good way or in a bad way (*bene vel male*) to passions or actions. For instance, through temperance we are related in a good way to sense desires (*bene ad concupiscentias*), whereas through intemperance we are related to them in a bad way; again, through knowledge we are related in a good way to acts of intellective understanding, whereas through the contrary habit we do badly with respect to the cognition of truth. But free choice is related indifferently to both choosing well and choosing badly (*indifferenter se habet ad bene eligendum vel male*). Hence, it is impossible for free choice to be a habit.

Therefore, it follows that free choice is a power.

**Reply to objection 1:** It is customary for a power to be signified by the name of its act. And so the power which is the principle of the act of free judgment is signified by the act. Otherwise, if 'free choice' named an act, then it would not always be present (*non semper maneret*) in a man.

**Reply to objection 2:** 'Faculty' sometimes names a power that stands ready to operate. And this is the sense in which 'faculty' occurs in the definition of free choice.

Now Bernard is taking 'habit' not in the sense in which it is divided off against 'power', but rather insofar as it signifies a relation (*habitudo*) by which someone is in some way related to an act—and this is either through a power or through a habit. For through a power a man is related as one who is able to act, whereas through a habit he is related as one who is ready to act well or as one who is ready to act badly.

**Reply to objection 3:** By sinning, a man is said to have lost free choice not with respect to his natural freedom, i.e., freedom from coercion, but with respect to that freedom which is freedom from sin and misery (*a culpa et a miseria*). This will be treated below in the tract on morals, in the second part of this work (*ST* 1–2, q. 85–89 and q. 109).

### Article 3

### Is free choice an appetitive power?

It seems that free choice is a cognitive power and not an appetitive power:
**Objection 1:** Damascene says, "Free choice immediately accompanies

the rational (*cum rationali confestim comitatur*)." But reason (*ratio*) is a cognitive power. Therefore, free choice is a cognitive power.

**Objection 2:** Free choice is, as it were, free judgment. But judging is an act of a cognitive power (*cognitiva virtus*). Therefore, free choice is a cognitive power.

**Objection 3:** Free choice (*liberum arbitrium*) mainly involves the act of choosing (*electio*). But the act of choosing seems to involve cognition, since choosing implies a sort of comparison of one alternative to another, and this is proper to a cognitive power (*proprium cognitivae virtutis*). Therefore, free choice is a cognitive power (*potentia cognitiva*).

**But contrary to this:** In *Ethics* 3 the Philosopher says that choice (*electio*) is "a desire for those things that are within our power (*desiderium eorum quae sunt in nobis*)." But desire is an act of an appetitive power. Therefore, so is the act of choosing. But free choice (*liberum arbitrium*) exists insofar as we choose. Therefore, free choice is an appetitive power (*virtus appetitiva*).

**I respond:** The act of choosing is what is proper to free choice (*proprium liberi arbitrii est electio*); for we are said to have free choice because we are able to take one thing while rejecting another, and this is what it is to choose. And so it is on the basis of the act of choosing that one must inquire into the nature of free choice.

Now in an act of choosing, something from the cognitive power comes together with something from the appetitive power. On the part of the cognitive power it is required that there be deliberation (*consilium*), through which one judges which of the alternatives is to be preferred, whereas on the part of the appetitive power it is required that the judgment made through deliberation be accepted by desiring it. And so in *Ethics* 6 Aristotle leaves it in doubt whether the act of choosing belongs mainly to the appetitive power or to the intellective power; for he says that choice "is either an appetitive understanding or an intellective desire (*intellectus appetitivus vel appetitus intellectivus*)."

However, in *Ethics* 3 he leans more to the view that it is an intellective desire, when he calls choice a 'deliberative desire' (*desiderium consiliabile*). The reason for this is that the proper object of an act of choosing is the means to an end. But the means to an end has, as such, the character of the sort of good that is called 'useful' (*bonum utile*). And so, since it is the good as such that is the object of the appetite, it follows that an act of choosing is mainly an act of the appetitive power. And so free choice is an appetitive power.

**Reply to objection 1:** Appetitive powers accompany apprehensive powers. And this is why Damascene says, "Free choice immediately accompanies the rational."

**Reply to objection 2:** Judgment is, as it were, the conclusion and determination of deliberation. But deliberation is made determinate, first of all, by the decision of reason (*per sententiam rationis*) and, secondly, by the approval of the appetite (*per acceptationem appetitus*). That is why in *Ethics* 3 the Philosopher says, "When we have judged on the basis of deliberating, we desire in accord with the deliberation." This is the sense in which the act of choosing is itself called a sort of judgment, from which comes the name 'free decision' (*liberum arbitrium*).

**Reply to objection 3:** The comparison that is implied by the name 'choice' pertains to the antecedent deliberation, which belongs to reason. For even though the appetite does not itself carry out a comparison, still, insofar as it is moved by a cognitive power that does carry out comparisons, it has a certain likeness to a comparison when it opts for one alternative over the other (*dum unum alteri praeoptat*).


## Article 4

### Is free choice a power distinct from the will?

It seems that free choice is a power distinct from the will:

**Objection 1:** In *De Fide Orthodoxa* 2 Damascene says that *thelesis* is one thing and *bulesis* another. But *thelesis* is the will (*voluntas*) and *bulesis* seems to be free choice (*liberum arbitrium*), since *bulesis*, according to Damascene, is a willing (*voluntas*) with respect to some aspect of one thing in comparison to another. Therefore, it seems that free choice is a power distinct from the will.

**Objection 2:** Powers are known through their acts. But choosing (*electio*), which is the act of free choice, is distinct from the act of willing (*aliud a voluntate*), as *Ethics* 3 says. For "the act of willing (*voluntas*) has to do with the end, whereas the act of choosing has to do with the means to the end." Therefore, free choice is a power distinct from the will (*liberum arbitrium est alia potentia a voluntate*).

**Objection 3:** The will is an intellective appetite. But the intellect has two powers, viz., the active intellect and the passive intellect (*agens et possibilis*). Therefore, the intellective appetite should likewise have another power besides the will. And there does not seem to be such a power except for free choice. Therefore, free choice is a separate power over and beyond the will (*alia potentia praeter voluntatem*).

**But contrary to this:** In *De Fide Orthodoxa* 3 Damascene says that free choice is nothing other than the will.

**I respond:** As was explained above (q. 80, a. 2), the appetitive powers have to be proportioned to the apprehensive powers. But, within the intellective appetite, the will and free choice, which is nothing other than the power of choosing (*vis electiva*), bear the same relation to one another that, within intellective apprehension, the intellect and reason bear to one another. This is clear from the relations among their objects and acts.

For to understand a thing intellectively (*intelligere*) implies a simple acceptance of it (*importat simplicem acceptionem*) of it, and so, properly speaking, what is said to be understood intellectively are principles that are known in their own right without any comparisons (*sine collatione per seipsa cognoscuntur*). By contrast, to reason discursively (*ratiocinari*) is, properly speaking, to come to the cognition of one thing on the basis of something else, and so, properly speaking, we have discursive reasoning with respect to conclusions that are known from principles (*proprie de conclusionibus ratiocinamur quae ex principiis innotescunt*).

Something similar holds for the appetite. An act of willing (*velle*) implies a simple desire (*importat simplicem appetitum*) for something, and so the will (*voluntas*) is said to be concerned with the end, which is desired for its own sake (*propter se appetitur*). On the other hand, to choose (*eligere*) is to desire something for the sake of attaining something else, and so, properly speaking, choice is directed toward the means to an end.

Now, in appetitive matters, the end is related to the means to the end, which are desired for the sake of the end, in the same way that, in cognitive matters, the principle is related to the conclusion, to which we assent because of the principles. Hence, it is clear that the will is related to the power to choose, i.e., to free choice, in the same way that the intellect is related to reason. But it was shown above (q. 79, a. 8) that understanding intellectively and reasoning discursively belong to the same power, just as coming to rest and being moved belong to the same power. Hence, an act of willing and an act of choosing likewise belong to the same power (*eiusdem potentiae est velle et eligere*). Because of this, the will and free choice are a single power and not two powers.

**Reply to objection 1:** *Bulesis* is distinguished from *thelesis* because of a difference between the acts and not because of a diversity of powers.

**Reply to objection 2:** As has been explained, choosing (*electio*) and willing (*voluntas*), i.e., the act itself of willing (*ipsum velle*), are diverse acts, and yet they belong to a single power, just as understanding intellectively (*intelligere*) and reasoning discursively (*ratiocinari*) likewise belong to the same power.

**Reply to objection 3:** The intellect is related to the will as its mover. And so there is no need to distinguish an active will from a passive will (*non oportet in voluntate distinguere agens et possibile*).

# QUESTION 84

## How the Conjoined Soul Understands Corporeal Things
## That Are Below Itself

Next we have to consider the acts of the soul with respect to the intel-lective and appetitive powers, since the other powers of the soul are not directly relevant to the theologian's inquiry. Now the acts of the appetitive part of the soul are relevant to moral knowledge (*moralis scientia*), and so they will be treated in the second part of this work (*ST* 1–2 and 2–2), in which moral matters will be discussed. At present, however, we will dis-cuss the acts of the intellective part.

In the consideration of these acts, we will proceed in the following way: We have to consider, first, how the soul has intellective understand-ing when it is conjoined to the body (questions 84–88), and, second, how the soul has intellective understanding when it is separated from the body (question 89).

The consideration of the first topic will have three parts: We will con-sider, first, how the soul has intellective understanding of corporeal things, which are below it (questions 84–86); second, how it has intellective under-standing of itself and of what is contained within itself (question 87); and, third, how it has intellective understanding of immaterial substances, which are above it (question 88).

As for the cognition of corporeal things, there are three matters to be considered: first, by what means (*per quid*) it has cognition of them (ques-tion 84); second, in what manner and order (*quomodo et quo ordine*) it has cognition of them (question 85); and, third, what (*quid*) it has cognition of in them (question 86).

On the first topic there are eight questions: (1) Does the soul have cog-nition of corporeal things through the intellect? (2) Does the soul have intellective understanding of them through its own essence or instead through species? (3) If through species, are the species of all intelligible things naturally inherent (*naturaliter innatae*) in the soul? (4) Do the species flow into the soul from immaterial separated forms? (5) Does our soul see in the eternal conceptions (*in rationibus aeternis*) all the things it has intellective understanding of? (6) Does it acquire intelligible cognition from the sensory power? (7) Can the intellect engage in actual intellective understanding through the intelligible species that it possesses without turning itself toward phantasms? (8) Is the intellect's judgment impeded when the sentient powers are impeded?

## Article 1

### Does the soul have cognition of bodies through the intellect?

It seems that the soul does not have cognition of bodies through the intellect:

**Objection 1:** In *Soliloquia* 2 Augustine says, "Bodies cannot be comprehended by the intellect; nor can a body be seen except by the senses." Also, in *Super Genesim ad Litteram* 12 he says that intellectual vision is of things that by their essence exist in the soul. But bodies are not things of this sort. Therefore, the soul cannot have cognition of bodies through the intellect.

**Objection 2:** The intellect is related to sensible things in the same way that the sensory power is related to intelligible things. But through the sensory power the soul cannot in any way have cognition of spiritual things, which are intelligible. Therefore, through the intellect the soul cannot in any way have cognition of bodies, which are sensible.

**Objection 3:** The intellect has as its objects things that are necessary and always remain the same way. But all bodies are changeable and do not remain the same way. Therefore, the soul cannot have cognition of bodies through the intellect.

**But contrary to this:** Scientific knowledge (*scientia*) exists in the intellect. Therefore, if the intellect does not have cognition of bodies, it follows that there is no scientific knowledge of bodies. And so natural science, which is about changeable bodies, will amount to nothing (*peribit*).

**I respond:** To make this question clear, note that the first philosophers who inquired into the natures of things thought that there was nothing in the world except bodies. And because they saw that all bodies are changeable and believed them to be in constant flux, they judged that we can have no certitude concerning the truth about things. For what is in continuous flux cannot be apprehended with certitude, because it perishes before the mind can reach a judgment about it; for instance, as the Philosopher reports in *Metaphysics* 4, Heraclitus claimed that "it is impossible to touch the water of a flowing stream twice."

Coming along later, and wishing to be able to salvage the claim that we can have stable cognition (*certam cognitionem*) of truth through the intellect, Plato posited, over and beyond corporeal things, another kind of entity separated from matter and movement, which he called *species* or *ideas* (*species sive ideas*), through participation in which each singular and sensible thing is said to be either a man or a horse or something else of that sort. In this way, then, he claimed that scientific knowledge, definitions, and whatever else pertains to the act of intellective understanding has to do not with sensible bodies but instead with those immaterial and separated entities. The result is that the soul does not have intellective understanding of corporeal entities, but instead has intellective understanding of the separated species of corporeal entities.

But there are two reasons why this view is evidently false:

First, since the species in question are immaterial and unchangeable, the cognition of motion and matter (which is proper to natural science), along with demonstration by means of moving causes and material causes, would be excluded from the sciences.

Second, it seems laughable that while we are seeking knowledge of things that are manifest to us, we should introduce other entities that cannot be the substances of those things, because they differ from them in *esse*; and so even if we do have cognition of the separated substances in question, we cannot on that account make judgments about sensible things.

Plato seems to have deviated from the truth in this matter because his view that every cognition involves some sort of likeness led him to believe that the form of a thing that is known must exist in the knower in the same way that it exists in the thing known. Now he thought that the form of a thing that is understood exists in the intellect in a way that is universal, immaterial, and without change. This is apparent from the very operation of the intellect, which has intellective understanding in a mode that is universal and in some sense necessary; for the mode of an action corresponds to the mode of the agent's form. And so he thought that the things that are understood must subsist in this same way in themselves, viz., immaterially and unchangeably.

However, this is not necessary. For we see even among sensible things that a form exists in one sensible thing in a way different from the way in which it exists in another sensible thing; for instance, in one thing whiteness is more intense (*intensior*) and in another it is less intense (*remissior*), and in one thing whiteness is combined with sweetness and in another thing it exists without sweetness. Along the same lines, a sensible form exists in one way in a thing that exists outside the soul and in another way in the sensory power, which receives the forms of sensible things without matter; for instance, it receives the color of the gold without the gold.

Similarly, the intellect receives the species of corporeal things, which are material and changeable, in its own way, viz., immaterially and without change. For what is received exists in the thing receiving it according to the mode of the thing receiving it.

Therefore, one must reply that the soul, through the intellect, has cognition of bodies by means of a cognition that is immaterial, universal, and necessary.

**Reply to objection 1:** Augustine's words should be taken to apply to the things *by which* our intellect has cognition and not to the things *of which* it has cognition. For the intellect has cognition by understanding bodies intellectively. But it understands not through the bodies, or through material and corporeal likenesses, but instead through immaterial and intelligible species, which by their essence (*per sui essentiam*) are able to exist in the soul.

**Reply to objection 2:** As Augustine says in *De Civitate Dei* 22, one should not claim that just as the senses have cognition only of bodies, so the intellect has cognition only of spiritual things. For then it would follow that God and angels have no cognition of corporeal things. The reason for this disanalogy (*diversitas*) is that the lower power does not extend to those things that belong to the higher power, but the higher power accomplishes in a more excellent way what belongs to the lower power.

**Reply to objection 3:** Every change (*motus*) presupposes something that perdures (*aliquid immobile*). For instance, when there is a change (*transmutatio*) with respect to a quality, the substance perdures; and when a substantial form is changed, the matter perdures. Also, there are unchanged relations involving changing things; for instance, even if Socrates is not always sitting, it is nonetheless unchangeably true that whenever he is sitting, he remains in one place. Because of this, nothing prevents us from having unchangeable scientific knowledge about changeable things.

## Article 2

### Does the soul have intellective understanding of corporeal things through its own essence?

It seems that the soul has intellective understanding of corporeal things through its own essence:

**Objection 1:** In *De Trinitate* 10 Augustine says that the soul "captures and collects images of bodies that are made in its very self and of its very self; for in forming them it communicates something of its own substance." But it is through likenesses of bodies that the soul has intellective understanding of bodies. Therefore, it is through its own essence, which it communicates in forming such likenesses and from which it forms them, that the soul has cognition of corporeal things.

**Objection 2:** In *De Anima* 3 the Philosopher says, "The soul is in some sense all things." Therefore, since like is known by like, it is through itself, it seems, that the soul has cognition of corporeal things.

**Objection 3:** The soul is higher than corporeal creatures. But as Dionysius says, lower things exist in a more eminent way in higher things than they do in themselves. Therefore, all corporeal creatures exist in a more noble way in the substance of the soul than they do in themselves. Therefore, it is through its own substance that the soul is able to have cognition of corporeal creatures.

**But contrary to this:** In *De Trinitate* 9 Augustine says, "The mind gathers knowledge of corporeal things through the body's sensory power." But the soul itself is not knowable through the bodily sensory power. Therefore, it does not have cognition of corporeal things through its own substance.

**I respond:** The ancient philosophers claimed that it is through its own essence that the soul has cognition of bodies. For it was generally instilled in the minds of all of them that like is known by like. And they believed that the form of the thing known exists in the knower in the same way that it exists in the thing known.

The Platonists, on the other hand, held a contrary opinion. For since Plato perceived that the intellective soul is immaterial and has cognition immaterially, he claimed that the forms of the things that are known subsist immaterially.

By contrast, since the prior naturalists had believed that the things known were corporeal and material, they claimed that the things known must also exist materially in the soul when it has cognition. And so, in order to attribute cognition of all things to the soul, they claimed that the soul has a nature in common with all things. And since the nature of things that have a beginning (*natura principiatorum*) is constituted from the principles, they attributed to the soul the nature of a principle, so that those who thought that fire was the principle of all things held that the soul has the nature of fire, and similarly for air and water. Empedocles, who posited four material elements and two principles that effect movement, likewise claimed that the soul was constituted by these. And so since they posited things materially in the soul, they held that all the soul's cognition is material, and they did not distinguish the intellect from the sensory power.

However, this opinion is disproved, first, by the fact that things that have a beginning exist only in potentiality in the material principle, which is what they were talking about. However, as is clear from *Metaphysics* 9, there is cognition of a thing only insofar as it exists in actuality and not insofar as it exists in potentiality, and so neither is the potentiality itself known except through the actuality. So, then, it would not be sufficient to attribute the nature of the principles to the soul in order for the soul to have cognition of all things—unless there existed within it the natures and forms of *all* the singular effects, e.g., bone and flesh and other things of this sort, as Aristotle argues, in opposition to Empedocles, in *De Anima* 1.

Second, if the thing known had to exist materially in the knower, then there would be no reason why entities subsisting materially outside the soul should themselves lack cognition; for instance, if it is by means of fire that the soul has cognition of fire, then fire which exists outside the soul would likewise have cognition of fire.

It follows, then, that material things that are known must exist in the knower not in a material way, but rather in an immaterial way. The reason for this is that an act of cognition extends to things that exist outside the one who has the cognition; for we have cognition even of those things that exist outside of us. But it is through matter that the form of an entity is determined to a singular thing (*determinatur ad aliquid unum*). Hence, it is clear that the nature of cognition stands in opposition to the nature of materiality. And so, as *De Anima* 2 says, things that receive forms only materially, such as plants, have no cognition at all (*nullo modo sint cognoscitiva*). But to the extent that something possesses the form of the thing known in a more immaterial way, its cognition is more perfect. Hence, our intellect, which abstracts species not only from matter but also from individuating material conditions, has more perfect cognition than does the sensory power, which receives without matter but with material conditions the forms of the things it has cognition of. And among the senses themselves, the sense of sight has the most perfect cognition (*est magis cognoscitivus*), since it is the least material—as was explained above (q. 78, a. 3). And among intellects themselves, any given one is more perfect to the extent that it is more immaterial.

From these considerations it is clear that if there is any intellect that has cognition of all things through its own essence, then its essence must possess everything within itself in an immaterial way—just as the ancients claimed that the soul's essence is actually composed of the principles of all material things, so that it might have cognition of all things. But it is proper to God that His essence should, in an immaterial way, comprehend all things in the sense in which effects preexist virtually in their cause. Therefore, it is God alone who has intellective understanding of all things through His own essence—and not the human soul or even the angels.

**Reply to objection 1:** Augustine is talking here about imaginative vision, which is effected by the images of bodies. In forming these images, the soul communicates something of its own substance in the sense in which a subject exists in order to be informed by some form. And so it makes images of this sort 'from' itself—not in the sense that the soul or something of the soul is converted into this or that image, but in the sense in which a body is said to become something colored when it is informed by a color.

This interpretation is clear from what follows the quoted passage. For he says, "It keeps something"—namely, something not formed by such an image "that freely judges concerning the species of such images"—and this, he says, is the mind or intellect. And he says that the part of the soul which is informed by images of this sort, viz., the imagination (*partem imaginativam*), "is common to us and to the beasts."

**Reply to objection 2:** Unlike the ancient naturalists, Aristotle did not claim that the soul is actually composed of all things. Rather, he said that "the soul is in some sense all things" insofar as it is in potentiality with respect to all things—in potentiality to sensible things through the senses and to intelligible things through the intellect.

**Reply to objection 3:** Every creature has finite and determinate *esse*. Hence, even if a higher creature's essence bears a certain likeness to a lower creature's essence insofar as they share in the same genus, it nonetheless does not bear a perfect likeness to it, since it is determined to a species that lies outside of the lower thing's species. By contrast, God's essence, as the universal principle of all things, is a perfect likeness of all things with respect to *everything* that is found in things.

### Article 3

### Does the soul have intellective understanding of all things through species that it is naturally endowed with?

It seems that the soul has intellective understanding of all things through species that it is naturally endowed with (*per species sibi natu-raliter inditas*):

**Objection 1:** In his homily on the feast of the Ascension Gregory says, "Man has intellective understanding in common with the angels." But the angels have intellective understanding through forms that they are natural-ly endowed with; thus, in the *Liber de Causis* it says, "Every intelligence is filled with forms." Therefore, the soul likewise has species of things which it is naturally endowed with and by means of which it has intellec-tive understanding of corporeal things.

**Objection 2:** The intellective soul is more noble than the primary mat-ter of a corporeal thing. But primary matter is created by God with forms that it is in potentiality with respect to. Therefore, *a fortiori*, the intellec-tive soul is created by God with intelligible species. And so the soul has intellective understanding of corporeal things through species that it is nat-urally endowed with.

**Objection 3:** No one can give true replies except about something he knows (*scit*). But even someone uneducated (*idiota*), who has not acquired any scientific knowledge (*scientiam*), gives true replies about singular things if he is interrogated in the right order—as is told of a certain man in Plato's *Meno*. Therefore, before someone acquires scientific knowledge, he has a cognition of things (*antequam aliquis acquirat scientiam, habet rerum cognitionem*). But this would not be so unless the soul had species that it is naturally endowed with. Therefore, the soul has intellective under-standing of corporeal things through species that it is naturally endowed with.

**But contrary to this:** In *De Anima* 3, talking about the intellect, the Philosopher says that it is "like a slate on which nothing has been written."

**I respond:** Since a form is a principle of action, a thing has to be relat-ed to the form that is the principle of an action in the same way that it is related to the action; for instance, if moving upwards derives from the form of being lightweight (*ex levitate*), then what is borne upwards only in potentiality is lightweight only in potentiality, whereas what is being car-ried upwards in actuality is lightweight in actuality.

Now we see that a man sometimes has cognition only in potentiality, both respect to the sensory power and with respect to the intellect. And from this potentiality he is led into actuality (a) by the actions of sensible things on the sensory power in order to have sensation and (b) by learning or discovery in order to have intellective understanding. Hence, one must claim that a soul with cognitive powers (*anima cognoscitiva*) is in potentiality both with respect to those likenesses that are principles of sensing and also with respect to those likenesses that are principles of intellective understanding. Because of this, Aristotle claimed that the intellect, by which the soul has intellective understanding, does not have any species that it is naturally endowed with, but is in potentiality at the beginning with respect to all species of this sort.

Now that which actually has a form is sometimes unable to act in accord with that form because of some impediment, as when a lightweight thing is impeded from being borne upwards. For this reason, Plato claimed that man's intellect is naturally full of all the intelligible species, but is prevented by its union with the body from being able to make the transition into actual [understanding] (*exire in actum*).

However, this claim does not seem right.

For, first, if the soul has a natural knowledge of all things, it does not seem possible to suffer such a great forgetfulness of this natural knowledge that one would not know that he possesses knowledge of this sort. For no man is oblivious of those things that he knows naturally, such as that a whole is greater than its part, and other things of this sort. This seems especially problematic if one claims, as we established above (q. 76, a. 1), that it is natural for the soul to be united to the body; for it is absurd that a thing's natural operation should be totally impeded by something that belongs to it by nature.

Second, the falsity of the claim in question is manifestly obvious from the fact that when one of the senses is inoperative (*deficiente aliquo sensu*), there is no knowledge (*scientia*) of the things apprehended by that sense; for instance, someone born blind cannot have knowledge of colors (*notitiam de coloribus*). This would not be the case if the soul were naturally endowed with the notions of all intelligible things.

And so one should reply that the soul does not have cognition of corporeal things through species that it is naturally endowed with.

**Reply to objection 1:** Man does, to be sure, agree with the angels in having intellective understanding, but he falls short of the eminence of their intellect, just as lower bodies, which *merely exist* according to Gregory, fall short of the sort of existence had by higher bodies. For the matter of the lower bodies is not totally perfected (*completa*) by their form, but instead remains in potentiality to forms that it does not now have, whereas the matter of the celestial bodies is totally perfected by their forms in such a way that it does not remain in potentiality with respect to any other form, as was established above (q. 66, a. 2). Similarly, an angel's intellect is by its own nature perfected by intelligible species, whereas the human intellect is in potentiality to species of this sort.

**Reply to objection 2:** Primary matter has substantival *esse* (*esse substantiale*) through form, and so it had to be created with some form; otherwise, it would not exist in actuality. Yet when it exists with one form, it remains in potentiality with respect to other forms. By contrast, the intellect does not have substantival *esse* through an intelligible species. And so the cases are not parallel.

**Reply to objection 3:** A well-ordered interrogation (*ordinata interrogatio*) proceeds from common principles, known *per se* (*per se notis*), to more particular matters (*ad propria*), and scientific knowledge is caused by such a progression in the learner's soul. Hence, when at a later point he gives true replies about the things concerning which he is being questioned, this is not because he knew those things beforehand; rather, it is because at that point he is learning them *de novo*. For regardless of whether it is by making a presentation or by asking a series of questions (*proponendo vel interrogando*) that the teacher proceeds from the common principles to the conclusions, in both cases the listener's mind becomes certain about the conclusions by means of the principles.

## Article 4

### Do the intelligible species flow into the soul from separated forms?

It seems that the intelligible species flow into the soul from separated forms (*effluant in animam ab aliquibus formis separatis*):

**Objection 1:** Everything that is such-and-such by participation is caused to be that way by something that is such-and-such by its essence; for instance, what is on fire is traced back to fire as a cause. But insofar as the intellective soul is actually engaged in intellective understanding, it participates in the intelligible things themselves; for the intellect in act is in a certain sense the thing understood in act. Therefore, the things that are actually understood in their own right and in their essence are causes of the intellective soul's actually having intellective understanding. But the things that are actually understood through their essence are forms that exist without matter. Therefore, the intelligible species by which the soul has intellective understanding are caused by separated forms.

**Objection 2:** Intelligible things are related to the intellect in the same way that sensible things are related to the sensory power. But sensible things, which exist in actuality outside the soul, are causes of the sensible species which exist in the sensory power and by which we have sensation. Therefore, the intelligible species by which our intellect has intellective understanding arc caused by actually intelligible things that exist outside the soul. But intelligible things of this sort are not anything other than forms separated from matter. Therefore, the intelligible forms that belong to our intellect flow from separated substances.

**Objection 3:** Everything that is in potentiality is led into actuality by what is actual. Therefore, if our intellect, at first being in potentiality, later has actual intellective understanding, this must be caused by some intellect that is always active. But this is a separated intellect. Therefore, the intelligible species by which we have actual intellective understanding are caused by separated substances.

**But contrary to this:** On the view just proposed we would not need the sensory powers in order to have intellective understanding. That this is false is clear mainly from the fact that someone who lacks one of the sensory powers can in no way have scientific knowledge of the sensible things that correspond to that sensory power.

**I respond:** Some have claimed that the intelligible species that belong to our intellect proceed from certain separated forms or substances—and this in one of two ways.

For Plato, as has been explained (a. 1), posited forms of sensible things that subsist in their own right without matter, e.g., the form of man, which he called *man per se*, and the form or idea of a horse, which he called *horse per se*, and so on for the others. Therefore, he claimed that these separated forms are participated in both by our soul and by corporeal matter—by our soul in order for the soul to have cognition, and by corporeal matter in order for corporeal matter to exist. So just as corporeal matter, by participating in the idea *rock* becomes *this* rock, so our intellect, by participating in the idea *rock*, comes to have an intellective understanding of *rock*. Now this participation is effected by a likeness of the idea itself in the thing that participates in it, in the way in which an exemplar is participated in by an example of it. Therefore, just as he claimed that the sensible forms that exist in corporeal matter flow from the ideas as certain likenesses of them, so too he claimed that our intellect's intelligible species are likenesses of the ideas that they flow from. Because of this, as was explained above (a. 1), he referred scientific knowledge and definitions to the ideas.

However, since, as Aristotle proves a number of times, it is contrary to the nature of sensible things that their forms should subsist without matter, Avicenna, having rejected this position, claimed that the intelligible species of all sensible things do not, to be sure, subsist *per se* without matter, but that instead they preexist in an immaterial way in separated intellects. Species of this sort flow from the first of these separated intellects into the next one, and so on for the others up to the last separated intellect, which he names 'the active intellect' (*intellectus agens*). From this active intellect, he says, intelligible species flow into our souls and sensible forms flow into corporeal matter. And so Avicenna agrees with Plato that our intellect's intelligible species flow from certain separated forms, but whereas Plato claims that these forms subsist *per se*, Avicenna places them in the active intelligence (*in intelligentia agente*). They also disagree in that Avicenna claims that the intelligible species do not remain in our intellect after our intellect ceases to have actual intellective understanding; instead, the intellect needs to turn itself [toward the active intelligence] once again in order to receive the intelligible species *de novo*. Hence, he does not posit a knowledge that our soul is naturally endowed with, as Plato does when he claims that participations in the ideas remain in the soul permanently (*immobiliter*).

However, given this position, no sufficient reason can be given for why our soul is united with a body. For one cannot claim that the intellective soul is united with a body for the sake of the body, since it is not the case that form exists for the sake of matter or that what effects movement exists for the sake of the thing moved; in fact, just the opposite is true. Now given that the soul does not depend on the body with respect to its *esse*, the body seems necessary to the intellective soul mainly for the soul's proper operation, i.e., intellective understanding. But if the soul were by its nature apt to receive intelligible species only through the influence of separated principles and did not take them from the sensory powers, then it would not need the body in order to have intellective understanding, and its union with the body would be pointless (*frustra corpori uniretur*).

Nor does it seem adequate to reply that our soul needs the sensory powers for intellective understanding because it is in some way stimulated by them to consider the things whose intelligible species it has received from the separated principles. For a stimulation of this sort does not seem necessary to the soul except insofar as it is in some sense sleepy or oblivious because of its union with the body, as the Platonists claim. And so the sensory powers would be of no use to the intellective soul except to remove an impediment that is posed for the soul because of its union with the body. Therefore, one still needs to ask what reason there is for the soul's union with the body.

On the other hand, if one claims, in accord with Avicenna, that the sensory powers are necessary for the soul because the soul is stimulated by them to turn itself toward the active intelligence, from which it receives the species, then this, too, is inadequate. For if it were in the soul's nature to have intellective understanding through species that flow from the active intelligence, it would follow that the soul is sometimes able to turn itself toward the active intelligence by an inclination of its own nature—or even that it is sometimes stimulated by one of the other senses to turn itself toward the active intelligence in order to receive the species of sensible things for which the man in question does not have [the appropriate] sensory power. And in this way someone born blind would be able to have knowledge of colors—which is manifestly false.

Hence, one should reply that the intelligible species by which our soul has intellective understanding do not flow from separated forms.

**Reply to objection 1:** The intelligible species that our intellect participates in are traced back, as to a first cause, to a principle that is intelligible through its essence, viz., God. But they proceed from that principle by the mediation of the forms of sensible and material things, from which, as Dionysius puts it, we gather knowledge.

**Reply to objection 2:** Given the *esse* that they have outside the soul, material things are able to be sensible in actuality, but not intelligible in actuality. Hence, there is no parallel between the sensory power and the intellect.

**Reply to objection 3:** Our passive intellect is led from potentiality into actuality by some actual being, viz., by the active intellect, which, as has been explained (q. 79, a. 4), is a certain power of our soul. But it is not led into actuality by any separated intellect as a proximate cause—though perhaps as a remote cause.


### Article 5

### Does the intellective soul have cognition of material things in the eternal conceptions?

It seems that the intellective soul does not have cognition of material things in the eternal conceptions (*in rationibus aeternis*):

**Objection 1:** That *in which* something is known is itself known to a greater extent and in a prior way. But in the state of the present life, man's intellective soul does not have cognition of the eternal conceptions, since it does not have cognition of God Himself, in whom the eternal conceptions exist, but is instead "conjoined to Him as something unknown," as Dionysius puts in *Mystica Theologia*, chap. 1. Therefore, the soul does not have cognition of all things in the eternal conceptions.

**Objection 2:** Romans 1:20 says, "The invisible things of God are clearly seen through the things that have been made." But the eternal conceptions are numbered among the invisible things of God. Therefore, it is the eternal conceptions that are known through material creatures, and not vice versa.

**Objection 3:** The eternal conceptions are nothing other than the ideas; for in *83 Quaestiones* Augustine says, "The ideas are stable conceptions of things that exist in God's mind." Therefore, if one claims that the intellective soul has cognition of all things in the eternal conceptions, there will be a return to the opinion of Plato, who claimed that all knowledge is derived from the ideas.

**But contrary to this:** In *Confessiones* 12 Augustine says, "If both of us see that what you say is true and if both of us see that what I say is true, then where, I ask, do we see it? Certainly, I do not see it in you, and you do not see it in me; rather, both of us see it in that immutable truth that lies beyond our minds." But immutable truth is contained in the eternal conceptions. Therefore, the intellective soul has cognition of all true things in the eternal conceptions.

**I respond:** As Augustine says in *De Doctrina Christiana* 2, "If those who are called philosophers have by chance made claims that are true and compatible with our Faith, then we must appropriate those truths from them, as from unjust possessors, for our own advantage. For the teachings of the Gentiles contain certain counterfeit and superstitious inventions (*simulata et superstitiosa figmenta*) that each of us who has left the company of the Gentiles should avoid." And so if Augustine, who had been imbued with the teachings of the Platonists, found anything consistent with the Faith in their sayings, he took it over, whereas when he found anything opposed to the Faith, he changed it into something better.

Now, as was explained above (a. 4), Plato claimed that the forms of things subsist in their own right separated from matter, and he claimed that through participation in these forms, which he called 'ideas', our intellect has cognition of all things. For instance, just as corporeal matter becomes a rock through participation in the idea *rock*, so too our intellect comes to have a cognition of *rock* through participation in that same idea. However, as Dionysius points out in *De Divinis Nominibus*, chap. 11, it seems alien to the Faith that the forms of things should subsist in their own right without matter, as the Platonists claimed when they said that *life per se* or *wisdom per se* were certain creative substances. So in *83 Quaestiones* Augustine posited, in place of these ideas that Plato had posited, the conceptions of all creatures existing in God's mind; all things are formed in accord with these conceptions, and, in addition, the human soul has cognition of all things in accord with these conceptions (*secundum quas rationes*).

Therefore, when the question arises whether the human soul has cognition of all things in the eternal conceptions, one should reply that there are two senses of 'having a cognition of something *in* something'.

The first sense is to have a cognition 'in something' as *in an object that is known*—as, for instance, when someone sees in a mirror those things whose images are reflected back in the mirror (*in speculo resultant*). And in this sense the soul, in the state of the present life, is unable to see all things in the eternal conceptions. However, the blessed in heaven, who see God and see all things in Him, do in this sense have cognition of all things in the eternal conceptions.

In the second sense, one is said to have a cognition of something 'in something' as *in a principle of cognition*, as if we were to say that we see 'in the sun' those things that we see because of the sun (*per solem*). And given this sense, one must claim that the human soul has cognition of all things in the eternal conceptions, by participation in which we have cognition of all things. For the intellectual light that exists in us is nothing other than a participated likeness of the uncreated light in which the eternal conceptions are contained. Hence, in Psalm 4:6–7 it says, "Many say, 'Who shows us good things?'" And to this question the Psalmist replies by saying, "The light of your countenance, O Lord, is signed upon us"—as if to say that all things are shown to us by the very mark (*sigillatio*) of the divine light in us.

Still, since in addition to the intellectual light in us, intelligible species taken from the things are necessary for having scientific knowledge of material things, it follows that it is not solely through participation in the eternal conceptions that we have knowledge of material things, in the way that the Platonists claimed that participation in the ideas was by itself sufficient for having knowledge. Hence, in *De Trinitate* 4 Augustine says, "Given that the philosophers prove with convincing arguments that all temporal things are caused by the eternal conceptions, have they been able because of this to see in these conceptions, or infer from them, how many kinds of animals there are, or what the origins (*semina*) of each are? Have they not instead looked for all these things through the history of places and times?"

Moreover, Augustine did not think that all things are known in the eternal conceptions, or in immutable truth, in such a way that the eternal conceptions themselves are seen; this is clear from what he himself says in *83 Quaestiones*: "Not each and every rational soul is claimed to be fit for that vision"—namely, the vision of the eternal conceptions—"but only one that is holy and pure"—as are the souls of the blessed in heaven.

**Reply to objection 1 and objection 2 and objection 3:** The replies to the objections are clear from what has been said.

## Article 6

### Is intellective cognition taken from sensible things?

It seems that intellective cognition is not taken from sensible things:

**Objection 1:** In *83 Quaestiones* Augustine says, "Purity of truth should not be expected from the sensory powers of the body." And there are two ways to prove this. First, from the fact that "everything that a corporeal sense touches is changing without any temporal intermission, and what does not remain the same cannot be perceived." Second, from the fact that "even when all the things we sense through the body are not present to the senses, we still have their images, as when we are sleeping or furiously angry; but we are unable to discern with the senses whether we are sensing the sensible things themselves or their misleading images, and nothing can be perceived that is not distinguished from what is false." And so he concludes that truth should not be expected from the sensory powers. But intellective cognition apprehends truth. Therefore, it is not the case that intellective cognition should be expected from the senses.

**Objection 2:** In *Super Genesim ad Litteram* 12 Augustine says, "Do not think that the body has an effect on the spirit, as if the spirit, instead of matter, might be subjected to the body's action; for what acts is in every way more excellent than what it acts on." Hence, he concludes that "the body does not cause an image of a body in the spirit, but that the spirit itself causes an image within itself." Therefore, intellective cognition is not derived from sensible things.

**Objection 3:** An effect does not extend beyond the power of its cause. But intellective cognition extends beyond sensible things; for we have intellective cognition of certain things that cannot be perceived by the sensory power. Therefore, intellective cognition is not derived from sensible things.

**But contrary to this:** In *Metaphysics* 1 and at the end of *Posterior Analytics* the Philosopher says that our cognition begins from the sensory power.

**I respond:** On this question philosophers have held three positions.

As Augustine explains in his letter *Ad Dioscorum,* Democritus claimed that "the only cause of our cognition is that images come from the bodies we are thinking about and enter into our souls." And in *De Somno et Vigilia* Aristotle likewise says that Democritus claimed that cognition is effected "by images and discharges (*per idola et defluxiones*)." As Aristotle explains in *De Anima,* the reason for this position was that Democritus himself and the other ancient naturalists did not believe that the intellect differs from the sensory power. And so since the sensory power is affected by the sensible thing, they thought that all of our cognition is brought about just by the changes caused by sensible things. Democritus asserted that these changes are effected through a discharge of images.

By contrast, Plato claimed that the intellect differs from the sensory power, and that the intellect is an immaterial power that does not use a corporeal organ in its own act. And because what is immaterial cannot be affected by what is corporeal, he claimed that intellective cognition comes about not through the intellect's being affected by the senses, but rather, as was explained above (aa. 4 and 5), through the intellect's participation in separated intelligible forms. Moreover, he claimed that the sensory power operates on its own (*operantem per se*). Hence, because the sensory power is a certain spiritual power, it is not affected by the sensible things; rather, the sensory organs are affected by the sensible things, and the soul is in some way stimulated by this change to form the species of sensible things within itself. This is the opinion that Augustine seems to be alluding to in *Super Genesim ad Litteram* 12, when he remarks, "The body does not sense, but instead the soul senses through the body, which it uses as a messenger in order to form within itself what is announced from the outside." So, then, according to Plato's opinion, intellective cognition does not proceed from the sensible thing; not even sentient cognition proceeds entirely from sensible things. Instead, sensible things stimulate the sentient soul to exercise sentient cognition and, similarly, the senses stimulate the intellective soul to exercise intellective understanding.

Aristotle, on the other hand, proceeded along a middle course. For with Plato he claimed that the intellect differs from the sensory power. But he claimed that the sensory power does not have a proper operation that the body does not share in (*sine communicatione corporis*), and so sensing is an act of the conjoined being and not of the soul alone; and he made a similar claim about all the operations of the sentient part of the soul. Therefore, since it is not unfitting that sensible things existing outside the soul should cause something in the conjoined being, Aristotle agreed with Democritus that the operations of the sentient part are caused by the impression sensible things make on the sensory power—not by way of discharges, as Democritus had held, but rather through a certain operation. (For as is clear from *De Generatione et Corruptione* 1, Democritus held that *every* action is effected by a discharge of atoms.) On the other hand, Aristotle held that the intellect has an operation that it does not share with the body. But nothing corporeal can leave an impression (*potest imprimere*) on an incorporeal entity. And so, according to Aristotle, the mere impression of sensible bodies is not enough to cause an intellectual operation; instead, what is required is something more noble, since "an agent is more honorable than a patient," as he himself puts it. However, it is not the case that intellectual operations are caused in us by the mere impression of some higher entities, as Plato had claimed. Instead, that higher and more noble agent, which Aristotle calls the 'active intellect' and which we have already talked about above (q. 79, aa. 3–4), makes the phantasms received from the senses intelligible in actuality, in the manner of a sort of abstraction (*per modum abstractionis cuiusdam*). Accordingly, as far as the phantasms are concerned, the intellectual operation is caused by the sensory power. But because (a) the phantasms are not sufficient to affect the passive intellect and because (b) they have to be made intelligible in actuality by the active intellect, it cannot be claimed that sentient cognition is the total and perfect cause of intellective cognition; instead, it is more like a material cause.

**Reply to objection 1:** What these words of Augustine's mean is that truth is not to be expected in its totality. What is required is the light of the active intellect, through which we have cognition in an unchangeable way of the truth in changeable things, and through which we distinguish those things from their likenesses.

**Reply to objection 2:** Augustine is talking here about imaginative cognition and not intellective cognition. And since, according to Plato's opinion, the power of imagining has an operation that belongs to the soul alone, Augustine used the same line of reasoning to show that bodies do not impress their likenesses on the power of imagining, but that the soul itself does this. Aristotle uses the same argument, viz., that an agent is more honorable than a patient, to prove that the active intellect is something separate. There is no doubt that, given Plato's position, it necessary to posit in the power of imagining not just a passive power, but an active power as well.

However, if we hold, in accord with Aristotle's opinion, that the operation of the power of imagining belongs to the conjoined being, then no difficulty ensues. For a sensible body is more noble than an animal's sensory organ, since it is related to the sensory organ as a being in actuality is related to a being in potentiality—for instance, as something colored in actuality is related to the pupil, which is colored in potentiality.

Still, one could claim that even though the first change in the power of imagining is effected by the sensible things—given that "an image (*phantasia*) is a movement effected in the sensory power (*motus factus secundum sensum*)," as *De Anima* says—nonetheless, there is an operation of man's soul which, by dividing and composing, fashions diverse images of things, even images that have not been received from the senses. And Augustine's words can be understood to be making this point.

**Reply to objection 3:** Sentient cognition is not the total cause of intellective cognition. And so it is no surprise that intellective cognition extends further than sentient cognition does.

### Article 7

### Can the intellect have actual intellective understanding through the intelligible species it has within itself, without turning itself to phantasms?

It seems that the intellect can have actual intellective understanding through the intelligible species it has within itself, without turning itself to phantasms:

**Objection 1:** The intellect becomes active (*fit in actu*) because of the intelligible species by which it is informed. But the intellect's becoming active is the very act of intellective understanding. Therefore, the intelligible species are sufficient for the intellect's actually engaging in intellective understanding, without turning itself to phantasms.

**Objection 2:** The imagination depends more on the sensory power than the intellect depends on the imagination. But the imagination can be actually engaged in imagining in the absence of sensible things. Therefore, *a fortiori*, the intellect can be actually engaged in intellective understanding without turning itself to phantasms.

**Objection 3:** There are no phantasms of incorporeal things, since the imagination does not transcend time and continuous quantity (*continuum*). Therefore, if our intellect were unable to have actual intellective understanding of anything without turning itself to phantasms, it would follow that it cannot have intellective understanding of anything incorporeal. But this is clearly false, since we have intellective understanding of truth itself and of God and of the angels.

**But contrary to this:** In *De Anima* 3 the Philosopher says, "The soul does not have intellective understanding of anything without a phantasm."

**I respond:** In the state of our present life, in which our intellect is joined to a passible body, it is impossible for it to have an actual intellective understanding of anything unless it turns itself toward phantasms. There are two indications that make this apparent.

First of all, given that the intellect is a power that does not use a corporeal organ, if no act of a power that uses a corporeal organ were required for its act, then the intellect would not in any way be impeded in its act by an injury to a corporeal organ. But the senses, the imagination, and all the other powers that belong to the sentient part of the soul use a corporeal organ. Hence, it is clear that in order for the intellect to be actually engaged in intellective understanding—not only for attaining knowledge *de novo*, but also for making use of already acquired knowledge—what is required are acts of the imagination and of the rest of the powers. For we see that when the act of the power of imagining is impeded by an injury to an organ, as in the case of those who are delirious (*in phreneticis*) or, similarly, when the act of the power of remembering is impeded, as in those who are groggy (*in lethargicis*), a man is prevented from having actual intellective understanding even of those things that he previously had scientific knowledge of.

Second, everyone can experience in his own case that when someone tries to have an intellective understanding of something, he forms for himself phantasms as examples in which he inspects, as it were, what he is trying to understand. And so, too, when we want to make someone else understand something, we propose to him examples from which he can form phantasms in order to understand the matter at hand. The reason for this is that a cognitive power is proportioned to the thing it has cognition of. Hence, the proper object of an angelic intellect, which is totally separated from a body, is an intelligible substance separated from a body, and it is through intelligible things of this sort that an angel has cognition of material things. By contrast, the proper object of the human intellect, which is conjoined to a body, is a 'what-ness' or nature existing in corporeal matter (*quidditas sive naturam in materia corporali existens*), and it is through these natures of visible things that it ascends to some sort of cognition of invisible things as well. But it is part of the conception of this sort of nature that it exists in an individual and not without corporeal matter; for instance, it is part of the conception of the nature of a rock that it exists in individual rocks (*de ratione naturae lapidis est quod sit in hoc lapide*), and part of the conception of the nature of a horse that it exists in individual horses, and so on for the others. Hence, the nature of a rock, or of any material entity, is such that there cannot be a complete and true cognition of it except insofar as it is thought of as existing in a particular. But we apprehend particulars through the sensory power and the imagination. And so for the intellect to have an actual intellective understanding of its own proper object, it is necessary that it turn itself to phantasms, in order that it might inspect the universal nature as it exists in the particular (*ut speculetur naturam universalem in particulari existentem*). On the other hand, if the proper object of our intellect were a separated form, or if the natures of sensible things did not subsist in particulars (as the Platonists held), then it would not be necessary that our intellect always turn itself to phantasms when engaging in intellective understanding.

**Reply to objection 1:** As was explained above (q. 79, a. 6), the species that are conserved in the passive intellect exist in it habitually when it is not actually engaged in intellective understanding. Hence, the conservation of these species is not itself sufficient for us to be actually engaged in intellective understanding; instead, it is necessary for us to make use of the species in a way appropriate to the entities whose species they are, and these entities are natures that exist in particulars.

**Reply to objection 2:** A phantasm is itself a likeness of a particular thing, and so the imagination does not need any other likeness of the particular in the way that the intellect does.

**Reply to objection 3:** We have cognition of incorporeal things, of which there are no phantasms, by way of a comparison to sensible bodies, of which there are phantasms. For instance, we come to an intellective understanding of truth by considering things with respect to which we see the truth, whereas, as Dionysius says, we have cognition of God (a) as a cause, and (b) through preeminence (*per excessum*), and (c) through negation (*per remotionem*). Again, other incorporeal substances are such that, in the state of our present life, we cannot have cognition of them except through negation or through some sort of comparison to corporeal things. And so when we have intellective understanding of something of this sort, we necessarily have to be turned toward the phantasms of bodies, even though there are no phantasms of these things themselves.

## Article 8

### Is the intellect's judgment impeded when the sensory power is inoperative?

It seems that the intellect's judgment is not impeded when the sensory power is inoperative (*per ligamentum sensus*):

**Objection 1:** Something higher is not dependent on something lower. But the intellect's judgment is higher than the sensory power. Therefore, the intellect's judgment is not impeded when the sensory power is inoperative.

**Objection 2:** Reasoning by means of a syllogism (*syllogizare*) is an act of the intellect. Now as *De Somno et Vigilia* says, during sleep the sensory power is inoperative; and yet it sometimes happens that someone who is sleeping reasons by means of a syllogism. Therefore, the intellect's judgment is not impeded by the fact that the senses are inoperative.

**But contrary to this:** As Augustine says in *Super Genesim ad Litteram* 12, morally illicit things that occur during sleep (*contingunt in dormiendo*) do not count as sins. But this would not be so if a sleeping man had the free use of his reason and intellect. Therefore, the use of reason is impeded when the sensory power is inoperative.

**I respond:** As has been explained (a. 7), the proper object proportioned to our intellect is the nature of a sensible thing. Now a perfect judgment cannot be made about a thing if not everything that pertains to that thing is known, and especially if the terminus or end of the judgment is unknown. But in *De Caelo* 3 the Philosopher says, "Just as the end of productive knowledge (*factiva scientia*) is a piece of work (*opus*), so the end of natural knowledge (*naturalis scientia*) is that which is apparent principally to the senses." For a craftsman seeks to have cognition of knives only for the sake of his work, so that he might make this particular knife; and, similarly, a natural scientist seeks to have cognition of the nature of a rock or of a horse only in order to know the natures of those things that are apparent to the senses.

Now it is obvious that the craftsman could not render a perfect judgment about a knife if he did not know how to make one (*si opus ignoraret*); and, similarly, no perfect judgment of natural knowledge can be made about natural things if sensible things are not known. But all the things we have intellective understanding of in our present state are such that we have cognition of them in relation to natural sensible things. Hence, it is impossible for a perfect judgment of the intellect to exist in us when the sensory power is inoperative, since it is through the sensory power that we have cognition of sensible things.

**Reply to objection 1:** Even though the intellect is higher than the sensory power, it nonetheless receives in a certain way from the sensory power, and its first and principal objects are grounded in sensible things (*fundatur in sensibilibus*). And so it is necessary that the intellect's judgment should be impeded when the sensory power is inoperative.

**Reply to objection 2:** As *De Somno et Vigilia* says, the sensory power is inoperative in those who are asleep because of the release of certain vapors and fumes. And so the sensory power can be more or less inoperative, depending on the disposition of such evaporations.

For instance, when there is a lot of movement of vapors, both the senses and the imagination are inoperative, so that there are no phantasms; this happens especially when someone goes to sleep after heavy eating or drinking.

However, if the movement of vapors is a bit less intense, then phantasms appear, but they are distorted and chaotic (*distorta et inordinata*); this occurs in those who are feverish.

Again, if the movement is still more sedate, then well-ordered phantasms appear; this occurs mainly near the end of the time of sleep and in men who are sober and have a strong imagination.

On the other hand, if the movement of the vapors is minimal, not only does the imagination remain free, but even the common sensory power is partly operative (*ex parte solvitur*), so that a man sometimes judges in his sleep that what he is seeing are dreams, as if he were distinguishing between things and their likenesses. But to some extent the common sensory power remains inoperative, and so even if he distinguishes certain likenesses from the things, he is nonetheless always deceived about some matters.

So, then, depending on the way in which the sensory power and imagination are operating in sleep, the intellect's judgment is freed up, but not entirely. Hence, those who engage in syllogistic reasoning while asleep always recognize, when they wake up, that they have made a mistake in some matter.

# QUESTION 85

## The Mode and Order of Intellective Understanding

Next we have to consider the mode and order of intellective understanding. And on this topic there are eight questions: (1) Does our intellect have intellective understanding by abstracting species from phantasms? (2) Are the intelligible species abstracted from the phantasms related to our intellective understanding as *that which* is understood or as *that by which* something is understood? (3) Does our intellect by its nature first have intellective understanding of what is more universal? (4) Can our intellect have intellective understanding of many things at once? (5) Does our intellect come to intellective understanding by composing and dividing? (6) Can our intellective understanding be mistaken? (7) Is it possible for someone to understand the same thing better than someone else? (8) Does our intellect understand what is indivisible prior to what is divisible?

### Article 1

### Does our intellect have intellective understanding of corporeal and material things through abstraction from phantasms?

It seems that our intellect does not have intellective understanding of corporeal and material things through abstraction from phantasms (*per abstractionem a phantasmatibus*):

**Objection 1:** If an intellect understands a thing otherwise than it is, then it has falsity. But the forms of material things are not abstracted from the particulars whose likenesses the phantasms are. Therefore, if we understand material things by means of the abstraction of species from phantasms, then falsity will exist in our intellect.

**Objection 2:** Material things are natural things that have matter as part of their definition (*in quarum definitione cadit materia*). But nothing can be understood intellectively in the absence of something that is part of its definition. Therefore, material things cannot be understood without matter. But matter is a principle of individuation. Therefore, material things cannot be understood by means of the abstraction of a universal from a particular—which is what it is to abstract intelligible species from phantasms.

**Objection 3:** *De Anima* 3 says that phantasms are related to the intellective soul in the way that colors are related to the power of vision. But an act of seeing occurs not by means of an abstraction of species from colors, but by the colors' leaving an impression on the power of vision (*per hoc quod colores imprimunt in visum*). Therefore, it is impossible to have intellective understanding by means of something's being abstracted from phantasms; instead, it must be had by means of the phantasms' leaving an impression on the intellect (*per hoc quod phantasmata imprimunt in intellectum*).

**Objection 4:** *De Anima* 3 says that there are two [cognitive powers] in the intellective soul, viz., the passive intellect and the active intellect (*intellectus possibilis et agens*). But the passive intellect's function is to receive the species that have already been abstracted and not to abstract the inteligible species from phantasms. Nor does abstracting the species belong to the active intellect. For the active intellect is related to the phantasms in the way that light (*lumen*) is related to colors; but light flows into the colors rather than abstracting anything from them (*non abstrahit aliquid a coloribus sed magis eis influit*). Therefore, there is no way in which we have intellective understanding by means of abstraction from phantasms.

**Objection 5:** In *De Anima* 3 the Philosopher says, "The intellect *understands* species in the phantasms"—and thus does not *abstract* them.

**But contrary to this:** *De Anima* 3 says, "Things are susceptible to intellective understanding (*circa intellectum sunt*) insofar as they are separable from matter." Therefore, it must be the case that material things are understood intellectively insofar as they are abstracted from matter and from material likenesses, i.e., phantasms.

**I respond:** As was explained above (q. 84, a. 7), an object of cognition (*obiectum cognoscibile*) is proportioned to the relevant cognitive power. Now there are three levels of cognitive power:

For there is a cognitive power, viz., *the sensory power*, that is the act of a corporeal organ. And so the object of any sentient power is *a form insofar as it exists in matter*. And since matter of this sort is a principle of individuation, it follows that every power of the sentient part of the soul has cognition only of particulars.

On the other hand, there is a cognitive power, viz., *the angelic intellect*, which is not the act of a corporeal power and is not conjoined in any way with corporeal matter. And so the object of this sort of cognitive power is a form that subsists without matter; for even though the angels have cognition of material things, they nonetheless have their intuitive vision of them (*ea intuentur*) 'in' immaterial things, viz., in themselves and in God (cf. q. 84, a. 5).

By contrast, human understanding (*intellectus humanus*) is situated in the middle. For as is clear from what was said above (q. 76, a. 1), human understanding is not the act of any [corporeal] organ. Yet it is a certain power belonging to a soul that is the form of a body, and so it is proper to it to have cognition of forms that exist individually in corporeal matter, though not insofar as they exist in such matter. But to have a cognition of what exists in a material individual, but not insofar as it exists in such matter, is to abstract the form from the individual matter represented by the phantasms. And so it is necessary to say that our intellect has intellective understanding of immaterial things by abstracting from the phantasms. And it is through material things considered in this way that we come to have a certain sort of cognition of immaterial things —just the opposite of the way that angels have cognition of material things through immaterial things.

However, Plato, who paid attention only to the immateriality of the human intellect, but not to the fact that it is united in some way to a body, claimed that the objects of the intellect are separated ideas and that we have intellective understanding not by abstracting but rather by participating in abstract entities. This was explained above (q. 84, a. 1).

**Reply to objection 1:** There are two ways in which it is possible to abstract: *first*, in the *mode of composition and division*, as when we understand intellectively that one thing does not exist in another, or that it is separated from it; *second*, in the *mode of simple and absolute consideration*, as when we have an intellective understanding of the one thing without considering the other at all.

Thus, in the *first* mode of abstraction, it involves falsity to abstract through intellection things that are not abstracted in reality (*secundum rem*). By contrast, in the *second* mode, it does not involve falsity to abstract through intellection things that are not abstracted in reality, as is manifestly obvious in the case of sensible things. For instance, if we think or say (*si intelligamus vel dicamus*) 'No color exists in a body that is colored', or 'Color is separated from a body that is colored', there will be falsity in what we think or in what we say (*in opinione vel in oratione*). On the other hand, if we are considering a color and its properties, paying no attention at all to the apple that is colored, then what we think or orally express in so doing will involve no falsity in thought or speech. For an apple is not part of the nature of a color (*pomum not est de ratione coloris*), and nothing prevents the color from being thought of without the apple's being thought of at all. Similarly, I claim that what belongs to the nature (*ratio*) of any species of material thing, e.g., *rock* or *man* or *horse*, can be considered without the individual principles, which do not belong to the nature (*ratio*) of the species. And to abstract the universal from the particular, or to abstract the intelligible species from the phantasms, is just this: to consider the nature (*natura*) of the species without considering the individual principles that are represented through the phantasms.

Therefore, when one says, 'An intellect has falsity when it understands a thing otherwise than it is', the sentence is true if 'otherwise' refers to the thing that is understood. For the intellect has falsity when it understands a thing to be otherwise than it is. Hence, the intellect would have falsity if it abstracted the species of a rock from matter in such a way that it understood this species not to exist in matter, as Plato posited.

However, the proposition 'The intellect has falsity when it understands a thing otherwise than it is' is not true if 'otherwise' is referred to the one who is doing the understanding (*accipiatur ex parte intelligentis*). For there is no falsity involved in the fact that the mode of the one who understands is, in his understanding, different from the mode of the thing in its existing. For in the one who is doing the understanding, the thing that is understood exists immaterially, in the manner of an intellect, and not materially, in the manner of a material thing.

**Reply to objection 2:** Some have thought that the species of a natural thing is the form alone, and that the matter is not part of the species. But according to this view, matter would have no place in the definitions of natural things.

And so one should reply in an alternative way that there are two types of matter, viz., (a) *common matter* and (b) *designated* (or *individual*) matter (*materia communis et signata vel individualis*)—where common matter is, e.g., *flesh* and *bone*, and individual matter is, e.g., *this flesh* and *these bones*.

Thus, the intellect abstracts the species of a *natural* thing from *individual* sensible matter, but not from *common* sensible matter. For instance, it abstracts the species *man* from *this* flesh and *these* bones, which, as *Metaphysics* 7 points out, are not part of the nature of the species but are instead parts of the individual; and so the nature can be thought about without them. However, the species *man* cannot be abstracted by the intellect from *flesh* and *bones*.

By contrast, *mathematical* species can be abstracted by the intellect not only from *individual* sensible matter but also from *common* sensible matter—and yet not from common *intelligible* matter, but only from individual *intelligible* matter. For sensible matter is called 'corporeal' matter insofar as it is subject to sensible qualities like hot and cold, hard and soft, and so on, whereas what is called intelligible matter is a substance insofar as it is subject to quantity. Now it is clear that quantity exists in a substance prior to its sensible qualities. Hence, quantities such as numbers, dimensions, and shapes (which are the limits of quantities) can be thought about without sensible qualities—which is what it is to abstract them from sensible matter. Now these quantities cannot be thought about without an understanding of a substance's being the subject of quantity—which would be to abstract them from *common* intelligible matter. But they can indeed be thought about without *this* or *that* substance—which is to abstract them from *individual* intelligible matter.

On the other hand, there are certain [species], e.g., *being, one, potentiality, actuality*, and others of this sort, that can be abstracted even from common intelligible matter. These can exist without any matter at all, as is clear in the case of immaterial substances.

And because Plato did not take into account what was said above about the two modes of abstraction, he posited as abstract entities, existing in reality, all the things that we have claimed to be abstracted by the intellect.

**Reply to objection 3:** Colors have the same mode of existing in a material corporeal individual as the power of sight does, and so colors can impress their likeness on the power of sight. But as is clear from what has been said, since phantasms are likenesses of individuals and exist in corporeal organs, they do not have the same mode of existing that the human intellect does. And so they cannot by their own power leave an impression on the passive intellect. Rather, by the power of the active intellect, a certain likeness results in the passive intellect from the active intellect's turning toward the phantasms; and this likeness is representative of those things that the phantasms are about, though only with respect to the nature of their species. This is the sense in which the intelligible species is said to be abstracted from the phantasms—and not in the sense that numerically the same form at first existed in the phantasms and later comes to exist in the passive intellect, in the way that a body is taken from one place and transferred to another.

**Reply to objection 4:** It is the case both that (a) the phantasms are illuminated by the agent intellect and, again, that (b) the intelligible species are abstracted from them by the power of the active intellect.

They are *illuminated* in the sense that just as the sentient part of soul is made more powerful by being conjoined to the intellect, so by the power of the active intellect the phantasms are rendered suitable for intelligible intentions to be abstracted from them.

And the active intellect *abstracts* the intelligible species from the phantasms in the sense that (a) by the power of the active intellect we are able, in our thinking, to grasp the natures of the species without their individual conditions, and that (b) the passive intellect is informed by the likenesses of these natures.

**Reply to objection 5:** On the one hand, our intellect *abstracts* intelligible species *from* the phantasms insofar as it considers the natures in general (*in universali*); on the other hand, it *understands* them *in* the phantasms, since, as was explained above (q. 84, a. 7), it is unable to understand even the things whose species it abstracts except by turning itself to the phantasms.

## Article 2

### Are the intelligible species abstracted from the phantasms related to our intellect as *that which* is understood intellectively?

It seems that the intelligible species abstracted from the phantasms are related to our intellect as *that which* (*id quod*) is understood intellectively:

**Objection 1:** A thing which is actually being understood (*intellectum in actu*) exists in the one who is engaged in understanding, since a thing which is actually being understood is the intellect itself insofar as it is acting (*ipse intellectus in actu*). But nothing of the things which is being understood, except the abstracted intelligible species, exists in an intellect actually engaged in understanding. Therefore, it is a species of this sort that is the very thing which is actually being understood.

**Objection 2:** A thing which is actually being understood has to exist in something; otherwise, it would be nothing at all. But it does not exist in the thing that is outside the soul; for since the thing outside the soul is material, nothing that is in it can be a thing which is actually being understood. Therefore, it follows that what is actually being understood exists in the intellect. And so the thing which is actually being understood is nothing other than the aforementioned intelligible species.

**Objection 3:** In *Perihermenias* 1 the Philosopher says, "Spoken words (*voces*) are signs of things received in the soul (*notae earum quae sunt in anima passionum*)." But spoken words signify the things which are understood; for we signify by spoken words what we understand intellectively. Therefore, the things received in the soul (*passiones animae*), i.e., the intelligible species, are themselves the things which are actually understood.

**But contrary to this:** Intelligible species are related to the intellect in the way that sensible species are related to the sensory power. But a sensible species is *that by which* (*id quo*) the sensory power senses and not *that which* (*illud quod*) is sensed. Therefore, the intelligible species is *that by which* the intellect understands intellectively and not *that which* (*quod*) is understood.

**I respond:** Some have claimed that the cognitive powers that exist in us have cognition of nothing except what they receive within themselves (*nihil nisi proprias passiones*); for instance, they claim that a sensory power senses only what is received in its corresponding organ (*passionem sui organi*). On this view, the intellect has intellective understanding of nothing except what is received within itself, i.e., the intelligible species received within it (*nisi suam passionem, idest speciem intelligibilem in se receptam*). Accordingly, this sort of species is itself what is understood.

However, there are two reasons why this opinion is manifestly false.

First, the things we have intellective understanding of are the same things that scientific knowledge is about. Therefore, if the things we have intellective understanding of were just the species that exist in the soul, then it would follow that all types of scientific knowledge are not about things that exist outside the soul, but only about the intelligible species that exist within the soul—just as, according to the Platonists, all types of scientific knowledge are about the ideas, which they claimed to be the things which are actually understood.

Second, this would entail the error of those ancients who claimed that "whatever seems to be the case is true," with the result that contradictories would be simultaneously true. For if a power has cognition only of what it receives within itself (*non cognoscit nisi propriam passionem*), then that is all it makes judgments about. But something seems to be the case insofar as the cognitive power is affected in a given way. Therefore, the cognitive power's judgment will always be a judgment about what it itself receives as such (*de propria passione, secundum quod est*); and so every judgment will be true. For instance, if the sense of taste senses only what it itself receives, then when someone with a healthy sense of taste judges that honey is sweet, he will be judging correctly; and, similarly, when someone with a diseased sense of taste judges that honey is bitter, he will be judging correctly. For each of them judges in accord with how his own sense of taste is affected. And so it follows that every opinion—and, in general, every instance of accepting a proposition (*omnis acceptio*)— will be equally true.

Therefore, one should reply instead that an intelligible species is related to the intellect as *that by which* (*quo*) the intellect has intellective understanding. This is made clear as follows:

As *Metaphysics* 9 says, there are two kinds of action, one of which *remains within the agent* (*manet in agente*), e.g., seeing and understanding intellectively, and the other of which *passes into an exterior thing* (*transit in rem exteriorem*), e.g., heating and cutting. Both kinds of action stem from some form. And just as the form from which an action tending toward an exterior thing arises is a likeness of the action's object—in the way that a heating agent's heat is a likeness of the thing that is made hot (*ut calor calefacientis est similitudo calefacti*)—so, similarly, the form from which an action remaining within the agent arises is a likeness of the object. Thus, the likeness of a visible thing is that in virtue of which the power of sight sees, and the likeness of a thing that is understood, i.e., the intelligible species, is the form in virtue of which the intellect has intellective understanding.

However, since the intellect reflects upon itself (*supra seipsum reflectit*), it is by the same act of reflection (*secundum eandem reflexionem*) that it understands both its own act of intellective understanding (*suum intelligere*) and the species by which it understands intellectively (*speciem qua intelligit*). And so the intellective species is in a secondary sense that which is understood intellectively. But that which is understood intellectively in the primary sense is the thing of which the intelligible species is a likeness.

This point is also made clear by the opinion of the ancients, who claimed that like is known by like. For they claimed that it is through the element earth that exists within the soul that the soul has cognition of the element earth as it exists outside the soul—and so on for the other elements. Therefore, if we substitute the intelligible species of the element earth for the element itself—in accord with the teaching of Aristotle, who said that "it is not a rock, but the species of a rock that exists within the soul"—then it will follow that it is by means of intelligible species that the soul has cognition of things that exist outside the soul.

**Reply to objection 1:** It is through its likeness that the thing which is being understood intellectively exists in the who is engaged in understanding. The sense in which it is said that a thing which is actually being understood is the intellect itself insofar as it is acting, is that a likeness of the thing which is being understood is the form of the intellect in the same way that the likeness of a sensible thing is the form of a sensory power that is acting. Hence, it does not follow that the abstracted intelligible species is the thing which is actually being understood; rather, what follows is that the abstracted intelligible species is a *likeness* of the thing which is actually being understood.

**Reply to objection 2:** When one says 'a thing which is actually being understood' (*intellectum in actu*), there are two things implied, viz., (a) the thing which is being understood and (b) the very fact of its being understood. Similarly, when one says 'the abstracted universal', there are two things implied, viz., (a) the nature itself of the thing and (b) its abstractness or universality.

Therefore, the nature which happens to be understood intellectively or to be abstracted, or to which the intention of universality accrues, does not itself exist except in singular things; but the intention of universality, or the very fact of the nature's being understood or abstracted exists in the intellect.

We can see this by a comparison with a sensory power. For the power of sight sees the color of an apple without seeing its smell. Therefore, if someone asked where the color is that is seen without the smell, it is obvious that the color which is seen exists only in the apple; however, the fact that it is perceived without its smell accrues to it because of the power of sight, since within the power of sight there exists a likeness of its color but not of its smell.

Similarly, the human-ness (*humanitas*) that is understood intellectively exists only in this or that man; but the fact that human-ness is apprehended without individual conditions—i.e., the fact that human-ness is abstracted, and that an intention of universality results from this—happens to human-ness insofar as it is perceived by the intellect, in which there is a likeness of the nature of the species without a likeness of the individual principles.

**Reply to objection 3:** There are two types of operation in the sentient part of the soul. One involves just [the sensory power's] *being affected* (*immutatio*), and on this score the sensory power's operation is perfected by its being affected by the sensible thing. The second operation is [the sensory power's] *being formed* (*formatio*), insofar as the power of imagining forms for itself an image (*idolum*) of an absent thing or even of a thing that has never been seen.

These two types of operation are joined together in the intellect. For the first thing to consider is the passive intellect's being acted upon insofar as it is informed by the intelligible species (*passio intellectus possibilis secundum quod informatur specie intelligibili*). Once it is formed by the intelligible species, it forms, in the second place, a definition or composition or division that is signified by spoken words.

Hence, the concept (*ratio*) that the spoken name (*nomen*) signifies is the definition. And the spoken sentence (*enuntiatio*) signifies the intellect's composition or division. Thus, it is not the case that spoken words signify the intelligible species themselves; instead, they signify the things that the intellect forms for itself in order to make its judgments about exterior things (*ea quae intellectus sibi format ad iudicandum de rebus exterioribus*).

## Article 3

### Is what is more universal prior in our intellective cognition?

It seems that what is more universal is not prior in our intellective cognition (*magis universalia non sint priora in nostra cognitione intellectuali*):

**Objection 1:** What is prior and better known by its nature (*secundum naturam*) is posterior and less well known as far as we are concerned (*secundum nos*). But universals are prior and better known by their nature, since "what is prior is such that there is no valid inference from it [to what is posterior] with respect to subsistence." Therefore, universals are posterior in our intellect's cognition.

**Objection 2:** Composites are prior to simples as far as we are concerned. But universals are more simple. Therefore, they are known later as far as we are concerned.

**Objection 3:** In *Physics* 1 the Philosopher says that, in our cognition, what is defined comes earlier than the parts of the definition. But the parts of a definition of what is less universal are more universal; e.g., *animal* is part of the definition of *man*. Therefore, universals are known later as far as we are concerned.

**Objection 4:** It is through effects that we arrive at causes and principles. But universals are a sort of principle. Therefore, universals are known later as far as we are concerned.

**But contrary to this:** *Physics* 1 says, "One must descend (*oportet devenire*) from universals to singulars."

**I respond:** In our intellect's cognition there are two things that have to be taken in account.

The first is that intellective cognition in some sense takes its origin from sentient cognition. And since the sensory power deals with singulars and the intellect with universals, it must be the case that, as far as we are concerned, the cognition of singulars is prior to the cognition of universals.

The second thing that has to be taken into account is that our intellect proceeds from potentiality to actuality. But everything that proceeds from potentiality to actuality first arrives at an incomplete actuality, which lies between the potentiality and the actuality, before arriving at perfect actuality. Now the perfect actuality at which the intellect arrives is *complete scientific knowledge* (*scientia completa*), through which it has a distinct and determinate cognition of things. And the incomplete actuality is *imperfect scientific knowledge* (*scientia imperfecta*), through which things are known indistinctly with a sort of murkiness (*indistincte sub quadam confusione*); for what is known in this way is known in some respect in actuality and in some sense in potentiality. Hence, in *Physics* 1 the Philosopher says, "What is first manifest and certain to us are things that are somewhat indistinct (*confusa*), but later on, by drawing distinctions, we come to have distinct cognition of principles and elements." And it is clear that to have cognition of something that contains many things without having a proper knowledge of each of the things contained in it is for our cognition of it to be somewhat indistinct. And it is possible for us to have this sort of indistinct cognition both of a *universal whole*, which contains its parts in potentiality, and also of an *integral whole*, since it is possible for there to be an indistinct cognition of both kinds of whole in the absence of a distinct cognition of the parts.

Now to have a distinct cognition of what is contained in a *universal whole* is to have a cognition of something less general (*de re minus communi*) than it. For instance, to have an indistinct cognition of an animal is to have a cognition of the animal insofar as it is an animal, whereas to have a distinct cognition of an animal is to have a cognition of the animal insofar as it is a rational animal or a non-rational animal—e.g., to have a cognition of it as a man or a lion.

Thus, what happens is that our intellect has the cognition *animal* prior to having the cognition *man*, and the same line of reasoning holds whenever we are comparing something more universal to something less universal. And since the sensory power goes from potentiality to actuality in the same way that the intellect does, this same order of cognition is evident in the case of the sensory power as well. For in accord with the sensory power, we judge what is more general prior to what is less general, both with respect to place and with respect to time. For instance, with respect to place, when something is seen from afar, it is perceived to be a body before it is perceived to be an animal, and it is perceived to be an animal before it is perceived to be a man, and it is perceived to be a man before it is perceived to be Socrates or Plato. Again, with respect to time, at the beginning a young child distinguishes a man from a non-man before distinguishing *this* man from *that* man; this is why, as *Physics* 1 points out, "at the beginning young children call all men 'father', whereas later on they mark each man as distinct (*determinant unumquemque*)."

The reason for this is clear. If someone knows something indistinctly, he is still in potentiality with respect to knowing a principle of division (*principium distinctionis*); for instance, someone who knows the genus is in potentiality with respect to knowing the specific differences. And so it is clear that indistinct cognition lies between potentiality and actuality.

Therefore, one should claim that, as far as we are concerned, the cognition of singulars is prior to the cognition of universals in the sense that sentient cognition is prior to intellective cognition. However, with respect to both the sensory power and the intellect, cognition that is more general (*communis*) is prior to cognition that is less general.

**Reply to objection 1:** A universal can be considered in two ways:

First, insofar as the universal nature is considered along with the intention of universality. Since the intention of universality, viz., one and the same thing's having a relation to many, arises from the intellect's act of abstracting (*proveniat ex abstractione intellectus*), the universal must be posterior when considered in this way. Hence, *De Anima* 1 says, "Either the universal *animal* is nothing or else it is posterior." By contrast, according to Plato, who posited subsistent universals, the universal, when considered in this first way, would be prior to the particular, which, on his view, exists only through participation in those subsistent universals that are called 'ideas'.

The second way in which a universal can be considered is with respect to the nature itself, e.g., *animal-ness* or *human-ness*, insofar as it is found in the particulars. When the universal is considered in this way, one should say that there are two orderings of nature:

The first is the *path of generation and time* (*via generationis et temporis*), and on this path the things that are imperfect and in potentiality are prior. In this sense, what is more general is prior in nature. This is obvious in the generation of man and animal; for "the animal is generated prior to the man," as *De Generatione Animalium* puts it.

The second is the *ordering of perfection* (*ordo perfectionis*), or the *ordering of nature's intention* (*ordo intentionis naturae*), in the sense that actuality is absolutely speaking prior in nature to potentiality, and the perfect is absolutely speaking prior in nature to the imperfect. Given this ordering, the less general is prior in nature to the more general, e.g., *man* is prior in nature to *animal*. For nature's intention does not stop at the generation of the animal; instead, nature tends toward generating the man.

**Reply to objection 2:** The more general universal is related to the less general universal as both a whole and a part:

As a whole, in the sense that the more universal contains in potentiality not only the less universal but other things as well. For instance, it is not only *man*, but also *horse*, that is contained under *animal*.

As a part, in the sense that in its definition (*ratio*) the less general contains not only the more general, but other things as well. For instance, *man* contains not only *animal*, but also *rational*.

So, then, considered in itself, *animal* is prior in our cognition to *man*, but *man* is prior in our cognition to *animal*'s being a part of the definition of man.

**Reply to objection 3:** There are two ways in which to have a cognition of a part:

First, *absolutely speaking*, according to what the part is in its own right. And in this sense nothing prevents there being a cognition of the parts prior to the cognition of the whole—e.g., a cognition of the rocks prior to a cognition of the house.

Second, *insofar as they are parts of this whole*. And in this sense it is necessary for us to have a cognition of the whole before a cognition of the parts; for instance, we first have a cognition of the house by means of an indistinct cognition, before we distinguish each of its parts from the others.

So, then, one should reply that the parts of a definition (*definientia*), *considered absolutely*, are known before that which is defined. Otherwise, what is defined would not be made known to us through those parts. On the other hand, *insofar as they are the parts of the definition*, they are known after what is defined; for instance, we know *man* in a sort of indistinct cognition before we know how to distinguish everything that belongs to the definition of *man*.

**Reply to objection 4:** Insofar as a universal is taken together with *the intention of universality*, it is in some sense a principle of cognition, since the intention of universality follows upon that mode of intellective understanding that occurs through abstraction. However, it is not the case that, as Plato thought, everything that is a principle of cognition has to be a principle of being; for sometimes we have cognition of a cause through its effect and of a substance through its accidents. Hence, according to

Aristotle, the universal, taken in this way, is neither a principle of being nor a substance; this is clear from *Metaphysics* 7.

On the other hand, if we consider the nature of the genus and the nature of the species (*natura generis et speciei*) *insofar as they exist in singulars*, then the universal taken in this way has the character of a formal principle with respect to the singulars; for something is singular because of the matter, whereas the nature of the species (*ratio speciei*) is taken from the form. However, the nature of the genus is related to the nature of the species more in the manner of a material principle, since the nature of the genus (*natura generis*) is taken from what is material in the thing, whereas the nature of the species (*ratio speciei*) is taken from what is formal; for instance, the notion (*ratio*) *animal* is taken from the sentient, whereas the notion *man* is taken from the intellective. And the reason why nature's ultimate intention is directed toward the species and not toward the individual or toward the genus is that the form is the end of generation, whereas the matter exists for the sake of the form.

However, it is not necessary for every cognition of a cause or principle to be posterior as far as we are concerned, since sometimes we come to a cognition of unknown effects through their sensible causes, and sometimes vice versa.

## Article 4

### Can we have an intellective understanding of many things at once?

It seems that we can have an intellective understanding of many things at once:

**Objection 1:** The intellect lies beyond time (*est supra tempus*). But *before* (*prior*) and *after* (*posterior*) have to do with time. Therefore, the intellect understands diverse things at once and not according to *before* and *after*.

**Objection 2:** Nothing prevents diverse forms that are not opposed to one another from actually existing in the same thing at the same time, in the way that a smell and a color exist in an apple. But intelligible species are not opposed to one another. Therefore, nothing prevents a single intellect from coming into act with respect to diverse intelligible species simultaneously, and in this way it can have an intellective understanding of many things at once.

**Objection 3:** The intellect has an intellective understanding of a whole, such as a man or a house, all at once. But many parts are contained in a whole. Therefore, the intellect can have an intellective understanding of many things at once.

**Objection 4:** As *De Anima* says, one cannot have a cognition of the difference between one thing and another without apprehending both of them at the same time; and the same line of reasoning holds for any comparison whatsoever. But our intellect has cognition of the differences between one thing and another, and of comparisons between one thing and another. Therefore, it has a cognition of many things at once.

**But contrary to this:** *Topics* says, "Intellective understanding is of one thing only, but scientific knowledge is of many things."

**I respond:** The intellect can have an intellective understanding of many things in the manner of one thing (*per modum unius*), but not in the manner of many things (*per modum multorum*)—and by 'in the manner of one thing (or many things)' I mean through one (or many) intelligible species. For the mode of an action follows upon the form that is the principle of that action.

On the other hand, if certain things are such that the intellect can understand them under a single intelligible species, then it can understand them all at once. For the reason why God sees all things at once is that He sees all things through one thing, viz., His own essence.

However, if certain things are such that the intellect understands them through diverse intelligible species, then it does not understand them all at once. The reason for this is that it is impossible for a subject to be perfected all at once by several forms that belong to the same genus but different species; for instance, it is impossible for the same body to be simultaneously colored in the same respect by diverse colors, or for it to have diverse shapes. But all intelligible species belong to one genus, since they are perfections of a single intellective power, even though the things that they are the species of belong to diverse genera. Therefore, it is impossible for a single intellect to be perfected all at once by diverse intelligible species in such a way as to have an actual intellective understanding of diverse things.

**Reply to objection 1:** The intellect lies beyond the time that measures the motion of corporeal things. But the plurality of intelligible species causes an alternation of intelligible operations (*quandam vicissitudinem intelligibilium operationum*), in accord with which one operation occurs before another. In *Super Genesim ad Litteram* 8 Augustine calls this alternation 'time' when he says, "God moves the spiritual creature through time."

**Reply to objection 2:** It is not only forms which are opposites that cannot exist all at once in the same subject; neither can forms of the same genus, even if they are not opposites. This is clear from the example adduced above about colors and shapes.

**Reply to objection 3:** Parts can be thought of in two ways:

First, they can be thought of with a certain *indistinctness* insofar as they exist in the whole, in which case they are being thought of through the single form of the whole and so are being thought of all at once.

Second, they can be thought of by a *distinct* cognition insofar as each is thought of through its own intelligible species, in which case they cannot all be understood intellectively at once.

**Reply to objection 4:** When the intellect understands a distinction between two things or a comparison of the one to the other, it has a cognition of the two distinct things, or of the two things being compared, under the notion *comparison* or *distinction* itself—just as it was claimed above that the intellect has a cognition of the parts under the notion *whole*.

## Article 5

### Does our intellect engage in intellective understanding by composing and dividing?

It seems that our intellect does not engage in intellective understanding by composing and dividing (*non intelligat componendo et dividendo*):

**Objection 1:** Composition and division [of subject and predicate] always involve many items. But the intellect cannot have an intellective understanding of many things at once. Therefore, the intellect cannot engage in intellective understanding by composing and dividing.

**Objection 2:** Either the present tense, the past tense, or the future tense (*tempus praesens, praeteritum vel futurum*) is adjoined to every composition and division. But the intellect abstracts from time, just as it abstracts from other particular conditions. Therefore, the intellect does not engage in intellective understanding by composing and dividing.

**Objection 3:** The intellect engages in intellective understanding by assimilating itself to the things (*per assimilationem ad res*). But there is no composition or division [of subject and predicate] among the things; for among the things there is nothing except what is signified by the predicate and by the subject—and this is one and the same thing if the composition is true. For a man is truly that which is an animal. Therefore, the intellect does not compose and divide.

**But contrary to this:** As the Philosopher says in *Perihermenias* 1, spoken words signify the intellect's conceptions (*conceptiones intellectus*). But in spoken language there is composition and division, as is clear in the case of affirmative and negative propositions (*in propositionibus affirmativis et negativis*). Therefore, the intellect composes and divides.

**I respond:** It is necessary for the human intellect to engage in intellective understanding by composing and dividing. For since the human intellect passes from potentiality into actuality, it has a certain likeness to generable things, which do not have their perfection immediately, but instead acquire it successively. In the same way, the human intellect does not immediately come to a perfect cognition of a thing in its first apprehension of it. Instead, it first apprehends an aspect of it (*aliquid de ipsa*), viz., the 'what-ness' (*quidditas*) of the thing itself, which is the first and proper object of the intellect; and then it comes to understand the properties, accidents, and relations associated with the thing's essence (*circumstantes rei essentiam*). Accordingly, it must necessarily (a) compose one apprehended thing with another or divide one apprehended thing from another and (b) proceed from one composition or division to another, i.e., reason discursively (*ratiocinari*).

By contrast, the angelic intellect and the divine intellect are incorruptible beings that have their total perfection immediately from the beginning. Hence, the angelic intellect and the divine intellect are immediately in perfect possession of a complete cognition of a thing. Thus, in having a cognition of a thing's 'what-ness', they have, with respect to that thing, an immediate cognition of whatever we ourselves can come to a cognition of by composing and dividing and reasoning discursively.

And so the human intellect engages in intellective cognition by composing and dividing, as well as by reasoning discursively. By contrast, the divine intellect and the angelic intellect do, to be sure, have a cognition of composition and division and discursive reasoning; however, they have this cognition not by themselves composing or dividing or reasoning discursively, but instead through an intellective understanding of their simple 'what-ness' (*quidditas*).

**Reply to objection 1:** The intellect's composing and dividing are effected through a sort of comparison or contrast. Hence, the sense in which the intellect, in composing and dividing, has a cognition of many things is the same sense in which it has a cognition of contrasts or comparisons between things.

**Reply to objection 2:** As was explained above (a. 1 and q. 84, a. 7), the intellect abstracts from phantasms, and yet it does not have actual intellective understanding except by turning itself back to the phantasms. And it is because the intellect turns itself back to the phantasms that tense is adjoined to the intellect's compositions and divisions.

**Reply to objection 3:** The likeness of a thing is received into the intellect according to the intellect's own mode and not according to the mode of the thing. Hence, even though there is something on the part of the thing that corresponds to the intellect's composition and division, it is not present in the thing in the same way that it is present in the intellect. For the proper object of the human intellect is the 'what-ness' (*quidditas*) of a material thing that falls under the sensory power and imagination.

Now there are two sorts of composition found in a material thing:

The first is the composition of *form* with respect to *matter*, and the intellect's composition corresponds to this sort of composition by a universal whole's being predicated of its part. For the genus is taken from the common matter, whereas the difference that completes the species is taken from the form, and the particular is taken from the material individual.

The second sort of composition is the composition of an *accident* with respect to its *subject*, and the intellect's composition corresponds to this sort of real composition by an accident's being predicated of its subject, as when one says, 'The man is white'.

On the other hand, the intellect's composition differs from the thing's composition by the fact that the items composed in the thing are diverse from one another, whereas the intellect's composition is a sign of the identity of the items that are composed. For the intellect does not compose in such a way as to affirm that the man is the whiteness (*homo est albedo*); rather, it composes in such a way as to affirm that the man is white, i.e., that the man is a thing that has the whiteness (*homo est albus, id est habens albedinem*). For that which is the man is the same subject as that which has the whiteness.

Something similar holds for the composition of form and matter. For 'animal' signifies that which has a sentient nature, 'rational' signifies that which has an intellective nature, and 'man' signifies that which has both a sentient nature and an intellective nature. But Socrates has all these things along with a material individual. And it is according to this notion of identity that our intellect composes one thing with another by predicating.

## Article 6

### Is there falsity in the intellect?

It seems that there can be falsity in the intellect (*intellectus possit esse falsus*):

**Objection 1:** In *Metaphysics* 6 the Philosopher says, "The true and the false exist in the mind." But as was explained above (q. 79), the mind and the intellect are the same thing. Therefore, there is falsity in the intellect.

**Objection 2:** Opinion and discursive reasoning belong to the intellect. But falsity is found in both of them. Therefore, there can be falsity in the intellect.

**Objection 3:** Sin exists in the intellective part of the soul. But sin is accompanied by falsity, since, as Proverbs 14:22 says, "Those err who work evil." Therefore, falsity can exist in the intellect.

**But contrary to this:** In *83 Quaestiones* Augustine says, "Everyone who makes a mistake fails to understand intellectively that which he is mistaken about." And in *De Anima* the Philosopher says, "Intellective understanding is always correct (*intellectus semper est rectus*)."

**I respond:** In *De Anima* 3 the Philosopher compares the intellect to the sensory power on the point at issue here. For the sensory power is not deceived with respect to its proper object; for instance, the power of sight is not deceived about color, except perhaps incidentally (*per accidens*) because of an impediment involving the organ—as when a feverish man's sense of taste judges sweet things as bitter because his tongue is full of bad humors.

In the case of the common sensibles, however, the sensory power makes mistakes in judging about size or shape, as when it judges that the sun is the size of a human foot, even though it is larger than the earth. Moreover, the sensory power makes many more mistakes with respect to things that are sensible *per accidens*, as when it judges that vinegar is honey because of a similarity in their color. The reason for this is clear. Each power is, as such, ordered *per se* toward its proper object, and things of this sort always behave in the same way. Hence, as long as the power remains, its judgment does not fail with respect to its proper object.

Now the proper object of the intellect is the 'what-ness' (*quidditas*) of a thing. Hence, with respect to the 'what-ness' of a thing the intellect does not make mistakes, speaking *per se*. But with respect to what accompanies a thing's essence or 'what-ness', the intellect can be mistaken when it relates one thing to another, either by composing or by dividing or by reasoning discursively.

For this reason, it is also the case that the intellect cannot err with respect to those propositions that it has an immediate cognition of once it has a cognition of the 'what-ness' of their terms. This occurs in the case of first principles, from which an infallibility of truth also arises, and in the case of conclusions in accord with the certitude of scientific knowledge. Still, it happens incidentally (*per accidens*) that the intellect is mistaken about what something is in the case of composite things. This is not because of any [bodily] organ, since the intellect is not a power that uses an organ; rather, it is because of compositions that intervene with respect to the definition in cases where either the definition of one thing is applied falsely to another thing, e.g., the definition of a circle is applied to a triangle, or when the definition is false in itself and implies an impossible composition, as would occur if, say, *rational animal with wings* were taken to be the definition of some entity.

Hence, in the case of simple things, where no composition can intervene in their definitions, we cannot be mistaken; rather, as *Metaphysics* 9 says, in such cases we are mistaken when we totally fail to grasp them (*deficimus in totaliter non attingendo*).

**Reply to objection 1:** The Philosopher is claiming that falsity exists in the mind with respect to composition and division.

**Reply to objection 2:** In this second objection, he is saying the same thing about opinion and discursive reasoning.

**Reply to objection 3:** As for the error of sinners, this consists in an application with respect to something desirable. However, the intellect is never deceived in its absolute consideration of the 'what-ness' of a thing and of those things that we have cognition of through the 'what-ness'. And this is what the passages [from Augustine and the Philosopher] that are adduced for the contrary position are talking about.

### Article 7

#### Can someone understand one and the same thing better than someone else does?

It seems that it cannot be the case that someone understands one and the same thing better (*melius*) than someone else does:

**Objection 1:** In *83 Quaestiones* Augustine says, "If anyone understands (*intelligit*) a thing to be otherwise than it is, then he does not understand (*intelligit*) it at all. Therefore, there is no doubt that there is a perfect understanding, unsurpassable in excellence. And so there are not infinitely many degrees of understanding a given thing; nor can one man understand it more (*plus*) than another."

**Objection 2:** When the intellect has intellective understanding, it has truth. But since truth is a sort of equality (*aequalitas quaedam*) between the intellect and the thing, it does not admit of more and less, since it is not proper to say that something is more equal or less equal. Therefore, neither is it proper to say that something is more understood or less understood intellectively.

**Objection 3:** The intellect is the most formal aspect of a man. But a difference in form causes a difference in species. Therefore, if one man has greater understanding than another man (*si unus homo magis alio intelligit*), it seems that they do not belong to the same species.

**But contrary to this:** Our experience indicates that some understand more deeply (*profundius*) than others; for instance, someone who can trace a conclusion back to its first principles and first causes understands it more deeply than someone who is able to trace it back only to its proximate causes.

**I respond:** There are two ways to interpret what it means for someone to understand one and the same thing more (*magis*) than someone else does.

On the first interpretation, 'more' modifies the act of intellective understanding *on the part of the thing that is understood*. And on this interpretation, it is not possible for someone to understand the very same thing more than someone else, since if he understood it to be otherwise than it is—whether better than it is or worse—he would be mistaken and, as Augustine argues, would not understand it at all.

On the second interpretation, 'more' determines the act of intellective understanding *on the part of the one who is engaged in understanding*. And on this interpretation, someone can understand the same thing better than someone else, in virtue of having more power of understanding—in the same way that someone who has a more perfect power and in whom the visual power is more perfect sees a given thing better by a corporeal act of seeing than someone else does.

There are two ways in which this occurs in the case of the intellect:

One way is on the part of the intellect itself, when it is more perfect.

For it is clear that to the extent that the body is better disposed, the soul is better. This is manifestly obvious in the case of beings that are diverse in species. The reason is that actuality and form are received into matter in accord with the matter's capacity. Hence, since even among men there are those who have a body that is better disposed, they receive a soul that has a greater power of intellective understanding. Hence, *De Anima* 2 says, "We notice that those with soft flesh are more mentally gifted."

The second way is on the part of the lower powers that the intellect needs for its own operation. For those in whom the power of imagining and the cognitive power and the power of remembering are better disposed are better disposed for intellective understanding.

**Reply to objection 1:** The reply to the first objection is obvious from what has been said.

**Reply to objection 2:** The same holds for the second objection. For the truth of the intellect consists in the thing's being understood intellectively as it is.

**Reply to objection 3:** A difference of form that arises only from the different dispositions of the matter makes for a diversity only in number and not in species. For diverse individuals have diverse forms that are diversified according to the matter.

## Article 8

### Does our intellect have cognition of what is indivisible prior to what is divisible?

It seems that our intellect has cognition of what is indivisible prior to what is divisible:

**Objection 1:** In *Physics* 1 the Philosopher says, "We have intellective understanding and scientific knowledge on the basis of our cognition of principles and elements." But indivisibles are the principles and elements of what is divisible. Therefore, indivisibles are known to us prior to what is divisible.

**Objection 2:** That which is posited in a thing's definition is such that we have a prior cognition of it, since, as *Topics* 6 says, a definition comes "from what is prior and more known." But indivisibles are posited in the definition of what is divisible; for instance, as Euclid says, "A line is a length without breadth whose extremities are two points." And oneness is posited in the definition of number, since, as *Metaphysics* 10 says, "Number is a multitude measured by *one*." Therefore, our intellect understands the indivisible prior to the divisible.

**Objection 3:** Cognition is by means of what is similar. But what is indivisible is more similar to the intellect than what is divisible, since, as *De Anima* 3 says, "The intellect is something simple." Therefore, our intellect first has a cognition of what is indivisible.

**But contrary to this:** *De Anima* 3 says, "What is indivisible is shown to be a privation." But a privation is known later. Therefore, what is indivisible is known later as well.

**I respond:** As is clear from what has gone before (a. 1 and q. 84, a. 7), in the state of the present life the object of our intellect is the 'what-ness' of a material thing, which the intellect abstracts from the phantasm. And since a cognitive power's proper object is that which it has cognition of in the first place and *per se*, the order in which we have intellective understanding of the indivisible can be thought about in terms of the indivisible's relation to a 'what-ness' of the sort in question.

Now as *De Anima* 3 says, 'indivisible' is used in three senses:

In one sense, a continuum is indivisible by virtue of the fact that it is actually undivided, even though it is divisible in potentiality. The indivisible in this sense is understood by us prior to its division into parts, since as was explained above (a. 3), an indistinct cognition is prior to a distinct cognition.

In a second sense, something is indivisible by its species, in the way that a man's reason is something indivisible. And in this sense, too, the indivisible is understood prior to its division into the parts of reason, as was explained above (a. 3), and likewise prior to the intellect's composing and dividing by affirming or negating.

The reason for this is that the intellect in its own right understands indivisibles of these two sorts as its proper object.

In a third sense, what is indivisible is altogether indivisible—e.g., a point (*punctus*) and oneness (*unitas*), which are divided neither in actuality nor in potentiality. And the indivisible in this sense is understood in a posterior way through the privation of divisibility (*per privationem divisibilis*). Hence, a point is defined by a privation (*privative*): A point is that which has no parts. Similarly, the definition of *one* is that which is not divisible, as *Metaphysics* 10 says. The reason is that an indivisible in this sense has a certain sort of opposition to a corporeal thing, whose 'what-ness' is what the intellect grasps in the first place and *per se*.

However, if, as the Platonists claimed, our intellect had intellective understanding by participating in separated indivisibles, then it would follow that what is indivisible in this third sense would be understood first. For according to the Platonists, things participate first in what is prior.

**Reply to objection 1:** In the acquisition of scientific knowledge, it is not always the principles and elements that are prior, since sometimes we go from sensible effects to a cognition of intelligible principles and causes.

On the other hand, in fully completed scientific knowledge (*in complemento scientiae*), the knowledge of the effects always depends on the cognition of principles and elements. For as the Philosopher says in the same place, "We are thought to have scientific knowledge when we are able to resolve what is derived from the principles into its causes."

**Reply to objection 2:** 'Point' does not occur in the commonly accepted definition of a line, since it is obvious that in an infinite line, or even in a circular line, there are no points except in potentiality. However, Euclid is here defining a finite straight line, and so he posits 'point' in the definition of a line in the way that a terminus occurs in the definition of what it terminates.

Oneness (*unitas*), on the other hand, is the measure of number and so occurs in the definition of a number that is measured. It does not, however, have a place in the definition of the divisible; instead, just the opposite occurs.

**Reply to objection 3:** The likeness through which we have intellective understanding is the species of what we have cognition of that exists in the one who understands. And so it is not because of the likeness of a nature to the cognitive power that something is understood first; rather it is because of the cognitive power's agreement with the object. Otherwise, the power of seeing would have cognition of the sense of hearing rather than of color.

# QUESTION 86

## What Our Intellect Has Cognition of in Material Things

Next we have to consider what our intellect understands in material things. And on this topic there are four questions: (1) Does our intellect have cognition of singulars? (2) Does our intellect have cognition of infinitely many things? (3) Does our intellect have cognition of contingent things? (4) Does our intellect have cognition of future things?

## Article 1

### Does our intellect have cognition of singulars?

It seems that our intellect has cognition of singulars (*cognoscat singularia*):

**Objection 1:** If someone has cognition of a composition, then he has cognition of the terms (*extrema*) of the composition. But our intellect has cognition of the composition 'Socrates is a man'; for it is the intellect's role to form a proposition. Therefore, our intellect has cognition of the singular thing that is Socrates.

**Objection 2:** The practical intellect directs one in acting. But acts have to do with singulars. Therefore, the intellect has cognition of singulars.

**Objection 3:** Our intellect has an intellective understanding of itself. But the intellect is itself a singular; otherwise, it would not have any acts at all, since acts belong to singular things. Therefore, our intellect has cognition of something singular.

**Objection 4:** A higher power is capable of whatever a lower power is capable of. But the sensory power has cognition of singulars. Therefore, *a fortiori*, so does the intellect.

**But contrary to this:** In *Physics* 1 the Philosopher says, "The universal is known in accord with reason (*secundum rationem*), the singular in accord with the sensory power (*secundum sensum*)."

**I respond:** Our intellect cannot have a direct and primary cognition of the singular in material things. The reason for this is that the principle of singularity in material things is individual matter (*materia individualis*), while, as was explained above (q. 85, a. 1), our intellect has intellective understanding by abstracting the intelligible species from individual matter. But it is the universal that is abstracted from individual matter.

Hence, our intellect has direct cognition only of the universals (*directe est cognoscitivus nisi universalium*).

However, our intellect can have cognition of the singular indirectly and, as it were, by a sort of turning back (*indirecte et quasi per quandam reflexionem*). For as was explained above (q. 84, a. 7), even after it has abstracted intelligible species, it cannot have actual intellective understanding except by turning itself to the phantasms, in which it has intellective understanding of the intelligible species, as *De Anima* 3 says.

So, then, our intellect understands the universal itself directly through the intelligible species, whereas it indirectly understands the singulars that the phantasms are phantasms of. And it is in this way that it forms the proposition 'Socrates is a man'.

**Reply to objection 1:** The reply to the first object is obvious from what was just said.

**Reply to objection 2:** As *Ethics* 7 puts it, the choice of a particular action (*electio particularis operabilis*) is, as it were, the conclusion of the practical intellect's syllogism. But a singular conclusion cannot be inferred directly from a universal proposition; rather, it is inferred by the mediation of some assumed singular proposition. Hence, as *De Anima* 3 says, the practical intellect's universal conception effects movement only through the mediation of a particular apprehension by the sentient part of the soul.

**Reply to objection 3:** The problem with a singular's being intelligible is not that it is *singular* but rather that it is *material*, since nothing is understood intellectively except in an immaterial mode. And so if a given singular, such as the intellect, is immaterial, there is no problem with its being intelligible (*hoc non repugnat intelligibilitati*).

**Reply to objection 4:** A higher power can do what a lower power does, but it does it in a more eminent way. Hence, what the sensory power has cognition of materially and concretely—which is what it is to have direct cognition of a singular—the intellect has cognition of immaterially and abstractly—which is what it is to have cognition of a universal.

### Article 2

#### Can our intellect have cognition of infinitely many things?

It seems that our intellect can have cognition of infinitely many things (*possit cognoscere infinita*):

**Objection 1:** God exceeds all infinities (*excedit omnia infinita*). But as was explained above (q. 12, a. 1), our intellect can have cognition of God. Therefore, *a fortiori*, our intellect can have cognition of all other infinities.

**Objection 2:** Our intellect is apt by nature to have cognition of genera and species. But some genera—e.g., *number*, *ratio*, and *shape*—have infinitely many species. Therefore, our intellect can have cognition of infinitely many things.

**Objection 3:** If one body did not prevent another body from being in one and the same place, then nothing would prevent infinitely many bodies from being in one place. But one intelligible species does not prevent another intelligible species from existing simultaneously in the same intellect, since it is possible to have habitual knowledge of many things (*multa scire in habitu*). Therefore, nothing prevents our intellect from having habitual knowledge of infinitely many things.

**Objection 4:** Since, as was explained above (q. 76, a. 1), our intellect is not a power that belongs to corporeal matter, it seems to be infinite in potentiality. But an infinite power ranges over infinitely many things (*virtus infinita potest super infinita*). Therefore, our intellect can have cognition of infinitely many things.

**But contrary to this:** *Physics* 1 says, "The infinite, insofar as it is infinite, is unknown."

**I respond:** Since a power is proportioned to its object, the intellect must be related to the infinite in the way that it is related to its object, viz., the 'what-ness' (*quidditas*) of a material thing. Now as *Physics* 3 explains, in material things there is no actual infinity (*infinitum in actu*), but only a potential infinity (*infinitum in potentia*) insofar as one thing succeeds another. And so a *potential infinity* is found in our intellect when it takes one thing after another, since our intellect never has an intellective understanding of so many things that it cannot have an intellective understanding of more things.

However, our intellect cannot have either an *actual* or a *habitual* cognition of infinitely many things.

Our intellect cannot have an *actual* cognition of infinitely many things, because it can have an actual cognition all at once only of that which it understands through a single species. But an infinity does not have a single species; otherwise, it would have the character of something total and complete. And so an infinity cannot be understood intellectively expect by taking one part after another. This is clear from the definition of an infinity given in *Physics* 3. For the infinite is "that which is such that when one takes a quantity from it, it is always possible to take more," and so it would be possible to have an actual cognition of an infinity only if all its parts were enumerated—which is impossible.

For the same reason, we cannot have a *habitual* intellective cognition of infinitely many things. For in our case a habitual cognition is caused by an actual thought, since as *Ethics* 2 says, it is by understanding intellectively that we become scientific knowers (*scientes*). Hence, we would not be able to have the habit of having a distinct cognition of infinitely many things unless we had thought of all the infinitely many things by enumerating them through a succession of cognitions—which is impossible.

And so our intellect cannot have either an actual or habitual cognition of infinitely many things; rather, as has been explained, it can have a cognition of infinitely many things only in potentiality.

**Reply to objection 1:** As was explained above (q. 7, a. 1), God is called infinite as a form that is not terminated by any *matter*, whereas among material things something is called infinite because of a lack of *formal* termination (*per privationem formalis terminationis*). And because form is known in its own right (*secundum se*), whereas matter without form is not known, it follows that a material infinite is unknown in its own right. By contrast, a formal infinite, i.e., God, is known in His own right (*notum secundum se*), but He is unknown as far as we are concerned (*ignotum quoad nos*) because of the weakness of our intellect, which in the state of the present life has a natural ability to understand material things. And so in our present state we cannot know God except through His material effects. However, in our future state this defect of our intellect will be removed by [the light of] glory, and at that time we will be able to see God Himself in His essence—though without comprehending Him.

**Reply to objection 2:** Our intellect is apt to have a cognition of species by abstracting them from phantasms. And so one cannot have either an actual or habitual cognition of those species of numbers or shapes which he has not imagined—except, perhaps, generically (*in genere*) and in their general principles, which is to understand them potentially and indistinctly.

**Reply to objection 3:** If two or more bodies were in one place, they would not have to enter that place successively in such a way that the located bodies would be enumerated by a succession of entrances. By contrast, intelligible species enter our intellect successively, since it is not the case that many of them are actually understood all at once. And so it is necessary for the species in our intellect to be numbered and not to be infinitely many.

**Reply to objection 4:** Our intellect has cognition of the infinite in the same sense in which it is infinite in power. For its power is infinite in the sense that it is not terminated by corporeal matter. And it has cognition of the universal, which is abstracted from the material individual, and, as a result, it is not terminated in any individual, but, as far it itself is concerned, it extends to infinitely many individuals.


## Article 3

### Does our intellect have cognition of contingent things?

It seems that our intellect does not have cognition of contingent things (*non sit cognoscitivus contingetium*):

**Objection 1:** As *Ethics* 6 says, understanding (*intellectus*), scientific knowledge (*scientia*), and wisdom (*sapientia*) have to do with necessary things and not contingent things.

**Objection 2:** As *Physics* 4 explains, "Things that exist at some times and not at others are measured by time." But the intellect abstracts from time in the same way that it abstracts from the other conditions of matter. Therefore, since it is a property of contingent things to exist at some times and not at others, it seems that our intellect cannot have cognition of contingent things.

**But contrary to this:** All scientific knowledge exists in the intellect. But some sciences have to do with contingent things—e.g., the moral sciences, which have to do with human acts subject to free choice, and the natural sciences, as regards that part of them which treats generable and corruptible things. Therefore, the intellect has cognition of contingent things.

**I respond:** Contingent things can be thought of in two ways: first, insofar as they are contingent and, second, insofar as something necessary is found in them. For nothing is contingent to such an extent that it has nothing necessary within itself. For instance, the very thing that is Socrates' running is, to be sure, contingent in itself, but the relation of running to movement is necessary, since it is necessary that Socrates is moving if he is running.

Each thing is contingent on the part of its matter. For the contingent is that which is able to be and able not to be, and potentiality has to do with matter. By contrast, necessity follows upon the nature of form, since what follows upon the form is in the thing by necessity. Matter is a principle of individuation, whereas the universal notion (*ratio universalis*) is obtained by the abstraction of the form from particular matter. It was explained above (a. 1) that the intellect has *per se* and direct cognition of universals and the sensory power has *per se* and direct cognition of singulars, which, as was said above (a. 1), are also understood intellectively in a certain indirect way.

So, then, contingent things, insofar as they are contingent, are such that the sensory power has direct cognition of them and the intellect has indirect cognition of them, whereas the intellect has cognition of the universal and necessary aspects of contingent things. Hence, if we attend to the universal aspects of knowable things, all scientific knowledge has to do with what is necessary. But if we attend to the things themselves, then some scientific knowledge has to do with necessary things and some has to do with contingent things.

**Reply to objection 1 and objection 2:** The reply to the objections is clear from what has been said.

## Article 4

### Does our intellect have cognition of future things?

It seems that our intellect has cognition of future things (*cognoscat futura*):

**Objection 1:** Our intellect has cognition through intelligible species, which abstract from the here and now, and so they are related indifferently to all times. But the intellect can have cognition of present things. Therefore, it can have cognition of future things.

**Objection 2:** When a man is bereft of his sensory powers, he is able to have cognition of some future things, as is clear in the case of those who are asleep and those who are delirious. But when someone is bereft of his sensory powers, his intellect becomes stronger. Therefore, the intellect, as far as it itself is concerned, has cognition of future things.

**Objection 3:** Man's intellective cognition is more efficacious than any sort of cognition on the part of brute animals. But there are certain animals that have cognition of some future things; for instance, crows that caw repeatedly signify that rain is coming soon. Therefore, *a fortiori*, the human intellect can have cognition of future things.

**But contrary to this:** Ecclesiastes 8:6–7 says, "There is a great affliction for man, because he is ignorant of things past; and things to come he cannot know by any messenger."

**I respond:** As with the cognition of contingent things, so in the same way we have to draw a distinction concerning the cognition of future things. For *insofar as they fall under a time*, future things are singulars, which, as was explained above (a. 1), the human intellect has cognition of only by turning back [to the phantasms] (*per reflexionem*). However, the *natures* of future things can be universal and perceptible by the intellect, and there can even be scientific knowledge of them.

Speaking in general about the cognition of future things, notice that there are two possible ways to have cognition of future things, viz., (a) *in themselves* and (b) *in their causes*.

Cognition of future things *in themselves* can be had only by God, to whom they are present even while they are future in the course of time; for as was explained above when we discussed God's knowledge (q. 14, a. 13), His eternal intuitive vision (*aeternus intuitus*) ranges over the whole course of time all at once.

However, even we can have cognition of future things insofar as they exist *in their causes*. And if they exist in their causes in such a way that they proceed from those causes with necessity, then our cognition has the certitude of scientific knowledge (*cognoscuntur per certitudinem scientiae*), as when an astronomer (*astrologus*) foreknows a future eclipse. On the other hand, if they exist in their causes in such a way that they proceed from those causes in most cases (*ut in pluribus*), then there can be cognition of them through a prediction that is more or less certain (*conjectura vel magis vel minus certa*), depending on whether the causes are more or less inclined toward the effects.

**Reply to objection 1:** This argument goes through for a cognition that involves the universal aspects of causes, on the basis of which there can be a cognition of future things that stems from the way in which an effect is ordered toward its cause (*secundum modum ordinis effectus ad causam*).

**Reply to objection 2:** As Augustine puts it in *Confessiones* 12, the soul has a certain power of prophecy, so that it is able, by its nature, to have cognition of future things; and so when it withdraws from the bodily senses and in a sense reverts to itself, it participates in the knowledge of future things.

And this opinion would indeed be reasonable if we held, as the Platonists do, that the soul receives its cognition of things by participating in the ideas. For in that case, if it were unimpeded by the body, the soul would by its nature have cognition of the universal causes of all effects. Hence, it knows future things when it is withdrawn from the body's senses.

However, since this mode of cognition is not connatural to our intellect, given that our intellect instead receives its cognition from the sensory powers, it follows that it is not because of the soul's nature that it has cognition of future things when it turns itself away from the senses, but rather because of the action of certain higher spiritual or corporeal causes (*per impressionem aliquarum causarum superiorum spiritualium et corporalium*).

Through *spiritual* causes, as when a human intellect is illuminated by God's power through the ministry of the angels and its phantasms are ordered toward the cognition of future things—or even, as was explained above (q. 57, a. 3), when through the action of demons there is a movement in the imagination toward foreknowing certain future things that the demons have cognition of. It is when it is turned away from the senses that the human soul is more susceptible to these impressions from spiritual causes; for in turning away from the senses it becomes more like the spiritual substances and more unimpeded by external disturbances.

This also happens through the action of higher *corporeal* causes. For it is clear that higher bodies act upon lower bodies. Hence, since the sentient powers are the acts of corporeal organs, it follows that the imagination is in some way affected by the action of the celestial bodies. Hence, since celestial bodies are a cause of many future things, certain signs of future things come to exist in the imagination. These signs are perceived more often at night and by those who are asleep than during the day and by those who are awake. For as *De Somno et Vigilia* says, "Impressions made by day more easily dissipate. The night air is calmer, because the nights are more silent. And within the body these impressions do the job of the sensory power because of sleep, since small interior movements are sensed more readily by those who are asleep than by those who are awake. And these movements produce phantasms, on the basis of which future things are foreseen."

**Reply to objection 3:** Brute animals do not have anything beyond the imagination to order their phantasms, in the way that men have reason. And so a brute animal's imagination is wholly led by the celestial impressions. Thus, some future things, like rain and others of this type, can be known better through movements of this sort in animals than through such movements in men, who are moved by the counsel of reason. Hence, in *De Somno et Vigilia* the Philosopher says, "Some extremely foolish men have the most foreknowledge. For their mind (*intelligentia*) is not affected by cares, but is, as it were, vacuous and empty of all anxiety and moves wherever it is led."

## How Our Intellect Has Cognition of Itself and of What Exists Within It

Next we have to consider how the intellective soul has cognition of itself and of what exists within it. And on this topic there are four questions: (1) Does the intellective soul have cognition of itself through its own essence? (2) How does it have cognition of the habits that exist within it? (3) How does the intellect have cognition of its own act? (4) How does it have cognition of an act of the will?

### Article 1

### Does the intellective soul have cognition of itself through its own essence?

It seems that the intellective soul has cognition of itself through its own essence:

**Objection 1:** In *De Trinitate* 9 Augustine says, "The mind knows itself through itself, because it is incorporeal."

**Objection 2:** An angel and a human soul share in the genus *intellectual substance*. But an angel has intellective understanding of himself through his own essence. Therefore, so does the human soul.

**Objection 3:** As *De Anima* 3 says, "In things that exist without matter, the intellect and what is understood are the same." But the human mind exists without matter, since, as was explained above (q. 76, a. 1), it is not the actuality of any body. Therefore, in the human mind the intellect and what is understood are the same. Therefore, it has intellective understanding of itself through its own essence.

**But contrary to this:** *De Anima* 3 says, "The intellect has intellective understanding of itself in the same way that it has intellective understanding of other things." But it has intellective understanding of other things through likenesses of those thing and not through their essence. Therefore, neither does it have intellective understanding of itself through its own essence.

**I respond:** As *Metaphysics* 9 says, each thing is such that there can be cognition of it insofar as it is actual and not insofar as it is potential. For something is a being and is true, i.e., falls under cognition, insofar as it is actual. This is manifestly obvious in the case of sensible things; for instance, the power of seeing perceives only what is actually colored and not what is potentially colored. Similarly, it is clear that insofar as the intellect has cognition of material things, it has cognition only of what is actual; and so, as *Physics* 1 says, the intellect does not have cognition of primary matter except in relation to form (*secundum proportionem ad formam*).

Hence, among immaterial substances, too, each of them bears the same relation to being intelligible through its essence that it bears to being actual through its essence.

Thus, God's essence, which is pure and perfect (*perfectus*) actuality, is simply and perfectly intelligible in its own right (*secundum seipsam*). Hence, it is through His essence that God has perfect intellective understanding not only of Himself but also of all things.

On the other hand, an angel's essence is, to be sure, in the genus of intelligible things as an actuality, but not as a pure and completely perfect (*completus*) actuality. Hence, an angel's act of intellective understanding (*eius intelligere*) is not completely perfected (*completur*) through his essence. For even though an angel has intellective cognition of himself through his essence, he nonetheless cannot have cognition of all things through his essence; instead, he has cognition of things other than himself through likenesses of those things.

By contrast, a human intellect is in the genus of intelligible things only as a being in potentiality, in the same way that primary matter is in the genus of sensible things; this is why the intellect is called the passive or potential intellect (*intellectus possibilis*) . Therefore, if the intellect is considered in its essence, it has intellective understanding in potentiality (*potentia intelligens*). Hence, of itself it has the power to have intellective understanding, but it is not itself understood intellectively except insofar as it becomes activated (*actu*).

On this score, the Platonists likewise held that the order of intelligible entities transcends the order of intellects; for the intellect has intellective understanding only through participation in what is intelligible, and, according to them, what participates is inferior to what it participates in. Therefore, if, as the Platonists held, the human intellect were activated (*fieret actu*) through participation in separated intelligible forms, then the human intellect would understand itself through this sort of participation in incorporeal things.

However, since, as was explained above (q. 86, a. 7), it is connatural to our intellect, in the state of the present life, to be directed toward material and sensible things, it follows that our intellect understands itself insofar as it is activated (*fit actu*) by species abstracted from sensible things through the light of the active intellect—and this is the actualization (*actus*) both of the intelligible things themselves and, through their mediation, of the passive intellect (*intellectus possibilis*).

Therefore, it is through its act, and not through its essence, that our intellect has cognition of itself. And this in two ways:

First, in a *particular* way (*particulariter*), insofar as Socrates or Plato perceives himself to have an intellective soul in virtue of the fact that he perceives himself to have intellective understanding.

Second, in a *general* way (*in universali*), insofar as we consider the nature of the human mind on the basis of the intellect's act. But, as was explained above (q. 84, a. 5), it is true that the discernment (*iudicium*) and efficacy of the cognition by which we grasp the nature of the soul belongs to us because of the derivation of our intellect's light from God's truth, in which the conceptions (*rationes*) of all things are contained. Hence, in *De Trinitate* 9 Augustine says, "We intuitively see (*intuemur*) inviolable truth, on the basis of which we perfectly define, as far as we are able to, not how each man's mind in fact is, but rather how it ought to be in light of the eternal conceptions."

However, there is a difference between these two types of cognition. For the mind's very presence, which is the principle of the act by which the mind perceives itself, is sufficient for the first type of cognition that is had of the mind. And it is for this reason that the mind is said to have a cognition of itself through its own presence. By contrast, the mind's presence is not itself sufficient for the second type of cognition that is had of the mind; instead, what is required is diligent and subtle inquiry. Hence, many are ignorant of the nature of the soul, and many have fallen into error about the nature of the soul. This is why, in *De Trinitate* 10, Augustine says of this sort of inquiry into the mind, "It is not as something absent that the mind seeks to discern itself; rather, it seeks to discern itself as something present"—that is, to have a cognition of how it differs from other things, which is what it is to have a cognition of its own 'what-ness' and nature.

**Reply to objection 1:** The mind knows itself through itself in the sense that it eventually (*tandem*) arrives at a cognition of itself, but through its own act. For the mind itself is what is known, because it loves itself, as Augustine adds in the place cited. For there are two possible reasons why something is said to be known in itself (*per se notum*): either (a) because there is nothing else through which one arrives at a knowledge of it, in the way that the first principles are said to be known in themselves, or (b) because it is not known *per accidens*—in the way in which color is *per se* visible, whereas a substance is visible *per accidens*.

**Reply to objection 2:** An angel's essence is an actuality in the genus of intelligible things, and so it is both an intellect and something that is understood intellectively. Hence, an angel apprehends his own essence through himself.

By contrast, this is not the case with a human intellect, which either (a) is entirely in potentiality with respect to intelligible things, as is the case with the passive intellect (*intellectus possibilis*), or else (b) is the actuality of the intelligible things which are abstracted from the phantasms, as is the case with the active intellect.

**Reply to objection 3:** This proposition (*verbum*) of the Philosopher's is true in general of all types of intellect. For just as an activated sensory power (*sensus in actu*) is the sensible thing, because of the likeness of the sensible thing that serves as the form of the activated sensory power, so too the activated intellect (*intellectus in actu*) is the thing as actually understood (*intellectum in actu*), because of the likeness of the thing understood that serves as the form of the activated intellect. And so the human intellect, which proceeds into act because of the species of the thing understood, is itself understood through that same species as through its own form.

Now to say that in those things without matter the intellect is the same as the thing understood is the same as saying that in things that are actually being understood the intellect and what is understood are the same. For something is actually being understood intellectively because it is without matter. But there is a difference here. For the essences of certain things exist without matter, e.g., the separated substances we call angels, and each of them is both something that is understood intellectively and something that understands intellectively. On the other hand, there are some things whose essences do not exist without matter; instead, all that exists without matter are the likenesses abstracted from them.

Hence, in *De Anima* 3 the Commentator says that the proposition adduced in the objection is true only in the case of the separated substances. For, as was just explained, the proposition is rendered true in their case in a way in which it is not rendered true in the case of other things.

## Article 2

### Does our intellect have cognition of the soul's habits through their essence?

It seems that our intellect has cognition of the soul's habits through their essence:

**Objection 1:** In *De Trinitate* 13 Augustine says, "Faith is not seen in the heart in which it exists in the same way that the soul of another man is seen from the movements of his body. Rather, a most certain knowledge grasps it, and the conscience calls out in testimony to it." And the same argument holds for the other habits of the soul. Therefore, the habits of the soul are perceived (*cognoscuntur*) through themselves and not through their acts.

**Objection 2:** We have cognition of material things that exist outside the soul in virtue of the fact that their likenesses are present in the soul, and this is why they are said to be understood (*cognoscuntur*) through their likenesses. But the soul's habits are present in the soul through their essence. Therefore, it is through their essence that they are understood.

**Objection 3:** That because of which a thing is such-and-such is itself such-and-such to a greater degree (*propter quod unumquodque tale, et illud magis*). But other things are understood by the soul because of its habits and intelligible species. Therefore, the soul's habits and intelligible species are understood by the soul to a greater degree through themselves.

**But contrary to this:** Habits are principles of acts, just as powers are. But as *De Anima* 2 says, "Acts and operations are conceptually prior (*priores secundum rationem*) to powers." For the same reason, therefore, acts and operations are prior to habits. And so habits are known through their acts, just as powers are.

**I respond:** In some sense a habit lies between a pure potentiality (*potentia pura*) and a pure actuality (*actus purus*). Now it has already been explained (a. 1) that nothing is understood except insofar as it is actual. So, then, insofar as a habit falls short of being a complete actuality, it falls short of being knowable through itself. Rather, it has to be known through its act—whether this be (a) when someone perceives himself to have a habit by virtue of perceiving himself to be producing the act proper to that habit, or (b) when someone is inquiring into the nature and character of a habit by considering its act. The first type of cognition of a habit is effected by the very presence of the habit, since by the very fact that it is present it causes the act in which it is immediately perceived. On the other hand, the second type of cognition of a habit comes about through diligent inquiry, as was explained above (a. 1) in the case of the mind.

**Reply to objection 1:** Even though faith is not perceived through exterior bodily movements, it is nonetheless perceived by the one in whom it exists through an interior act of the heart. For no one knows that he has faith unless he perceives himself to be making an act of faith (*nisi per hoc quod se credere percipit*).

**Reply to objection 2:** Habits are not present in our intellect as objects of the intellect, since, as was explained above (q. 84, a. 7), in the state of the present life the object of our intellect is the nature of a material thing. Instead, habits are present in the intellect as things by which the intellect engages in intellective understanding.

**Reply to objection 3:** The dictum 'That because of which (*propter quod*) a thing is such-and-such is itself such-and-such to a greater degree' is true if it is understood to apply to things that belong to the same order, e.g., things in the same genus of cause. For instance, if one claimed that health exists for the sake of life (*propter vitam*), it would follow that life is desirable to a greater degree.

However, the dictum is not true if it is applied to things that belong to diverse orders. For instance, if one claimed that health exists because of medicine (*propter medicinam*), it would not thereby follow that medicine is more desirable; for health belongs to the order of ends, while medicine belongs to the order of efficient causes.

So, then, if we take two things, both of which belong *per se* to the order of the objects of cognition, the one because of which the other is known (*cognoscitur*) will itself be known (*notum*) to a greater degree—in the way that principles are known to a greater degree than their conclusions are. However, a habit does not, insofar as it is a habit, belong to the order of objects of cognition. Furthermore, it is not because of a habit as an *object* of cognition that certain things are known; instead, certain things are known because of a habit as a *disposition* or *form* by which the knower understands. And so the argument does not go through.

### Article 3

### Does the intellect have cognition of its own act?

It seems that the intellect does not have cognition of its own act (*non cognoscat proprium actum*):

**Objection 1:** It is the object of a cognitive power (*cognoscitiva virtus*) that is properly speaking such that there is cognition of it. But an act differs from its object. Therefore, the intellect does not have cognition of its own act.

**Objection 2:** If there is a cognition of something, then there is an act by which that cognition takes place. Therefore, if the intellect has a cognition of its own act, then there is an act by which it has the cognition of that act; and, again, the cognition of this latter act will take place by means of yet another act. Therefore, there will be an infinite regress (*erit procedere in infinitum*)—which seems impossible.

**Objection 3:** The intellect is related to its own act in the same way that a sensory power is related to its own act. But a proper sensory power does not sense its own act; rather, as *De Anima* says, this is the role of the common sensory power. Therefore, neither does the intellect have intellective cognition of its own act.

**But contrary to this:** In *De Trinitate* 10 Augustine says, "I understand that I understand."

**I respond:** As has already been explained (a. 1), there is cognition of a thing insofar as it is actual. Now the ultimate perfection of an intellect is its operation. For this operation is not like an action which tends toward something else (*tendens in alterum*) and which is a perfection of the thing acted upon, in the way that an act of building is a perfection of the thing built. Rather, as is explained in *Metaphysics* 9, the intellect's action remains within the agent as the agent's own perfection and actuality.

Therefore, the first thing that is understood about an intellect is its very act of intellective understanding. But this applies in different ways to the different types of intellects:

For there is one type of intellect, viz., God's intellect, which is its very act of intellective understanding. And so in the case of God, His understanding that He understands is the same as His understanding His own essence, since His essence is His very act of intellective understanding.

On the other hand, there is another type of intellect, viz., the angelic intellect, which, as was explained above (q. 79, a. 1), is not its own act of intellective understanding, but is nonetheless such that the first object of its act of understanding is its own essence. Hence, even though, in an angel, his understanding that he understands is conceptually different from his understanding his own essence, he nonetheless understands both of them together and in a single act; for his understanding his own essence is a proper perfection of his essence, and an entity taken together with its perfection is understood all at once and by a single act.

But there is another type of intellect, viz., the human intellect, which (a) is not its own act of understanding and which (b) is such that the primary object of its act of understanding is not its own essence but instead something extrinsic, viz., the nature of a material thing. And so what is understood in the first place by the human intellect is an object of this latter sort, and what is understood in the second place is the very act by which the [primary] object is understood. Furthermore, by this act the intellect itself is understood, since the intellect's perfection is the very act of intellective understanding. This is why the Philosopher says that objects are understood prior to their acts, and acts prior to their powers.

**Reply to objection 1:** The object of the intellect is something general, viz., *being* and *true*, under which is also included the very act of intellective understanding. Hence, the intellect is able to have intellective understanding of its own act. But it does not understand its own act in the first place, since in the state of the present life the primary object of our intellect is not just any being or any true thing but rather, as was explained above (q. 84, a. 7), *being* and *true* as thought of in material things (*ens et verum consideratum in rebus materialibus*). And it is on this basis that our intellect arrives at the cognition of all other things.

**Reply to objection 2:** The human act of intellective understanding is not itself the actuality and perfection of the material nature that is understood, in the sense that the nature of the material thing and the very act of understanding it could be understood in a single act, in the way that a thing together with its perfection is understood by a single act. Hence, the act by which the intellect understands a rock is different from the act by which it understands that it understands the rock, and so on. Nor, as was explained above (q. 86, a. 2), is it problematic for there to be a potential infinity in the intellect.

**Reply to objection 3:** A proper sensory power has an act of sensing (*sentit*) because of a change effected in the material organ by a sensible exterior thing. But it is impossible for something material to effect a change within itself; instead, one material thing is affected by another. And so the act of a proper sensory power is perceived through the common sensory power.

By contrast, the intellect does not have intellective understanding through any material change in an organ, and so the cases are not parallel.

## Article 4

### Does the intellect have intellective understanding of acts of willing?

It seems that the intellect does not have intellective understanding of acts of willing (*non intelligat actum voluntatis*):

**Objection 1:** The intellect does not have cognition of anything that is not in some way present in the intellect. But an act of willing is not present in the intellect, since the intellect and the will are diverse powers. Therefore, the intellect does not have cognition of acts of willing.

**Objection 2:** An act takes its species from its object. But the object of the will differs from the object of the intellect. Therefore, an act of willing has a species different from that of an object of the intellect. Therefore, the intellect does not have cognition of it.

**Objection 3:** In *Confessiones* 10 Augustine says of the soul's affections that they are perceived "neither through images, in the way that bodies are, nor through their presence, in the way that crafts (*artes*) are, but through certain notions (*per quasdam notiones*)." But it does not seem to be possible for there to be notions of things in the soul other than the essences of the things perceived or likenesses of those things. Therefore, it seems impossible for the intellect to have cognition of the soul's affections, i.e., of acts of willing.

**But contrary to this:** In *De Trinitate* 10 Augustine says, "I understand myself to have an act of willing (*intelligo me velle*)."

**I respond:** As was explained above (q. 59, a. 1), an act of willing is nothing other than a certain inclination that follows upon an understood form, in the same way that a natural desire (*appetitus naturalis*) is an inclination that follows upon a natural form. But a thing's inclination exists within the thing itself in the way appropriate to it (*per modum eius*). Hence, a natural inclination exists naturally in a natural thing; and an inclination which is a sentient desire exists in a sensible way in a thing that has sentience; and, similarly, an intelligible inclination, which is an act of willing, exists intelligibly, as in its source and proper subject, in someone who has intellective understanding. This is why, in *De Anima* 3, the Philosopher employs the following manner of speaking: "The will exists in reason." But if something exists intelligibly in someone who has intellective understanding, then it follows that that thing is understood by him.

Hence, an act of willing is understood by the intellect both (a) insofar as someone perceives himself to be willing (*inquantum aliquis percipit se velle*) and also (b) insofar as someone has cognition of the nature of this act (*inquantum aliquis cognoscit naturam huius actus*) and, as a result, cognition of the nature of its source (*principium*), which is either a habit or a power.

**Reply to objection 1:** This argument would go through if the will and the intellect differed in subject in addition to being diverse powers. For in that case what exists in the will would be absent from the intellect. As things stand, however, since both of them are rooted (*radicetur*) in the same substance of the soul and the one is in some sense a principle of the other, it follows that what exists in the will somehow exists in the intellect as well.

**Reply to objection 2:** The good and the true, which are the objects of the will and the intellect, do, to be sure, differ conceptually, but, as was explained above (q. 16, a. 4 and q. 82, a. 4), the one is contained under the other. For the true is something good, and the good is something true. And so what belongs to the will falls under the intellect, and what belongs to the intellect is able to fall under the will.

**Reply to objection 3:** The soul's affections do not exist in the intellect just through a likeness, as bodies do, or through their presence in the subject, as crafts do. Rather, they exist in the intellect in the way that something that is derived from a principle exists in a principle that is such that a notion of what is derived exists in it (*principiatum est in principio in quo habetur notio principiati*). And this is why Augustine says that the soul's affections exist in memory through certain notions (*per quasdam notiones*).

# QUESTION 88

## How the Human Soul Understands Things That are Above It

Next we have to consider how the human soul has cognition of things that are above it, viz., immaterial substances. And on this topic there are three questions: (1) Can the human soul, in the state of the present life, have intellective understanding of the immaterial substances which we call angels through themselves? (2) Can the human soul come to a knowledge (*notitia*) of immaterial substances through its cognition of material things? (3) Is it God that is understood by us in the first place?

### Article 1

### Can the human soul, in the state of the present life, have intellective understanding of immaterial substances through themselves?

It seems that the human soul, in the state of the present life, can have intellective understanding of immaterial substances through themselves (*possit intelligere substantias immateriales per seipsas*):

**Objection 1:** In *De Trinitate* 9 Augustine says, "Just as the mind itself gathers knowledge of corporeal things through the bodily senses, so it gathers knowledge of incorporeal things through its very self (*per semetipsam*)." But things of this latter sort are immaterial substances. Therefore, the mind has intellective understanding of immaterial substances.

**Objection 2:** What is similar is known by means of what is similar to it. But the human mind is more similar to immaterial things than to material things, since, as is clear from what was said above (q. 76, a. 1), the mind is itself immaterial. Therefore, since our mind has intellective understanding of material things, *a fortiori* it has intellective understanding of immaterial things.

**Objection 3:** The fact that things that are maximally sensible in their own right (*secundum se maxime sensibilia*) are not maximally sensible by us stems from the fact that excesses in the case of sensibles (*excellentiae sensibilium*) damage our sensory power. But as *De Anima* 3 says, excesses in the case of intelligibles (*excellentiae intelligibilium*) do not damage our intellect. Therefore, things that are maximally intelligible in their own right are likewise maximally intelligible to us. But since material things are intelligible only because we make them actually intelligible through abstraction from matter, it is clear that substances that are immaterial are by their nature more intelligible in their own right. Therefore, *a fortiori*, we have a much better intellective understanding of them than of material things.

**Objection 4:** In *Metaphysics* 2 the Commentator says that if we could not understand abstract substances intellectively, then "nature would have acted pointlessly (*otiose*), since it would have rendered what is naturally intelligible in its own right (*intellectum in se*) unintelligible by anyone (*non intellectum ab aliquo*)." But there is nothing pointless or useless (*otiosum sive frustra*) in nature. Therefore, we can have intellective understanding of immaterial substances.

**Objection 5:** The intellect is related to intelligible things in the same way that the sensory power is related to sensible things. But our sense of sight can see all bodies, regardless of whether they are higher and incorruptible bodies or lower and corruptible bodies. Therefore, our intellect can have intellective understanding of all intelligible substances, even higher and immaterial substances.

**But contrary to this:** Wisdom 9:16 says, "Who will investigate the things in the heavens?" But substances of the sort in question are said to be 'in the heavens' (*in caelis*)—this according to Matthew 18:10 ("Their angels in heaven (*in caelis*) . . ."). Therefore, immaterial substances cannot be understood through human inquiry (*per investigationem humanam*).

**I respond:** According to Plato's opinion, not only are immaterial substances understood by us intellectively, but they are the very first things understood by us. For Plato claimed that immaterial subsistent forms, which he called 'ideas', are the proper object of our intellect, and so they are understood by us in the first place and *per se* (*primo et per se*). However, the soul's cognition is applied to material things insofar as the imagination and sensory power are mixed in with intellection (*intellectui permiscetur phantasia et sensus*). Hence, the more the soul has been purified (*depuratus*), the more it perceives the intelligible truth that belongs to the immaterial things.

By contrast, according to Aristotle's position, which is closer to our experience (*quam magis experimur*), in the state of the present life our intellect has a natural relation to the natures of material things. Hence, as is clear from what has been said (q. 84, a. 7), our intellect does not understand anything except by turning itself toward the phantasms. And so it is clear that given the mode of cognition that we experience, we cannot have intellective understanding in the first place and *per se* of immaterial substances, which do not fall under the sensory power or the imagination.

However, in his commentary on *De Anima* 3, Averroes claims that in this life man can in the end arrive at an intellective understanding of separated substances because of our continuity or union with a certain separated substance which he calls the active intellect and which, because it is a separated substance, naturally understands separated substances. Hence, when the active intellect has been perfectly united with us in such a way that we are able to have perfect intellective understanding through it, then we will understand separated substances in the same way that we now understand material substances through the passive intellect that is united with us.

Now Averroes claimed that the active intellect is united with us in the following way: Since we have intellective understanding through the active intellect and through the contemplated intelligibles (*per intelligibilia speculata*), as is clear when we understand conclusions through their understood principles, the active intellect has to be related to the contemplated intelligibles either (a) as a principal agent to its instruments or (b) as a form to its matter. For these are the two ways in which an action is attributed to two principles. That is, the action is attributed either (a) to a principal agent and to its instrument, as when the action of cutting is attributed to the craftsman and to his saw, or (b) to a form and its subject, as when the action of heating is attributed to the heat and to the fire. But in both these ways the active intellect will be related to the contemplated intelligibles as a perfection to what is perfectible, and as an actuality to a potentiality. Now what is perfected is received along with the perfection itself all at once in something; for instance, what is actually visible is received along with the light all at once in the pupil. Therefore, the contemplated intelligibles are received along with the active intellect all at once in the passive intellect. And the greater the number of contemplated intelligibles we receive, the closer we get to the active intellect's being perfectly united with us—so that when we have had cognition of all the contemplated intelligibles, the agent intellect will be perfectly united with us and we will be able to have cognition of all things, material and immaterial, through it. This is what he posits as ultimate human happiness. Moreover, as far as this proposal is concerned, it does not matter (a) whether in that state of happiness the passive intellect understands separated substances through the active intellect, as Averroes himself thinks, or (b) whether instead—a view Averroes attributes to Alexander—the man understands separated substances through the

active intellect, and the passive intellect never understands separated substances (because he posits a corruptible passive intellect).

However, the positions just laid out cannot stand.

First of all, if the active intellect is a separated substance, it is impossible for us to formally have intellective understanding through it. For that
by which an agent formally acts is a form and actuality that belongs to the
agent, since every agent acts insofar as it is actualized—just as was
explained above (q. 76, a. 1) concerning the passive intellect.

Second, given the position in question, if the active intellect is a separated substance, then it is not united with us in its substance. Instead, only
its light is united to us to the extent that there is a participation in the contemplated intelligibles (*secundum quod participatur in intellectis specu-
latis*); and the active intellect is not united to us with respect to its other
actions, so that we might thereby be able to understand immaterial substances. This is like the fact that when we see colors illuminated by the sun,
it is not the sun's substance that is united with us, so that we might be able
to perform the sun's actions. Instead, it is only the sun's light that is united
with us for seeing colors.

Third, even on the assumption that the active intellect's substance is
united with us along the lines explained above, they themselves do not
claim that the active intellect is totally united with us after one or two intelligibles—instead, it is totally united with us after *all* the contemplated
intelligibles. But all the contemplated intelligibles together fall short of the
active intellect's power, since it takes much more power to understand separated substances intellectively than to understand all material substances.
Hence, it is clear that even if all material substances were understood intellectively, the active intellect would not be united with us in such a way that
we would be able to understand separated substances through it.

Fourth, it is scarcely possible for anyone in this world to have an intellective understanding of all material intelligibles, and so no one—or at
most very few—would attain happiness. But this contradicts the
Philosopher in *Ethics* 1, where he says that happiness is "a general good
that is accessible to all who are not bereft of virtue." It is likewise contrary
to reason that the end of a species should be attained only by a few members of the species (*ut in paucioribus consequantur ea quae contintentur
sub specie*).

Fifth, in *Ethics* 1 the Philosopher explicitly says that happiness "is an
operation in accord with perfect virtue." And having enumerated many
virtues, he concludes in *Ethics* 10 that ultimate happiness, which consists

in the cognition of the most intelligible things, is in accord with the virtue of wisdom, which he had claimed in *Ethics* 6 is "the chief among the speculative virtues." Hence, it is clear that Aristotle located man's ultimate happiness in cognition of separated substances of a sort that can be had through the speculative sciences—and not through the sort of continuity with the active intellect fabricated by some.

Sixth, it was shown above (q. 79, a. 4) that the active intellect is not a separated substance, but a certain power of the soul that extends actively to the same things that the passive intellect extends to passively. For as *De Anima* 3 says, the passive intellect "is that by which the intellect becomes all things," whereas the active intellect is "that by which the intellect makes all things." Therefore, both the active intellect and the passive intellect extend, in the state of the present life, only to material things, which the active intellect makes actually intelligible and which are received in the passive intellect.

Hence, in the state of the present life, we cannot understand immaterial substances through themselves either by means of the passive intellect or by means of the active intellect.

**Reply to objection 1:** From this quotation from Augustine one can infer that what our mind is capable of attaining by way of cognition of incorporeal things is such that the mind can have this cognition through itself. And this is true to the extent that even among the philosophers one finds the claim that knowledge concerning the soul is a certain source of cognition about separated substances. For by understanding itself, our soul takes a step toward having the sort of cognition of incorporeal substances that it is possible for it to have. But it does not, by understanding itself, understand them absolutely speaking or perfectly.

**Reply to objection 2:** Likeness to a nature is not a sufficient explanation for cognition; otherwise, one would have to say what Empedocles said, viz., that the soul shares in the nature of all things in order to have cognition of all things. Instead, what is required for cognition is that a likeness of the thing understood should exist in the one having the cognition as a certain form of his own. Now in the state of the present life our passive intellect is apt to be informed by the likenesses of material things abstracted from phantasms, and so it has a better cognition of material substances than of immaterial substances.

**Reply to objection 3:** The object must have a certain proportion to the cognitive power—more specifically, a proportion of what is active to what is passive, and a proportion of what is perfect to what is perfectible. Hence, the fact that excessive sensibles (*excellentia sensibilia*) are not grasped by the sensory power is explained not only by the fact that they damage the sensory organs but also by the fact that they are disproportionate to the sentient powers. And it is in this latter way that immaterial substances are disproportionate to our intellect, in its present state, with the result that they cannot be understood by it.

**Reply to objection 4:** This argument of the Commentator's is defective in several ways.

First, from the fact that separated substances are not understood by us, it does not follow that they are not understood by any intellect. For they are understood by themselves and by one another.

Second, separated substances do not have being understood by us as their end. But what is called 'pointless' or 'useless' is that which does not attain the end for which it exists. And so even if immaterial substances were not understood in any way by us, it would not follow that they are useless.

**Reply to objection 5:** The sensory power has cognition of higher and lower bodies in the same way, viz., through an organ's being affected by the sensible thing. But we do not have intellective cognition of material substances, which are understood by means of abstraction, in the same way that we have intellective cognition of immaterial substances, which cannot be understood in this way by us, since there are no phantasms of them.

## Article 2

### Can our intellect arrive at an intellective understanding of immaterial substances through its cognition of material things?

It seems that our intellect can arrive at an intellective understanding of immaterial substances through its cognition of material things:

**Objection 1:** In *De Caelesti Hierarchia*, chap. 1, Dionysius says, "It is impossible for the human mind to be stimulated upward to the immaterial contemplation of the heavenly hierarchies unless in its own right it uses material guidance." Therefore, it follows that we can be led by material things to an intellective understanding of immaterial substances.

**Objection 2:** Scientific knowledge exists in the intellect. But there are sciences about immaterial substances, along with definitions. For instance, Damascene defines an angel, and certain texts about angels are proposed in both the theological and philosophical disciplines. Therefore, immaterial substances can be understood by us.

**Objection 3:** The human soul belongs to the genus of immaterial substances. But it itself can be understood intellectively by us through its own act, by which it understands material things. Therefore, other immaterial substances, too, can be understood by us through their effects on material things.

**Objection 4:** The only sort of cause that cannot be comprehended through its effects is one which lies at an infinite distance from its effects. But this is proper to God alone. Therefore, other immaterial substances, which are created, can be understood by us through material things.

**But contrary to this:** In *De Divinis Nominibus*, chap. 1, Dionysius says, "Intelligible things cannot be understood by means of sensible things, and simples cannot be understood by means of composites, and incorporeal things cannot be understood by means of corporeal things."

**I respond:** As Averroes reports in *De Anima* 3, a thinker by the name of Avempace held that through the understanding of material substances we are able to arrive, through true philosophical principles, at an intellective understanding of immaterial substances. For given that our intellect is able to abstract the 'what-ness' (*quidditas*) of a material thing from matter, if there is still something material left in that 'what-ness', our intellect will be able to do another abstraction; and since this process does not go on to infinity, it will be able at last to arrive at an understanding of a 'what-ness' that is wholly without matter. And this is what it is to understand an immaterial substance intellectively.

This argument would be effective if, as the Platonists held, immaterial substances were the forms and species of the material things around us. However, if we do not hold this but presuppose instead that immaterial substances have a nature that is altogether different from the 'what-nesses' of material things, then no matter how much our intellect abstracts the 'whatness' of a material thing from matter, it will never arrive at anything like an immaterial substance. And so it is not the case that through material substances we can perfectly (*perfecte*) understand immaterial substances.

**Reply to objection 1:** We can ascend from material things to some sort of cognition of immaterial things, but not to perfect cognition, since there is not enough likeness (*comparatio*) between material things and immaterial things. Instead, as Dionysius points out in *De Caelesti Hierarchia*, chap. 2, if the likenesses taken from material things are used for understanding immaterial things, they turn out to be very dissimilar.

**Reply to objection 2:** In the sciences the higher things are treated principally through the way of negation (*per viam remotionis*). So, for instance, Aristotle makes the celestial bodies known by negating the properties of lower bodies. Hence, *a fortiori*, we cannot have cognition of immaterial substances in such a way as to apprehend their 'what-nesses'. Instead, the treatments proposed to us in the sciences about immaterial substances proceed by appeal to the way of negation and to certain of their relations to material things.

**Reply to objection 3:** The human soul has intellective cognition of itself through its own act of understanding, which is the act proper to it and which perfectly reveals its power and nature. By contrast, the human soul is not able, either through its own act or through any other features found in material things, to have a perfect cognition of the power or nature of immaterial substances. For material things do not measure up to (*non adaequant*) the powers of immaterial substances.

**Reply to objection 4:** Created immaterial substances do not share the same *natural* genus with material substances, since immaterial substances do not have the same type of power or matter. However, they do share the same *logical* genus with material substances, since even immaterial substances are in the category of *substance*, given that their 'what-ness' is not the same as their *esse*.

By contrast, God does not share with material substances either a *natural* genus or a *logical* genus, since, as was explained above (q. 3, a. 5), there is no sense in which God is in a genus. Hence, through the likenesses of material things something affirmative can be understood of the angels in accord with a common conception (*secundum rationem communem*), though not in accord with any conception of a species (*secundum rationem speciei*); but this cannot occur in any way in the case of God.

## Article 3

### Is God the first thing that the human mind has cognition of?

It seems that God is the first thing (*primum*) that the human mind has cognition of:

**Objection 1:** That in which all other things are understood and by appeal to which we pass judgment on other things is the first object understood by us—in the way that light is sensed by the eye, and in the way that first principles are understood by the intellect. But as Augustine says in *De Trinitate* and in *De Vera Religione*, we have cognition of all things in the light shed by the first truth, and it is through this truth that we pass judgment on all things. Therefore, God is that which is first understood by us.

**Objection 2:** That because of which a thing is such-and-such is itself such-and-such to a greater degree (*propter quod unumquodque, et illud magis*). But God is a cause of all of our cognitions, since as John 1:9 says, "He is the true light, which enlightens every man who comes into the world." Therefore, God is that which is understood by us in the first place and to the greatest degree.

**Objection 3:** That which is first understood in an image is the exemplar by reference to which the image is formed (*exemplar quo imago formatur*). But as Augustine says, the image of God exists in our mind. Therefore, God is that which is first understood in our mind.

**But contrary to this:** John 1:18 says, "No one has ever seen God."

**I respond:** Since, as has been explained (a. 1), the human intellect cannot, in the state of the present life, have cognition of created immaterial substances, *a fortiori* it cannot have cognition of the essence of the uncreated substance. Hence, one should reply simply that God is not the first object understood by us; instead, we come to a cognition of God through creatures—this according to the Apostle in Romans 1:20 ("The invisible things of God are clearly seen, being understood through the things that have been made").

Now, as has been explained many times above (q. 84, a. 7 and q. 85, a. 8 and q. 87, a. 2), in the state of the present life the first thing understood by us is the 'what-ness' of a material thing, which is the object of our intellect.

**Reply to objection 1:** The sense in which we understand and pass judgment on all things in the light of the first truth is that, as was explained above (q. 12, a. 2 and q. 84, a. 5), the intellect's very light—whether its natural light (*lumen naturale*) or the light of grace (*lumen gratuitum*)—is nothing other than the imprint of the first truth. Hence, since our intellect's light is itself related to our intellect not as *that which* is understood but as *that by which* things are understood, *a fortiori* God is not that which is first understood by our intellect.

**Reply to objection 2:** As was explained above (q. 87, a. 2), the dictum 'That because of which a thing is such-and-such is itself such-and-such to a greater degree' must be thought of as applying to things that belong to the same order.

Now the sense in which other things are understood 'because of God' is not that God is the first object, but rather that He is the first cause of our cognitive power.

**Reply to objection 3:** If the image of God in our soul were perfect, in the way that the Son is the perfect Image of the Father, then our mind would immediately have an intellective understanding of God. However, our mind is an imperfect image. Hence, the argument does not go through.

# QUESTION 89

## A Separated Soul's Cognition

Next we have to consider a separated soul's cognition. And on this topic there are eight questions:

(1) Can a soul that has been separated from its body have intellective understanding? (2) Does a separated soul have intellective understanding of separated substances? (3) Does a separated soul have intellective understanding of all natural things? (4) Does a separated soul have cognition of singulars? (5) Does a habit of knowledge acquired here remain in a separated soul? (6) Can a separated soul make use of a habit of knowledge acquired here? (7) Does spatial distance impede a separated soul's cognition? (8) Do souls separated from their bodies have cognition of what is happening here?

## Article 1

### Can a separated soul have intellective understanding of anything at all?

It seems that a separated soul cannot have intellective understanding of anything at all:

**Objection 1:** In *De Anima* 1 the Philosopher says, "Understanding is corrupted when something is corrupted interiorly." But everything interior that belongs to a man is corrupted by death. Therefore, understanding is itself likewise corrupted.

**Objection 2:** As was explained above (q. 84, a. 7 and 8), the human soul is prevented from understanding by impediments in the sensory power (*per ligamentum sensus*) and by an unruly imagination. But as is clear from what was said above (q. 77, a. 8), the sensory power and imagination are totally corrupted by death. Therefore, after death the soul does not have intellective understanding of anything at all.

**Objection 3:** If a separated soul has intellective understanding, then it must have this understanding by means of certain [intelligible] species. But it does not have understanding by means of innate species, since in the beginning the soul "is like a slate on which nothing has been written." Nor does it have understanding by means of species that it abstracts from things, since it no longer has the organs associated with the sensory power and imagination, by the mediation of which intelligible species are abstracted from things. Nor does it have understanding by means of species that have been previously abstracted and are now conserved in the soul; for in that case a child's soul would not understand anything after death. Nor does it have understanding even by means of intelligible species that flow into it from God (*per species intelligibiles divinitus influxas*), since this sort of cognition would not be natural cognition—which is what we are talking about now—but would instead be a cognition associated with grace. Therefore, a soul separated from its body cannot have intellective understanding of anything.

**But contrary to this:** In *De Anima* 1 the Philosopher says, "If the soul had no proper operations, then it would not be possible for the soul to be separated." But it is possible for the soul to be separated. Therefore, it has proper operations—and especially that operation which is intellective understanding (*intelligere*). Therefore, it has intellective cognition when it exists without its body.

**I respond:** This question derives its difficulty from the fact that as long as a soul is conjoined with its body, it cannot have intellective understanding of anything except by turning itself toward phantasms. This is clear from experience.

Now if, as the Platonists held, this fact were not due to the nature of the soul, but instead belonged to the soul incidentally (*per accidens*) because it is tied to a body, then the question could easily be answered. For once the impediment of the body were removed, the soul would revert to its own nature, so that it would understand intelligible things directly (*simpliciter*) and without turning itself to phantasms—just as happens in the case of other separated substances.

However, on this view, the soul would not be united to its body for the soul's own good, given that its intellective understanding would be poorer (*peius*) when it is united with the body than when it is separated. Instead, the union would be solely for the sake of the betterment of the body. But this is ludicrous (*irrationabile*), since the matter exists for the sake of the form, and not vice versa.

By contrast, if we hold that it is by its nature that the soul has to turn itself toward phantasms in order to have intellective understanding, then, since the soul's nature is not changed by the death of the body, it seems that a [separated] soul cannot have intellective understanding of anything. For there are no phantasms at hand toward which it might turn itself.

So to remove this difficulty, note that since nothing operates except insofar as it actualized, each thing's mode of operating (*modus operandi*) follows upon its mode of being (*modus essendi ipsius*). But even while a soul's nature remains the same, its mode of being when it is united with a body is different from its mode of being when it is separated from its body—not in such a way that the soul's being united to a body is incidental (*accidentale*) to it, but rather in such a way that it is by reason of its nature that the soul is united to a body. In the same way, the nature of something lightweight is not changed when it goes from being in its proper place, which is natural to it, to being outside its proper place, which lies beyond its nature (*est ei praeter naturam*). Therefore, corresponding to the mode of being by which a soul is united to a body, the soul has a mode of understanding that involves turning toward the phantasms of bodies that exist in the bodily organs. But when a soul is separated from its body, it has a mode of understanding that involves turning toward those things that are intelligible absolutely speaking—just like the mode of understanding had by the other separated substances. Hence, the mode of understanding that involves turning toward phantasms is natural to a soul in the same way that being united to a body is likewise natural to it, whereas being separated from its body lies outside the conception of its nature (*praeter rationem suae naturae*), just as understanding without turning toward phantasms lies outside its nature. And so a soul is united to a body in order that it might exist and operate in accord with its nature.

However, this reply once again provokes a doubt. For since (a) nature is always ordered toward what is better, and since (b) the mode of understanding that involves turning toward intelligible things absolutely speaking is better than the mode of understanding that involves turning toward phantasms, God should have constituted the soul's nature in such a way that (a) the more noble mode of understanding would be natural to it and that (b) for this reason it would not need to be united to a body.

Notice, then, that even if intellective understanding by turning toward higher things is more noble, absolutely speaking, than understanding by turning toward phantasms, nonetheless, the former mode of understanding was less perfect as a possibility for the soul (*prout erat possibilis animae erat imperfectior*). This is made clear as follows:

In all intellectual substances the intellective power comes through the influence of the divine light. This light is unitary and simple in the first principle, and the further away intellectual creatures are from the first principle, the more this light is divided and differentiated, like lines emanating from a central point. And so it is that God understands all things through His own unitary essence. The higher intellectual substances, on the other hand, even if they have intellective understanding through more than one form (*per plures formas*), nonetheless understand through forms that are fewer and more universal and more potent for comprehending things because of the efficacy of the intellective power that exists in them, whereas in the lower intellectual substances, to the extent that they fall short of the intellective power of the higher substances, the forms are greater in number, less universal, and less efficacious for comprehending things. Therefore, if the lower substances had forms with the same degree of universality that the higher substances do, then because they have weaker intellects, they would not receive through those forms a perfect cognition of things, but would instead have a cognition that was somewhat general and indistinct. In a certain way, this same thing is apparent among men; for those of weaker intellect do not receive perfect cognition through the universal conceptions had by more intelligent men, unless each individual case is specifically (*in speciali*) explained to them.

Now it is clear that, according to the order of nature, human souls are the lowest among intellectual substances. The perfection of the universe requires this, so that diverse grades might exist among things. Therefore, if human souls had been constituted by God in such a way as to have intellective understanding in the mode in which separated substances have it, then they would not have had perfect cognition, but would instead have had indistinct cognition in general. Therefore, in order for them to be able to have perfect and proper cognition of things, they were naturally constituted in such a way as to be united to bodies and so to receive their proper cognition of sensible things from the things themselves, in much the same way that uneducated men cannot be led to scientific knowledge except through sensible examples.

So, then, it is clear that it is for the soul's own good that it should be united to a body and have intellective cognition by turning itself toward phantasms. And yet the soul is able to be separated and to have a different mode of intellective understanding.

**Reply to objection 1:** If the Philosopher's words are carefully unpacked (*diligenter discutiantur*), the Philosopher asserted this claim after having first made a certain assumption, viz., that the act of intellective understanding is a certain movement of the conjoined being in the same way that the act of sensing is. For he had not yet shown the difference between intellective understanding and sensing.

An alternative reply is that he is speaking of the mode of intellective understanding which involves turning toward phantasms.

**Reply to objection 2:** The second objection is about this same mode of intellective understanding.

**Reply to objection 3:** A separated soul has intellective understanding neither through innate [intelligible] species, nor through species that it abstracts during the time it is separated, nor solely through conserved species, as the objection proves. Instead, it has intellective understanding through participated species which come from the influence of God's light and which the soul comes to participate in just as the other separated substances do, though in an inferior mode. Hence, as soon as it ceases to turn itself toward the body, the soul turns itself toward higher things. And yet the cognition is not for this reason non-natural. For God is the source not only of the influence of the light of grace, but also of the influence of the natural light.

## Article 2

### Does a separated soul have intellective understanding of separated substances?

It seems that a separated soul does not have intellective understanding of separated substances:

**Objection 1:** A soul that is joined to a body is more perfect than a soul separated from a body, since the soul is naturally part of a human nature, and every part is more perfect within its own whole. But as was established above (q. 88, a. 1), a soul conjoined to a body does not have intellective understanding of separated substances. Therefore, *a fortiori*, it does not have such understanding when it has been separated from its body.

**Objection 2:** If anything is understood, it is understood either through its presence or through a species of it. But separated substances cannot be understood by the soul through their presence, since nothing penetrates the soul except God alone. Nor can they be understood by the soul through any species of them that the soul is able to abstract from an angel, since an angel is more simple than the soul is. Therefore, there is no way in which a separated soul is able to have cognition of separated substances.

**Objection 3:** Certain philosophers have held that man's ultimate happiness consists in the cognition of separated substances. Therefore, if a separated soul is able to have intellective understanding of separated substances, it will attain happiness solely by virtue of being separated. But this is absurd.

**But contrary to this:** Separated souls have cognition of other separated souls. For instance, the rich man in hell sees Lazarus and Abraham, according to Luke 16:23. Therefore, separated souls also see both demons and angels.

**I respond:** As Augustine says in *De Trinitate* 9, "Our mind receives cognition of incorporeal things through itself," i.e., by having cognition of itself, as was explained above (q. 88, a. 1). Therefore, by appeal to the fact that a separated soul has cognition of itself, we are able to grasp the way in which it understands other separated substances.

Now it was explained above (a. 1) that as long as a soul is united to its body, it has intellective understanding by turning itself toward phantasms. And so it cannot even understand itself except insofar as it comes to be actually engaged in intellective understanding through a species abstracted from phantasms. For as was explained above (q. 87, a. 1), it is through its own act that it understands itself. However, when it has been separated from its body, it will have intellective understanding by turning itself not toward phantasms but toward things that are intelligible in their own right, and so it will understand itself through itself.

Now it is common to each separated substance that it understands what lies above it and what lies below it in a mode that corresponds to its own substance. For a thing is understood intellectively insofar as it exists in the one who is engaged in understanding, and something exists in another in accord with the mode of thing that it exists in. Now the mode of a separated soul's substance is lower than an angelic substance's mode, but it is similar to the mode of other separated souls. And so a separated soul has perfect cognition of other separated souls, whereas it has imperfect and deficient cognition of the angels.

Now I am speaking here of the *natural* cognition had by a separated soul; there is a different account of the cognition associated with [the light of] *glory*.

**Reply to objection 1:** A separated soul is indeed less perfect if one considers the nature that it shares in common with the nature of the body (*natura qua communicat cum natura corporis*). However, a separated soul is nonetheless more free with respect to intellective understanding, since the soul is kept from a purity of understanding by the burdensomeness of the body and its care for it (*per gravedinem et occupationem corporis*).

**Reply to objection 2:** A separated soul has intellective understanding of the angels through divinely impressed likenesses (*per similitudines divinitus impressas*). However, these likenesses fall short of a perfect representation of the angels, because the soul's nature lies below that of an angel.

**Reply to objection 3:** Man's ultimate happiness does not consist in the cognition of just any separated substances; rather, it consists solely in the cognition of God, who cannot be seen except through grace. However, there is indeed a great, even if not ultimate, happiness in the cognition of other separated substances—if, that is, they are understood perfectly. However, as has been explained, a separated soul does not understand them perfectly by its natural cognition.

### Article 3

#### Does a separated soul have cognition of all natural things?

It seems that a separated soul has cognition of all natural things:

**Objection 1:** In separated substances there are conceptions (*rationes*) of all natural things. But separated souls have cognition of the separated substances. Therefore, they have cognition of all natural things.

**Objection 2:** If someone has intellective understanding of something more intelligible, then, *a fortiori*, he can have intellective understanding of something less intelligible. But a separated soul has intellective understanding of the separated substances, which are the greatest among intelligible things. Therefore, *a fortiori*, it can have intellective understanding of all natural things, which are less intelligible.

**But contrary to this:**

**1.** Natural cognition is more vigorous in the demons than in a separated soul. But the demons do not have cognition of all natural things; instead, as Isidore says, they learn many things by experience over a long period of time. Therefore, neither do separated souls have cognition of all natural things.

**2.** If as soon as a soul were separated, it had cognition of all natural things, then it would be pointless for men to study diligently in order to gain scientific knowledge of things. But this is absurd. Therefore, it is not the case that a separated soul has cognition of all natural things.

**I respond:** As was explained above (a. 1), a separated soul has intellective understanding through species that it receives by the influence of the divine light, just as angels do. However, since the soul's nature lies below the nature of an angel, for whom this mode of cognition is connatural, a separated soul does not acquire perfect cognition of things through species of this sort, but instead receives a cognition that is general and indistinct. Therefore, a separated soul bears the same relation to imperfect and indistinct cognition of natural things through these species that angels bear to perfect cognition of natural things.

Now through species of this sort angels understand all natural things by a perfect cognition, since, as Augustine says in *Super Genesim ad Litteram*, God effects in the angelic understanding whatever He effects in the proper natures of things. Hence, separated souls likewise have a cognition of all things—not a certain and proper cognition, but a general and indistinct cognition.

**Reply to objection 1:** As was explained above (q. 55, a. 1 and q. 87, a. 4), an angel has cognition of all natural things through [intelligible] species and not through his own substance. And so from the fact that a soul has some sort of cognition of a separated substance it does not follow that it has cognition of all natural things.

**Reply to objection 2:** Just as a separated soul does not have a perfect intellective understanding of the separated substances, so neither does it have a perfect intellective understanding of all natural things. Instead, as has been explained, it has a sort of indistinct cognition of natural things.

**Reply to argument 1 for the contrary:** Isidore is here talking about the cognition of *future* things, which angels and demons and separated souls have cognition of only in their causes or through divine revelation. By contrast, we ourselves are talking about the cognition of *natural* things.

**Reply to argument 2 for the contrary:** Cognition that is acquired in this life through study is proper and perfect cognition, whereas the cognition in question is indistinct. Hence, it does not follow that an eagerness for learning is pointless.

## Article 4

### Does a separated soul have cognition of singulars?

It seems that a separated soul does not have cognition of singulars:
**Objection 1:** As is clear from what was said above (q. 77, a. 8), the

only cognitive power that remains in a separated soul is the intellect. But as was established above (q. 86, a. 1), the intellect does not have cognition of singulars. Therefore, a separated soul does not have cognition of singulars.

**Objection 2:** A cognition by which something is understood as a singular (*in singulari*) is more determinate than a cognition by which something is understood in general (*in universali*). But a separated soul does not have determinate cognition of the species of natural things. Therefore, *a fortiori*, it does not have cognition of singulars.

**Objection 3:** If a separated soul had cognition of singulars and not through the sensory power, then by parity of reasoning it would have cognition of all singulars. But it does not have cognition of all singulars. Therefore, it does not have cognition of any singulars.

**But contrary to this:** In Luke 16:27 the rich man situated in hell said, "I have five brothers."

**I respond:** Separated souls have cognition of some singulars, but not all of them, not even all of the ones that exist at the present time (*quae sunt praesentia*). To see this clearly, note that there are two modes of intellective understanding. One mode is through abstraction from phantasms and, in accord with this mode, singulars cannot be understood directly by the intellect; instead, they are understood indirectly, as was explained above (q. 86, a. 1). The second mode of intellective understanding is through an influx of species from God, and, in accord with this mode, the intellect can have cognition of singulars. For just as in accord with what was explained above (q. 14, aa. 5–8), God Himself has cognition of all things, both universals and singulars, through His essence and insofar as He is a cause of all universal and individual principles, so too, through the species that are certain participated likenesses of the divine essence, separated substances are able to have cognition of singulars.

However, on this score there is a difference between angels and separated souls. For through species of this sort angels have perfect and proper cognition of things, whereas separated souls have indistinct cognition. Hence, because of the efficacy of their intellect angels have, through species of this sort, a perfect and proper cognition not only of the natures of things at the level of a species (*in speciali*) but also of the singulars contained under those species. By contrast, through species of the sort in question separated souls can have cognition only of those singulars on which they are in some way fixed (*ad quae quodammodo determinantur*), viz., either by a previous cognition or by some affective tie (*per aliquam affectionem*) or by a natural relation or by divine ordination. For everything that is received in a entity has determinate conditions (*determinatur*) that correspond to the mode of the recipient.

**Reply to objection 1:** The intellect does not have cognition of singulars by way of abstraction. But this is not the manner in which a separated soul has intellective understanding; instead, that manner is the one that has been explained.

**Reply to objection 2:** As has been explained, a separated soul's cognition is fixed on the species of those things that it bears some determinate relation to, or on individuals belonging to those species.

**Reply to objection 3:** A separated soul is not related in the same way to all singulars; instead, it has a relation to some of them that it does not have to others. And so there is no universally applicable reason (*aequalis ratio*) why a separated soul should have cognition of all singulars.

## Article 5

### Does a habit of scientific knowledge acquired here remain in a separated soul?

It seems that a habit of scientific knowledge acquired here does not remain in a separated soul:

**Objection 1:** In 1 Corinthians 13:8 the Apostle says, "Knowledge shall be destroyed."

**Objection 2:** In this world some less virtuous men (*quidam minus boni*) abound in scientific knowledge, while other more virtuous men lack scientific knowledge. Therefore, if a habit of scientific knowledge remained in the soul after death, it would follow that some less virtuous men would be more competent (*potiores*) in the future state than some more virtuous men. But this seems absurd.

**Objection 3:** Separated souls will have scientific knowledge because of the influx of the divine light. Therefore, if scientific knowledge acquired here remains in the separated soul, it follows that two forms of the same species will exist in the same subject. But this is impossible.

**Objection 4:** In the *Categories* the Philosopher says that "a habit is a quality that is difficult to change, whereas scientific knowledge is sometimes corrupted by illness or something else of this sort." But no change in this life is as powerful as the change effected by death. Therefore, it seems that a habit of knowledge is corrupted by death.

**But contrary to this:** In his letter to Paulinus Jerome says, "Let us learn on earth things such that the knowledge of them will survive for us in heaven."

**I respond:** Some have claimed that (a) a habit of scientific knowledge exists not in the intellect itself but in the sentient powers—more specifically, in the power of imagining, in the cogitative power, and in the power of remembering—and that (b) intelligible species are not conserved in the passive intellect. And if this opinion were true, then it would follow that once the body is destroyed, any habit of scientific knowledge acquired here would be totally destroyed.

However, since scientific knowledge exists in the intellect, which, as *De Anima* 3 says, is "the locus of species," a habit of scientific knowledge acquired here exists partly in the aforementioned sentient powers and partly in the intellect itself. This can be thought about by appeal to the very acts by which a habit of scientific knowledge is acquired, since, as *Ethics* 2 says, "habits are similar to the acts by which they are acquired." Now the acts of the intellect by which scientific knowledge is acquired in the present life involve the intellect's turning itself toward phantasms, which exist in the aforementioned sentient powers. Hence, through such acts the passive intellect itself acquires a certain capacity (*facultas*) for thinking by means of the species it has received, and the aforementioned lower powers acquire a certain aptitude (*habilitas*) such that the intellect, by turning toward them, is more easily able to think about intelligible things. But just as an act of the intellect principally and formally exists in the intellect itself, whereas it exists materially and dispositively in the lower powers, so too the same thing must be said about the corresponding habit.

Therefore, as regards what someone has of present scientific knowledge in the lower powers, this will not remain in a separated soul; on the other hand, what he has in the intellect itself must remain. For as *De Longitudine et Brevitate Vitae* says, there are two ways in which a form is corrupted, viz., (a) *per se*, when it is corrupted by its contrary, e.g., hot by cold, and (b) *per accidens*, viz., through the corruption of its subject. Now it is clear that the scientific knowledge that exists in a human intellect cannot be corrupted through the corruption of its subject; for as was shown above (q. 79, a. 2), the intellect is incorruptible. Similarly, neither can the intelligible species that exist in the passive intellect be corrupted by a contrary; for there is no contrary to an intelligible intention, especially with respect to the simple understanding by which one understands a thing's 'what-ness' (*praecipue quantum ad simplicem intelligentiam, qua intelligitur quod quid est*). On the other hand, as regards the operation by which the intellect composes and divides, or even as regards the operation by which it reasons discursively, contrariety is found in the intellect in the sense that falsity in a proposition or argument is contrary to truth. And in this sense scientific knowledge is sometimes corrupted by a contrary, viz., when someone is drawn away from knowledge of the truth by false argumentation. And so the Philosopher, in the book already cited, claims that there are two ways in which scientific knowledge is corrupted *per se*, viz., through forgetfulness on the part of the memory and through deception by false argumentation. But these have no relevance in the case of a separated soul.

Hence, one should reply that to the extent that a habit of scientific knowledge exists in the intellect, it remains in a separated soul.

**Reply to objection 1:** In this passage the Apostle is speaking not about scientific knowledge as a habit, but about the act of cognition. Hence, he adds by way of proof: "Now I know in part . . ."

**Reply to objection 2:** Just as someone who is less virtuous will be greater in bodily stature than someone who is more virtuous, so too nothing prevents someone who is less virtuous from having in the future a habit of scientific knowledge that someone more virtuous does not have. But this is of no importance in comparison with the other prerogatives that more virtuous men will have.

**Reply to objection 3:** The two types of knowledge do not have the same nature. Hence, nothing absurd follows.

**Reply to objection 4:** This argument goes through in the case of the corruption of scientific knowledge as regards that part of it that belongs to the sentient powers.


## Article 6

### Does an act of scientific knowledge acquired here remain in a separated soul?

It seems that an act of scientific knowledge acquired here does not remain in a separated soul:

**Objection 1:** In *De Anima* 1 the Philosopher says that when the body is corrupted, the soul "neither remembers nor loves." But to remember is to think about things that one previously knew. Therefore, a separated soul cannot have an act of the scientific knowledge which it acquired here.

**Objection 2:** Intelligible species will not be more powerful in a separated soul than they are in a soul united to a body. But as was established above (q. 84, a. 7), we are at present able to have an act of intellective understanding through intelligible species only by turning ourselves toward phantasms. Therefore, a separated soul will not be able to do this. And so there is no way in which a separated soul will be able to have an act of intellective understanding through intelligible species acquired here.

**Objection 3:** In *Ethics* 2 the Philosopher says, "Habits give rise to acts that are similar to the acts through which they are acquired." But a habit of scientific knowledge is acquired here through acts of an intellect that is turning itself toward phantasms; therefore, this habit cannot give rise to any other sort of act (*alios actus reddere*). But acts of the sort in question do not belong to a separated soul. Therefore, a separated soul will not have any acts of the scientific knowledge that has been acquired here.

**But contrary to this:** In Luke 16:25 the following is said to the rich man who is in hell: "Remember that you received good things in your life."

**I respond:** There are two things to consider in an act, viz., the species of the act and its mode. The species of an act is thought of by reference to the object which the act of the cognitive power is directed toward through the [intelligible or sensible] species that is a likeness of the object, whereas the mode is thought of by reference to the agent's power. For instance, the fact that someone sees a rock depends on the species of a rock that exists in the eye, but the fact that he sees it in a sharp-sighted way (*acute*) depends on the eye's visual power.

Therefore, since, as has been explained (a. 5), the intelligible species remain in a separated soul despite the fact that a separated soul's status is not the same as it is at present, it follows that a separated soul is able to understand the things that it previously understood through the intelligible species acquired here. However, it does not understand them in the same mode, viz., through turning toward phantasms. Instead, it understands them in a mode appropriate to a separated soul. And so an act of scientific knowledge acquired here remains in a separated soul, but not with the same mode.

**Reply to objection 1:** The Philosopher is talking about memory (*reminiscentia*) insofar as memory (*memoria*) belongs to the sentient part of the soul, but not insofar as memory exists in a certain way in the intellect, as was explained above (q. 79, a. 6).

**Reply to objection 2:** Different modes of intellective understanding stem from the different states of the soul that is engaged in understanding and not from different levels of power (*ex diversa virtute*) on the part of the [intelligible] species.

**Reply to objection 3:** It is with respect to the species of the acts, but not with respect to the mode of acting, that the acts through which a habit is acquired are similar to the acts which the habit causes. For instance, performing just deeds without performing them in a just way (*operari iusta sed non iuste*), i.e., with delight, causes a habit of political justice, through which one operates with delight.

## Article 7

### Does spatial distance impede a separated soul's cognition?

It seems that spatial distance (*distantia localis*) impedes a separated soul's cognition:

**Objection 1:** In *De Cura pro Mortuis Agenda* Augustine says, "The souls of the dead are in a place where they cannot know what is happening here." But they do know what is happening among themselves. Therefore, spatial distance impedes a separated soul's cognition.

**Objection 2:** In *De Divinatione Daemonum* Augustine says, "Because of their swift movement, the demons report certain things that are unknown to us." But agility of movement would not matter if spatial distance did not impede the demons' cognition. Therefore, *a fortiori*, spatial distance impedes the cognition of a separated soul, which is inferior in nature to a demon.

**Objection 3:** In the same way that someone is distant with respect to place, so too he can be distant with respect to time. But temporal distance impedes a separated soul's cognition, since a separated soul does not have cognition of future things. Therefore, it seems that distance with respect to place likewise impedes a separated soul's cognition.

**But contrary to this:** Luke 16:23 says, "When the rich man was in torment, he raised his eyes and saw Abraham in the distance." Therefore, spatial distance does not impede a separated soul's cognition.

**I respond:** Some have claimed that a separated soul has cognition of singulars by abstracting from sensible things. If this were true, then one could claim that spatial distance impedes a separated soul's cognition. For it would be required either that sensible things act on a separated soul or that a separated soul acts on sensible things—and in either case determinate distances would be required.

But the position just described is impossible, since the abstraction of species from sensible things is effected by means of the senses and other sentient powers, which do not remain as actualities in a separated soul.

Now a separated soul has intellective understanding of singulars through an influx of species from the divine light, and this light is related in the same way to what is distant as to what is close by. Hence, spatial distance does not in any way impede a separated soul's cognition.

**Reply to objection 1:** Augustine is not claiming that the reason why the souls of the dead cannot see things *here* is that they are *there*, as if he believed spatial distance to be the cause of this ignorance. Rather, the ignorance can be due to something else, as will be explained below (a. 8).

**Reply to objection 2:** In this passage Augustine is speaking in accord with the opinion by which some had claimed that demons have bodies naturally united to them. According to this position, they can even have sentient powers whose cognition requires determinate distances.

Augustine also touches on this position explicitly in the same book, though he seems to do so by reciting the position rather than by asserting it. This is clear from what he says in *De Civitate Dei* 21.

**Reply to objection 3:** Future things, which are distant with respect to time, are not actual entities (*entia in actu*). Hence, they are unknowable in themselves, since something lacks knowability in the same way that it lacks being (*entitas*). But things that are distant with respect to place are actual entities and knowable in their own right. Hence, the argument from spatial distance is not the same as the argument from temporal distance.


### Article 8

### Do separated souls have cognition of what is happening here?

It seems that separated souls have cognition of what is happening here:

**Objection 1:** If they did not have cognition of these things, then they would not care about them. But they do care about what is happening here—this according to Luke 16:28 ("I have five brothers . . . so that he might give witness to them, lest they, too, come into this place of torment"). Therefore, separated souls have cognition of what is happening here.

**Objection 2:** The dead frequently appear to the living, whether asleep or awake, and warn them about what is happening here—in the way that

Samuel appeared to Saul, as 1 Kings 28:11 reports. But this would not be the case if they had no cognition of what is happening here. Therefore, they have cognition of what is happening here.

**Objection 3:** Separated souls have cognition of what is happening around them. Therefore, if they did not have cognition of what is happening among us, then it would be the case that their cognition is impeded by spatial distance. But this was denied above (a. 7).

**But contrary to this:** Job 14:21 says, "He will not know whether his children turn out noble or ignoble."

**I respond:** As regards natural cognition, which is what we are now talking about, the souls of the dead do not know what is happening here. The reason for this can be gathered from what has already been said (a. 4). For a separated soul has cognition of singulars by being in some sense directed toward them (*determinata ad illa*), either through a vestige of some previous cognition or affective tie, or else through divine ordination. Now it is both because of divine ordination and because of their mode of being that the souls of the dead are segregated off from fellowship with the living and joined in fellowship with spiritual substances that are separate from bodies. Hence, they are ignorant of what is happening among us. In *Moralia* 12 Gregory gives this explanation: "The dead do not know how life after them in the flesh is going among the living. For the life of the spirit is far from the life of the flesh, and just as the corporeal and the incorporeal are diverse in genus, so too they are distinct in cognition." Augustine seems to touch on this, too, in *De Cura pro Mortuis Agenda*, when he says, "The souls of the dead are not involved (*non intersunt*) in the affairs of the living."

However, there seems to be a disagreement between Gregory and Augustine as far as the souls of the blessed in heaven are concerned.

For in the same place Gregory adds, "Yet do not think the same way about the saintly souls, for since they see interiorly the clarity of almighty God, it is impossible to believe that there is anything exterior that they do not know."

By contrast, in *De Cura pro Mortuis Agenda* Augustine explicitly says, "The dead, even the saints, do not know what the living are doing, even their own children"—as we have it in the Gloss on Isaiah 63:16 ("Abraham has not known us . . ."). Augustine confirms this claim by appeal to the fact that he was not visited by his mother or consoled by her in his sorrows, as he was when she was alive, and it is unlikely that she is less kind in her happier life. He also confirms it by the fact that the Lord promised king Josiah that he would die first, lest he see the evils that were going to befall his people (4 Kings 22:20). However, Augustine says this with hesitation; that is why he prefaces his remarks by saying, "Let each one take as he wishes what I am about to say."

Gregory, on the other hand, speaks with confidence (*assertive*), as is evident from the fact that he says, "It is impossible to believe . . ." But according to Gregory's opinion, it seems that the souls of the saints, seeing God, have cognition of all present things that are happening here. For these souls are equal to the angels, of whom even Augustine asserts that they are not ignorant of what is happening among the living. But because the souls of the saints are most perfectly joined to God's justice, they do not grieve; nor do they enter into the affairs of the living, except insofar as the order of divine justice requires it.

**Reply to objection 1:** The souls of the dead can care about the affairs of the living, even if they do not know their condition—just as we ourselves exercise care for the dead by offering suffrages for them, even though we do not know their condition.

It is also possible for the souls of the dead to have cognition of the deeds of the living not on their own, but through the souls of those who join them from here, or through the angels or demons, or even when God's Spirit reveals these things to them, as Augustine says in the same book.

**Reply to objection 2:** When the dead appear in some way to the living, either (a) this happens because of God's specially arranging for the souls of the dead to enter into the affairs of the living, in which case it is counted among God's miracles, or (b) apparitions of this sort are effected by the actions of good or bad angels, even when the dead do not know about it—just as the living likewise, without knowing it, appear in the dreams of others among the living, as Augustine says in the aforementioned book.

Hence, one can say of Samuel that he appeared through a divine revelation—this according to Ecclesiasticus 46:23 ("He slept, and he made known to the king . . . the end of his life"). Or else, if one does not accept the authority of Ecclesiasticus because it was not counted by the Hebrews among the canonical writings, one can claim that the apparition was arranged by demons.

**Reply to objection 3:** This sort of ignorance occurs for the reasons explained above and not because of spatial distance.

# QUESTION 90

## The Initial Production of Man with Respect to His Soul

After what has gone before, we have to consider the initial production of man. And on this topic there are four things to consider: first, the production of man himself (questions 90–92); second, the goal of this production (question 93); third, the status and condition of man as he was first produced (questions 94–101); fourth, his location (question 102).

As far as the production is concerned, there are three topics to consider: first, the production of man with respect to his soul (question 90); second, the production of the man with respect to the male body (question 91); third, the production of the woman (question 92).

On the first topic there are four questions: (1) Is the human soul something made, or is it part of God's substance? (2) Assuming that it is made, is it created? (3) Is the soul produced by the mediation of angels? (4) Was the soul produced before the body?

### Article 1

#### Is a [human] soul made, or is it part of God's substance?

It seems that a [human] soul is not made, but is instead part of God's substance (*sit de substantia Dei*):

**Objection 1:** Genesis 2:7 says: "The Lord God formed man from the slime of the earth, and breathed into his face the breath of life, and man became a living soul." But when one breathes, he emits something from himself. Therefore, the soul by which man lives is part of God's substance.

**Objection 2:** As was established above (q. 75, a. 5), a [human] soul is a simple form. But a form is an actuality. Therefore, a soul is a pure actuality—a feature that belongs to God alone. Therefore, a soul is part of God's substance.

**Objection 3:** If things exist and do not differ from one another in any way, then they are the same. But God and a [human] mind exist, and they do not differ from one another in any way—since they would have to differ from one another in virtue of certain differences, and if that were so, they would be composite. Therefore, God and a human mind are the same.

**But contrary to this:** In *De Origine Animae* Augustine enumerates certain positions that he takes to be "exceedingly and openly perverse and

opposed to the Catholic Faith," the first among which is the claim, asserted by some, that "God made the soul from Himself and not from nothing."

**I respond:** There is an obvious implausibility in the claim that a
[human] soul is part of God's substance. For as is clear from what has been
said (q. 77, a. 2 and q. 79, a. 2 and q. 84, a. 6), the human soul (a) sometimes has intellective understanding [only] in potentiality, (b) in some
sense acquires scientific knowledge from the things themselves, and (c)
has diverse powers—all of which are foreign to the nature of God, who, as
was proved above (q. 3), (a) is pure actuality, (b) acquires nothing from
another, and (c) has no differentiation within Himself.

Now the error in question seems to have originated in two positions
held by the ancients.

Those who first began to consider the natures of things were unable to
transcend the imagination and so claimed that there is nothing beyond bodies. So they claimed that God is a certain body that they judged to be the
source of other bodies. And since, as *De Anima* 1 reports, they claimed that
the soul is part of the nature of that body said to be the source, it followed
as a result that the soul is part of the nature of God. Verging on this position, the Manicheans, who took God to be a certain sort of corporeal light,
claimed that the soul is a part of this light that is tied down to a body.

Second, things progressed to the point that certain thinkers apprehended that something incorporeal exists—not something separated from a
body, but something that is the form of a body. Hence, as Augustine reports
in *De Civitate Dei* 7, Varro claimed that God is a soul that governs the
world by motion and reason. Accordingly, there were some who claimed
that a man's soul is a part of this whole soul in the same way that a man is
a part of the whole world; for they were unable to reach the point intellectually of distinguishing the different grades of spiritual substances except
by reference to the distinctions among bodies.

But as was proved above (q. 3), all these claims are impossible. Hence,
it is manifestly false that a [human] soul is a part of God's substance.

**Reply to objection 1:** 'Breathe' should not be taken in a corporeal
sense here. Instead, God's 'breathing' is the same as His making a spirit—
though it is true in any case that in breathing corporeally a man emits
something extraneous to himself and not something of his own substance.

**Reply to objection 2:** Even though a [human] soul is a simple form in
its essence, it is not its own *esse*; instead, it is a being by participation, as
is clear from what was said above (q. 75, a. 5). And so, unlike God, a
human soul is not pure actuality.

**Reply to objection 3:** Things that *differ* in the proper sense differ *in* something (*differt aliquo*); this is why a difference is sought in cases where there is agreement. Because of this, things that differ from one another must be composite in some sense, since they differ in something and agree in something.

Given this, as *Metaphysics* 10 points out, even if it is the case that all things that *differ* from one another are *diverse*, it is nonetheless not the case that all things that are *diverse* also *differ* from one another (*licet omne differens est diversum, non tamen omne diversum est differens*). For simple things are diverse in their own right (*seipsis*), but they do not differ by any differences out of which they might be composed. For instance, a man and a donkey differ by the differences *rational* and *non-rational*, but one cannot say of these differences themselves that they differ from one another by still other differences.

## Article 2

### Is a [human] soul brought into being through creation?

It seems that a [human] soul is not brought into being (*producta in esse*) through creation:

**Objection 1:** That which has something material within itself is made from matter. But a soul has something material within itself, since it is not pure actuality. Therefore, a soul is made from matter. Therefore, it is not created.

**Objection 2:** Every actuality that belongs to some matter seems to be brought forth from the matter's potentiality (*educi de potentia materiae*); for since matter is in potentiality with respect to actuality, every actuality preexists in potentiality within the matter. But a soul is the actuality of corporeal matter, as is clear from the definition of a soul. Therefore, a soul is brought forth from the potentiality of matter.

**Objection 3:** A soul is a certain form. Therefore, if a soul is made through creation, then by parity of reasoning all other forms are likewise made through creation. And so no form will come into being through generation—which is absurd.

**But contrary to this:** Genesis 1:27 says, "God created man in His own image." But man is "in God's image" because of the soul. Therefore, the soul came into being through creation.

**I respond:** A rational soul can be made only through creation—something that is not true of other forms. The reason for this is that since being-made (*fieri*) is a path to *esse*, being-made belongs to a given thing in the same way that *esse* belongs to it.

Now what is properly said to exist is that which itself has *esse* in the sense of subsisting in its own *esse* (*quasi in suo esse subsistens*); hence, it is only substances that are properly and truly called beings (*entia*). By contrast, an accident does not have *esse*, but is that *by which* something is such-and-such (*eo aliquid est*). This is the sense in which it is called a being (*ens*); for instance, a whiteness is called a being because by it something is white (*quia ea aliquid est album*). It is for this reason that *Metaphysics* 7 says that an accident "is said to be 'of-a-being' (*entis*) rather than 'a being' (*ens*)." Moreover, the same line of reasoning holds for every other non-subsistent form. And so being-made does not properly belong to any non-subsistent form; instead, such forms are said to be made by virtue of the fact that subsistent composites are made.

By contrast, as was shown above (q. 75, a. 2), a rational soul is a subsistent form. Hence, both being-made and *esse* belong to it properly speaking. And since a soul cannot be made from preexistent matter—either corporeal matter, since in that case it would have a corporeal nature, or spiritual matter, since in that case spiritual substances would be transformed into one another—one must claim that a soul can be made only through creation.

**Reply to objection 1:** In a soul the simple essence itself is akin to the material aspect (*sicut materiale*), whereas the formal aspect in it (*formale in ipsa*) is the participated *esse*, which is necessarily simultaneous with the essence of the soul, since *esse* follows *per se* upon form.

The same line of reasoning would hold if one claimed—as some do—that [a human soul] is composed of spiritual matter. For like celestial matter, spiritual matter is not in potentiality with respect to any other [substantial] form; otherwise, a soul would be corruptible.

Hence, there is no way in which a [human] soul can be made from pre-existing matter.

**Reply to objection 2:** For an actuality to be drawn from the potentiality of matter (*actum extrahi de potentia materiae*) is nothing other than for something that previously existed in potentiality to be brought into actuality (*aliquid fieri actu quod prius erat in potentia*). However, since a rational soul has subsistent *esse* and not *esse* that depends on corporeal matter, and since, as was explained above (q. 75, a. 2), a rational soul exceeds the capability of corporeal matter, it follows that it is not brought forth from the potentiality of matter.

**Reply to objection 3:** As has been explained, there is no parallel between a rational soul and other forms.

## Article 3

### Is a rational soul produced directly by God, or is it produced through the mediation of angels?

It seems that a rational soul is not produced directly (*immediate*) by God, but is instead produced through the mediation of angels (*mediantibus angelis*):

**Objection 1:** There is more order among spiritual things than among corporeal things. But as Dionysius says in *De Divinis Nominibus*, chap. 4, lower bodies are produced through higher bodies. Therefore, lower spirits, i.e., rational souls, are likewise produced through higher spirits, i.e., angels.

**Objection 2:** The end of things corresponds to their source; for instance, God is both the source and the end of things. Therefore, it is also the case that a thing's issuing forth from its source (*exitus a principio*) corresponds to its being brought back to its end (*reductio in finem*). But as Dionysius says, "the lowest things are brought back to their end through the first things." Therefore, the lowest things likewise proceed into *esse* through the first things; more specifically, souls proceed into being (*procedunt in esse*) through angels.

**Objection 3:** As *Meteorologia* 4 says, "The perfect is that which can make what is similar to itself." But spiritual substances are much more perfect than corporeal substances are. Therefore, since bodies make things that are similar in species to themselves, *a fortiori* angels will be able to make something that is lower than they are in its natural species (*secundum speciem naturae*), viz., a rational soul.

**But contrary to this:** Genesis 2:7 says that God Himself "breathed into man's face the breath of life."

**I respond:** Some have claimed that angels, acting in the power of God, cause rational souls. But this opinion is altogether impossible and alien to the Faith.

For it has been shown (a. 2) that a rational soul can be produced only through creation. But God alone is able to create. For it belongs to the first agent alone to act without presupposing anything, since, as was established above (q. 65, a. 3), a secondary agent always presupposes something that comes from the first agent. But if an agent effects something out of what is presupposed (*quod agit aliquid ex aliquo praesupposito*), then it acts by transforming (*transmutando*). And so every other agent acts only by *transforming*, whereas God acts by *creating*. And since a rational soul cannot be produced by the transformation of any matter, it follows that it cannot be produced except directly by God.

**Reply to objection 1 and objection 2 and objection 3:** The reply to the objections is clear from what has been said. For the fact that bodies cause what is similar to themselves or what is lower than themselves, and the fact that lower beings are brought back [to their end] through higher beings—all of this occurs through one or another sort of transformation.

## Article 4

### Was the human soul produced before the human body?

It seems that the human soul was produced before the human body:

**Objection 1:** As was established above (q. 66, a. 1 and q. 70, a. 1), the work of creation preceded the work of division and the work of adornment. But the soul was brought into being (*producta in esse*) through creation, whereas the body was made at the end of the work of adornment. Therefore, the soul of man was produced before the body.

**Objection 2:** A rational soul shares more in common (*magis convenit*) with angels than with brute animals. But angels were created either before bodies or right at the beginning along with corporeal matter, whereas the human body was formed on the sixth day, after the brute animals had already been produced. Therefore, the human soul was created before the human body.

**Objection 3:** The end is proportionate to the beginning. But the soul remains in the end after the body. Therefore, it was likewise created at the beginning before the body.

**But contrary to this:** A proper actuality is effected in a proper potentiality. Therefore, since the soul is the proper actuality of the body, the soul was produced in the body (*anima producta est in corpore*).

**I respond:** Origen claimed that not only the first man's soul, but the souls of all men, were created along with the angels before bodies—and he made this claim because he believed that all spiritual substances, both souls and angels, were equal in the status of their natures and unequal only in merit (*solum merito distare*). The result is that some of these spiritual substances were tied to bodies—these are the souls of men and the souls of the celestial bodies—whereas others remained in their purity, divided into diverse orders (*secundum diversos ordines*).

We have already replied to this opinion above (q. 47, a. 2), and so we will leave it aside at present.

However, in *Super Genesim ad Litteram* 7 Augustine has a different reason for claiming that the soul of the first man was created along with the angels and before the body, viz., because he holds that (a) in the work of the six days man's body was produced only with respect to its causal principles (*solum secundum causales rationes*) and not in actuality, whereas (b) this cannot be said of the soul, because the soul was not made from any preexisting matter, whether corporeal or spiritual, and because the soul could not have been produced by any created power. And so it seems that (a) the soul itself was created along with the angels during the work of the six days, when all things were made, and that (b) afterwards it was directed by its own will to be in charge of a body (*propria voluntate inclinata fuit ad corpus adminstrandum*).

However, Augustine does not make these claims by way of assertion, as his words demonstrate. For he says, "As long as no Scriptural passage or sound argument contradicts it, it is permissible to believe that man was made on the sixth day in the sense that the causal principle of the human body was created in the elements of the world, whereas the soul itself had already been created."

Now this view could indeed be tolerated according to those who claim that the soul has a complete species and nature in its own right (*per se*) and is united to the body not as its form, but only in order to be in charge of the body. However, if the soul is united to the body as its form and is naturally a part of a human nature, then this view is altogether impossible. For it is clear that God instituted the first things in a state of natural perfection (*in perfecto statu suae naturae*), in the way required by the species of each thing. But since a soul is part of a human nature, it does not have its natural perfection except insofar as it is united to a body. Hence, it would not have been appropriate for the soul to be created without a body.

Therefore, in order to sustain Augustine's opinion about the work of the six days (cf. q. 74, a. 2), one could claim that (a) in the work of the six

days the human soul came beforehand (*praecessit*) by way of a certain likeness of genus, in the sense that it agrees with the angels in being an intellectual nature, but that (b) it itself was created simultaneously with the
body. By contrast, according to the other saints, both the soul and the body
of the first man were produced during the work of the six days.

**Reply to objection 1:** If the soul's nature had a complete species, so
that it might be created in its own right (*secundum se*), then the argument
that the soul was created by itself (*per se*) at the beginning would go
through. However, since the soul is naturally the form of a body, it must not
have been created separately (*non fuit seorsum creanda*), but instead it had
to be created in a body.

**Reply to objection 2:** The reply to the second objection is similar. If
a soul had a species in its own right (*per se*), it would share more in common with the angels. However, because a soul is the form of a body, it
belongs, as a formal principle, to the genus *animal*.

**Reply to objection 3:** The fact that a soul remains after its body stems
from a defect of the body, i.e., death. This defect was not supposed to exist
at the beginning of the soul's creation (cf. q. 97, a. 1).

# QUESTION 91

## The Production of the First Man's Body

The next thing we have to consider is the production of the first man's body. On this topic there are four questions: (1) What was the matter from which it was produced? (2) Which agent was it produced by? (3) What sort of constitution (*dispositio*) was given it through its production? (4) What was the manner and order of its production?

## Article 1

### Was the first man's body made from the slime of the earth?

It seems that the first man's body was not made from the slime of the earth (*de limo terrae*):

**Objection 1:** It takes more power to make something from nothing (*ex nihilo*) than to make it from something, since non-being (*non ens*) is more distant from actuality than is being-in-potentiality (*ens in potentia*). But since man is the most dignified of the lower creatures (*dignissima creaturarum inferiorum*), it was fitting that God's power should be manifested to the highest degree in the production of man's body. Therefore, it ought to be the case that man's body was made from nothing and not from the slime of the earth.

**Objection 2:** Celestial bodies are more noble than earthly bodies are. But the human body has the greatest nobility, since it is perfected by the most noble form, viz., the rational soul. Therefore, it ought to be the case that it was made from a celestial body rather than from an earthly body.

**Objection 3:** As is clear from their subtlety, fire and air are more noble bodies than earth and water. Therefore, since the human body is the most dignified of all bodies, it ought to be the case that it was made from fire and air rather than from the slime of the earth.

**Objection 4:** The human body is composed of the four elements. Therefore, it was made from all the elements and not from the slime of the earth.

**But contrary to this:** Genesis 2:7 says, "God formed man from the slime of the earth."

**I respond:** Since God is perfect, He has given to His works a perfection corresponding to their mode [of being]—this according to

Deuteronomy 32:4 ("God's works are perfect"). Now He Himself is perfect absolutely speaking because He contains all things within Himself antecedently—not in the mode of composition, but "in a simple and unified way (*simpliciter et unite*)," as Dionysius puts it, in the manner in which diverse effects preexist in a cause in accord with its unified essence (*secundum unam eius essentiam*).

Now this perfection flows into the angels insofar as all the things produced by God in nature fall within their cognition through diverse [intelligible] forms. By contrast, perfection of this sort flows into man in a lower-level way (*inferiori modo*). For man does not have within his natural cognition a knowledge of all natural things. Instead, he is in a certain sense *composed of* all things. For (a) he has within himself a rational soul from the genus of spiritual substances, and (b) he is, by way of likeness to the celestial bodies, far removed from contraries because of the exceptional balance of his constitution (*habet elongationem a contrariis per maximam aequalitatem complexionis*), whereas (c) he has the elements with respect to his substance. However, he has the elements in such a way that the higher elements, viz., fire and air, dominate in him with respect to their *power* (since life consists principally in heat, which comes from fire, and in moistness, which comes from air), whereas the lower elements are abundant in him with respect to their *substance*. For a balanced mixture would not be possible if the lower elements, which have less power, were not quantitatively more abundant in man; and the reason why man's body is said to have been formed from the slime of the earth is that slime is earth mixed with water. And because all the creatures of the world are in some sense found in him, man is called a 'miniature world' (*minor mundus*).

**Reply to objection 1:** God's creative power is manifested in man's body because its matter was produced through creation.

Now the human body had to be made from the matter of the four elements in order that man might share something in common with the lower bodies (*haberet convenientiam cum inferioribus corporibus*), constituting, as it were, a certain middle ground between spiritual substances and corporeal substances.

**Reply to objection 2:** Even though a celestial body is, absolutely speaking, more noble than an earthly body, nonetheless, a celestial body shares less in common with the activity of the rational soul. For the rational soul takes its knowledge of truth in a certain way from the sensory powers, whose organs cannot be formed from a celestial body, because a celestial body cannot be acted upon (*cum sit impassibile*).

Nor is it true that a bit of the fifth essence (*aliquid de quinta essentia*) enters materially into the composition of the human body; this claim is made by some who hold that the soul is united to the body by the mediation of a certain sort of light (cf. q. 76, a. 7).

First of all, their claim that light is a body is false (cf. q. 67, a. 2).

Second, it is impossible for any part of the fifth essence to be divided off from a celestial body or to be mixed in with the elements—and this because of the celestial body's impassibility. Hence, a celestial body can enter into the composition of mixed bodies only through the effect of its power.

**Reply to objection 3:** If fire and air, which are more powerful in their action, also abounded quantitatively in the composition of the human body, then they would completely draw the other elements to themselves, and it would be impossible to fashion the balanced mixture that man's composition needs in order to have a good sense of touch, which is the foundation for the other senses. For the organ associated with each sense must have only in potentiality—and not in actuality—the contraries which are perceived by that sense. This must be so either in such a way that (a) the organ lacks the whole genus of relevant contraries, in the way that the pupil lacks color, so that it might be in potentiality with respect to all colors—something not possible in the case of the organ of touch, since it is composed of the elements, whose qualities the sense of touch perceives—or in such a way that (b) the organ is midway between the contraries, as is necessary in the case of the sense of touch. For the middle is in some sense in potentiality with respect to both extremes.

**Reply to objection 4:** The slime of the earth contains both earth and also water cementing the parts of earth together. Scripture does not make mention of the other [two] elements, both because (a) they are quantitatively less abundant in man's body, as has been explained, and also because (b) in the whole account of the production of things Scripture, which was handed down to an uneducated people, does not make mention of fire and air, which uneducated people do not perceive with their sensory power.

## Article 2

### Was the human body produced directly by God?

It seems that the human body was not produced directly by God (*non sit immediate a Deo*):

**Objection 1:** In *De Trinitate* 3 Augustine says that God takes care of corporeal things through the angelic creature. But, as has been explained (a. 1), the human body was formed from corporeal matter. Therefore, it ought to be the case that it was produced by the mediation of angels and not directly by God.

**Objection 2:** It is unnecessary for anything that can be effected by a created power to be produced directly by God. But the human body can be produced through the created power of a celestial body; for instance, certain animals are generated by putrefaction through the active power of a celestial body, and Albumasar says that men are generated only in places with temperate climates (*in locis temperatis tantum*) and not in places where heat or cold is excessive. Therefore, it was unnecessary for the human body to be formed directly by God.

**Objection 3:** Nothing is made from corporeal matter except through matter's being transformed (*per aliquam materiae transmutationem*). But every corporeal transformation has as a cause that movement of a celestial body that is the first of the movements. Therefore, since the human body is produced from corporeal matter, it seems that a celestial body contributed something to the human body's being formed.

**Objection 4:** In *Super Genesim ad Litteram* Augustine says that man's body was made during the work of the six days in the sense that God placed certain causal principles within corporeal creation (*secundum causales rationes quas Deus inseruit creaturae coporali*), whereas later on man's body was formed in actuality. But that which preexists by means of its causal principles in corporeal creation can be produced through a corporeal power. Therefore, the human body was produced by some created power and not directly by God.

**But contrary to this:** Ecclesiasticus 17:1 says, "God created man out of the earth."

**I respond:** The first formation of the human body could not have occurred through any created power, but was instead directly from God.

To be sure, some have claimed that the forms existing in corporeal matter are derived from certain immaterial forms. But as has already been explained (q. 65, a. 4), the Philosopher fends off this position in *Metaphysics* 7 by appeal to the fact that it is composite things, and not forms, that are made *per se*. And since an agent is similar to what it makes, it is not fitting that a pure form, which exists without matter, should produce a form which exists in matter and which is made only in virtue of the fact that the relevant composite is made. And so it has to be the case that the cause of a form that exists in matter is itself a form that exists in matter; for what is composite is generated from what is composite.

On the other hand, even though God is altogether immaterial, it is He alone who through His power can produce matter by creating it. Hence, it belongs to Him alone to produce a form in matter without the assistance of a preexisting material form. For this reason, angels cannot transform bodies with respect to any form unless they are aided by certain 'seeds', as Augustine puts it in *De Trinitate* 3.

Therefore, since the human body—by the power of which another similar in species might be formed by way of generation—had never previously been formed, it was necessary for the first human body to be formed directly by God.

**Reply to objection 1:** Even if angels provide some sort of ministry to God in what He does with respect to bodies, it is nonetheless the case that God does certain things among corporeal creatures that angels cannot in any way do—e.g., bringing back the dead and giving sight to the blind. It was likewise this sort of power by which He formed the body of the first man from the slime of the earth.

Still, it could have happened that angels provided some sort of ministry in the formation of the body of the first man—like the ministry they will provide at the last resurrection by collecting the dust.

**Reply to objection 2:** Perfect animals, which are generated from semen, cannot be generated solely through the power of a celestial body in the way that Avicenna imagines—this, despite the fact that the power of a celestial body does cooperate in the natural generation of perfect animals, in keeping with the Philosopher's claim in *Physics* 2 that "a man and the sun generate a man from matter." This is why a place with a temperate climate is required for the generation of men and other perfect animals.

However, the power of celestial bodies is indeed sufficient for generating certain imperfect animals from properly disposed matter, since it is clear that more is required for the production of a perfect entity than for the production of an imperfect entity.

**Reply to objection 3:** The movement of the heavens is a cause of natural transformations, but not of transformations that are effected outside the order of nature (*praeter naturae ordinem*) and by God's power alone, e.g., raising the dead and giving sight to the blind. It is these transformations that are similar to a man's being formed from the slime of the earth.

**Reply to objection 4:** There are two ways in which, among creatures, something is said to preexist through its causal principles.

In the first way it preexists in virtue of both an active and a passive power; that is, the thing preexists not only in the sense that it can be made out of preexisting matter, but also in the sense that there is some preexisting creature that is able to make it.

In the second way it preexists in virtue of a passive power alone, i.e., in the sense that it can be made by God from preexisting matter. It is in this sense that, according to Augustine, the human body preexisted through causal principles in the works that were produced.

## Article 3

### Is the human body appropriately constituted?

It seems that the human body is not appropriately constituted (*non habuerit convenientem dispositionem*):

**Objection 1:** Since man is the most noble of the animals, the human body should be optimally constituted for doing what is proper to animals, viz., sensing and moving about. But some animals have a more acute sensory power than man, and some have swifter movement; for instance, dogs have a better sense of smell than man, and birds move more swiftly. Therefore, man's body is not appropriately constituted.

**Objection 2:** The perfect is that which is lacking in nothing. But the human body lacks more things than do the bodies of other animals, which have hides and natural weapons for their protection—something that man lacks. Therefore, the human body is very imperfectly constituted.

**Objection 3:** Man is more distant from the plants than from the brute animals. But plants have an upright stature, whereas brute animals are on all fours. Therefore, it ought not to have been the case that man has an upright stature.

**But contrary to this:** Ecclesiastes 7:30 says, "God made man upright."

**I respond:** All natural things have been produced by God's craftsmanship (*ab arte divina*), and so they are in a certain sense the artifacts of God Himself (*sunt quodammodo artificiata ipsius Dei*). Now every craftsman intends to give the best constitution to his work—not the best constitution absolutely speaking, but the best constitution relative to its end. And if such a constitution has some defect associated with it, the craftsman does not care. For instance, a craftsman who makes a saw for cutting makes it out of iron in order that it might be fit for cutting, and he does not care to make it out of glass, which is a more beautiful material, since such beauty would pose an obstacle to its end.

So, then, God gave the best constitution to each natural thing—not, to be sure, the best constitution absolutely speaking, but rather the best constitution relative to its being ordered toward its proper end. As the Philosopher puts it in *Physics* 2, ". . . because it is more worthy—not absolutely speaking, but relative to the substance of each one."

Now the proximate end of the human body is the rational soul and its operations, since matter is for the sake of form and instruments are for the sake of the agent's actions. Therefore, I claim that God made (*instituit*) the human body with the best constitution as far as appropriateness for this sort of form and its operations is concerned. And if there seems to be any defect in the constitution of the human body, notice that such a defect follows by material necessity from what is required in the body in order for it have a due proportion to the soul and to the soul's operations.

**Reply to objection 1:** The sense of touch, which is the basis for the other sensory powers, is more perfect in man than in any other animal, and for this reason it was necessary for man to have the most balanced physical constitution (*haberet temperatissimam complexionem*) of all the animals. Moreover, as is clear from what was said above (q. 78, a. 4), man is superior to all the other animals with respect to the interior sentient powers.

On the other hand, as far as some of the exterior sensory powers are concerned, it happens by a certain necessity that man falls short of the other animals. For instance, among all the animals, man has the worst sense of smell. For it was necessary that man, among all the animals, should have the largest brain in relation to his body (*respectu sui corporis haberet maximum cerebrum*), both in order to perfect in a less restricted way (*liberius*) the operations of the interior sentient powers—which, as was explained above (q. 84, a. 7), are necessary for the intellect's operation—and in order for the brain's cool temperature (*frigiditas cerebri*) to moderate the heart's heat, which has to abound in man in order for him to have an upright stature. But because of the brain's moistness, its size is an impediment to the sense of smell, which requires dryness.

In this same way, one can likewise give reasons for why certain animals have more acute vision or more sensitive hearing than man—because the obstacles to these senses must follow in man from the perfect balance of his constitution. And the same reason is also to be given for why other animals are swifter than man; for the balance of the human constitution is incompatible with excessive swiftness.

**Reply to objection 2:** Horns and hooves, which are the weapons of certain animals, along with a toughness of hide and a multitude of hair or feathers, which are the coverings of animals, attest to an abundance of the element earth, which is incompatible with the balance and tenderness of the human constitution. And so such things were not fitting for man. Rather, in place of these things man has his reason and his hands, by which he can make for himself, in an unlimited number of ways, weapons and coverings and the other things necessary for life. Hence, in *De Anima* 3 the hand is called "the organ of organs." This was more appropriate for a rational nature, which has an unlimited number of ideas, with the result that it has the capacity to make an unlimited number of instruments.

**Reply to objection 3:** There are four reasons why having an upright stature was appropriate for man.

First, the sensory powers were given to man not only, as with the other animals, in order to procure the necessities of life, but also in order to have cognition. Hence, whereas the other animals do not delight in sensible things except in their relation to food and sexual attraction, man alone takes delight in the very beauty of sensible things in its own right. And so since the sensory powers are particularly strong in the facial area, the other animals have their faces turned toward the earth, as if in order to seek food and provide nourishment for themselves, whereas man has his face held up, in order that through the senses—and chiefly through the sense of sight, which is more subtle and reveals the many differences among things—he might be able in an unrestricted way (*libere*) to have cognition of sensible things, both earthly and celestial, from every angle, so that he might gather intelligible truth from all things.

Second, he has an upright stature so that the interior powers might have their operations more freely, given that the brain, in which the interior powers are in some sense activated (*perficiuntur*), is not close to the ground (*non depressum*) but is instead elevated over all the parts of the body.

Third, if man had a prone posture, he would have to use his hands as front feet. And so the hands would cease to be useful for performing diverse works.

Fourth, if man had a prone posture and used his hands as front feet, then he would have to capture food with his mouth. And so, as is clear from the case of the other animals, he would have an oblong mouth, and hard and large lips, and a hardened tongue as well, so as not to be harmed by exterior things. And this sort of arrangement would completely impede speech, which is a proper work of reason.

And yet even though he has an upright stature, man is still maximally remote from plant life. For man has his superior part, i.e., the head, facing the higher part of the world, and he has his inferior part facing the lower part of the world, and so he is optimally arranged in his entire constitution. By contrast, plants have their superior part facing the lower part of the world (for their roots are, as it were, their mouths), whereas their inferior part is found in the higher part of the world. On the other hand, brute animals lie between the two, since the superior part of an animal is the part which takes in nourishment, whereas the inferior part is the part that emits waste products.

## Article 4

### Is the production of the human body appropriately described in Scripture?

It seems that the production of the human body is not appropriately described in Scripture:

**Objection 1:** Just as the human body was made by God, so too were the other works of the six days. But in the case of the other works it says, "God said, 'Let such-and-such be made', and it was made." Therefore, something similar should have been said concerning the production of man.

**Objection 2:** As was explained above (a. 2), the human body was made directly by God. Therefore, it is inappropriate to say, "Let *us* make man."

**Objection 3:** The form of the human body is the soul itself, which is the breath of life. Therefore, after it had said, "God formed man from the slime of the earth," it was not appropriate to add, ". . . and He breathed into his face the breath of life."

**Objection 4:** The soul, which is the breath of life, is in the whole body and most especially in the heart. Therefore, it was inappropriate to say, "He breathed into his face the breath of life."

**Objection 5:** The male and female sexes have to do with the body, whereas the image of God has to do with the soul. But according to Augustine, the soul was made before the body. Therefore, after it had said, "To His image He made him," it was not appropriate to add, ". . . male and female He created them."

**But contrary to this** is the authority of Scripture.

**I respond** [by replying to the objections]:

**Reply to objection 1:** As Augustine says in *Super Genesim ad Litteram* 6, the reason why man is preeminent over other things is not that God Himself made man—as if He Himself did not make the other things. For it is written, "The heavens are the works of your hands" (Psalm 101:26), and in another place, "His hands laid down the dry land" (Psalm 94:5). Rather, man is preeminent over other things because man was made to the image of God.

Nonetheless, in the case of the production of man Scripture uses a special way of speaking in order to indicate that the other things were made for the sake of man. For we normally make with greater thought and care those things that we principally intend.

**Reply to objection 2:** This phrase should not be taken to mean—as some have perversely taken it to mean—that God was saying to the *angels*, "Let us make man." Instead, this is said in order to signify the plurality of the divine persons, whose image is found explicitly in man.

**Reply to objection 3:** Some have claimed that the [first] man's body was formed antecedently in time, and that later on God infused a soul into the already formed body. But it is contrary to the nature of the perfection of the first institution of things that God would make either the body without the soul or the soul without the body; for each of them is a part of human nature.

It is especially inappropriate to make the body without the soul, since the body depends on the soul, but not vice versa. And so to rule this out, some have claimed that (a) when it says, "God formed man," this means that the production of the body was simultaneous with the soul, and that (b) when it is added, ". . . and He breathed (*inspiravit*) into his face the breath of life," this is referring to the Holy Spirit—just as our Lord breathed (*insufflavit*) on the Apostles, saying, "Receive the Holy Spirit" (John 20:22).

However, as Augustine points out in *De Civitate Dei*, this reading is ruled out by the words of Scripture. For the following is added to what was just cited: "And man was made a living soul"—but in 1 Corinthians 15:45 the Apostle relates this phrase to man's animal life and not to his spiritual life. Therefore, the words "breath of life" refer to the soul, so that when it says, "He breathed into his face the breath of life," this serves as an explanation, so to speak, of what had gone before; for the soul is the form of the body.

**Reply to objection 4:** The reason why it says that the breath of life was breathed into the man's face is that the vital operations (*operationes vitae*) are more manifest in man's face because of the sensory powers that exist there.

**Reply to objection 5:** According to Augustine, all the works of the six days were effected simultaneously. Hence, he does not hold that the first man's soul, which he claims to have been made simultaneously with the angels, was made before the sixth day. Instead, he claims that on the sixth day itself (a) the first man's soul was made in actuality and (b) his body was made with respect to its causal principles.

By contrast, the other doctors claim that both the man's soul and his body were made in actuality on the sixth day.

# QUESTION 92

## The Production of the Woman

The next thing we have to consider is the production of the woman. On this topic there are four questions: (1) Was it fitting for the woman to be produced in this [initial] production of things? (2) Was it fitting for the woman to be made from the man? (3) Was it fitting for the woman to be produced from the man's rib? (4) Was the woman made directly by God?

### Article 1

### Was it fitting for the woman to be produced in the initial production of things?

It seems that it was not fitting for the woman to be produced in the initial production of things [*in prima rerum productione*]:

**Objection 1:** In *De Generatione Animalium* the Philosopher says, "The female is an inadvertently caused male (*femina est mas occasionatus*)." But it was not fitting for anything inadvertent and deficient to exist in the initial institution of things. Therefore, it was not fitting for the woman to be produced in that initial production of things.

**Objection 2:** Subjection and abasement are the result of sin; for it is after the sin that the woman is told, "You shall be under the man's power" (Genesis 3:16), and Gregory says, "When we do not sin, we are all equal." But the woman has less natural power and dignity than the man, since, as Augustine says in *Super Genesim ad Litteram* 12, "What acts is always more honorable than what is acted upon." Therefore, it was not fitting for the woman to be produced in the initial production of things, before the sin.

**Objection 3:** The occasions of sin should be eliminated. But God foreknew that the woman would be an occasion of sin for the man. Therefore, He should not have produced the woman.

**But contrary to this:** Genesis 2:18 says, "It is not good for the man to be alone; let us make him a helper like to himself."

**I respond:** As Scripture says, it was necessary for the woman to be made as a helper to the man—more specifically, as a helper in the work of generation and not as a helper for just any other work, as some have claimed, since for any other work a man can be helped more appropriately by another man than by a woman.

This can be made clearer if one considers the modes of generation among living things:

For some living things do not have within themselves the active power of generation, but are instead generated by an agent of another species, e.g., those plants and animals that are generated from the appropriate matter without seed (*sine semine*) by the active power of the celestial bodies.

On the other hand, other living things have the active and passive powers of generation joined together [within themselves], as in the case of plants that are generated from seeds. For in plants there is no vital work that is more noble than the work of generation, and so it is appropriate in their case for the active power of generation to be joined with the passive power of generation at all times.

By contrast, perfect animals have the active power of generation in the male sex and the passive power of generation in the female sex. And because in animals there is a vital work which is more noble than generation and which their life is principally ordered toward, the masculine sex is not joined at all times to the female in perfect animals, but is joined only at the time of coitus. So we might imagine that through coitus the male and the female become one in a way similar to that in which the masculine and feminine powers are joined at all times in a plant—even though in some plants the one power is more abundant, and in others the other power is more abundant.

Now man is ordered toward an even more noble vital work, viz., intellective understanding. And so in the case of man there is an even stronger reason for why there ought to be a distinction between the two powers, with the result that the female is produced separately from the male and yet they are joined together as one carnally (*carnaliter in unum*) for the work of generation. And this is why, immediately after the formation of the woman, Genesis 2:24 says, "They will be two in one flesh."

**Reply to objection 1:** In relation to *a particular nature*, the female is something deficient and inadvertent (*aliquid deficiens et occasionatum*). For the active power that exists in the male's seed aims at producing something complete and similar to itself in the masculine sex, and the fact that a female is generated is due either to a weakness in the active power, or to some indisposition on the part of the matter, or even to some transformation from without, e.g., from the southern winds (*a ventis australibus*), which are humid, as *De Generatione Animalium* says.

However, in relation to *nature as a whole* (*per comparationem ad naturam universalem*), the female is not something inadvert, but is instead ordered by the intention of nature toward the work of generation. Now the intention of nature as a whole depends on God, who is the universal author of nature. And so in instituting the nature, He produced not only the male but also the female.

**Reply to objection 2:** There are two kinds of subjection:

The first kind is *servile subjection*, according to which the one who presides makes use of his subjects for his own advantage. This kind of subjection was introduced after the sin.

The second kind is *civil* or *economic subjection*, according to which the one who presides makes use of his subjects for their own advantage and good. This kind of subjection existed even before the sin. For the good of order would have been lacking within the human multitude if some had not been governed by others who were wiser. And so it is by this sort of subjection that the woman is naturally subject to the man (*ex tali subiectione naturalitur femina subiecta est viro*), since the discernment of reason (*discretio rationis*) naturally abounds more in the man. Nor, as will be explained below (q. 96, a. 3), is inequality among men (*inaequalitas hominum*) excluded by the state of innocence.

**Reply to objection 3:** If God had removed from the world everything that man (*homo*) has turned into an occasion of sin (*omnia ex quibus homo sumpsit occasionem peccandi*), the universe would have remained incomplete (*imperfectum*). Nor should the common good have been destroyed in order that a particular evil might be avoided, especially in light of the fact that God is powerful enough to order every evil toward the good.

### Article 2

#### Was it fitting for the woman to be made from the man?

It seems that it was not fitting for the woman (*mulier*) to be made from the man (*vir*):

**Objection 1:** The sexes are common to both man (*homo*) and the other animals. But in the case of the other animals the females (*feminae*) were not made from the males (*mares*). Therefore, this should not have been the case with man, either.

**Objection 2:** Things that belong to the same species have the same type of matter. But the male (*mas*) and the female (*femina*) belong to the same species. Therefore, since the man was made from the slime of the earth, the woman (*femina*) should have been made from the same thing, and not from the man (*vir*).

**Objection 3:** The woman (*mulier*) was made as a helper to the man in the work of generation. But excessively close kinship renders a person unsuitable for generation, and this is why closely related persons are excluded from matrimony, as is clear from Leviticus 18:6. Therefore, the woman should not have been made from the man.

**But contrary to this:** Ecclesiasticus 17:5 says, "He created from him"— that is, from the man—"a helper like to himself"—that is, the woman.

**I respond:** In the initial institution of things it was fitting for the woman (*mulier*) to be formed from the man (*vir*)—more so than in the case of the other animals.

It was fitting, first of all, in order that a certain dignity might be preserved for the first man (*primus homo*), viz., that, by way of likeness to God, he himself would be the source of his whole species in the way that God is the source of the whole universe. Hence, in Acts 17:26 Paul says that God "made the whole human race from one."

It was fitting, second, in order that the man might love the woman more and adhere to her in a more inseparable way, given his realization that she had been produced from him. Hence, Genesis 2:23–24 says, ". . . she was taken out of man. Wherefore a man shall leave father and mother, and shall cleave to his wife." This was especially necessary in the case of the human species, in which the male and the female remain together throughout their whole life (*per totam vitam*)—something that does not happen in the case of the other animals.

Third, it was fitting because, as the Philosopher says in *Ethics* 8, in the case of human beings, the male and the female are conjoined not only because of the necessity for generation, as with the other animals, but also for the sake of their domestic life, in which the other works of the man and the woman take place and in which the man is the head of the woman (*in qua vir est caput mulieris*). Hence, it was fitting for the woman to be formed from the man as her source.

Fourth, there is a reason having to do with the mysteries [of the Faith] (*ratio sacramentalis*). For [the woman's being made from the man] is a figure of the Church's taking her origin from Christ. Hence, in Ephesians 5:32 the Apostle says, "This is a great mystery (*sacramentum magnum*); I mean in Christ and in the Church."

**Reply to objection 1:** The reply to the first objection is clear from what has been said.

**Reply to objection 2:** The matter is that from which something is made. But a created nature has a determinate source, and since it is determined to one outcome, it also has a determinate process. Hence, it produces from determinate matter something that belongs to a determinate species.

By contrast, since God's power is infinite, He can make something that is the same in species from any kind of matter whatsoever, e.g., the man from the slime of the earth and the woman from the man.

**Reply to objection 3:** The sort of close kinship that is an impediment to matrimony comes from natural generation. But the woman was produced from the man solely by God's power and not through natural generation. This is why Eve is not called Adam's daughter. For this reason, the argument is invalid (*non sequitur*).

## Article 3

### Was it fitting for the woman to be formed from the man's rib?

It seems that it was not fitting for the woman to be formed from the man's rib:

**Objection 1:** The man's rib was much smaller than the woman's body. But more can be made from less only either (a) through *addition*—but if this had happened, then the woman would be said to be made from what was added rather than from the rib—or (b) through *rarefaction*, since, as Augustine says in *Super Genesim ad Litteram*, it is impossible for a body to increase unless it becomes rarified. But a woman's body (*corpus mulieris*) is not more rarified than a man's, at least not in the proportion that a rib has to Eve's body. Therefore, Eve was not formed from Adam's rib.

**Objection 2:** There was nothing superfluous in the works that were initially created. Therefore, Adam's rib contributed to the perfection of his body. Therefore, when it was taken away, what remained was imperfect. But this seems wrong.

**Objection 3:** A rib cannot be separated from a man without pain. But there was no pain before the sin. Therefore, the rib should not have been separated from the man so that the woman might be formed from it.

**But contrary to this:** Genesis 2:22 says, "The Lord God built the rib which He had taken from Adam into a woman."

**I respond:** It was fitting for the woman (*mulier*) to be formed from the man's rib (*ex costa viri*).

It was fitting, first, in order to signify that there should be social union (*socialis coniunctio*) between the man and the woman. For instance, the woman should not dominate over the man, and so she was not formed from his head. But neither should she be looked down upon by the man as if she were under servile subjection (*tamquam serviliter subiecta*) (cf. a. 1), and so she was not formed from his feet.

Second, it was fitting because of a mystery [of the Faith] (*propter sacramentum*). For the sacraments—i.e., the blood and water by which the Church was instituted—flowed from the side of Christ in dormition on the cross.

**Reply to objection 1:** Some claim that the woman's body was formed by the multiplication of the matter without any other addition, in the way in which our Lord multiplied the five loaves.

But this is altogether impossible. For the multiplication of the loaves occurred either through a transformation of the substance of the matter itself or through a transformation of its dimensions. But it did not occur through a transformation of the substance of the matter itself, both because (a) matter, considered in itself, is wholly unable to change as long as it exists in potentiality and has only the character of a subject, and also because (b) multitude and magnitude lie outside of the essence of matter itself. And so the multiplication of matter is not in any way intelligible as long as the same matter remains without addition—unless the matter takes on bigger dimensions. But as the Philosopher explains in *Physics* 4, for the matter to be rarefied is just for it to take on bigger dimensions. Therefore, to claim that the matter is multiplied without rarefaction is to posit contradictories simultaneously, viz., the definition without the thing defined.

Hence, since rarefaction does not seem to be present in the multiplications under discussion, it is necessary to posit an *addition to* the matter, either through creation or (what is more probable) through conversion. Hence, in *Super Ioannem* Augustine says, "Christ satisfied the five thousand men with the five loaves in the way that from a few seeds He produces a field full of corn"—which happens through the conversion of nutrients (*per conversionem alimenti*).

Yet we still say, "He fed the five thousand *with five loaves*," or "He formed the woman *from the man's rib*," because the addition was made to the preexisting matter of the loaves or of the rib.

**Reply to objection 2:** The rib contributed to Adam's perfection not insofar as he was a certain *individual*, but insofar as he was the source of the *species*—in the same way that semen, which is released by a natural operation accompanied by pleasure, contributes to the perfection of the one that generates. Hence, *a fortiori*, by God's power the woman's body was able to be formed from the man's rib without pain.

**Reply to objection 3:** From this the reply to the third objection is clear.

## Article 4

### Was the woman formed directly by God?

It seems that the woman was not formed directly (*immediate*) by God:

**Objection 1:** No individual produced from something similar to it in species is made directly by God. But the woman was made from the man, who was of the same species as she was. Therefore, she was not made directly by God.

**Objection 2:** In *De Trinitate* 3 Augustine says that corporeal things are managed by God through the angels. But the woman's body was formed from corporeal matter. Therefore, it was made by the ministry of the angels and not directly by God.

**Objection 3:** Among creatures the things that preexist through their causal principles are produced by the power of another creature and not directly by God. But as Augustine says in *Super Genesim ad Litteram* 9, the woman's body was produced in its causal principles in the initial works. Therefore, the woman was not produced directly by God.

**But contrary to this:** In the same book Augustine says, "Only God, from whom all of nature subsists, was able to form or shape the rib in such a way that it would be a woman."

**I respond:** As was explained above (a. 2), natural generation in any given species is from a determinate matter. But the matter from which man is generated is the human seed of a male or a female (*semen humanum viri vel feminae*). Hence, an individual of the human species cannot be naturally generated from any other type of matter. Rather, only God, who institutes nature, can bring things into being outside of the order of nature. And so only God was able to form the man from the slime of the earth or the woman from the man's rib.

**Reply to objection 1:** This argument goes through for a case in which the individual is generated by a natural generation from something similar to it in species.

**Reply to objection 2:** As Augustine says in *Super Genesim ad Litteram* 9, we do not know whether angels provided service to God in the formation of the woman. However, it is certain that just as the man's body was not formed by angels from the slime of the earth, so neither was the woman's body formed by angels from the man's rib.

**Reply to objection 3:** As Augustine says in the same book, "The initial state of things was not such that the female was going to be formed wholly in this way, but it was only such that she *could* be formed in this way." And so with respect to its causal principles the woman's body preexisted in the initial works not in virtue of an active power, but only in virtue of a passive power ordered toward the creator's active power.

# QUESTION 93

## The End or Terminus of the Production of Man

The next thing we have to consider is the end or terminus of the production of man, insofar as man is said to be made to the image and likeness of God (*ad imaginem et similitudinem Dei*) (Genesis 1:26). On this topic there are nine questions: (1) Does the image of God exist in man? (2) Does the image of God exist in non-rational creatures? (3) Does the image of God exist more in an angel than in a man? (4) Does the image of God exist in every man? (5) Is the image of God in man related to [God's] essence, or to all the divine persons, or to just one of the divine persons? (6) Is the image of God found in man only with respect to man's mind? (7) Does the image of God exist in man because of man's powers, or because of his habits, or because of his acts? (8) Does the image of God exist in man in relation to all objects? (9) What is the difference between an image and a likeness?

## Article 1

### Does the image of God exist in man?

It seems that the image of God does not exist in man:

**Objection 1:** Isaiah 40:18 says, "To whom have you likened God? Or what image will you make for Him?"

**Objection 2:** Being an image of God is proper to the Firstborn, of whom the Apostle says in Colossians 1:15, "He is the Image of the invisible God, the Firstborn of every creature." Therefore, the image of God is not found in man.

**Objection 3:** In *De Synodis* Hilary says, "An image is not different in species (*species indifferens*) from the thing it is an image of." And, again, he says, "An image is an undivided and unified likeness of a thing, meant to equate that thing with another thing." But God and man do not share the same species (*non est species indifferens Dei et hominis*); nor can man have equality with God. Therefore, the image of God cannot exist in man.

**But contrary to this:** Genesis 1:26 says, "Let us make man to our image and likeness."

**I respond:** In *83 Quaestiones* Augustine says, "Where there is an image (*imago*), there is always a likeness (*similitudo*), but where there is a likeness, there is not always an image." From this it is clear that *likeness* is part of the concept *image*, and that *image* adds something beyond the concept *likeness*, viz., that an image is modeled after something else (*sit ex alio expressum*). For the word 'image' (*imago*) is derived from something's being done in imitation of another (*agitur ad imitationem alterius*). Hence, even if one egg is similar to and equal to a second egg, nonetheless, it is not called an image of that other egg, because it is not modeled after it.

Moreover, equality is not part of the concept *image*. For as Augustine says in the same place, "It does not follow that where there is an image, there is equality." This is clear in the case of the image of someone in a mirror (*in speculo relucente*). Still, equality is part of the concept *perfect image*, since a perfect image lacks nothing that exists in the thing after which it is modeled (*in perfecta imagine non deest aliquid imagini quod insit illi de quo expressa est*).

Now it is clear that in man there is some sort of likeness to God that is derived from God as its exemplar (*sicut ab exemplari*); however, it is not a likeness of equality, since in this case the exemplar infinitely exceeds that which it is the exemplar of. And so the image of God is said to exist in man not as a perfect image, but as an imperfect image. Scripture signifies this when it says that man was made "to the image of God (*ad imaginem Dei*)." For the preposition 'to' (*ad*) signifies the approach of something that is far off in the distance (*accessum quendam qui competit rei distanti*).

**Reply to objection 1:** The prophet is talking about corporeal images fabricated by man, and this is why he expressly says, "What image will you make for Him?" But it is God Himself who has placed a spiritual image of Himself in man.

**Reply to objection 2:** The "Firstborn of every creature" is the perfect Image of God, perfectly matching (*perfecte implens*) that of which He is the Image (cf. q. 35). This is why He is said to be "the Image" and never "to the image" (*dicitur imago et numquam ad imagem*).

By contrast, man is called an image because of a likeness, and he is said to be made "to the image" because of the imperfection of the likeness. And since a perfect likeness of God cannot exist except by an identity of nature, the Image of God exists in His Firstborn Son in the way that the image of a king exists in his connatural son, whereas in man the image of God exists in a different nature, in the way that the king's image exists in a silver coin. This is clear from Augustine in *De Decem Chordis*.

**Reply to objection 3:** Since *one* is [the same as] *undivided being*, a species is called 'non-different' (*indifferens*) in the same way that it is called 'one'. But a thing is said to be *one* not only in number or in species or in genus, but also in accord with a certain analogy or proportion (*secundum analogical vel proportionem quandam*); and this is the sort of oneness or agreement that a creature has with respect to God.

On the other hand, what [Hilary] says about equating the one thing with the other has to do with the concept *perfect image*.

### Article 2

### Is the image of God found in non-rational creatures?

It seems that the image of God is found in non-rational creatures (*in irrationalibus creaturis*):

**Objection 1:** In *De Divinis Nominibus* Dionysius says, "Things that have causes bear contingent images of their causes." But God is a cause not only of rational creatures, but also of non-rational creatures. Therefore, the image of God is found in non-rational creatures.

**Objection 2:** The more explicit (*expressior*) a likeness is in a thing, the closer it approaches the nature of an image. But in *De Divinis Nominibus*, chap. 4, Dionysius says that a solar ray has a maximal likeness to God's goodness. Therefore, it is made to the image of God.

**Objection 3:** The more perfect a thing is in goodness, the more like God it is. But the universe as a whole is more perfect in goodness than man is, since even if each particular thing is good, all of them together are called "very good" in Genesis 1:31. Therefore, the whole universe—and not just man—is made to the image of God.

**Objection 4:** In *De Consolatione Philosophiae* Boethius says of God, ". . . holding the world in His mind and forming it in a like image." Therefore the whole world—and not just the rational creature—is made to the image of God.

**But contrary to this:** In *Super Genesim ad Litteram* 6 Augustine says, "This reaches its peak in man, since God made man to His own image by giving him an intellectual mind by which he stands out from the beasts." Therefore, things that do not have an intellect are not made to the image of God.

**I respond:** Not just any likeness, even if it is modeled after another, is enough for the concept *image*. For if the likeness corresponds only to a genus or to some common accident, the thing in question will not thereby be said to be made "to the image" of the other. For instance, one could not say that a worm which comes out of a man is an image of the man because of the likeness in genus. Nor, again, can one say that if something becomes white and so like another thing, it is thereby made to that thing's image; for whiteness is an accident common to many species.

What is required for the concept *image* is that the likeness be either (a) with respect to the species, in the way that the image of a king exists in his son, or (b) at least with respect to some accident that is proper to the species—especially its shape—in the way that an image of a man is said to exist in copper. This is why Hilary explicitly says, "An image is not different in species." And it is clear that a likeness in species has to do with the last difference [contained in the definition].

Now first, and most generally, some things are like God insofar as they *exist*. Second, some are like Him insofar as they are *alive*. Third, some are like him insofar as they *have knowledge or intellective understanding* (*sapiunt vel intelligunt*). These last ones are, as Augustine puts it in *83 Quaestiones*, "so close to God in likeness that nothing among creatures is closer."

So, then, it is clear that, properly speaking, only intellectual beings are made to the image of God.

**Reply to objection 1:** Everything imperfect is a sort of participation (*quaedam participatio*) in what is perfect. And so even those things that fall short of the concept *image* still participate to some extent in the nature of an image insofar as they have some sort of likeness to God. This is why Dionysius says that things that have causes bear "contingent images" of their causes; that is, they bear the images not absolutely speaking, but to the extent that this is possible for them.

**Reply to objection 2:** Dionysius compares a solar ray to God's goodness with regard to its causality, but not with respect to the dignity of its nature—which is what is required for the concept *image*.

**Reply to objection 3:** In the extensive and diffusive sense (*extensive et diffusive*), the universe is more perfect in goodness than an intellectual creature is. However, in the intensive and concentrated sense (*intensive et collective*), the likeness of the divine perfection is found to a greater degree in an intellectual creature, which has a capacity for the highest good (*capax summi boni*).

An alternative reply is that a part is contrasted not with the whole, but with other parts. Hence, when one claims that intellectual natures alone are made to the image of God, this rules out other parts of the universe from being made to God's image, but it does not rule out the universe's being made to the image of God in some of its parts.

**Reply to objection 4:** Boethius is taking 'image' here as a kind of likeness by which an artifact imitates the pattern (*species*) of art that exists in the craftsman's mind; and in this sense every creature is an 'image' of the exemplary conception that it has in God's mind.

However, this is not the sense of 'image' that we are talking about in the present context. Instead, we are talking now about images that have a likeness in their nature. More specifically, all things are like the First Being insofar as they are beings, and some are like the First Life insofar as they are alive, and some are like the Highest Wisdom insofar as they have intellective understanding.

## Article 3

### Is an angel made to the image of God to a greater degree than a man is?

It seems that an angel is not made to the image of God to a greater degree than a man is:

**Objection 1:** In his sermon *De Imagine* Augustine says that God did not grant to any creature other than man that it should be made to His image. Therefore, it is not true that an angel is made to the image of God to a greater degree than a man is.

**Objection 2:** According to Augustine in *83 Quaestiones*, "Man is made to the image of God in such a way that he is formed by God without any other creature intervening. And so nothing is more closely conjoined to God than he is." But a creature is called an image of God to the extent that it is conjoined to God. Therefore, an angel is not made to the image of God to a greater degree than a man is.

**Objection 3:** A creature is made to the image of God insofar as it has an intellectual nature. But there is no such thing as more of an intellectual nature or less of an intellectual nature (*intellectualis natura non intenditur nec remittitur*), since intellectual nature is in the genus *substance* and does not belong to the genus *accident*. Therefore, an angel is not made to the image of God to a greater degree than a man is.

**But contrary to this:** In one of his homilies Gregory says, "An angel is called 'a seal of likeness', because in him the likeness of the divine image is imprinted more explicitly."

**I respond:** There are two ways of talking about the image of God:

First, with respect to what the notion of an image is *primarily* thought of as existing in, viz., an intellectual nature. And in this sense the image of God exists to a greater degree in angels than in men, since, as is clear from what was said above (q. 58, a. 3), a more perfect intellectual nature exists in angels.

Second, the image of God in a man can be thought of with respect to what the image is *secondarily* thought of as existing in. More specifically, a certain imitation of God can be found in a man (a) insofar as man is from man in the way that God is from God, and (b) insofar as a man's soul is a whole in his whole body and also a whole in each part of the body, in the same way that God is related to the world. As far as these and other such likenesses are concerned, the image of God is found to a greater degree in a man than in an angel. However, the nature of God's image in man is associated with these likenesses *per se* only insofar as they presuppose the first sort of imitation, which has to do with the intellectual nature. Otherwise, brute animals would likewise be made to God's image.

And so since as far as the intellectual nature itself is concerned, an angel is made to God's image to a greater degree than a man is, one should grant that (a) absolutely speaking (*simpliciter*) an angel is made to God's image to a greater degree than a man is, but that (b) in a certain sense (*secundum quid*) a man is made to God's image to a greater degree than an angel is.

**Reply to objection 1:** Augustine is here excluding from God's image other lower creatures that lack intellective understanding. He is not, however, excluding the angels.

**Reply to objection 2:** The claim that nothing is more closely conjoined to God than the human mind is asserted with respect to the genus *intellectual nature*, in the same way that fire is, as a species, the most subtle of bodies, even though one instance of fire is more subtle than another. For as Augustine had said earlier, "Those who have knowledge bear such a close likeness to Him that there is nothing closer among creatures." Hence, this does not rule out the claim that an angel is made to God's image to a greater degree.

**Reply to objection 3:** The assertion, "A substance does not admit of more and less," does not imply that one species of substance is not more perfect than another. Instead, it implies that (a) one and the same individual does not participate more in its own species at some times and less at other times, and also that (b) different individuals [of the same species] do not participate to greater and lesser degrees in that species of substance.

## Article 4

### Is the image of God found in every man?

It seems that the image of God is not found in every man (*in quolibet homine*):

**Objection 1:** In 1 Corinthians 11:7 the Apostle says, "The man (*vir*) is the image of God, while the woman (*mulier*) is the image of the man." Therefore, since the woman is an individual of the human species, not every individual is an image of God.

**Objection 2:** In Romans 8:29 the Apostle says, "Those whom God foreknew, He also predestined to be conformed to the image of His Son." But not all men have been predestined. Therefore, not all men are conformed to the image.

**Objection 3:** As was explained above (a. 1), *likeness* (*similitudo*) is part of the concept *image* (*imago*). But through sin a man becomes unlike God (*Deo dissimilis*). Therefore, he loses the image of God.

**But contrary to this:** Psalm 38:7 says, "Surely man passes as an image."

**I respond:** Since it is because of his intellectual nature that man is said to be made to the image of God, it follows that he is made to God's image to the highest degree to the extent that his intellectual nature is able to imitate God to the highest degree. But it is with respect to God's knowing and loving Himself that an intellectual nature especially imitates God. Hence, there are three possible ways to think of the image of God in man:

In the first way, a man has a natural capacity to understand and to love God, and this capacity resides in the *very nature of the mind* (*consistit in ipsa natura mentis*), which is common to all men.

In the second way, a man actually or habitually understands and loves God, but still imperfectly; and this is the image associated with *the conformity of grace* (*imago per conformitatem gratiae*).

In the third way, a man has actual and perfect understanding of and love for God, and the image so taken is associated with *the likeness of glory* (*imago secundum similitudinem gloriae*).

This is why the Gloss on Psalm 4:7 ("The light of your countenance, O Lord, is signed upon us") distinguishes three images: (a) the image of *creation*, (b) the image of *re-creation*, and (c) the image of *likeness*. The first image is found in all men, the second image is found only in the justified (*tantum in iustis*), and the third image is found only in the blessed in heaven (*solum in beatis*).

**Reply to objection 1:** The image of God is found in both the man and the woman with respect to what the character of an image primarily consists in, viz., an intellectual nature. Hence, after Genesis 1:27 had said, "He created him"— viz., man (*homo*)—"to the image of God," it adds, ". . . male and female He created them." And as Augustine explains, it says "them" in the plural, lest it be thought that both sexes had been joined in one individual.

On the other hand, there is a certain secondary sense in which the image of God is found in the man and not in the woman. For the man is the source and the end of the woman in the way that God is the source and the end of the whole creation. Hence, after the Apostle had said, "The man is the image and glory of God, while the woman is the glory of the man," he explained why he had said this by adding, "For the man is not from the woman, but the woman is from the man; and the man is not created for the sake of the woman, but the woman is created for the sake of the man."

**Reply to objection 2 and objection 3:** These arguments proceed from the type of image that has to do with the conformity of grace and glory.

## Article 5

### Does the image of God in man bear upon the Trinity of divine persons?

It seems that the image of God in man does not bear upon the Trinity of divine persons (*non sit quantum ad Trinitatem divinarum personarum*):

**Objection 1:** In *De Fide ad Petrum* Augustine says, "There is a unified divine essence of the Holy Trinity, and there is a unified image to which man was made." And in *De Trinitate* 5 Hilary says, "Man is made to the common image of the Trinity." Therefore, the image of God in man bears upon the divine essence and not upon the Trinity of persons.

**Objection 2:** *De Ecclesiasticis Dogmatibus* says that the image of God in man bears upon [God's] eternity. Also, Damascene says, "Man's being made to the image of God signifies *per se* the intellect, the free will, and the power." Again, Gregory of Nyssa says that when Scripture said that man was made to God's image, "this amounts to saying that human nature was made a participant in every good; for the divine nature (*divinitas*) is the plenitude of goodness." But all of this pertains to the oneness of the essence and not to the distinction among the persons. Therefore, in man the image of God bears upon the oneness of the essence and not upon the Trinity of persons.

**Objection 3:** An image leads to the cognition of the one whose image it is. Therefore, if the image of God in man bore upon the Trinity of persons, then since man is able to know himself through his natural reason, it would follow that man could know the Trinity of divine persons through his natural reason. But as was shown above (q. 32, a. 1), this is false.

**Objection 4:** The name 'image' belongs only to the Son and not to each of the three Persons; for in *De Trinitate* 6 Augustine says, "The Son alone is the Image of the Father." Therefore, if the image of God in man were associated with a [divine] person, there would be just an image of the Son in man and not an image of the whole Trinity.

**But contrary to this:** In *De Trinitate* 4 Hilary says, "Man's being made to the image of God shows the plurality of the divine persons."

**I respond:** As was established above (q. 40, a. 2), the distinctions among the divine persons stem only from origins or, better, from the relations of origin. But the mode of origin is not the same in all things; instead, each thing's mode of origin is appropriate to its nature. For instance, living things are produced in one way and non-living things in another way; animals are produced in one way and plants in another way.

Hence, it is clear that the distinction among the divine persons is appropriate to the divine nature. Thus, being made to the image of God in imitation of the divine nature does not rule out being made to the image of God in a sense that represents the three persons. Instead, the one follows upon the other.

So, then, one should reply that the image of God exists in man in a way that bears upon both the divine nature and the Trinity of persons. For in God Himself the one nature exists in three persons (*in ipso Deo in tribus personis una existit natura*).

**Reply to objection 1 and objection 2:** The reply to the first two objections is clear from what has been said.

**Reply to objection 3:** This argument would go through if the image of God in man represented God perfectly. But as Augustine says in *De Trinitate* 15, there is a huge difference (*maxima est differentia*) between the trinity that exists in us and the divine Trinity. And so, as he says in the same place, "We see, rather than believe, the trinity that is in us, whereas we believe, rather than see, that God is a Trinity."

**Reply to objection 4:** Some have claimed that only the image of the Son exists in man. But Augustine disproves this claim in *De Trinitate* 12.

First, since the Son is similar to the Father by an equality of essence, it is necessary that if man is made to the likeness of the Son, then he is made to the likeness of the Father.

Second, if man had been made only to the image of the Son, then the Father would have said, "Let us make man to *your* image and likeness," and not "to *our* image and likeness."

Therefore, when it says, "He made him to the image of God," one should not, as some have, interpret this to mean that the Father made man only to the image of the Son, who is God. Instead, it should be interpreted to mean that the Triune God (*Deus Trinitas*) made man to His own image, i.e., to the image of the whole Trinity.

Now there are two readings of the sentence, 'God made man to His image (*Deus fecit hominem ad imaginem suam*)'.

On the first reading, the preposition 'to' (*ad*) designates the terminus of the act of making, so that the sentence has this meaning: "Let us make man in such a way that the image exists in him."

On the second reading, the preposition 'to' can designate the exemplary cause, as when one says, "This book is made to [conform to] that book." On this reading the image of God is the divine essence itself —improperly (*abusive*) called an 'image'—insofar as 'image' is being used for 'exemplar'. Alternatively, in keeping with what some have claimed, the divine essence is being called an 'image' because one [divine] person is like the other with respect to the divine essence.

## Article 6

### Does the image of God exist in man only because of his mind?

It seems not to be the case that the image of God exists in man only because of his mind (*non solum secundum mentem*):

**Objection 1:** In 1 Corinthians 11:7 the Apostle says, "The man (*vir*) is the image of God." But the man is not only the mind. Therefore, the image of God is not associated only with the mind.

**Objection 2:** Genesis 1:27 says, "God created man to His own image. To the image of God He created him. Male and female He created them." But the distinction of male from female has to do with the body. Therefore, the image of God in man is associated with the body and not just with the mind.

**Objection 3:** An image seems mainly to have to do with shape. But shape pertains to bodies. Therefore, the image of God in man is associated with the body, too, and not just with the mind.

**Objection 4:** According to Augustine in *Super Genesim ad Litteram* 12, we have three types of vision, viz., (a) corporeal, (b) spiritual or imaginative, and (c) intellectual. Therefore, if, because of our intellectual vision, which pertains to the mind, there is a 'trinity' (*aliqua trinitas*) in us by virtue of which we are made to the image of God, then by parity of reasoning the same should hold for the other types of vision as well.

**But contrary to this:** In Ephesians 4:23–24 the Apostle says, "Be renewed in the spirit of your mind and put on the new man." From this we are given to understand that our renewal, which is effected by our putting on the new man, pertains to the mind. But Colossians 3:10 says, ". . . putting on the new man, who is renewed in the knowledge of God according to the image of Him who created him . . . ," where he attributes the renewal which is effected by putting on the new man to the image of God. Therefore, being an image of God involves just the mind.

**I respond:** As was explained above (a. 2), even though there is some sort of likeness to God in all creatures, it is only in the rational creature that one finds a likeness to God in the manner of an *image*, whereas in other creatures there is a likeness in the manner of a *trace* (*vestigium*). But it is his intellect or mind (*intellectus sive mens*) in which the rational creature exceeds other creatures. Hence, it follows that the image of God is found in the rational creature himself only because of his mind (*non nisi secundum mentem*).

Moreover, if the rational creature in question has any other parts, then the likeness of a trace is found in those parts, just as it is in the other creatures that this rational creature is similar to in virtue of those parts. The reason for this can be seen clearly if one looks carefully at the way in which a trace represents and the way in which an image represents. For as has been explained (a. 2), an image's representation involves a likeness of species. By contrast, a trace represents in the manner of an effect that represents its cause in such a way that it does not attain to a likeness of species; for instance, the footprints left behind by the movement of animals are called traces, and ash is likewise called the trace of a fire, and the desolation of the land is called the trace of a hostile army.

One can see a difference of this sort between rational creatures and other creatures—both with respect to how a likeness to the divine *nature* is represented in the creatures and also with respect to how a likeness of the uncreated *Trinity* is represented in creatures. For as far as the likeness to the divine nature is concerned, rational creatures seem in some sense to attain a representation of the species insofar as they imitate God not only in existing and in living but also in having intellective understanding—as was explained above (a. 2). By contrast, the other creatures do not have intellective understanding; instead, what appears in them is a certain trace of a productive intellect (*vestigium intellectus producentis*), if the way they are arranged is taken into account (*si earum dispositio consideretur*).

Similarly, since, as was established above (q. 28, a. 3), the uncreated Trinity is distinguished by the procession of the Word (*Verbum*) from the Speaker (*Dicens*) and by the procession of the Love (*Amor*) from the two of them, in the rational creature, in which there is a procession of a word stemming from (*secundum*) the intellect and a procession of love stemming from the will, one can say that there is an image of the uncreated Trinity through a certain representation of the species. By contrast, in the other creatures one does not find either a *source of a word*, or a *word*, or *love*; rather, what one finds is a certain trace, because the cause that produces these other creatures has within itself a Source of the Word, and the Word, and the Love. For the very fact that a creature has a limited and finite substance (*substantiam modificatam et finitam*) demonstrates that it comes from some Source, whereas a creature's species points to its Maker's Word in the same way that the form of a house points to the craftsman's conception; and the creature's being ordered points to its Maker's Love, by which the effect is ordered toward the good, in the same way that the use of a building points to the craftsman's will.

So, then, in man the likeness of God is found in the manner of an image because of his mind, whereas in his other parts the likeness of God is found in the manner of a trace.

**Reply to objection 1:** Man is called an image of God not because he is an image in his essence, but because the image of God is imprinted on him in virtue of his mind—in the way that a denarius is called an image of Caesar in virtue of bearing Caesar's image. Hence, it is not necessary that the image of God be received with respect to every part of a man.

**Reply to objection 2:** As Augustine reports in *De Trinitate* 12, some have claimed that the image of the Trinity in man is borne not by one individual man, but by several individuals together (*secundum plura*). They say that "a man (*vir*) intimates the person of the Father, whereas the person of the Son is intimated by one who proceeds from the man in such a way as to be generated from him (*de illo nasceretur*); and they claim that the third person, corresponding to the Holy Spirit, is the woman, who proceeds from the man in such a way that she is neither his son nor his daughter."

On the surface, this seems absurd. First, it would follow that the Holy Spirit is a source of the Son in the way that the woman is a source of the child who is generated from the man. Second, a man (*homo*) would be the image of just one person. Third, on this view Scripture ought not to have mentioned the image of God in man until after offspring had been produced.

And so one should reply that after Scripture had said "He created him to the image of God," it added "male and female He created them" not in order to associate the image of God with the distinction between the sexes, but because the image of God is common to both sexes, since it stems from the mind, in which there is no distinction between sexes. Hence, in Colossians 3:10, after the Apostle had said, ". . . according to the image of Him who created him," he adds, "where there is neither male nor female."

**Reply to objection 3:** Even though the image of God in man does not involve the shape of the body, still, as Augustine says in *83 Quaestiones*, "since man's body, alone among the bodies of the land animals, does not lie face downward (*non prostratum est*), with its belly close to the ground, but is instead such that it is more suitable for contemplating the heavens, it can rightly seem to be made to the image and likeness of God to a greater degree than the other animal bodies." However, this should be understood to mean not that there is an image of God in man's body, but that the very shape of the human body represents, in the manner of a trace, the image of God in the soul.

**Reply to objection 4:** As Augustine says in *De Trinitate*, in both corporeal vision and imaginative vision there is a certain trinity.

For in corporeal vision there is first the *species* of the exterior body; second, the *act of seeing* itself, which is effected by the impression of a likeness of the species in question on the faculty of sight; and, third, the *will's intention* in applying the faculty of sight to the act of seeing and keeping the act of seeing fixed on the thing seen.

Similarly, in the case of imaginative vision, one finds, first, a *species* reserved in memory; second, the *very act of imaginative seeing*, which stems from the fact that the soul's glance, i.e., the very power of imagining, is informed by the species in question; and, third, there is the *will's intention*, which joins the two.

However, both of these trinities fall short of the concept *image of God*.

For the species itself of the exterior body lies outside the nature of the soul, whereas even if the species that exists in memory does not exist outside the soul, it is nonetheless incidental to the soul. And so in both these cases the representation of the connaturality and coeternality of the divine persons is lacking.

Again, corporeal vision proceeds not only from the species of the exterior body but, along with this, from the sensory power of the one who sees; and, similarly, imaginative vision proceeds not only from the species that is conserved in the memory, but also from the power of imagining. And this does not appropriately represent the procession of the Son from the Father alone.

Again, the will's intention, which connects the species and the power, does not proceed from them in the case of either corporeal vision or spiritual vision, and so it does not appropriately represent the procession of the Holy Spirit from the Father and Son.

## Article 7

### Is the image of God found in the soul's acts?

It seems that the image of God is not found in the soul's acts (*non inveniatur in anima secundum actus*):

**Objection 1:** In *De Civitate Dei* 11 Augustine says that man was made to the image of God "insofar as we exist, and know that we exist, and love our existence (*esse*) and our knowing (*nosse*)." But 'existence' (*esse*) does not signify an act. Therefore, the image of God in the soul is not associated with the soul's acts.

**Objection 2:** In *De Trinitate* 9 Augustine assigns the image of God in the soul to three things, viz., mind (*mens*), knowledge (*notitia*), and love (*amor*). But 'mind' signifies not an act, but rather a power of—or even the essence of—the intellective soul. Therefore, the image of God is not associated with acts.

**Objection 3:** In *De Trinitate* 10 Augustine assigns the image of the Trinity in the soul to memory (*memoria*), intellective understanding (*intelligentia*), and will (*voluntas*). But as the Master says in *Sentences* 1, dist. 3, these are "natural powers of the soul." Therefore, the image is associated with powers and not with acts.

**Objection 4:** The image of the Trinity remains in the soul continuously (*semper manet*). But the acts do not remain continuously. Therefore, the image of God in the soul is not associated with the acts.

**But contrary to this:** In *De Trinitate* 11 Augustine associates the trinity in the lower parts of the soul with the sentient *act* of seeing and the imaginative *act* of seeing (*secundum actualem visionem sensibilem et imaginariam*). Therefore, the trinity that exists in the mind, in accord with which man is made to the image of God, should likewise be associated with the act of seeing (*debet attendi secundum actualem visionem*).

**I respond:** As was explained above (a. 2), some type of representation of the species is part of the concept *image*. Therefore, if the image of the divine Trinity is going to be received in the soul, then it must be associated principally with what comes as close as possible to representing the species of the divine persons.

Now the divine persons are distinguished from one another by the procession of the Word from the Speaker and the procession of the Love that joins the two of them (*secundum processionem Verbi a Dicente et Amoris connectentis utrumque*). But as Augustine says in *De Trinitate* 14, the word in our soul cannot exist in the absence of actual thinking. Therefore, the image of the Trinity in our mind is primarily and principally associated with the act. More specifically, on the basis of the knowledge (*notitia*) we have, we form an interior word by thinking (*cogitando interius verbum formamus*) and from this we break out into love (*in amorem prorumpimus*).

However, since habits and powers are the principles of acts and since each thing exists virtually in its principles, there can be in the soul a secondary and, as it were, implied (*ex consequenti*) image of the Trinity that is associated with the soul's powers and mainly with its habits, insofar as the acts exist virtually in the habits.

**Reply to objection 1:** Our existence (*esse*) pertains to the image of God because it is proper to us above and beyond the other animals; for *esse* belongs to us insofar as we have a mind. And so the trinity mentioned here is the same one that Augustine posits in *De Trinitate* 9, consisting of *mind, knowledge,* and *love*.

**Reply to objection 2:** Augustine at first finds in the mind the trinity mentioned in the objection. However, the mind is such that even if it in some sense knows itself as a whole, it is also in some sense ignorant of itself, viz., insofar as it is distinct from other things; and so it also seeks itself, as Augustine later shows in *De Trinitate* 10. Hence, given that *knowledge* (*notitia*) is not entirely the same as *mind* (*mens*), he takes three things in the soul—viz., memory (*memoria*), intellective understanding (*intelligentia*), and will (*voluntas*)—which are proper to the mind and which no one is ignorant of having. And it is to these three things that he then ascribes the image of the Trinity, given that his first ascription was in some sense deficient.

**Reply to objection 3:** As Augustine shows in *De Trinitate* 14, we are said to understand and to will (or love) certain things both when we are actually thinking of them and when we are not actually thinking of them. But when they exist in the absence of thought, they belong only to the memory, which in itself is nothing other than the habitual retention of knowledge and love. "But since," as he himself puts it, "the word cannot exist there in the absence of thought (for we think everything that we say, at least by means of that interior word which does not belong to the language of any nation), the image in question is known instead in these three things, viz., memory, intellective understanding, and will. I mean the intellective understanding by which we understand when we are thinking; and I mean the will (or love (*amor*) or higher affection (*dilectio*)) which joins that parent and that offspring." From this it is clear that he locates the image of the Trinity in actual understanding and actual willing rather than in their habitual retention in memory—even though in habitual retention there is also a certain image of the Trinity in the soul, as he says in the same place. And so it is clear that 'memory', 'intellective understanding', and 'will' are not being used here for three powers, as they are in the *Sentences*.

**Reply to objection 4:** Someone could reply by citing the fact that in *De Trinitate* 14 Augustine says, "The mind always remembers itself, always understands itself, and always loves itself." Some take this to mean that actual intellective understanding of itself and actual love for itself are [always] present in the soul.

However, Augustine undermines this interpretation when he adds, "[The mind] is not always thinking of itself as discrete from those things that are not what it itself is." From this it is clear that the soul is always understanding and loving itself *habitually* and not *actually*—though one can also say that because it perceives its own act, it understands itself whenever it understands anything at all.

However, since the soul is not always actually engaged in intellective understanding, as is clear in the case of someone who is sleeping, one must say that even if its acts do not in themselves remain continuously, they nonetheless do always remain in their principles, viz., the powers and habits. Hence, in *De Trinitate* 14 Augustine says, "If the rational soul is made to the image of God because it is *able to* use reason and intellect to understand and contemplate God, then from the very beginning of its existence the image of God existed within it."

## Article 8

### Does the image of the divine Trinity exist in the soul only in relation to the object which is God?

It seems that it is not the case that the image of the divine Trinity exists in the soul only in relation to the object which is God (*non solum per comparationem ad obiectum quod est Deus*):

**Objection 1:** As has been explained (a. 6–7), the image of the divine Trinity is found in the soul because the *word* in us proceeds from the *speaker* and the *love* in us proceeds from both the *speaker* and the *word*. But [these processions] are found in us with respect to every object whatsoever. Therefore, the image of the divine Trinity is found in our mind with respect to every object whatsoever.

**Objection 2:** In *De Trinitate* 12 Augustine says, "When we are looking for the Trinity in the soul, we look in the whole soul, not separating rational action in the realm of temporal things from the contemplation of eternal things." Therefore, the image of the Trinity is found in the soul even with respect to temporal objects.

**Objection 3:** The fact that we understand and love God belongs to us by a gift of grace. Therefore, if the image of the Trinity in the soul is associated [only] with the memory of God, the understanding of God, and the willing (or loving) of God, then the image of God will exist in man only by grace and not by nature. Therefore, it will not be something common to all men.

**Objection 4:** The saints who dwell in heaven are maximally conformed to the image of God by the vision of glory (*secundum gloriae visionem*); this is why 2 Corinthians 3:18 says, "We are being transformed into the same image from glory to glory (*a claritate in claritatem*)." But temporal things are known through the vision of glory. Therefore, it is also in relation to temporal objects that the image of God exists in us.

**But contrary to this:** In *De Trinitate* 14 Augustine says, "It is not because the mind remembers itself and understands itself and loves itself that the image of God exists in it; rather, it is because the mind is able to remember, understand, and love the God by whom it was made." Therefore, even less is it the case that the image of God in the mind is associated with objects other [than God or the mind itself].

**I respond:** As was explained above (a. 2), *image* implies a likeness that somehow involves a representation of the species. Hence, the image of the divine Trinity in the soul must be associated with something that represents the divine persons by a representation of their species, insofar as this is possible for a creature. Now as has been said (a. 6–7), the divine persons are distinguished by the procession of the Word from the Speaker and the procession of the Love from the two of them. And the Word of God is begotten of God insofar as He knows Himself (*secundum notitiam sui ipsius*), and the Love proceeds from God insofar as He loves Himself. Now it is clear that it is the diversity of the objects that differentiates the species of words and the species of love. For instance, the word *rock* conceived in the human heart is not the same in species as the word *horse*; nor is the love of a rock the same in species as the love of a horse. Therefore, the divine image in man is associated with (a) the word that is conceived from knowledge about God and (b) the love that is derived from that word. And so the image of God is present in the soul insofar as the soul is drawn—or is capable of being drawn—toward God.

Now there are two ways in which the mind is drawn toward something: (a) *directly and immediately*, and (b) *indirectly and mediately*, as when someone looking at a man's image in a mirror is said to be drawn toward the man himself. This is why, in *De Trinitate* 14 Augustine says, "The mind remembers itself, understands itself, and loves itself. If we discern this, we discern the Trinity—not yet God Himself, but even now an image of God." This is not because the mind is drawn toward itself, absolutely speaking, but rather because by being drawn toward itself, it can be drawn further toward God. This is clear from the passage just quoted.

**Reply to objection 1:** As far as the concept *image* is concerned, one must attend not only to the fact that something proceeds from something, but also to what exactly proceeds from what, viz., that the word *God* proceeds from knowledge about God.

**Reply to objection 2:** There is a sort of trinity in the whole soul—not, to be sure, such that, in addition to action regarding temporal things and the contemplation of eternal things, "there is some third thing to look for by which the trinity is completed," as Augustine adds in the same place. Instead, as he explains later, "Even if a trinity could be found in the part of reason that is derived from the side of temporal things, the image of God would still not be found there," because this sort of knowledge of temporal things is incidental to the soul.

Moreover, the habits by which temporal things are known are not themselves always present in the soul; instead, they are sometimes there in the present and sometimes there only in memory, even after they have begun to be present. This is clear, for instance, in the case of faith, which comes to us temporally in the present life but which in the state of future beatitude will no longer be faith, but a memory of faith.

**Reply to objection 3:** The meritorious cognition and love of God occur only through grace. However, as was established above (q. 12, a. 12), there is such a thing as a natural cognition and love of God.

And it is likewise natural for the mind *to be able* to use reason to understand God, and because of this we have claimed that the image of God remains continuously (*permanere semper*) in the mind, regardless of whether (a) "this image of God is so thinned out"—clouded over, as it were— "as to amount to almost nothing," as in those who do not have the use of reason, or whether (b) "it is darkened or deformed," as in sinners, or whether (c) "it is bright and beautiful," as in the justified—as Augustine says in *De Trinitate* 14.

**Reply to objection 4:** Through the vision of glory temporal things will be seen in God Himself, and so this sort of vision of temporal things will be relevant to the image of God. This is what Augustine is talking about in *De Trinitate* 14: "In the nature to which the mind will happily adhere, the mind will see as immutable everything that that nature sees. For the conceptions of all creatures exist in the uncreated Word Himself."

## Article 9

### Is it appropriate to distinguish the likeness [of God] from the image [of God]?

It seems that it is not appropriate to distinguish the likeness [of God] from the image [of God] (*similitudo ab imagine non convenienter distinguatur*):

**Objection 1:** It is not appropriate to distinguish a genus from its species. But *likeness* is related to *image* in the way that a genus is related to its species, since "where there is an image, there is always a likeness, but not vice versa," as *83 Quaestiones* puts it. Therefore, it is inappropriate to distinguish the likeness from the image.

**Objection 2:** The concept *image* involves not only a representation of the divine persons, but also a representation of the divine essence, where immortality and indivisibility are relevant to the latter. Therefore, it is not appropriate to claim that "the likeness exists in the essence [of the soul], since it is immortal and indivisible, whereas the image exists in other things" [*Sentences* 2, dist. 16].

**Objection 3:** As was established above (a. 4), there are three images of God in man, viz., the image of *nature*, the image of *grace*, and the image of *glory*. But innocence and justification pertain to grace. Therefore, it is not appropriate to say that "the image is associated with *memory*, *intellective understanding*, and *will*, whereas the likeness is associated with *innocence* and *justification*" [*Sentences* 2, dist. 16].

**Objection 4:** The cognition of truth belongs to intellective understanding, whereas the love of virtue belongs to the will—and these are two parts of the image. Therefore, it is not appropriate to say that "the image exists in the cognition of truth, whereas the likeness exists in the love of virtue" [*Sentences* 2, dist. 16].

**But contrary to this:** In *83 Quaestiones* Augustine says, "It is not in vain that some understand that two things are being spoken of in the phrase 'to [our] image and likeness' (Genesis 1:26); for if there were just one thing, then a single name could have sufficed."

**I respond:** A likeness is a certain sort of oneness (*quaedam unitas*); for as *Metaphysics* 5 says, "Oneness (*unum*) is a cause of likeness in quality." Now since *one* is a transcendental and common to all things, it can be adapted to each individual (*ad singula potest aptari*) in the same way that *good* and *true* can be.

Hence, just as *good* can be applied to a particular thing both (a) as preliminary to it (*ut praeambulum ad ipsam*) and also (b) as subsequent to it (*ut subsequens*), viz., insofar as *good* designates some perfection it has, so it is with the relation of *likeness* to *image*. For instance, *good* is preliminary to *man* insofar as a man is a certain particular good and, again, *good* is subsequent to *man* insofar as we say that some individual man is good within his species (*bonum specialiter*) because of the perfection of his virtue. Similarly, *likeness* is thought of as preliminary to *image* insofar as *likeness* is more general than *image*, as was explained above (a. 1); and *likeness* is thought of as subsequent to *image* insofar as *likeness* signifies a certain perfection in an image, in the sense in which we say that an image of someone is like or unlike the one whose image it is, depending on whether the image represents him more perfectly or less perfectly.

So, then, there are two possible ways to distinguish *likeness* from *image*.

In the first way, *likeness* is preliminary to *image* and exists in more things. And in this sense, the likeness [of God] involves those things that are more general than the properties of the intellectual nature that *image* is properly associated with. Accordingly, *83 Quaestiones* says, "No one doubts that spirit"—i.e., mind—"is made to the image of God, whereas, according to what some want to say, the rest of a man"—viz., those things that belong to the lower parts of the soul or even to the body itself—"are made to the likeness [of God]." It is also in keeping with this reading that *De Quantitate Animae* says that the likeness of God in the soul is associated with the soul's being incorruptible, since *corruptible* and *incorruptible* are differences of *being-in-general*.

In the second way in which it can be thought of, *likeness* signifies the vividness (*expressio*) and perfection of an image. It is in accord with this reading that Damascene says, "What is relevant to the *image* signifies an intellectual power and a power that is *per se* free because of choice, whereas what is relevant to the *likeness* is a likeness of virtue, to the extent that it is possible for virtue to exist in a man." And this is equivalent to saying that the likeness pertains to the love of virtue; for there is no virtue without a love of virtue.

**Reply to objection 1:** A likeness is distinguished from an image not with respect to the general concept *likeness* (for this concept is included within the concept *image* itself), but rather insofar as a given likeness either (a) falls short of the concept *image* or (b) is perfective of an image.

**Reply to objection 2:** The soul's essence is relevant to the image to the extent that the image represents the divine essence in what is proper to an intellectual nature, e.g., being simple and being indissoluble—though not in the conditions that follow upon being in general (*conditiones consequentes ens in communi*).

**Reply to objection 3:** Certain virtues exist in the soul naturally, at least as far as their seeds are concerned, and a natural likeness could be associated with these virtues. However, it is not inappropriate for something that is called an image by one criterion (*secundum assignationem unam*) to be called a likeness by some other criterion.

**Reply to objection 4:** Love for the Word (*dilectio verbi*), i.e., knowledge that is loved (*amata notitia*), pertains to the concept *image*, but the love of virtue pertains to the concept *likeness*, as does virtue as well.

# QUESTION 94

## The State of the First Man with respect to His Intellect

The next thing we have to consider is the state or condition of the first man, first with respect to his soul (questions 94–96) and then with respect to his body (questions 97–101). On the first point there are two things to be considered: first, the condition of man with respect to his intellect (question 94) and second, the condition of man with respect to his will (questions 95–96).

On the first topic there are four questions: (1) Did the first man see God through His essence? (2) Was he able to see the separated substances, i.e., the angels? (3) Did he have knowledge (*scientia*) of all things? (4) Was he able to be mistaken or to be deceived?

## Article 1

## Did the first man see God through His essence?

It seems that the first man saw God through His essence:

**Objection 1:** Man's beatitude consists in the vision of the divine essence. But as Damascene says in *De Fide Orthodoxa* 2, "When the first man was living in Paradise, he had a life that was happy and rich in all things." And in *De Civitate Dei* 14 Augustine says, "If men had affections of the sort we have now, then how were they happy in that place of ineffable happiness, i.e., Paradise?" Therefore, in Paradise the first man saw God through His essence.

**Objection 2:** In *De Civitate Dei* 14 Augustine says, "The first man did not lack anything that a good will desires." But a good will can desire nothing better than the vision of God's essence. Therefore, the man saw God through His essence.

**Objection 3:** The vision of God through His essence is a vision by which God is seen directly and without any enigma (*sine medio et sine aenigmate*). But as the Master says in *Sentences* 4, dist. 1, man in the state of innocence "saw God directly." He also saw Him without any enigma, since 'enigma' implies obscurity and, as Augustine says in *De Trinitate* 15, obscurity  was introduced through sin. Therefore, in his initial state man saw God through His essence.

**But contrary to this:** In 1 Corinthians 15:46 the Apostle says, "It is not what is spiritual that is first, but what is animal." But to see God through His essence is maximally spiritual. Therefore, in the initial state of animal life the first man did not see God through His essence.

**I respond**: The first man did not see God through His essence, given the general state of his life—unless, perhaps, one claims that he saw God in a rapture when "God cast a deep sleep over Adam" (Genesis 2:21). The reason for this is that since God's essence is beatitude itself, the intellect of one who sees the divine essence is related to God in the same way that every man is related to beatitude. But it is clear that no man can voluntarily (*per voluntatem*) turn away from beatitude, since he naturally and necessarily wills beatitude and flees from unhappiness. Hence, no one who sees God through His essence can voluntarily (*voluntate*) turn away from God, i.e., sin. Because of this, everyone who sees God through His essence is so stable in his love for God that he is unable to sin for all eternity. Therefore, since Adam sinned, it is clear that he did not see God through His essence.

However, he did have a certain higher cognition of God than we ourselves have, and so in a way his cognition stood midway between the cognition associated with our present state and the cognition associated with heaven, by which God is seen through His essence.

To see this clearly, note that the vision of God through His essence is distinct from the vision of God through a creature. Now the higher a creature is and the more like God, the more clearly God is seen through that creature—just as a man is more perfectly seen in a mirror in which his image is reflected more distinctly. And so it is clear that God is seen much more prominently through His intelligible effects than through His sensible and corporeal effects. In his present state, man is kept from the full and lucid consideration of intelligible effects by the fact that he is distracted by sensible things and occupies himself with them. But as Ecclesiastes 7:30 says, "God made man upright (*rectus*)." And the rectitude of man, as he was instituted by God, consists in the fact that his lower powers were subject to his higher powers and that his higher powers were not impeded by his lower powers. Hence, the first man was not impeded by exterior things from a clear and firm contemplation of God's intelligible effects, which he perceived by the illumination (*irradiatio*) of the first truth, whether by natural cognition or graced cognition (*sive naturali cognitione sive gratuita*). Thus, in *Super Genesim ad Litteram* 11 Augustine says, "Perhaps God earlier spoke with the first men in the way that He speaks with the angels, illuminating their minds with the unalterable truth itself, though not with so great a participation in the divine essence as the angels have." So, then, through these intelligible effects of God's, man had a clearer cognition of God than we now have.

**Reply to objection 1:** Man was happy in Paradise, but not with that perfect beatitude to which he was going to be transported and which consists in the vision of the divine essence. Yet, as Augustine points out in *Super Genesim ad Litteram* 11, he had "a particular type of happy life" insofar as he had a certain natural integrity and perfection.

**Reply to objection 2:** A good will is a well-ordered will (*ordinata voluntas*). But the first man's will would not have been well-ordered if he had willed to have in the state of merit what was promised to him as a reward.

**Reply to objection 3:** There are two types of medium (*duplex est medium*):

One of them is such that what is said to be seen through the medium is seen at the very same time in the medium, as when a man is seen through a mirror and is seen at the very same time as the mirror itself is seen.

The other type of medium is such that through our knowledge of it we arrive at something unknown, as is the case with the medium [or middle term] of a demonstration.

God was seen without this latter sort of medium, but not without the former sort of medium. For the first man did not have to arrive at a cognition of God through a demonstration taken from some effect, as we ourselves have to. Instead, in his own way he had a cognition of God immediately in His effects, especially in His intelligible effects.

Similarly, one should note that there are two possible ways to understand the obscurity implied by the name 'enigma'.

In one sense, each creature is somewhat obscure if it is compared with the immensity of God's splendor (*ad immensitatem divinae claritatis*). And in this sense Adam saw God "in an enigma" (*in aenigmate*) because he saw God through a created effect.

In the second sense, one can mean the obscurity that follows upon sin; more specifically, man is impeded from the consideration of intelligible things by his occupation with sensible things. On this reading, it is not the case that [Adam] saw God "in an enigma."

## Article 2

### Did Adam in the state of innocence see angels through their essence?

It seems that Adam in the state of innocence saw angels through their essence:

**Objection 1:** In *Dialogi* 4 Gregory says, "In Paradise man used to enjoy God's words and, with cleanness of heart and loftiness of vision, to have commerce with the spirits of the holy angels."

**Objection 2:** In its present state the soul is impeded from a cognition of separated substances by the fact that it is united to a corruptible body that "weighs down the soul," as Wisdom 9:15 puts it. This is why, as was explained above (q. 89, a. 2), a separated soul is able to see separated substances. But the soul of the first man was not weighed down by his body, since his body was not corruptible. Therefore, he was able to see separated substances.

**Objection 3:** As it says in the *Liber de Causis*, one separated substance has cognition of another separated substance by having cognition of itself. But the first man's soul had cognition of itself. Therefore, it had cognition of the separated substances.

**But contrary to this:** Adam's soul was of the same nature as our souls. But our souls cannot now have intellective understanding of the separated substances. Therefore, neither could the first man's soul.

**I respond:** The state of the human soul can be thought of in two ways:

(a) In one way, with respect to the *diverse modes of its natural esse*, and on this score the state of a separated soul is distinct from the state of a soul conjoined to a body.

(b) In the second way, the state of the soul is thought of in terms of *integrity and corruption*, while keeping its mode of natural *esse* fixed; and on this score the state of innocence is distinct from man's state after the sin.

In the state of innocence, man's soul was applied to perfecting and directing the body, just as it is now, and this is why the first man is said to have been made "a living soul " (Genesis 2:7), i.e., a soul giving life to a body and, more specifically, an animal soul. But as was explained above (a. 1), [the first man] had integrity of life in the sense that his body was totally subject to his soul and in no way impeded it. And it is clear from what has gone before (q. 84, a. 7 and q. 85, a. 1) that because the soul is applied to directing and perfecting the body in its animal life, what belongs to our soul is a mode of intellective understanding that involves turning toward phantasms. Hence, this mode of intellective understanding likewise belonged to the soul of the first man.

Now given this mode of intellective understanding, there are, as Dionysius says in *De Divinis Nominibus*, chap. 4, three levels of movement in the soul: In the *first* of them "the soul is gathered into itself and away from exterior things." The *second* level occurs when the soul ascends to the point of "being united with the united higher powers," viz., the angels. In the *third* level the soul "is led to the good that surpasses all goods, viz., God."

Therefore, with the first movement of the soul, which is away from exterior things and toward itself, our cognition of the soul is brought to perfection. For as was explained above (q. 87, a. 3), the soul's intellective operation has a natural ordering toward those things that lie outside itself, and so through the cognition of those things we can have a perfect cognition of our own intellectual operation, since an act is known through its object. And through the intellectual operation itself we can have a perfect cognition of the human intellect, since a power is known through its proper act.

By contrast, no perfect cognition is found in the second movement, since, as was explained above (q. 55, a. 2), an angel has intellective understanding not by turning toward phantasms, but in a far more eminent way. So the mode of cognition just explained, by which the soul has cognition of itself, is not sufficient to lead to the cognition of an angel.

*A fortiori*, the third movement does not lead to perfect knowledge, since even the angels themselves are not able, by having cognition of themselves, to attain to the cognition of the divine substance—and this because of its surpassing nature (*propter eius excessum*).

So, then, the first man's soul could not have seen the angels through their essence. However, it nonetheless had cognition of them in a more excellent mode than we ourselves have. For its cognition was more certain and more fixed with respect to interior intelligible things than our cognition is. And it is because of this great eminence that Gregory says that the first man's soul "had commerce with the spirits of the angels."

**Reply to objection 1:** The reply to the first objection is clear from what was just said.

**Reply to objection 2:** The fact that the first man's soul fell short of an intellective understanding of the separated substances stemmed not from the body's weighing it down, but instead from the fact that its connatural object fell short of the excellence of the separated substances. We ourselves, on the other hand, fall short for both these reasons.

**Reply to objection 3:** As was just explained, the first man's soul was not able through its cognition of itself to attain to a cognition of the separated substances. For even in the case of the separated substances, each has a cognition of other separated substances in a mode peculiar to itself (*per modum sui ipsius*).

## Article 3

### Did the first man have scientific knowledge of all things?

It seems that the first man did not have scientific knowledge of all things (*non habuerit scientiam omnium*):

**Objection 1:** Either (a) he had such knowledge through acquired [intelligible] species or (b) he had it through connatural species or (c) he had it through infused species. But not through acquired species, since, as *Metaphysics* 1 says, cognition of the sort in question is caused by experience, whereas he had not at that time experienced all things. Again, not through connatural species, since he had the same nature that we have and, as *De Anima* 3 says, our soul is "like a tablet on which nothing has been written." On the other hand, if he had such knowledge through infused species, then the knowledge he had of things was not of the same nature as our scientific knowledge, which we acquire from things.

**Objection 2:** The same mode of reaching perfection is present in all individuals of the same species. But other men do not at their inception have scientific knowledge of all things; instead, they acquire it in their own way over a period of time (*per temporis successionem*). Therefore, neither did Adam, immediately upon being formed, have scientific knowledge of all things.

**Objection 3:** The state of the present life is granted to man in order that his soul might make progress both with respect to cognition and with respect to merit; for this seems to be the reason why the soul is united to the body. But in that [initial] state man would have been making progress with respect to merit. Therefore, he would likewise have been making progress with respect to the cognition of things. Therefore, he did not have scientific knowledge of all things.

**But contrary to this:** He himself imposed names on the animals, as Genesis 2:20 says. But names have to fit the natures of things. Therefore, Adam knew the natures of all the animals and, by parity of reasoning, he had scientific knowledge of all other things.

**I respond:** In the order of nature, the perfect precedes the imperfect in the sense that actuality precedes potentiality; for what exists in potentiality is not led into actuality except by some actual being. And since things were originally instituted by God not only as they exist in themselves, but also as principles of other things, it follows that they were produced in a perfect state, in which they were able to be principles of other things.

Now man can be a principle of another not only through corporeal generation but also through instructing and governing (*per instructionem et gubernationem*). And so just as the first man was instituted in a perfect state with respect to his body, so that he could immediately generate, so also he was instituted in a perfect state with respect to his soul, so that he could immediately instruct and direct others. But no one can instruct unless he has scientific knowledge. And so the first man was instituted by God in such a way that he had scientific knowledge of all the things in which a man is apt to be instructed. And these are all the things which exist virtually in the first principles that are known *per se*—in other words, whatever a men can have natural cognition of.

Now what is required for governing his own life and the lives of others is not only cognition of those things that can be naturally known, but also cognition of things that exceed natural cognition. For man's life is ordered toward a supernatural end. Similarly, in our own case, in order to govern our lives we must have cognition of what belongs to the Faith. Hence, the first man received cognition of these supernatural matters to the extent that this was necessary to direct human life in his state.

However, the first man did not have cognition of other things which cannot be known by man's natural efforts and which are not necessary for governing human life, e.g., the thoughts of men, future contingents, and singular facts such as, for instance, how many pebbles there are in a stream, and other things of this sort.

**Reply to objection 1:** The first man had scientific knowledge of all things through species that were infused by God. And yet his knowledge was not different in nature from our knowledge—just as the eyes that Christ gave to the man born blind were not different in nature from the eyes which nature produced.

**Reply to objection 2:** As is clear from what has been said, since Adam was the first man—something not true of the rest of men—it was fitting for him to have a modicum of perfection (*aliquid perfectionis*).

**Reply to objection 3:** In his scientific knowledge of naturally knowable things Adam made progress not with respect to the number of things known, but with respect to his mode of knowing them. For what he knew intellectually, he later came to know through experience.

On the other hand, as regards the supernatural things he had cognition of, he made progress, through new revelations, with respect to the number of things known, just as the angels make progress through new instances of enlightenment. However, progress in merit is unlike progress in knowledge, since it is not the case that one man is a principle of meriting for another man, whereas it is the case that one man is a principle of knowing for another man.

## Article 4

### Was man in his initial state able to be deceived?

It seems that man in his initial state was able to be deceived (*decipi potuisset*):

**Objection 1:** In 1 Timothy 2:14 the Apostle says, "The woman, having been deceived, was in sin."

**Objection 2:** In *Sentences* 2, dist. 21, the Master says, "The woman was not afraid of the serpent who was speaking to her, because she thought that he had received from God the role of speaking." But this was false. Therefore, the woman was deceived before the sin.

**Objection 3:** It is natural that the farther away something seems, the smaller it seems. But the nature of the eye is not changed because of sin, and so the same thing would have been true in the state of innocence. Therefore, a man would have been deceived about the size of something he saw, just as happens even now.

**Objection 4:** In *Super Genesim ad Litteram* 12 Augustine says that in a dream the soul clings to a likeness as if it were something real. But in the state of innocence man ate and, as a result, slept and had dreams. Therefore, he was deceived by clinging to likenesses as if they were real things.

**Objection 5:** As was explained above (a. 3), the first man did not know men's thoughts or future contingents. Therefore, if someone had spoken falsely to him about these matters, he would have been deceived.

**But contrary to this:** Augustine says, "It is not the nature of man as instituted, but the punishment of the damned, to take truths for falsehoods."

**I respond:** Some have claimed that there are two things that can be understood in the name 'deception': (a) a sort of cursory judgment (*qualiscumque existimatio levis*) by which someone clings to something false as if it were true, but without assent to the false belief (*sine assensu credulitatis*), and (b) a firm false belief (*firma credulitas*). Thus, with respect to things Adam had scientific knowledge of, man could not, before the sin, be deceived in either of these ways. But with respect to those things he did not have scientific knowledge of, he was able to be deceived, taking 'deception' in the broad sense for a sort of judgment that does not involve assent to a false belief (*pro existimatione qualicumque sine assensu credulitatis*). They make this claim because judging falsely in such matters is not harmful to a man; nor is it culpable, since assent is not rashly given.

However, this position is not consonant with the integrity of the initial state; for as Augustine says in *De Civitate Dei* 14, in that state "there was a tranquil avoidance of sin such that, while the state remained, no evil at all could exist." But it is clear that, as *Ethics* 6 explains, what is false is an evil for the intellect in the same way that what is true is its good. Hence, for as long as the state of innocence remained, it could not have been the case that man's intellect should acquiesce in something false as if it were true. For just as there was a lack of a certain perfection, e.g., splendor (*claritas*), in the first man's bodily parts and yet no evil could exist in him, so too in his intellect it was possible for there to be a lack of some sort of knowledge and yet there could not be any false judgment there (*nulla tamen poterat ibi esse existimatio falsi*).

The same point is also clear from the rectitude of the initial state. In accord with this rectitude, as long as the soul remained subject to God, man's lower powers were subject to his higher powers and the higher powers were not impeded by the lower powers. But it is clear from what was said above (q. 85, a. 6) that the intellect always has truth with respect to its proper object. Hence, the intellect is never deceived in its own right; instead, every deception in the intellect stems from some lower power, viz., the imagination or some other such power. Hence, we see that as long as the power of natural judgment (*naturale iudicatorium*) is not rendered inoperative, we are not deceived by appearances; rather, we are deceived only when that power is rendered inoperative, as is clear in the case of those who are asleep. Hence, it is clear that the rectitude of the initial state is not compatible with any deception in the intellect.

**Reply to objection 1:** Even though the seduction of the woman preceded the sin of deed (*peccatum operis*), it was subsequent to a sin of interior elation. For in *Super Genesim ad Litteram* 11 Augustine says, "The woman would not have believed the serpent's words if she had not already had in her mind a love for her own power and a proud presumptuousness regarding that power."

**Reply to objection 2:** What the woman believed was that the serpent had received the role of speaking (*officium loquendi*) not through its own nature, but by some supernatural act.

In any case, it is not necessary to follow the Master's authority on this point.

**Reply to objection 3:** If something had been represented to the first man's sensory power or imagination otherwise than it was in reality, he would not thereby have been deceived; for he would have discerned the truth through his reason.

**Reply to objection 4:** What happens in a dream is not imputed to a man, since he does not at that time have the use of reason, which is man's proper operation.

**Reply to objection 5:** When someone told a falsehood about future contingents or the thoughts of the heart, a man in the state of innocence would not have believed that it was so; instead, he would have believed that it was possible—and this would not have been to make a false judgment.

An alternative reply is that he was divinely assisted, lest he be deceived in matters that he did not have scientific knowledge of. Nor does it count against this, as some have asserted, that in the temptation he was not assisted in not being deceived, even though he especially needed to be assisted at that point. For a sin had already taken place in his mind, and he did not have recourse to God's assistance.

# QUESTION 95

## Things Relevant to the First Man's Will, viz., Grace and Justice

The next thing we have to consider is what pertains to the first man's will. On this point there are two topics: first, concerning the grace and justice or moral rectitude of the first man (*de gratia et iustitia primi hominis*) (question 95) and, second, concerning the use of justice in his dominion over other things (question 96).

On the first topic there are four questions: (1) Was the first man created in grace? (2) Did the soul have passions in the state of innocence? (3) Did the soul have all virtues in the state of innocence? (4) Were the first man's works as efficacious for meriting as our works are now?

## Article 1

## Was the first man created in grace?

It seems that the first man was not created in grace (*creatus in gratia*):

**Objection 1:** In 1 Corinthians 15:45 the Apostle, distinguishing Adam from Christ, says, "The first Adam was made a living soul; the last Adam was made a life-giving spirit." But the spirit's life-giving occurs through grace. Therefore, it is peculiar to Christ that he was made in grace.

**Objection 2:** In *Quaestiones Veteris et Novi Testamenti* Augustine says, "Adam did not have the Holy Spirit." But whoever has grace has the Holy Spirit. Therefore, Adam was not created in grace.

**Objection 3:** In *De Correptione et Gratia* Augustine says, "God ordered the lives of angels and men in such a way that He demonstrated in them, first, what their free choice was capable of and, second, what the gift of grace and the judgment of justice were capable of." Therefore, He first established men and angels with only their natural freedom of choice, and afterwards He conferred grace on them.

**Objection 4:** In *Sentences* 2, dist. 24 the Master says, "In creation man was given assistance through which he was able to hold his own but was not able to make progress (*datum est auxilium per quod stare poterat sed non poterat proficere*)." But whoever has grace is able to make progress through merit. Therefore, the first man was not created in grace.

**Objection 5:** In order for someone to receive grace, consent is required on the part of the recipient, since a sort of spiritual marriage is thereby consummated between God and the soul. But the consent to grace can belong only to someone who already exists. Therefore, man did not receive grace at the first instant of his creation.

**Objection 6:** Nature is more distant from grace than grace is from glory, which is nothing other than consummated grace. But in man grace preceded glory. Therefore, *a fortiori*, nature preceded grace.

**But contrary to this:** Men and angels are equally ordered toward grace. But angels were created in grace; for in *De Civitate Dei* 12 Augustine says, "God was in them, simultaneously creating them and giving them grace." Therefore, man was likewise created in grace.

**I respond:** Some claim that the first man was not created in grace, but that instead grace was conferred on him later—though before he sinned, since many passages from the saints attest that man had grace in the state of innocence.

However, as others claim, the very rectitude of the initial state in which God made man seems to require that man was created in grace—this according to Ecclesiastes 7:30 ("God made man upright"). For this rectitude involved reason's being subject to God, the lower powers' being subject to reason, and the body's being subject to the soul, where the first sort of subordination (*subjectio*) was a cause of both the second and the third. For, as Augustine says, as long as reason remained subject to God, the lower powers were subject to reason.

However, it is obvious that the subjection of the body to the soul and of the lower powers to reason was not natural; otherwise, it would have remained after the sin, since even among the demons their natural gifts remained after their sin, as Dionysius points out in *De Divinis Nominibus*, chap. 4. Hence, it is clear that the first sort of subjection, by which reason was subject to God, likewise did not stem from nature, but stemmed instead from the supernatural gift of grace, since it is impossible for an effect to be more potent than its cause. Thus, in *De Civitate Dei* 13 Augustine says, "After they had committed the transgression against the precept, and after God's grace had deserted them, they were immediately ashamed of the nakedness of their bodies; for they sensed the urges of their disobedient flesh as a punishment that corresponded to their own disobedience." From this we can see that if the flesh's obedience to the soul was lost when grace deserted them, then it was through the presence of grace in their soul that the lower powers had been subject to the soul.

**Reply to objection 1:** The Apostle adduces these words in order to show that there is a spiritual body if there is an animal body, since the life of the spiritual body began in Christ, who is "the firstborn from the dead" (Colossians 1:18), just as the life of the animal body began in Adam. Therefore, the Apostle's words imply not that Adam was not spiritual with respect to his soul, but rather that he was not spiritual with respect to his body.

**Reply to objection 2:** As Augustine points out in the same place, it is not being denied that the Holy Spirit was in Adam in some way, just as He is in the rest of those who are justified. Rather, the claim is that the Holy Spirit "was not in Adam in the same way that He is now in the faithful," who are admitted to the reception of their eternal inheritance immediately after death.

**Reply to objection 3:** On the basis of this passage from Augustine one may conclude not that angels or men were created in a natural freedom of choice before they had grace, but that He made manifest in them (a) what free choice was capable of before their confirmation [in the good] and (b) what they would attain afterwards through the assistance of confirming grace.

**Reply to objection 4:** The Master is speaking in accord with the opinion of those who claimed that man was created in a natural state only (*in naturalibus tantum*) and not in grace.

An alternative reply is that even if man was created in grace, he still had his ability to make progress through merit from additional grace (*ex superadditione gratiae*) and not from the creation of his nature.

**Reply to objection 5:** Since the will's movement is not continuous, nothing prevents it from being the case that the first man consented to grace at the very first instant of his creation.

**Reply to objection 6:** We merit glory through an act of grace, but we do not merit grace through an act of nature. Therefore, the cases are not parallel.

## Article 2

### Did the passions of the soul exist in the first man?

It seems that the passions of the soul did not exist in the first man:

**Objection 1:** It is because of the passions of the soul that "the flesh lusts against the spirit" (Galatians 5:17). But this did not occur in the state of innocence. Therefore, in the state of innocence there were no passions of the soul.

**Objection 2:** Adam's soul was more noble than his body. But Adam's body was impassible. Therefore, there were no passions in his soul, either.

**Objection 3:** The passions of the soul are suppressed (*comprimuntur*) by moral virtue. But in Adam there was perfect moral virtue. Therefore, the passions were totally excluded from him.

**But contrary to this:** In *De Civitate Dei* 14 Augustine says that [our first parents] had "an untroubled love for God" and certain other passions of the soul.

**I respond:** The passions of the soul exist in the sentient appetite (*in appetitu sensuali*), the object of which is the good and the bad. Hence, among all the passions of the soul, some, e.g., love (*amor*) and joy (*gaudium*), are related to what is good, and some, e.g., fear (*timor*) and sorrow (*dolor*), are related to what is bad. And since, as is clear from Augustine in *De Civitate Dei* 14, in the initial state (a) there was nothing bad that was either present or threatening and (b) there was nothing good which was absent and which a good will would at that time have desired to possess, none of the passions that are related to what is bad, e.g., fear, sorrow, and others of this kind, existed in Adam, and, similarly, neither did those passions which are related to something good that is not had and yet should be had at present, e.g., an urgent desire (*cupiditas aestuans*).

However, those passions that can relate to a present good, e.g., joy and love, or to a future good to be had in its own time, e.g., a non-distressed desire or hope, did exist in the state of innocence—though otherwise than they exist in us. For in us the sentient appetite, in which the passions exist, is not totally subject to reason. And so the passions sometimes exist in us in a way that precedes reason's judgment and impedes it, whereas sometimes they follow upon reason's judgment, so that the sentient appetite obeys reason in some way. By contrast, in the state of innocence the lower appetite was totally subject to reason, and so the only passions in it were ones that follow upon the judgment of reason.

**Reply to objection 1:** The flesh "lusts against the spirit" in the sense that the passions fight against reason—something that did not occur in the state of innocence.

**Reply to objection 2:** In the state of innocence the human body was impassible with respect to those passions that undermine its natural disposition (*removent dispositionem naturalem*); this will be explained below (q. 97, a. 2). Similarly, the soul was impassible with respect to those passions that impede reason.

**Reply to objection 3:** Perfect moral virtue does not totally eliminate the passions, but instead orders them. For instance, as *Ethics* 3 says, "It belongs to the temperate man to desire what is necessary as is necessary."

## Article 3

### Did Adam have all the virtues?

It seems that Adam did not have all the virtues:

**Objection 1:** Certain virtues are ordered toward constraining immoderation in the passions, in the way that immoderate desire (*immoderata concupiscentia*) is constrained by temperance (*temperantia*) and immoderate fear (*immoderatus timor*) is constrained by fortitude (*fortitudo*). But in the state of innocence immoderation in the passions did not exist. Therefore, neither did the aforementioned virtues exist.

**Objection 2:** Certain virtues have to do with passions that are related to what is bad—for instance, mildness (*mansuetudo*) has to do with instances of anger (*irae*) and fortitude has to do with instances of fear. But as has been explained (a. 2), such passions did not exist in the state of innocence. Therefore, neither did virtues of this type.

**Objection 3:** Repentance (*poenitentia*) is a virtue having to do with a previously committed sin; likewise, mercy (*misericordia*) is a virtue having to do with unhappiness (*miseria*). But in the state of innocence there was neither sin nor unhappiness. Therefore, neither were there virtues of this sort.

**Objection 4:** Perseverance (*perseverantia*) is a virtue. But as his later sin demonstrated, Adam did not have this virtue. Therefore, it is not the case that he had all the virtues.

**Objection 5:** Faith (*fides*) is a virtue. But it did not exist in the state of innocence; for it implies an enigmatic cognition (*importat aenigmaticam cognitionem*), which seems to be incompatible with the perfection of the initial state.

**But contrary to this:** In one of his homilies Augustine says, "The prince of vices conquered Adam, who had been made to God's image from the slime of the earth and who was armed with modesty (*pudicitia armatum*), restrained by temperance (*temperantia compositum*), and refulgent with splendor (*claritate splendidum*)."

**I respond:** There is a certain sense in which man had all the virtues in the state of innocence. This can be made clear from what has already been said. For it was explained above (a. 1) that the rectitude of the initial state was such that reason was subject to God and the lower powers were subject to reason. But the virtues are nothing other than certain perfections by which reason is ordered to God and by which the lower powers are disposed to following the rule of reason; this will become clearer when we discuss the virtues (*ST* 1–2, qq. 55–70). Hence, the rectitude of the initial state required that man in some sense have all the virtues.

However, note that certain virtues, e.g., *charity* and *justice*, are such that by their nature they involve no imperfection. Virtues of this sort existed absolutely speaking in the state of innocence, both with respect to their habits and with respect to their acts.

By contrast, there are some virtues that involve imperfection by their very nature, either on the part of their act or on the part of their matter. If the imperfection in question is not incompatible with the perfection of the initial state, then virtues of this sort could still have existed in the initial state. Examples are *faith*, which is directed toward things that are not seen, and *hope*, which is directed toward things that are not had. For the perfection of the first state did not extend to seeing God through His essence or to having Him with the enjoyment of final beatitude, and so faith and hope were able to have existed in the initial state, both with respect to their habits and with respect to their acts.

But if the imperfection that has to do with the nature of a given virtue is incompatible with the perfection of the initial state, then that virtue was able to have existed in the initial state with respect to its habit but not with respect to its act. This is clear, for instance, in the case of *repentance*, which is sorrow (*dolor*) for a sin that has been committed, and in the case of *mercy*, which is sorrow at the unhappiness of another; for sorrow, along with guilt and unhappiness, are incompatible with the perfection of the initial state. Hence, virtues of this sort existed in the first man with respect to their habits, but not with respect to their acts. For the first man was disposed in such a way that if he had previously sinned, he would be sorrowful, and, similarly, if he were to see unhappiness in another, he would dispel it as far as he was able to. For as the Philosopher says in *Ethics* 4, "Shame"—which has to do with one's own bad deeds—"occurs in a virtuous man only conditionally. For he is so disposed that he would feel shame if he were to commit some bad deed."

**Reply to objection 1:** It is incidental to temperance and fortitude to *repel* excessive passions; this occurs [only] to the extent that there are excessive passions in their subject. By contrast, what belongs *per se* to virtues of this sort is to *moderate* the passions.

**Reply to objection 2:** The passions directed toward what is bad are incompatible with the perfection of the initial state if, like fear and sorrow, they are directed toward something bad that exists in the one having the passion.

By contrast, passions that have a relation to something bad that exists in someone else are not incompatible with the perfection of the initial state; for instance, in the initial state man was able to have hated the malice of the demons in the same way that he loved the goodness of God. Hence, the virtues that have to do with such passions were able to have existed in the initial state, both with respect to their habit and with respect to their act.

However, virtues having to do with passions that are directed toward what is bad in the same subject are such that, if they have to do only with passions of the sort in question, then they were able to have existed in the initial state only with respect to their habit and not with respect to their act—as has been explained concerning repentance and mercy.

On the other hand, there are certain virtues that have to do not only with these passions but also with other passions—e.g., temperance, which has to do not only with types of sadness (*circa tristitias*), but also with pleasures (*circa delectationes*), and fortitude, which has to do not only with types of fear (*circa timores*), but also with audacity and hope (*circa audaciam et spem*). Hence, an act of temperance could have existed in the initial state insofar as it was moderating pleasures; and the same holds for fortitude insofar as it was moderating audacity or hope, though not insofar as it was moderating sadness or fear.

**Reply to objection 3:** The reply to the third objection is clear from what has been said.

**Reply to objection 4:** 'Perseverance' is taken in two ways:

In one way, insofar as it is a *virtue*, and in this sense it signifies a habit by which someone chooses to persevere in the good. On this reading, Adam had perseverance.

In the second way, insofar as it is a *circumstance modifying a virtue*, and in this sense it signifies a certain continuity of virtue without interruption. On this reading, Adam did not have perseverance.

**Reply to objection 5:** The reply to the fifth objection is clear from what has been said.

## Article 4

### Were the first man's works less efficacious
### for meriting than our works are?

It seems that the first man's work were less efficacious for meriting than our works are:

**Objection 1:** Grace is given out of God's mercy, which grants more help to those who are more needy. But we ourselves need grace more than the first man did in the state of innocence. Therefore, grace is poured into us more copiously. Since grace is the root of merit, our works are rendered more efficacious for meriting.

**Objection 2:** A certain struggle and difficulty is required for merit. For 2 Timothy 2:5 says, "He who does not legitimately struggle will not be crowned," and in *Ethics* 2 the Philosopher says, "Virtue has to do with the difficult and the good." But there is more struggle and difficulty now. Therefore, there is also more efficacy for meriting now.

**Objection 3:** In *Sentences* 2, dist. 24 the Master says, "Man would not have merited by resisting temptation, but now one who resists temptation merits." Therefore, our works are more efficacious for meriting than were works in the initial state.

**But contrary to this:** On this view, man would be in a better condition after the sin.

**I respond:** The quantity of merit can be thought of in two ways:

In one way, in terms of its *root* in charity and grace (*ex radice caritatis et gratiae*). And on this reading, the quantity of merit corresponds to the *essential* reward (*praemio essentiali*), which consists in the enjoyment of God; for someone who does something out of greater charity enjoys God more perfectly.

In the second way, the quantity of merit can be thought of in terms of the quantity of the *work* (*ex quantitate operis*); and this is twofold, viz., *absolute* quantity and *proportional* quantity (*quantitas absoluta et proportionalis*). For the widow who put two mites into the treasury did a lesser work in terms of absolute quantity than those who put in large sums, but in terms of proportional quantity the widow did more in our Lord's view, because she exceeded her means to a greater degree (Mark 12:41, Luke 21:1). Still, both of these sorts of quantity of merit correspond to an *incidental* reward (*praemio accidentali*), viz., joy with respect to a created good.

So, then, one should say that the works of man were more efficacious for meriting in the state of innocence than after the sin, if what is meant is the quantity of merit on the part of grace; for grace was more copious at that time, when no obstacle to it existed in human nature. The same thing holds if one considers the *absolute quantity* of the work. For since man had greater virtue, he did greater works.

However, if one considers *proportional quantity*, then more of the character of merit is found after the sin because of man's weakness. For a small work exceeds the power of someone who does it with difficulty to a greater degree than a great work exceeds the power of someone who does it without difficulty.

**Reply to objection 1:** After the sin man needed grace for more works than before the sin, but he did not have more of a need for grace. For even before the sin man needed grace to attain eternal life, which is the main reason why grace is necessary. But beyond this, after the sin man also needs grace for the remission of his sins and for support in his weakness.

**Reply to objection 2:** As has been explained, difficulty and struggle have to do with the quantity of merit in the sense of the proportional quantity of the works. For it is a sign of the will's promptitude that it tries to do what is difficult for itself, and the will's promptitude is caused by the magnitude of its charity. However, it can happen that, because someone is prepared to do even something that is difficult for himself, he does an easy work with as prompt a will as someone else does a difficult work. Still, to the extent that the actual difficulty has the character of punishment, it also has the character of satisfying for sin (*inquantum est poenalis habet etiam quod sit satisfactoria pro peccato*).

**Reply to objection 3:** According to the opinion of those who hold that the first man did not have grace, it would not have been meritorious for him to resist temptation, just as this is not now meritorious for someone who does not have grace. But there is a difference here, since in the initial state there was nothing interior that impelled man toward what is bad, as there now is. Hence, man would have been able to resist temptation more easily without grace at that time than he is now.

# The Sort of Dominion That Belonged to the First Man in the State of Innocence

The next thing we have to consider is the sort of dominion that belonged to man in the state of innocence. And on this topic there are four questions: (1) Did man in the state of innocence have dominion over the animals? (2) Did he have dominion over every creature? (3) Would all men have been equal in the state of innocence? (4) Did one man have dominion over another in the state of innocence?


## Article 1

### Did Adam in the state of innocence have dominion over the animals?

It seems that in the state of innocence Adam did not have dominion over the animals (*Adam in statu innocentiae animalibus non dominabatur*):

**Objection 1:** In *Super Genesim ad Litteram* 9 Augustine says that it was by the ministry of the angels that the animals were brought to Adam, so that he might impose names on them. But the ministry of the angels would not have been necessary in this case if man had had dominion over the animals in his own right. Therefore, in the state of innocence man did not have dominion over the other animals.

**Objection 2:** It is not right to bring together under one dominion things that are in conflict with one another (*discordant ad invicem*). But many animals, e.g. the sheep and the wolf, are naturally in conflict with one another. Therefore, it is not the case that all the animals were included under man's dominion.

**Objection 3:** Jerome says, "God gave man dominion over the animals before the sin even though man did not need it, because He foreknew that after the Fall man would be helped by the support of the animals." Therefore, before the sin it was at least the case that man did not make use of his dominion over the animals.

**Objection 4:** It seems proper to a master (*dominus*) to rule (*praecipere*). But rule (*praeceptum*) is appropriately exercised only over those who have reason. Therefore, man did not have dominion over the non-rational animals.

**But contrary to this:** Genesis 1:26 says of man, "Let him have dominion over the fish of the sea, and over the birds of the air and over the beasts of the earth."

**I respond**: As was explained above (q. 95, a. 1), disobedience against man on the part of those things that should be subject to him followed as his punishment for his own disobedience against God. And so in the state of innocence, before this act of disobedience, nothing that should naturally be subject to man put up any opposition against him. But all the animals were naturally subject to man.

This is made clear in three ways:

First, from *the very manner in which nature proceeds*. For just as in the generation of things one sees a certain order by which nature proceeds from the imperfect to the perfect (since matter exists for the sake of form, and a less perfect form exists for the sake of a more perfect form), so too this holds with respect to the use that is made of natural things; more specifically, the less perfect are made use of by the more perfect. For instance, for their nourishment plants make use of the earth, and animals make use of plants, and men make use of both plants and animals. Hence, man by nature has dominion over the animals. Thus, the Philosopher says in *Politics* 1 that it is just and natural to hunt wild animals, because man thereby lays claim to what is naturally his.

Second, the same point is clear from *the order of God's providence*, which always governs lower things by means of higher things. Hence, since man is higher than the rest of the animals, given that he is made to the image of God, it is appropriate for the other animals to be subject to his governance.

Third, the same point is clear from *the properties of man and the other animals*. For in the other animals what one finds, in accord with their natural judgment, is a certain participation in prudence with respect to some particular acts, whereas in man one finds general prudence, i.e., reason with respect to all actions (*ratio omnium agibilium*). But whatever is such-and-such by participation is subject to that which is such-and-such through its essence and in a general way.

Hence, it is clear that the subjection of the other animals to man is something natural.

**Reply to objection 1:** A higher power can do many things to his subjects that a lower power cannot do. But an angel is naturally higher than a man. Hence, some effect with respect to animals that was not able to be brought about by human power was able to be brought about by angelic power, viz., that all the animals should be brought together at once.

**Reply to objection 2:** Some claim that the animals that are now ferocious and kill other animals were tame in that initial state not only with respect to men but also with respect to the other animals.

However, this claim is wholly unreasonable. For the nature of the animals was not changed through man's sin in such a way that certain animals, e.g., lions and falcons, for whom it is now natural to eat the flesh of other animals, lived off of plants at that time. Moreover, Bede's gloss on Genesis 1:30 says that trees and plants were given not to *all* the animals and birds as food, but to *some* of them. Therefore, there would have been natural conflict among certain animals.

However, the animals were not thereby removed from man's dominion, just as they are not now thereby removed from the dominion of God, by whose providence all of this is arranged. Moreover, man executed this providence, even as is now obvious in the case of domestic animals. For men give hens as food to domesticated falcons.

**Reply to objection 3:** In the state of innocence men did not need animals (a) for bodily necessities, or (b) for clothing, since they were naked and unashamed and untroubled by any movement of disordered desire, or (c) for food, since they fed on the trees of Paradise, or (d) for transportation, because of their own bodily strength.

However, they did need the animals in order to gain experiential cognition of the animals' natures. This is indicated by the fact that God brought the animals to Adam, so that he might impose upon them names that designate their natures.

**Reply to objection 4:** The other animals have a certain participation in prudence and reason because of their natural judgment (*secundum aestimationem naturalem*), by which cranes follow their leader and bees obey their ruler. And they obeyed man at that time in the same way that certain domestic animals obey him now.

## Article 2

### Did man have dominion over all other creatures?

It seems that man did not have dominion over all other creatures:

**Objection 1:** Angels are naturally more powerful than men. But as Augustine says in *De Trinitate* 3, "Corporeal matter did not obey even the holy angels at their will." Therefore, *a fortiori*, it did not obey man in the state of innocence.

**Objection 2:** The only powers of the soul had by plants are the nutritive power, the augmentative power, and the generative power. But these powers are not apt by nature to obey reason, as in clear within one and the same man. Therefore, since dominion belongs to man because of his reason, it seems that in the state of innocence man did not have dominion over plants.

**Objection 3:** Whoever has dominion over a thing can change that thing. But man was not able to change the course of the celestial bodies, since this belongs to God alone, as Dionysius says in his letter to Polycarp. Therefore, he did not have dominion over them.

**But contrary to this:** Genesis 1:26 says of man, ". . . that he might have dominion over every creature."

**I respond:** In a certain sense all things exist within man, and so he has dominion over other things in the sense that he has dominion over what exists within himself.

Now there are four things to take account of within man, viz., *reason*, in accord with which he is like the angels; *the sentient powers*, in accord with which he is like the animals; *the natural powers*, in accord with which he is like the plants; and *the body itself*, in accord with which he is like inanimate things.

Now within man reason plays the role of that which has dominion and is not subject to any dominion. Hence, in his initial state man did not have dominion over the angels; and when it says "every creature," what this means is "every creature that is not made to God's image."

On the other hand, the soul, by commanding, has dominion over the sentient powers, such as the irascible and concupiscible powers, which in some sense obey reason. Hence, in the state of innocence man likewise had dominion over the other animals through his command.

Again, man has dominion over the natural powers, and the body itself, by making use of them rather than by commanding them. And so in the state of innocence man likewise had dominion over plants and inanimate things in this way—not by commanding them or changing them, but by using their help without impediment.

**Reply to objection 1 and objection 2 and objection 3:** The replies to the objections are clear from what has been said.

## Article 3

### Would all men have been equal in the state of innocence?

It seems that all men would have been equal in the state of innocence (*homines omnes fuissent aequales*):

**Objection 1:** Gregory says, "When we do not commit crimes (*ubi non delinquimus*), we are all equal (*pares*)." But there was no crime in the state of innocence. Therefore, everyone was equal.

**Objection 2:** Likeness and equality are the reason for mutual love (*ratio mutuae dilectionis*)—this according to Ecclesiasticus 13:19 ("Every animal loves what is like itself, and so too every man loves his neighbor"). But love among men, which is a bond of peace, abounded in the state of innocence. Therefore, everyone would have been equal in the state of innocence.

**Objection 3:** When a cause ceases, its effect ceases. But the cause of inequality among men at present seems to be (a) from the side of God, given that He rewards some for merits and punishes others, and (b) from the side of *nature*, given that some are born disabled or deprived because of a natural defect while some are born strong and perfect. These things would not have occurred in the initial state.

**But contrary to this:** Romans 13:1 says, "What is from God is ordered toward God." But order seems to consist especially in inequality; for in *De Civitate Dei* 19 Augustine says, "Order is an arrangement of equal and unequal things, assigning places to each." Therefore, in the initial state, which would have been the most orderly, there was inequality.

**I respond:** One must claim that there would have been some inequality in the initial state, at least with respect to sex, since without diversity of sex there would have been no generation. Likewise, there would have been inequality with respect to age, since some would have been born from others; nor would those who had sexual relations have been sterile.

But there would also have been diversity in the soul, both with respect to moral rectitude (*quantum ad iustitiam*) and with respect to knowledge. For man would have acted by free choice and not by necessity, and because of this men would have been able to apply themselves in greater or lesser degrees to doing or willing or knowing something. Hence, some would have made more progress than others in moral rectitude and knowledge.

Again, there could have been inequality on the part of the body. For the human body was not wholly exempt from the laws of nature in the sense that it would not receive greater or lesser help or assistance from exterior agents, since the life of men would likewise have been sustained by food. So nothing prevents one from saying that, given the diverse climatic conditions and the diverse arrangements of the stars, some would have been born more robust and bigger and more beautiful and more attractive in body than others. Yet in those who were surpassed in such things, there would have been no defect or flaw (*defectus sive peccatum*), either with respect to the soul or with respect to the body.

**Reply to objection 1:** With these words Gregory intends to rule out an inequality that stems from differences in moral rectitude and sin, on the basis of which some have to be subjected to others as a punishment.

**Reply to objection 2:** Equality is the reason why mutual love is equal. However, it is possible for there to be greater love among unequals than among equals, even though this sort of love does not come from both parties equally. For instance, a father naturally loves his child more than a brother loves his brother—even though a child does not love his father to the same degree that he is loved by him.

**Reply to objection 3:** The reason for the inequality could have been from the side of God, not in the sense that He punished some and rewarded others, but in the sense that He elevated some to a greater degree and some to a lesser degree, so that the beauty of order would better shine through among men. And the inequality could also have been caused in the way explained above from the side of nature—and this without any defect of nature.

## Article 4

### Did one man have dominion over another in the state of innocence?

It seems that one man did not have dominion over another in the state of innocence (*homo homini non dominabatur*):

**Objection 1:** In *De Civitate Dei* 19 Augustine says, "God wanted rational man, made to His own image, to have dominion only over non-rational beings; He wanted man to have dominion over the beasts and not over man."

**Objection 2:** Anything introduced as a punishment for sin would not have existed in the state of innocence. But man's being subject to man was introduced as a punishment for sin; for instance, after the sin the woman was told, "You will be under the man's power" (Genesis 3:16). Therefore, in the state of innocence it was not the case that one man was subject to another.

**Objection 3:** Subordination is opposed to freedom. But freedom is one of the principal goods that was not lacking in the state of innocence, where "nothing was lacking that a good will could desire," as Augustine puts it in *De Civitate Dei* 14. Therefore, it is not the case that one man had dominion over another in the state of innocence.

**But contrary to this:** The condition of men in the state of innocence was not more dignified than the condition of the angels. But among the angels there are some who have dominion over others; thus, one order of angels is even called Dominations. Therefore, it is not contrary to the dignity of the state of innocence that one man should have dominion over another.

**I respond:** 'Dominion' (*dominium*) is taken in two senses:

(a) In one sense, dominion is opposed to servitude, and in this sense a lord (*dominus*) is one to whom someone is subject as a servant (*servus*).

(b) In the second sense, dominion is related in general to any kind of subject at all, and in this sense even someone who has the role of governing and directing free men (*liberi*) can be called a lord.

Thus, if we take 'dominion' in the first sense, then it is not the case that one man had dominion over another in the state of innocence, whereas if we take 'dominion' in the second sense, then it was possible for one man to have dominion over another in the state of innocence. The reason for this is that a servant differs from a free man in that "a free man is a cause of himself (*causa sui*)," as it says at the beginning of the *Metaphysics*, whereas a servant is ordered toward another.

Thus, someone has dominion over another *as a servant* when the one who has dominion looks to the one over whom he has dominion for his usefulness to himself, i.e., to the one who has dominion. And since everyone desires his own good and consequently finds it deplorable to have to give exclusively to someone else a good that ought to have been his own, it follows that this sort of dominion cannot exist without suffering on the part of the subjects *(sine poena subiectorum)*. Consequently, this sort of dominion of one man over another would not have existed in the state of innocence.

On the other hand, someone has dominion over another *as a free man* when he directs him either to the proper good of the one who is being directed or to the common good. And this sort of dominion of one man over another would have existed in the state of innocence—and this for two reasons.

First, man is naturally a social animal, and so in the state of innocence men would have lived in society (*vixissent socialiter*). But it would not be possible for a multitude to live in society unless there were someone in charge who looked toward the common good (*nisi aliquis praesideret qui ad bonum commune intenderet*); for the many necessarily look toward many goods, while the one looks toward one good. This is why the Philosopher says at the beginning of the *Politics* that whenever the many are ordered toward one thing, that one thing will always be found to be central and directive (*unum ut principale et dirigens*).

Second, if one man had preeminence over another in knowledge and moral rectitude, then it would not have been fitting for him not to act for the benefit of the others—this according to 1 Peter 4:10 ("As every man has received grace, ministering the same one to another"). Thus, in *De Civitate Dei* 19 Augustine says, "Those who are just rule not out of a desire to dominate, but because it is their duty to give counsel (*officio consulendi*). The natural order of things prescribes this, and thus did God make man."

**Reply to objection 1 and objection 2 and objection 3:** From what has been said it is clear how to reply to all the objections, which are based on the first sense of 'dominion'.

# QUESTION 97

## The Conservation of the Individual in the Initial State

The next thing we have to consider is what pertains to the state of the first man with respect to the body: first, as regards the conservation of the individual (question 97); and, second, as regards the conservation of the species (questions 98–101).

On the first topic there are four questions: (1) Was man immortal in the state of innocence? (2) Was man impassible in the state of innocence? (3) Did man need food in the state of innocence? (4) Did he attain immortality through the tree of life?

## Article 1

### Was man immortal in the state of innocence?

It seems that man was not immortal in the state of innocence:

**Objection 1:** *Mortal* is part of the definition of man. But when a definition is denied, the thing defined is denied. Therefore, if he was a man, then he could not have been immortal.

**Objection 2:** As *Metaphysics* 10 says, "What is corruptible differs in genus from what is incorruptible." But there is no transmutation of things differing in genus into one another. Therefore, if the first man was incorruptible, then man would not be able to be corruptible in the present state (*in statu isto*).

**Objection 3:** If man was immortal in the state of innocence, this was so either by nature or by grace. But it was not by nature; for since nature remains the same in species, he would also be immortal now. Similarly, it was not by grace, since the first man recovered grace through repentance—this according to Wisdom 10:2 ("He brought him out of his sins"). Therefore, he would have recovered his immortality, too. But this is obviously false. Therefore, man was not immortal in the state of innocence.

**Objection 4:** Immortality is promised to man as a reward—this according to Apocalypse 21:4 ("Death will be no more"). But man was not created in a state of reward; rather, he was created in order to merit a reward. Therefore, man was not immortal in the state of innocence.

**But contrary to this:** Romans 5:12 says, "Through sin death entered into the world." Therefore, before the sin man was immortal.

**I respond**: There are three senses in which a thing can be said to be incorruptible:

(a) First, *because of matter* (*ex parte materiae*), viz., either because it does not have matter, as in the case of the angels, or because it has matter that is in potentiality only to a single [substantial] form, as in the case of the celestial bodies. This is called *being incorruptible by nature*.

(b) Second, a thing is said to be incorruptible *because of a form* (*ex parte formae*), viz., when a thing corruptible by nature has a disposition by which it is absolutely prevented from being corrupted (*dispositio per quam totaliter a corruptione prohibetur*). This is called *being incorruptible by glory*, since as Augustine says in his letter *Ad Dioscorum*, "God made the soul so powerful by nature that the fullness of its health, i.e., the vigor of its incorruption, spills over from its beatitude into its body."

(c) Third, a thing is said to be incorruptible *because of an efficient cause* (*ex parte causae efficientis*). This is the sense in which man was incorruptible and immortal in the state of innocence. For as Augustine says in *Quaestiones Veteris et Novi Testamenti*, "God made man to live immortally as long as he did not sin, so that he would be the source of life or death for himself." For his body was not incorruptible (*indissolubile*) through any sort of vigor of immortality that existed within it; instead, his soul had a certain power, given supernaturally by God, through which, as long as it remained subject to God, it was able to preserve the body from all corruption. This made good sense. For since, as was explained above (q. 76, a. 1), the rational soul exceeds the proportion of corporeal matter, it was fitting that at the beginning a power should be given to it by which it was able to conserve the body in a way that exceeded the nature of corporeal matter.

**Reply to objection 1 and objection 2:** These arguments go through in the case of what is incorruptible and immortal by nature.

**Reply to objection 3:** The power of preserving the body from corruption was not natural to the human soul, but stemmed from a gift of grace. And even though the soul would regain grace with respect to having its sins remitted and meriting glory, it would nonetheless not regain it with respect to the effect of its lost immortality. For this effect was reserved for Christ, through whom, as will be explained below (*ST* 3, q. 14, a. 4), the defect of nature was to be remade into something better (*naturae defectus in melius reparandus erat*).

**Reply to objection 4:** The immortality of glory, which is promised as a reward, is different from the immortality which was given to man in the state of innocence.

## Article 2

### Was man passible in the state of innocence?

It seems that man was passible in the state of innocence:

**Objection 1:** To sense something is a sort of being acted upon (*pati quoddam*). But in the state of innocence man was able to have sensation. Therefore, he was passible.

**Objection 2:** Sleeping is a sort of being acted upon (*passio quaedam*). But man slept in the state of innocence—this according to Genesis 2:21 ("God cast a deep sleep upon Adam"). Therefore, he was passible.

**Objection 3:** In the same place it adds, "He took one of his ribs." Therefore, he was passible even to the point of the having part of his body removed.

**Objection 4:** Man's body was soft. But what is soft is naturally passive in relation to what is hard. Therefore, if a hard body had struck the first man's body, he would have been acted upon by it. And so the first man was passible.

**But contrary to this:** If he was passible, then he was also corruptible, since being acted upon, if amplified, brings a substance to ruin (*passio magis facta abiicit a substantia*).

**I respond:** There are two senses of 'being acted upon' (*passio*):

(a) The first sense is the proper one, and in this sense 'is acted upon' is said of something that is taken out of its natural disposition (*a sua naturali dispositione removetur*). For a passion is the effect of an action, and among natural things contraries act on one another and are acted upon by one another, and one takes another out of its natural disposition.

(b) In the second sense, 'is acted upon' is taken in a general way for any sort of change, even if it contributes to the perfection of the nature. It is in this sense that an act of intellective understanding or an act of sensing is said to be an instance of being acted upon.

Therefore, in the second sense, man was passible in the state of innocence, and he was acted upon, both with respect to his body and with respect to his soul. By contrast, in the first sense of 'being acted upon', he was impassible both with respect to his body and with respect to his soul, just as he was immortal. For he was able to prevent his being acted upon—just as he was likewise able to prevent his death—as long as he persisted without sin.

**Reply to objection 1 and objection 2:** This makes clear the reply to objections one and two. For sensing and sleeping do not take a man out of his natural disposition, but instead order him toward the good of nature.

**Reply to objection 3:** As was explained above (q. 92, a. 3), the rib existed in Adam insofar as he was the source of the human race, just as semen exists in a man insofar as he is a source through generation. Therefore, just as the release of semen is not accompanied by an instance of being acted upon which takes a man out of his natural disposition, so one should say the same thing about the removal of the rib in question.

**Reply to objection 4:** In the state of innocence man's body was able to persist without suffering injury from anything hard—partly because of man's own reason, through which he was able to avoid dangers, and partly because of God's providence, which protected him in such a way that nothing unexpected would happen to him by which he might be injured.

# Article 3

### Did man need food in the state of innocence?

It seems that man did not need food in the state of innocence (*non indigebat cibis*):

**Objection 1:** Man needs food in order to restore what has been lost. But in Adam's body, it seems, there was no loss, since he was incorruptible. Therefore, he did not need food.

**Objection 2:** Food is necessary for nutrition. But nutrition does not occur without one's being acted upon. Therefore, since man's body was impassible, food was not, it seems, necessary for him.

**Objection 3:** For us food is necessary for the conservation of our life. But there was another way in which Adam was able to conserve his life, since he was not going to die as long as he did not sin. Therefore, food was not necessary for him.

**Objection 4:** The discharge of excess materials (*emissio superfluitatum*) follows upon the consumption of food; but this excess material has a foulness that does not befit the dignity of the initial state. Therefore, it seems that in the initial state man did not make use of food.

**But contrary to this:** Genesis 2:16 says, "You shall eat of every tree that is in Paradise."

**I respond:** In the state of innocence man had an animal life in need of food, whereas after the resurrection he will have a spiritual life that is not in need of food.

To see this clearly, note that the rational soul is both a *soul* (*anima*) and a *spirit* (*spiritus*). It is called a *soul* with respect to what is common to it and the other souls, viz., giving life to a body; hence Genesis 2:7 says, "Man was made into a living soul," i.e., a soul giving life to a body. On the other hand, it is called a *spirit* with respect to what is proper to itself and not to the other souls, viz., that it has an immaterial intellective power.

Therefore, in the initial state the rational soul communicated to the body what belonged to the soul insofar as it is a *soul*, and so the body was called an animal insofar as it had life from the soul. But as the *De Anima* says, among the lower things here below the first source of life is the vegetative soul, whose operations are to make use of food and to generate and to grow. And hence these works belonged to man in the initial state.

However, in the last state, after the resurrection, the soul will in some way communicate to the body those things that are proper to the soul insofar as it is a spirit—immortality for everyone, but also impassibility, glory, and power for the blessed (*quantum ad bonos*), whose bodies will be called 'spiritual'.

Hence, after the resurrection men will not need food, but in the state of innocence they did need food.

**Reply to objection 1:** As Augustine put it in *Quaestiones Veteris et Novi Testamenti*, "How is it that an immortal body was sustained by food? For what is immortal does not need food or drink."

Now it was explained above (a. 1) that the immortality that belonged to the initial state stemmed from a certain supernatural power residing in the soul—and not from any disposition inhering in the body. Hence, some of the body's moisture was able to be lost through the action of heat; and so it was necessary for man to help himself by taking food, lest the moisture be totally consumed.

**Reply to objection 2:** In the act of nutrition there is an alteration and an instance of being acted upon, viz., on the part of the food, which is converted into the substance of the one that is nourished. Hence, one can infer from this not that the man's body was passible, but rather that the food that was taken was passible—though it is also true that such an instance of being acted upon contributed to the perfection of the nature.

**Reply to objection 3:** If the man had not helped himself to food, he would have sinned—just as he did sin by taking the forbidden food. For at one and the same time he was commanded both to abstain from the tree of the knowledge of good and evil and to eat from every other tree in Paradise.

**Reply to objection 4:** Some claim that in the state of innocence man took only as much food as was necessary for him, so that there was no emission of excess material.

But it seems hard to believe that in the food that was consumed there was no excess material that was unable to be converted into human nourishment. Hence, it was necessary for the waste excess to be emitted. However, God saw to it (*divinitus provisum*) that this did not involve anything foul.

## Article 4

### Could the tree of life have been a cause of immortality?

It seems that the tree of life could not have been a cause of immortality:

**Objection 1:** Nothing is able to act beyond its own species, since an effect does not exceed its cause. But the tree of life was corruptible; otherwise it could not have been taken in nourishment, since, as has been explained (a. 3), food is converted into the substance of the one that is nourished. Therefore, the tree of life could not have conferred incorruptibility or immortality.

**Objection 2:** Effects that are caused by the powers of plants and other natural things are natural. Therefore, if the tree of life had caused immortality, the immortality in question would have been natural.

**Objection 3:** This seems to go back to the fables of the ancients, who claimed that the gods who ate of a certain food became immortal; but the Philosopher ridicules these ancients in *Metaphysics* 3.

**But contrary to this:**

**1.** Genesis 3:22 says, ". . . lest perhaps he put forth his hand, and take also of the tree of life, and eat, and live for ever."

**2.** In *Quaestiones Veteris et Novi Testamenti* Augustine says, "Tasting of the tree of life held back the corruption of the body, and even then, after the sin, he would have been able to remain uncorrupted if he had been permitted to eat of the tree of life."

**I respond:** The tree of life caused immortality in a certain way, but not absolutely speaking. To see this clearly, note that in the initial state man had two remedies, directed against two defects, for conserving his life. The first defect is the loss of moisture due to the action of natural heat, which is an instrument of the soul. And against this defect man helped himself by eating of the other trees in Paradise, in the sameway that we now help ourselves by the food we eat.

However, the second defect is that, as the Philosopher puts it in *De Generatione Animalium* 1, whatever is generated from what is extraneous and is added to what was previously moist diminishes the active power of the species. For instance, water added to wine is at first converted into the taste of the wine, but as more and more water is added, it weakens the strength of the wine, and finally the wine becomes watery. So, then, we see that at the beginning the active power of the species is so strong that it can convert food in a way that is sufficient not only to restore what was lost but also to add to it. However, afterwards, what is assimilated is sufficient not for an increase, but only for restoring what was lost. And, finally, in the state of old age, it is not even sufficient for this, and so a loss of size follows, and, finally, the natural dissolution of the body.

Man was helped by the tree of life against this defect, since the tree of life had the power to fortify the power of the species against the sort of weakness that stems from the admixture of what is extraneous. Hence, in *De Civitate Dei* 14 Augustine says, "Food was there for man, lest he get hungry; drink was there, lest he get thirsty; and the tree of life was there, lest old age destroy him." And in *Quaestiones Veteris et Novi Testamenti* he says, "In the manner of medicine the tree of life prevented men from dying."

However, it was not a cause of immortality absolutely speaking. For the power that existed in the soul to conserve the body was not caused by the tree of life. Nor was the tree of life able to confer on the body even the disposition for immortality, so that it might never be destroyed. This is clear from the fact that the power of a body is finite. Hence, the power of the tree of life was able to reach as far as to give the body the power to endure up to some determinate time, but not for an infinitely long time. For it is clear that the greater the power, the more durable the effect it imparts. Hence, since its power was finite, once the tree of life was eaten from, it preserved the body from corruption up to some determinate time. And when that time ended, either the man would be transferred to a spiritual life or he would need to eat from the tree of life once again.

**Reply to objection 1 and objection 2 and objection 3 and argument to the contrary 1 and argument to the contrary 2:** The replies to the objections are clear from what has been said. For the first set of arguments reach the conclusion that the tree of life did not cause incorruptibility absolutely speaking, whereas the other arguments reach the conclusion that it did cause incorruptibility by impeding corruption in the way explained above.

# QUESTION 98

## The Conservation of the Species in the Initial State: Generation

The next thing to consider is what pertains to the conservation of the species: first, with respect to generation itself (question 98) and, second, with respect to the condition of the generated offspring (questions 99–101).

On the first topic are two questions: (1) Would there have been generation in the state of innocence? (2) Would the generation have been through sexual union?

## Article 1

### Would there have been generation in the state of innocence?

It seems that in the state of innocence there would not have been generation:

**Objection 1:** As *Physics* 5 says, "Corruption is contrary to generation." But contraries have to do with the same thing, and in the state of innocence there would not have been corruption. Therefore, there would not have been generation, either.

**Objection 2:** Generation is ordered toward conserving within the species what cannot be conserved with respect to the individual; hence, generation is not found among those individuals that last forever. But in the state of innocence man would have lived forever without death. Therefore, generation would not have existed in the state of innocence.

**Objection 3:** It is through generation that men are multiplied. But when owners are multiplied (*muliplicatis dominis*), there has to be a division of possessions in order to avoid confusion about ownership (*ad evitandam confusionem dominii*). Therefore, since man was set up as the owner of the animals, if a multiplication of the human race had been made through generation, then a division of ownership would have ensued. But this seems contrary to the natural law, according to which all things are held in common, as Isidore says. Therefore, there would not have been generation in the state of innocence.

**But contrary to this:** Genesis 1:28 says, "Grow and multiply, and fill the earth." But multiplication of the sort in question here could not have occurred without new generation, since only two human beings were made at the beginning. Therefore, there would have been generation in the initial state.

**I respond**: In the state of innocence there would have been generation for the multiplication of the human race. Otherwise, man's sin would have been absolutely necessary in order that such a great good might follow from it.

Therefore, note that man by nature is constituted as a sort of middle ground between corruptible creatures and incorruptible creatures. For his soul is naturally incorruptible, whereas his body is naturally corruptible. But notice that what nature intends (*intentio naturae*) relates to corruptible creatures in a way different from the way it relates to incorruptible creatures. For it seems that it is what exists always and forever that belongs *per se* to nature's intention. By contrast, what exists only for some temporal interval does not seem to stem chiefly from what nature intends, but is instead ordered toward something else; otherwise, when it is corrupted, nature's intention would cease. Therefore, since among corruptible things the only thing that remains forever or is everlasting is the species, what nature principally intends has to do with the good of the species, whose conservation natural generation is ordered toward. By contrast, incorruptible substances remain forever not only with respect to the species but also with respect to the individuals, and so what nature principally intends has to do with the individuals themselves as well.

So, then, generation belongs to man with respect to his body, which is corruptible by its nature. But on the part of the soul, which is incorruptible, what belongs to man is that a multitude of individuals is intended *per se* by nature—or, better, by the author of nature, who alone is the creator of human souls. And so for the multiplication of the human race He established generation within the human race—even in the state of innocence.

**Reply to objection 1:** In the state of innocence man's body, taken just by itself, was corruptible, but it was able to be preserved from corruption by the soul. And this is why generation, which is appropriate for corruptible things, was not to be taken away from man.

**Reply to objection 2:** Even if generation in the state of innocence was not for the sake of the conservation of the species, it was nonetheless for the sake of the multiplication of the individuals.

**Reply to objection 3:** In our present state, it is necessary for there to be a division of possessions when the owners are multiplied. For as the

Philosopher says in *Politics* 2, the holding of possessions in common (*communitas possessionis*) is an occasion for discord.

However, in the state of innocence men's wills were ordered in such a way that, without any danger of discord, they would have had, to the extent appropriate for each, common use (*communiter usi fuissent*) of the goods that fell under their ownership. For this practice is observed even now among many good men.

### Article 2

### Would there have been generation through sexual union in the state of innocence?

It seems that in the state of innocence there would not have been generation through sexual union (*per coitum*):

**Objection 1:** As Damascene says, in the earthly Paradise man was "like an angel." But in the future state of resurrection, when men will be similar to angels, "they will neither marry nor be given in marriage," as Matthew 22:30 says. Therefore, neither would there have been generation through sexual union in Paradise.

**Objection 2:** The first men were created at a perfect age. Therefore, if among them there had been generation through sexual union before the sin, then they would have been carnally joined even in Paradise—which is clearly false according to Scripture.

**Objection 3:** In carnal union (*in coniuctione carnali*) man becomes especially like the beasts, because of the vehemence of the pleasure; this is why there is praise for celibacy (*continentia*), through which men abstain from pleasures of this sort. But it is because of sin that man is compared to the beasts—this according to Psalm 48:21 ("Man, when he was in honor, did not understand; he is compared to senseless beasts, and is become like to them"). Therefore, before the sin there would have been no carnal union between male and female.

**Objection 4:** In the state of innocence there would have been no corruption. But virginal integrity is corrupted through sexual union. Therefore, there would not have been sexual union in the state of innocence.

**But contrary to this:**

**1.** According to Genesis 1:27 and 2:22, it was before the sin that God made them male and female. But nothing in the works of God is in vain. Therefore, even if man had not sinned, there would have been sexual union, which the difference between the sexes is ordered toward.

**2.** Genesis 2:18–20 says that the woman was made to help the man— but not for anything if not for the generation that is effected through sexual union, since for any other sort of work the man could be helped more fittingly by a man rather than by a woman. Therefore, even in the state of innocence there would have been generation through sexual union.

**I respond:** Some ancient doctors, reflecting on the shamefulness of the concupiscence associated with sexual union in our present state (*considerantes concupiscentiae foeditatem quae invenitur in coitu in isto statu*), claimed that in the state of innocence there would not have been generation through sexual union. Hence, in his book *De Homine* Gregory of Nyssa says that in Paradise the human race would have been multiplied in some other way—just as the angels are multiplied without sexual intercourse (*absque concubitu*) through the operation of God's power. Furthermore, he claims that God made them male and female before the sin with an eye toward the mode of generation that would exist after the sin, which God had foreknowledge of.

But this is unreasonable. For what is natural to man is neither taken away from nor added to man because of sin. But it is clear that because of his animal life—which, as was explained above (q. 97, a. 3), he had even before the sin—it is natural to man to generate through sexual union, just as it is natural to the other perfect animals as well. And this is made clear by the natural members of the body deputed for this use. So just as with the other bodily members, one should not claim that the use of these natural members did not exist before the sin.

Thus, there are two things to take into account concerning sexual union in our present state:

The first is what belongs to *nature*, viz., the union of the male and the female in order to generate. For every instance of generation requires an active power and a passive power. Hence, since in all the animals in which there is a distinction between the sexes, the active power exists in the male and the passive power in the female, the order of nature requires that the male and the female come together through sexual union in order to generate.

The other thing that can be taken into account is the *deformity of unbridled concupiscence* (*quaedam deformitas immoderatae concupiscentiae*). This did not exist in the state of innocence, wherein the lower powers were altogether subject to reason. Hence, in *De Civitate Dei* 14 Augustine says, "Far be it from us to suspect that offspring could not have been brought forth without the sickness of disordered desire (*sine libidinis morbo*). Instead, the members in question were moved at will just like the other members—and this without burning desire or seductive stimulation, but with tranquility of mind and body."

**Reply to objection 1:** In Paradise man was like the angels because of his spiritual mind, even though he had an animal life with respect to his body. However, after the resurrection man will be a spiritual effect like the angels, both with respect to his soul and with respect to his body. Hence, the arguments are not parallel.

**Reply to objection 2:** As Augustine says in *Super Genesim ad Litteram* 9, the reason why the first parents did not have sexual intercourse in Paradise was either (a) that, because of their sin, they were ejected from Paradise shortly after the woman was formed, or (b) that they were waiting for God's authority, from which they had received the general command [to multiply], to specify a determinate time for sexual intercourse (*ad determinatum tempus commixtionis*).

**Reply to objection 3:** The beasts lack reason. Hence, man becomes bestial in sexual union to the extent that he cannot by means of his reason moderate the pleasure of sexual union and the fervor of sensual desire.

However, in the state of innocence there was nothing of this sort that was not moderated by reason. This was not, as some claim, because there was less sensual pleasure. (For the sensual pleasure would have been greater to the extent that the nature was purer and the body more sensitive.) Instead, it was because the concupiscible power would not have indulged in pleasure of this sort in a disordered way, given that it was regulated by reason—which implies not that there is less pleasure in the senses, but rather that the concupiscible power does not cling (*inhaeret*) to the pleasure in an unbridled way (*immoderate*). (By 'unbridled' I mean 'beyond the measure of reason'.) In like manner, one who is temperate with respect to food taken in moderation (*sobrius in cibo moderate assumpto*) does not have less pleasure than a glutton; instead, his concupiscible power lingers less over this sort of pleasure (*minus super delectatione huiusmodi requiescit*).

This is consonant with the passage from Augustine, which does not rule out a great deal of pleasure (*magnitudinem delectationis*) in the state of innocence, but instead rules out feverish disordered desire (*ardorem libidinis*) and disquietude of mind. And so in the state of innocence celibacy (*continentia*) would not have been praiseworthy—even though in our times it is praised not because of its lack of fecundity, but because of its exclusion of disordered desire. For in the state of innocence fecundity would have existed without disordered desire.

**Reply to objection 4:** As Augustine says in *De Civitate Dei* 14, in the state of innocence "there was no corruption of virginal integrity involved in sexual intercourse (*nulla corruptione integritatis infunderetur gremio maritus uxoris*). For the man's seed was able to be emitted into his wife's uterus in such a way that the integrity of the female genitalia was preserved—just as, even now, a menstrual flow can be emitted from a virgin's uterus while that same integrity is preserved. For just as it is not the groan of pain but the sense of completion (*impulsus maturitatis*) that relaxes a woman's viscera in order for her to give birth, so too it was not lustful desire (*libidinis appetitus*) but the voluntary use [of the organs] (*voluntarius usus*) that united the two natures in order for them to conceive."

# QUESTION 99

## The Condition of the Generated Offspring with Respect to their Body

The next thing to consider is the condition of the offspring that are generated: first, with respect to their body (question 99); second, with respect to their justice or moral rectitude (*quantum ad iustitiam*) (question 100); and, third, with respect to their knowledge (question 101).

On the first topic there are two questions: (1) In the state of innocence, would children have had full corporeal power immediately upon birth? (2) Would all children have been born males?

### Article 1

### In the state of innocence, would children have had full power over the movement of their limbs immediately upon birth?

It seems that in the state of innocence children would have had full power over the movement of their limbs (*virtutem perfectam ad motum membrorum*) immediately upon birth:

**Objection 1:** In *De Baptismo Pavulorum* Augustine says, "To the weakness of mind corresponds that weakness of body"—viz., the weakness of body that is apparent in children. But in the state of innocence there would have been no weakness of mind. Therefore, neither would there have been weakness of body in little children.

**Objection 2:** Certain animals are such that they have enough power to use their limbs immediately upon being born. But man is more noble than the other animals. Therefore, *a fortiori*, it is natural for man to have the power to use his limbs immediately upon birth. And so [the lack of such power] seems to be a punishment that followed upon sin.

**Objection 3:** The inability to attain something pleasant presented to one is a source of affliction. But if children had not had the power to move their limbs, then oftentimes they would have been unable to attain something pleasant presented to them. Therefore, they would have been afflicted. But this could not have been the case before sin. Therefore, in the state of innocence children would not have lacked the power to move their limbs.

**Objection 4:** The weakness of old age (*defectus senectutis*) seems to correspond to the weakness of childhood (*defectus pueritiae*). But in the state of innocence there would not have been any weakness of old age. Therefore, there would not have been any weakness of childhood, either.

**But contrary to this:** Every generated thing is imperfect before it becomes perfect. But in the state of innocence children would have been produced through generation. Therefore, at the beginning they would have been imperfect both in size and in bodily power.

**I respond**: Truths that are supernatural (*ea quae super naturam*) we hold by faith alone, and what we hold on faith (*credimus*) we owe to some authority. Hence, in all our assertions we ought to be guided by (*sequi debemus*) the nature of things, except with respect to what is handed down to us by God's authority and lies beyond nature.

Now it is clearly natural—in the sense of belonging to the principles of human nature—for children not to have enough power to move their limbs immediately upon birth. For man has by nature a brain that is larger in size, relative to his body, than the other animals do. Hence, it is natural that because of the great moisture of the brain in children, the nerves, which are the instruments of movement, are not fit for moving the limbs.

From the other side, no Catholic doubts that it could happen by God's power that children have the full power to move their limbs immediately upon birth. But it is clear from the authority of Scripture that "God made man upright" (Ecclesiastes 7:30) and that, as Augustine says, this uprightness consists in the full subjection of the body to the soul. Therefore, just as there could not have been in the initial state anything in a man's limbs that conflicted with the man's well-ordered will, so too a man's limbs could not have failed to do the human will's bidding.

However, a well-ordered human will is one that tends toward acts that are appropriate for the man, and it is not the case that the very same acts are appropriate for a man at every age. Therefore, one should claim that immediately upon birth the children would have had enough power to move their limbs not for just any acts at all, but for the acts appropriate to a child, e.g., sucking at the breast and other acts of this sort.

**Reply to objection 1:** Augustine is talking about the sort of weakness that now appears in some children even with respect to those acts that are appropriate for children. This is clear from his previous remark that "even when they are hungrey and close to the breast, they are more apt to cry than to suck."

**Reply to objection 2:** The fact that certain animals have the use of their limbs immediately upon birth does not stem from their nobility, since other animals more perfect than they are do not have such use of their limbs. Rather, this happens to them because of the dryness of their brains and because the acts proper to such animals are imperfect, so that even a little power is sufficient for them.

**Reply to objection 3:** The reply to this objection is clear from what was said in the body of this article.

An alternative reply is that the children would have desired nothing except what was appropriate for a well-ordered will in their particular state.

**Reply to objection 4:** In the state of innocence man would have been generated but would not have been corrupted. And so in that state it would have been possible for there to be some childhood weaknesses that followed upon generation, but there could not have been any weaknesses of old age that were ordered toward corruption.

## Article 2

### In the state of innocence, would any females have been born?

It seems that in the state of innocence no female would have been born:

**Objection 1:** In *De Generatione Animalium* 2 the Philosopher says, "A female is an inadvertent male"—in the sense that a female is produced outside of the intention of nature. But in the state of innocence nothing unnatural (*innaturale*) would have occurred in human generation. Therefore, no females would have been born.

**Objection 2:** Every agent generates what is similar to itself, unless it is impeded either because of a defect in its power or because the matter is not well disposed, as when a small fire is unable to ignite green wood. But in generation the active power resides in the male. Therefore, since in the state of innocence the male's power would not have been defective and the female's matter would not have been indisposed, it seems that males would always have been born.

**Objection 3:** In the state of innocence generation was ordered toward the multiplication of men (*ad multiplicationem hominum*). But men could have been multiplied to a sufficient degree through the first man and the first woman, since they were going to live forever. Therefore, in the state of innocence it would have been unnecessary for females to be born.

**But contrary to this:** Nature would have proceeded in generation in the way that God had instituted it. But as Genesis 1:27 and 2:22 say, within human nature God made them male and female. Therefore, in the state of innocence males and females would likewise have been generated.

**I respond:** Nothing relevant to the fullness of human nature (*ad complementum humanae naturae*) would have been lacking in the state of innocence. But just as diverse grades of things contribute to the perfection of the universe, so too the difference between the sexes contributes to the perfection of human nature. And so in the state of innocence both sexes would have been produced through generation.

**Reply to objection 1:** The female is called an 'inadvertent male' because she lies outside the intention of a *particular* nature. But, as was explained above (q. 92, a. 1), the female does not lie outside the intention of nature *as a whole* (*non praeter intentionem naturae universalis*).

**Reply to objection 2:** The generation of a female does not occur just because of a defect in the active power or because of the matter's indisposition, as the objection implies. Rather, it sometimes occurs because of an extrinsic accident; for instance, in *De Animalibus* the Philosopher says, "The northern wind (*ventus septentrionalis*) favors the generation of males, and the southern wind (*ventus australis*) the generation of females."

Moreover, the generation of a female sometimes occurs because of a thought on the part of the soul (*ex conceptione animae*) at which the body is readily changed. This could have happened especially in the state of innocence, when the body was more subject to the soul, so that the sex of the offspring might be determined by the will of the one generating.

**Reply to objection 3:** The offspring would have been generated with an animal life (*vivens vita animali*), which involves generating as well as making use of food. Hence, it was appropriate for all of them to generate, and not just the first parents. It seems to follow from this that as many females would have been generated as males.

# QUESTION 100

## The Condition of the Generated Offspring with Respect to Justice

The next thing to consider is the condition of the offspring with respect to justice or moral rectitude (*quantum ad justitiam*). On this topic there are two questions: (1) Would men have been born with justice? (2) Would they have been born confirmed in justice?

## Article 1

### Would men have been born with justice?

It seems that men would not have been born with justice or moral rectitude (*cum iustitia nati*):

**Objection 1:** Hugo of St. Victor says, "Before the sin the first man generated children who were without sin but who did not inherit their father's justice."

**Objection 2:** As the Apostle says in Romans 5:16 and 21, justice or justification comes through grace (*iustitia est per gratiam*). But grace is not bequeathed [by the parents to the children] (*non transfunditur*), since in that case it would be natural; instead, it is infused by God alone. Therefore, the children would not have been born with justice.

**Objection 3:** Justice exists in the soul. But the soul is not passed on [from the parents to the children] (*anima non est ex traduce*). Therefore, neither was justice passed on from the parents to the children.

**But contrary to this:** In *De Conceptu Virginali* Anselm says, "Along with having a rational soul, those whom the man would generate would be just if they did not sin."

**I respond:** Man naturally generates what is similar to himself in species. Hence, any accidents that follow upon the nature of the species are such that the children must be similar in those accidents to the parents, unless there is some error in the operation of nature—which there would not have been in the state of innocence. But in individual accidents the children did not have to be similar to the parents.

Now original justice (*iustitia originalis*), in the rectitude of which the first man was made, was an accident belonging to the nature of the species—not in the sense that it was caused by the principles of the species, but in the sense that it was a special gift given by God to the nature as a whole. This is clear from the fact that opposites belong to a single genus, and original sin (*peccatum originale*), which is opposed to original justice, is called a sin of the nature. That is why it is passed down from the parents to their posterity. Because of this, the children would have been like the parents with respect to original justice as well.

**Reply to objection 1:** The passage from Hugo should be taken not to be about the habit of justice, but rather about the execution of the act of justice.

**Reply to objection 2:** Some claim that the children would have been born not with the justice of grace (*cum iustitia gratuita*), which is a principle of meriting, but rather with original justice.

However, the root of original justice, in the rectitude of which man was made, consists in the supernatural submission of reason to God (*in subiectione supernaturali rationis ad Deum*)—a submission which, as was explained above (q. 95, a. 1), is effected by habitual grace (*per gratiam gratum facientem*). Hence, one must claim that if the children had been born with original justice, then they would likewise have been born with grace—just as we explained above (q. 95, a. 1) that the first man was made with grace. Still, the grace would not for this reason have been natural, since it would not have been bequeathed by the power of the semen, but would instead have been conferred on man as soon as he had a rational soul—just as it is also the case that even though the rational soul is not passed on [from the parents to the children], it is nonetheless infused by God as soon as the body is disposed for it.

**Reply to objection 3:** The solution to the third objection is clear from what was just said.

## Article 2

### In the state of innocence, would the children have been born confirmed in justice?

It seems that in the state of innocence the children would have been born confirmed in justice (*in iustitia confirmati*):

**Objection 1:** In *Moralia* 4, commenting on Job 3:13 ("For now I should have been asleep, etc."), Gregory says, "If none of the rottenness of sin (*putredo peccati*) had corrupted the first parent, then he would in no way have generated of himself the children of Gehenna; but those who now have to be saved by the Redeemer would have been born of him only as the elect." Therefore, all of them would have been born confirmed in justice.

**Objection 2:** In *Cur Deus Homo* Anselm says, "If the first parents had lived in such a way that, though tempted, they did not sin, then they, along with all their progeny, would have been confirmed in the sense that they would no longer have been able to sin." Therefore, the children would have been born confirmed in justice.

**Objection 3:** Good is more powerful than evil. But from the sin of the first man there followed a necessity of sinning on the part of those who were born of him. Therefore, if the first man had persisted in justice, the necessity of preserving justice would have redounded to his posterity.

**Objection 4:** An angel who adheres to God while others are sinning is immediately confirmed in justice, so that he is no longer able to sin. Therefore, if man had resisted the temptation, he too would have been confirmed. But he would have generated others who were such as he was. Therefore, his children would likewise have been born confirmed in justice.

**But contrary to this:** In *De Civitate Dei* 14 Augustine says, "Human society would have been happy as a whole if they"—viz., the first parents—"had not committed the evil that they passed on to their descendants, and if none of their posterity had perpetrated the iniquity that merited condemnation." From this one is given to understand that even if the first parents had not sinned, some of their posterity would have been able to perpetrate iniquity. Therefore, they would not have been born confirmed in justice.

**I respond:** It does not seem possible that in the state of innocence children should have been born confirmed in justice. For it is clear that at their birth the children would not have had more perfection than their parents had in the state of generating them. But for as long as the parents were generating, they would not have been confirmed in justice. For a rational creature is confirmed in justice by the fact that he is beatified (*efficitur beata*) through the clear vision of God, who is such that one is unable not to inhere in Him when He is seen; for He is the very essence of goodness, from which no one can turn away, since nothing is desired and loved except under the notion of the good. (I say this as a general rule, since it can happen otherwise by a special privilege, as we believe happened in the case of the virgin mother of God (*sicut creditur de virgine matre Dei*).) But as soon as Adam had arrived at that beatitude by which he saw God through

His essence, he would have been made spiritual in both mind and body, and his animal life, in which alone he would have made use of generation, would have ceased. Hence, it is clear that the children would not have been born confirmed in justice.

**Reply to objection 1:** If Adam had not sinned, he would not have generated from himself children of Gehenna, i.e., children who would have contracted from him the sin that is the cause of Gehenna. Yet they would have been able to become children of Gehenna by sinning through their own free choice. Or, if they did not become children of Gehenna through sin, this would not have been because they were confirmed in justice. Instead, it would have been because of divine providence, through which they would have been preserved immune from sin.

**Reply to objection 2:** Anselm said this not by way of assertion (*asserendo*), but by way of conjecture (*opinando*). This is clear from his very mode of speaking when he says, "It *seems that* if they had lived, etc."

**Reply to objection 3:** This argument is not efficacious even though, as is apparent from his words, Anselm seems to have been moved by it. For through their sin the first parents did not impose on their descendants a *necessity of sinning* in the sense that they would have been unable to return to justice; for this holds only in the case of the damned. Hence, neither would they have transmitted to their descendants a *necessity of not sinning* in the sense that they would have been altogether unable to sin; for this holds only in the case of the blessed in heaven.

**Reply to objection 4:** There is no similarity here between men and angels. For men have a power of free choice that can turn either way (*vertibile*) both before an act of choice and after an act of choice; by contrast, as was explained above when we were discussing the angels (q. 64, a. 2), this is not the case with angels.

# QUESTION 101

## The Condition of the Generated Offspring
## with Respect to Knowledge

The next thing to consider is the condition of the offspring with respect to knowledge (*quantum ad scientiam*). On this topic there are two questions: (1) Would the children have been born perfect in knowledge? (2) Would they have had the full use of reason immediately upon birth?

## Article 1

### In the state of innocence, would the children
### have been born perfect in knowledge?

It seems that in the state of innocence the children would have been born perfect in knowledge (*in scientia perfecti*):

**Objection 1:** Adam would have generated children who were like himself. But as was explained above (q. 94, a. 3), Adam was perfect in knowledge. Therefore, children would have been born from him perfect in knowledge.

**Objection 2:** As Bede says, ignorance is caused by sin. But ignorance is a privation of knowledge. Therefore, before sin the children would have had every sort of knowledge (*omnem scientiam*) immediately upon birth.

**Objection 3:** The children would have had justice at their birth. But knowledge, which directs actions (*dirigit in agendis*), is required for justice. Therefore, they would have had knowledge as well.

**But contrary to this:** As *De Anima* 3 says, our soul is by nature "like a blank slate on which nothing has been written." But the nature of the soul is the same now as it would have been then. Therefore, the souls of the children would have lacked knowledge at the beginning.

**I respond:** As was explained above (q. 99, a. 1), what is supernatural is such that one has faith in it on authority alone (*soli auctoritate creditur*); hence, in a case where such authority is lacking, we ought to be guided by what is natural (*sequi debemus naturae conditionem*).

Now as was explained above (q. 84, a. 6), it is natural for man to acquire knowledge (*scientia*) through his senses, and so the soul is united to a body because it needs the body for its own proper operation. This would not be the case if right at the very beginning the soul had knowledge that was not acquired through the sentient powers.

So one should claim that in the state of innocence children would not have been born perfect in knowledge, but that instead they would have acquired knowledge without difficulty as time went on, by discovery or by being taught.

**Reply to objection 1:** Being perfect in knowledge was an *individual* accident of the first parent—more specifically, insofar as he was established as the father and instructor of the whole human race. And so it was not with respect to this accident that he generated children who were similar to him, but only with respect to the natural or grace-related accidents that belong to *the whole nature*.

**Reply to objection 2:** Ignorance (*ignorantia*) is a privation of the knowledge that ought to be had at a given time—which would not have been the case with the children immediately upon birth, since they would have had the knowledge that was appropriate for them at that time. Hence, it was not ignorance (*ignorantia*) that existed in them, but rather an absence of knowledge (*nescientia*) with respect to certain things—something that Dionysius likewise posits in the holy angels in *De Caelesti Hierarchia* 7.

**Reply to objection 3:** The children would have had enough knowledge to direct them in those works of justice in which men are directed by the universal principles of the law, and they would have had this knowledge much more fully at that time than we have it by nature now. The same thing holds for other universal principles as well.


## Article 2


### In the state of innocence, would the children
### have had the full use of reason immediately upon birth?


It seems that in the state of innocence the children would have had the full use of reason (*usum perfectum rationis*) immediately upon birth:

**Objection 1:** Children now do not have the perfect use of reason because their soul is weighed down (*aggravatur*) by their body. But this would not have been the case at that time, since, as Wisdom 9:15 says, "The corruptible body is a load upon the soul." Therefore, before the sin and the corruption that followed upon the sin, children would have had the full use of reason immediately upon birth.

**Objection 2:** Certain other animals have the use of their natural talents immediately upon birth; for instance, a lamb immediately flees from a wolf. Therefore, *a fortiori*, in the state of innocence men would have had the full use of reason immediately upon birth.

**But contrary to this:** Nature proceeds from the imperfect to the perfect in all generated things. Therefore, the children would not have had the full use of reason immediately from the beginning.

**I respond:** As is clear from what was said above (q. 84, a. 7), the use of reason depends in a certain sense on the use of the sentient powers; hence, when the sensory power is inoperative and the interior sensory powers are impeded, a man does not have the full use of reason, as in obvious in the case of those who are asleep (*in dormientibus*) and those who are delirious (*in phreneticis*). But the sentient powers are powers of corporeal organs, and so when their organs are impeded, their acts must likewise be impeded and, as a result, the use of reason is impeded.

Now in children these powers are impeded because of the brain's excessive moisture. And so children do not have the full use of reason, just as they do not have the full use of their other bodily members.

So in the state of innocence the children would not have had the full use of reason in the way that they were going to have it at a mature age. However, they would have had a more perfect use of reason than children do now with regard to those things that were appropriate to them in their state—just as was claimed above (q. 99, a. 1) about the use of their limbs as well.

**Reply to objection 1:** 'Weight' is added by the corruption of the body in the sense that the use of reason is impeded even with respect to what is appropriate for a man at each particular age.

**Reply to objection 2:** The other animals likewise do not have as perfect a use of their natural talents immediately at the beginning as they will later on. This is clear from the fact that birds teach their young to fly; and similar examples are found among the other kinds of animals. Yet, as was explained above (q. 99, a. 1), in the case of man there is a special impediment because of the abundance of moisture in the brain.

# QUESTION 102

## Man's Location, i.e., Paradise

The next thing to consider is man's location, i.e., Paradise. On this topic there are four questions:

(1) Is Paradise a corporeal place? (2) Is Paradise a place fit for human habitation? (3) What was man placed in Paradise for? (4) Was it fitting for man to be made in Paradise?

## Article 1

## Is Paradise a corporeal place?

It seems that Paradise is not a corporeal place:

**Objection 1:** Bede says, "Paradise reaches to the lunar circle." But no earthly place can be like that, both because (a) it is contrary to earth's nature that it should be so high up (*tantum elevaretur*), and also because (b) the region of fire, which consumes earth, lies under the lunar globe (*sub globo lunari*). Therefore, Paradise is not a corporeal place.

**Objection 2:** As is clear from Genesis 2:10–15, Scripture mentions that four rivers have their source in Paradise. But the rivers that are named in that passage have obvious sources in other places, as is likewise clear from the Philosopher in *Meteorologia*. Therefore, Paradise is not a corporeal place.

**Objection 3:** Some have very diligently inquired into all the places in the habitable regions of the earth (*omnia loca terrae habitabilis*), but they make no mention of the location of Paradise. Therefore, Paradise does not seem to be a corporeal place.

**Objection 4:** The tree of life is described as existing in Paradise. But the tree of life is something spiritual; for Proverbs 3:18 says of Wisdom, "She is a tree of life for those who lay hold of her." Therefore, Paradise is likewise a spiritual place and not a corporeal place.

**Objection 5:** If Paradise is a corporeal place, then the trees in Paradise must be corporeal. But this does not seem to be the case, since corporeal trees were produced on the third day, whereas Genesis 2:8–9 talks of the trees being planted in Paradise after the work of the six days. Therefore, Paradise is not a corporeal place.

**But contrary to this:** In *Super Genesim ad Litteram* 8 Augustine says, "There are three general opinions about Paradise: One is held by those who claim that Paradise is to be understood only corporeally; the second is held by those who claim that it is to be understood only spiritually; and the third is held by those who take Paradise in both ways. This last opinion, I acknowledge, seems right to me."

**I respond:** As Augustine says in *De Civitate Dei* 13, "Let no one silence what can plausibly be said by way of a spiritual understanding of Paradise—as long as there is a belief in the most faithful truthfulness, preserved by the narrative, of the history of the events." For what is said about Paradise in Sacred Scripture is proposed in the manner of a historical narrative (*per modum narrationis historicae*), and in everything that Scripture hands down in this way there is a historical truth (*veritas historiae*) which should be held on to as the foundation and upon which the spiritual interpretations are to be built.

Therefore, as Isidore says in *Etymologiae*, Paradise is "a place set up in the East, the word for which is from the Greek and is translated by the Latin for 'garden' (*hortus*)." Now the site is appropriately said to be in the East. For it is necessary to believe that Paradise was set up in the most noble part of the whole earth. And since, as the Philosopher makes clear in *De Caelo* 2, the East is the right side of the heavens, and since the right (*dextera*) is more noble than the left (*sinistra*), it was appropriate for God to situate the earthly Paradise in the East.

**Reply to objection 1:** Bede's words are not true if they are taken in their most obvious sense. However, they could be taken to mean that Paradise rises up to the place of the lunar globe not in terms of its height, but according to a certain likeness. For in Paradise "the air is at a constant moderate temperature (*perpetua aeris temperies*)," as Isidore says, and in this it is like the celestial bodies, which are not subject to contrary extremes (*quae sunt absque contrarietate*). And the reason why the lunar globe is mentioned more often than the other spheres is that the lunar globe is the boundary of the celestial bodies closest to us (*versus nos*) and, in addition, of all the celestial bodies it is the moon that is most like the earth. It even has nebulous shadows, as if it were verging on opaqueness.

Now there are some who claim that Paradise was reaching up to the lunar globe in the sense that it reached up to the middle part of the atmosphere, where rain and wind and things of this sort are generated. For control over these evaporations is attributed especially to the moon.

However, if this were true, then the place would not be fit for human habitation, both because the weather is especially inclement there (*ibi est maxima intemperies*), and also because that place is not congenial to the human constitution, in the way that the lower atmosphere closer to the earth is.

**Reply to objection 2:** As Augustine says in *Super Genesim ad Litteram* 8, "One should hold that since the place of Paradise is very far removed from human cognition, the rivers whose sources are said to be known went underground at some point and after a long course through many regions came up to the surface in other places. For who is ignorant of the fact that this is what many streams commonly do?"

**Reply to objection 3:** The place in question was cut off from where we live by obstacles—such as mountains or oceans or some very hot region—which cannot be crossed. And this is why the writers of various regions made no mention of the place.

**Reply to objection 4:** The tree of life is a material tree that is so called because, as was explained above (q. 97, a. 4), its fruit had the power to conserve life. And yet it signified something spiritually, just as the rock in the desert was something material and yet signified Christ (see 1 Corinthians 10:4).

Similarly, the tree of the knowledge of good and evil was a material tree that was so named because of something that would happen in the future. For after man ate of it, he learned, through the experience of punishment, what the difference was between the good of obedience and the evil of disobedience. And yet, spiritually, the tree was also able to signify free choice, as some claim.

**Reply to objection 5:** According to Augustine, on the third day plants were produced not in actuality but only with respect to certain seminal natures (*rationes seminales*), and after the work of the six days both the plants in Paradise and the other plants were produced in actuality.

By contrast, according to the other saints, one must claim that all the plants were produced in actuality on the third day, including the trees of Paradise, and that what is said about the planting of the trees in Paradise after the work of the six days is to be understood as having been said by way of a recapitulation. This is why our text says, "And the Lord God *had planted* a Paradise of pleasure from the beginning" (Genesis 2:8).

### Article 2

#### Was Paradise a place fit for human habitation?

It seems that Paradise was not a place fit for human habitation (*non fuerit locus conveniens habitationi humanae*):

**Objection 1:** Men and angels are both alike ordered toward beatitude.

But angels were immediately, from the beginning, made inhabitants of the place of the blessed, viz., the empyrean heaven. Therefore, that is where man's place to live should have been set up as well.

**Objection 2:** If a place is fitting for man (*debetur homini*), then it is fitting for him either by reason of his soul or by reason of his body. If by reason of his soul, then the place that is fitting for him is heaven, which seems to be the soul's natural place, since the desire for heaven is instilled into everyone. On the other hand, if by reason of his body, then the place that is fitting for him is no different from the place that is fitting for the other animals. Therefore, there is no way in which Paradise was a place fit for human habitation.

**Objection 3:** A place that contains nothing located within it is senseless. But after the sin Paradise was not a place of human habitation. Therefore, if it is a place fit for human habitation, then it seems that it has been made by God for nothing.

**Objection 4:** A place with a temperate climate (*locus temperatus*) is fitting for man because he has a temperate constitution. But the place of Paradise did not have a temperate climate. For it is said to be located on the equator (*sub aequinoctiali circulo*), which seems to be a very hot place, since twice a year the sun passes over the tops of the heads of those who live there. Therefore, Paradise is not a place fit for human habitation.

**But contrary to this:** Damascene says of Paradise, "It was a Godly region, and it was a worthy dwelling place for the one who was made in God's image (*secundum imaginem Dei*)."

**I respond:** As was explained above (q. 97, a. 1), man was incorruptible and immortal not because his body had a disposition for incorruptibility, but because he had a power of the soul for preserving the body from corruption. Now the human body can be corrupted both from within and from without. As was explained above (q. 97, a. 4), it is corrupted from within by the loss of moisture through old age, and the first man was able to counteract this sort of corruption by taking nutrition. Among the things that corrupt the body from without, the main one seems to be an extreme air temperature (*distemperatus aer*), and so this sort of corruption is counteracted mainly by the temperateness of the air.

Now in Paradise both these types of counteraction are found, since, as Damascene says, Paradise "is a place shining through with very temperate, very fine, and very pure air, always decorated with flowering plants." Hence, it is clear that Paradise is a place fit for human habitation, in keeping with the state of initial immortality.

**Reply to objection 1**: The empyrean heaven (a) is the highest of all corporeal places and (b) lies beyond all mutability.

Given the first of these features, it is a place congenial to the angelic nature, since, as Augustine says in *De Trinitate* 3, "God governs the corporeal creature through the spiritual creature." Hence, it is fitting that the spiritual nature should be set up above everything corporeal, as if presiding over it.

On the other hand, given the second of these features, it is a place appropriate for the state of beatitude, which is grounded in maximal stability. So, then, the place of beatitude is fit for angels according to their nature, and that is why they were created there.

However, the place of beatitude does not befit man according to his *nature*, since he does not preside over all corporeal creatures in the sense of governing them; instead, it befits him only by reason of *beatitude*. Hence, he was not put into the empyrean heaven at the beginning, but instead he was to be transported there in the state of ultimate beatitude.

**Reply to objection 2:** It is ridiculous to claim that there is a natural place for the soul or for any spiritual substance. However, a special place may be attributed to an incorporeal creature because of some sort of fittingness (*per congruentiam quandam*).

Thus, the earthly Paradise is a place that is fit for man both with respect to his soul and with respect to his body, viz., insofar as his soul had a power for preserving the human body from corruption—something that did not belong to the other animals. And so, as Damascene says, "Nothing non-rational lived in Paradise," even though by a certain dispensation the animals were brought there to Adam by God, and even though the serpent entered there by an act of the devil.

**Reply to objection 3:** It is not the case that this place is senseless because men do not live there after the sin—just as it is likewise not senseless for man to have been given a certain sort of immortality that was not going to be preserved. For things of this sort make God's kindness manifest to man, and they also make manifest what man lost by sinning.

Still, it is said that Enoch and Elijah are now living in that Paradise.

**Reply to objection 4:** Those who claim that Paradise is located on the equator are of the opinion that a place on the equator has a thoroughly temperate climate, because day and night are equal all of the time, and because the sun is never so far from the inhabitants that they would have an abundance of cold weather. Neither—so the claim goes—do they have an excess of hot weather, since even if the sun passes directly overhead, it nonetheless does not stay in that position for a long time.

However, in *Meteorologia* Aristotle explicitly claims that the region in question is uninhabitable because of its heat. This seems more likely, since some lands in which the sun is never directly overhead are intemperately hot just because of their closeness to the sun.

But whatever the truth might be about this, one should believe that Paradise was set up in a place with a very temperate climate, either on the equator or somewhere else.

### Article 3

#### Was man put into Paradise to cultivate it and to guard it?

It seems that man was not put into Paradise to cultivate it and to guard it (*ut operaretur et custodiret illum*):

**Objection 1:** What was introduced as a punishment for sin would not have existed in Paradise in the state of innocence. But as Genesis 3:17 says, the cultivation of the soil (*agricultura*) was introduced as a punishment for sin. Therefore, man was not put into Paradise to cultivate it.

**Objection 2:** Guarding is unnecessary where there is no fear of a violent invader. But in Paradise there was no fear of a violent invader. Therefore, it was unnecessary to guard Paradise.

**Objection 3:** If man was put into Paradise to cultivate it and to guard it, then it seems to follow that man was made for the sake of Paradise, and not vice versa—which seems false. Therefore, man was not put into Paradise to work in it and to guard it.

**But contrary to this:** Genesis 2:15 says, "The Lord God took the man, and put him into the Paradise of pleasure as something to cultivate and guard (*posuit illum in Paradiso voluptatis ut operaretur et custodiret illum*)."

**I respond:** As Augustine points out in *Super Genesim ad Litteram* 8, there are two ways to understand this passage from Genesis.

On one interpretation, God put man into Paradise in order for God Himself to cultivate and to guard man—to cultivate him, I repeat, by justifying man, in order that He might guard man against every sort of corruption and evil. For if God's operation withdraws from man, then man is continually in the dark (*continuo obtenebratur*), just as the air becomes dark if the influx of light ceases.

The second possible interpretation is that man is the one who is to cultivate Paradise and guard it. Nor would this work have been laborious, as it was to be after the sin. Rather, it would have been pleasant, because of the experience of the nature of virtue. Moreover, the sort of guarding in question would not have been against invaders, but would instead have been for the purpose of man's guarding Paradise for himself, lest he lose it by sinning. And all of this redounded to man's good, and in this sense Paradise is ordered to the good of man, and not vice versa.

**Reply to objection 1 and objection 2 and objection 3:** The replies to the objections are clear from what has been said.

## Article 4

### Was the man made in Paradise?

It seems that the man was made in Paradise (*homo factus est in Paradiso*):

**Objection 1:** The angels were created in the place of their habitation, viz., the empyrean heaven. But before the sin Paradise was a place fit for human habitation. Therefore, it seems that the man ought to have been made in Paradise.

**Objection 2:** The other animals are conserved in the place of their generation, e.g., fish in water and walking animals on the earth, from which they were produced. But as has been explained (q. 97, a. 4), man would have been conserved in Paradise. Therefore, he ought to have been made in Paradise.

**Objection 3:** The woman was made in Paradise. But the man has more dignity than the woman. Therefore, *a fortiori*, the man ought to have been made in Paradise (*multo magis vir debuit fieri in Paradiso*).

**But contrary to this:** Genesis 2:15 says, "The Lord God took the man, and put him into Paradise."

**I respond:** Paradise was a place fit for human habitation, given the lack of corruption in the initial state. But this lack of corruption belonged to man not by his nature, but by a supernatural gift from God. Therefore, in order that this gift might be imputed to God's grace and not to human nature, God made man outside of Paradise and afterwards put him into Paradise, in order that he might live there for the whole time of his animal life. Afterwards, when he had attained his spiritual life, he was to be transported to heaven.

**Reply to objection 1:** The empyrean heaven is a place fit for the angels even with respect to their nature, and that is why they were created there.

**Reply to objection 2:** The same thing should be said in reply to the second objection. For the places in question were fit for the animals with respect to their nature.

**Reply to objection 3:** The woman was made in Paradise not because of her own dignity, but because of the dignity of the principle from which her body was formed. The children likewise would have been born in Paradise, because the parents had already been put there.

# Index

intellect's cognition, 172; intellect's defect, 190; intellect's immateriality, 84; intellect's intelligible species, 149, 151; intellect's judgment, 140, 160–61; intellect's object, 93, 123–24, 140, 165, 181, 185, 200, 202–4; intellect's operation, 21, 78, 82, 84, 141, 184, 201, 246; intellect's perfection, 202; passive (potential) intellect, 21, 27, 83–89, 91–92, 94, 101, 136, 151, 156, 159, 164, 167–68, 171, 196–98, 207–9, 225; practical intellect, 79, 102–3, 188; productive intellect, 270; separated intellect, 87, 90, 149–51; speculative intellect, 79, 102–3

intellective understanding, 4–7, 10, 14–15, 20–23, 26–28, 37–38, 47, 57–58, 64, 79–82, 84–88, 91, 93–97, 100–102, 104–5, 110, 116, 121, 125, 127, 134, 137–39, 141–43, 145–51, 156–61, 163–65, 169–70, 175–81, 183–90, 195–97, 200–3, 205–8, 210–11, 214–24, 227, 229, 233, 252, 262–64, 270, 272, 274, 278, 283–84, 309

intelligible species, 11, 20–21, 27–28, 91–93, 139, 142, 146–51, 153, 157, 163, 166–72, 176–78, 187–90, 192, 199, 215–16, 219, 222, 225, 227–28, 285

Isaiah, Book of, 230, 259

Isidore of Seville, 221–22, 315; *Etymologiae*, 333

Jeremiah, Book of, 130

Jerome, 104–5, 107, 299; Letter to Paulinus, 225; *Super Matthaeum*, 114, 128

Jesus Christ, *see* God (God the Son)

Job, Book of, 230, 326

John, Gospel of, 85, 213, 249

Josiah, King, 231

justice, 290, 295, 321, 325–30; divine (God's) justice, 231; original justice, 325–26; political justice, 228

justification, 278, 325

1 Kings (1 Samuel in most Bibles), *see* 1 Samuel

4 Kings (2 Kings in most Bibles), 231

Lazarus, 220

Leviticus, Book of, 254

*Liber de Causis*, 146, 283

light: celestial light, 42; corporeal light, 233; divine (God's) light, 153, 217, 219, 222, 224, 229; intellectual (intellect's) light, 87, 153, 197, 213; intelligible light, 84; light of the active intellect, 156, 197, 208; light of the first truth, 213; light of glory, 190, 220; light of grace, 213, 219; natural light, 213, 219; true light, 87, 213; uncreated light, 153

likeness (*as relates to cognition and sensing*), 2–3, 21, 28, 66–67, 78, 84–85, 88, 91, 141–43, 147, 149, 156–57, 159, 161–64, 167–68, 170–71, 180, 186, 195–96, 198–99, 203–4, 209, 211–12, 221, 223, 227, 271, 279, 287; likeness (*as relates to image*), 259–66, 268, 276–79; likeness (*as a similarity in general*), 2, 136, 145, 179, 211, 239, 241, 259, 269, 303, 333; likeness of the divine perfection/nature, 262, 270; likeness of the Father, 268; likeness of glory, 265; likeness of God, 51–52, 109, 254, 259–60, 262, 264, 269–71,

319; corporeal power, 14, 56, 65, 164, 243, 321; created power, 238, 243; creative power, 241; desirous power, 128; estimative power, 75–78, 103, 115–17; natural estimative power, 77; feminine power, 252; generative power (*see also,* generation), 68–70, 302; God's power, 48, 194, 236, 240, 244, 255, 257, 318, 322; human power, 259, 301; immaterial power, 84, 155; infinite power, 189, 235; intellective (intellectual) power, 19, 23, 47, 56, 64–66, 79–81, 86, 90, 95, 102–3, 121, 133, 135, 177, 217–18, 279, 311; irascible power, 104, 112–17, 119, 127–29, 302; masculine power, 251–52, 305; moving power (power to effect movement), 7–8, 35, 40, 43, 46, 64–67, 102–03, 110–11, 113, 116–17; natural power, 68, 126, 133, 273, 302; nutritive power, 30, 56, 63, 68–70, 80, 85, 302; operative power, 57; passive power, 53, 69, 71, 79, 81–83, 86, 94–95, 101, 110–11, 157, 245, 252, 258, 318; power of active intellect, *see* intellect: active intellect; power of hearing, 46, 110; power of imagining (imaginative power), *see* imagination; power of the intellect, *see* intellect; power of the intellective appetite, *see* appetite: intellective appetite; power of passive intellect, *see* intellect: passive intellect; power of remembering, *see* memory; power of reminiscing, *see* reminiscence; power of the sentient appetite, *see* appetite: sentient appetite; power of (intellective) understanding, *see* intel-

lective understanding; power of the will, *see* will; rational power (power of reason), *see* reason; sensory power (power of sensing), 7, 26, 37, 54, 61–62, 65, 67, 70–78, 80, 83–85, 90, 93–96, 100, 109–11, 115, 117, 121, 123, 129, 139–41, 143–44, 146, 149–51, 154–62, 164, 169–74, 180–81, 187–88, 192, 194, 201, 205–7, 210, 215–16, 223, 241–42, 245–47, 250, 272, 289, 331; activated sensory power, 198; common sensory power, 53, 74–78, 161, 201–2; exterior sensory power, 64, 70–71, 74, 76, 117, 246; interior sensory power, 64, 74–75, 77, 331; proper sensory power, 76–78, 201–2; sentient power (power of sentience), 7, 11, 26, 33, 38, 47, 51, 54, 56–57, 61–66, 70, 74–77, 80, 88, 95, 103, 115, 122, 128, 140, 164, 194, 210, 225–26, 229, 302, 330–31; interior sentient power, 74–75, 77, 246; primary sentient power, 74, 78; spiritual power, 155; supernatural power, 311; vegetative power, 64–68, 81, 83, 123; visual power (power of seeing/sight/vision), 21, 23, 44–46, 53, 88, 94, 103, 109, 112–13, 126, 128, 164, 167, 170–71, 181, 183, 186, 196, 227
primary matter, 10–11, 33–34, 47, 49, 82, 146, 148, 196
principle: active principle, 53, 60–61; causal principle, 238, 243–45, 250, 257–58; common principle, 148; corporeal principle, 6; essential principle, 50; exterior principle, 65; extrinsic principle, 120; final principle, 61; first principle,

# Thomas Aquinas's
## *Summa Theologiae*
### Translated by Alfred J. Freddoso

---

**Get your full purchase price for**
***The Treatise on Human Nature***
**as a credit toward the purchase of**
***The Summa Theologiae of Thomas Aquinas***
**translated by Alfred J. Freddoso.**

(Now, the small print)

This translation of the *Treatise on Human Nature* is part of a complete translation of St. Thomas's *Summa Theologiae*, to be published by St. Augustine's Press, now scheduled for publication in 2013. It is the first such translation by one man, so it avoids the problems of multiple translators having different terms for a given word. While it is more accessible and understandable than other translations, its hallmark is accuracy and fidelity to the text of St. Thomas.

Your entire purchase price for this book may be used as a credit for your future purchase from St. Augustine's Press of *The Summa Theologiae* when it comes out. To get credit, you must register your copy of *Treatise on Law* by contacting the publisher, as follows.

E-mail summa@staugustine.net and give us your name and the book you purchased. You will be notified when *The Summa Theologiae* is about to be published and given full credit for the price of the *Treatise* toward your purchase of the *Summa*. Please note that by writing us, *you are under no obligation* to buy the *Summa*. Moreover, your name and e-mail address will be secure with us; we will not rent or sell it elsewhere.